Skip·Beat!

Shojo Beat

Skip·Beat!

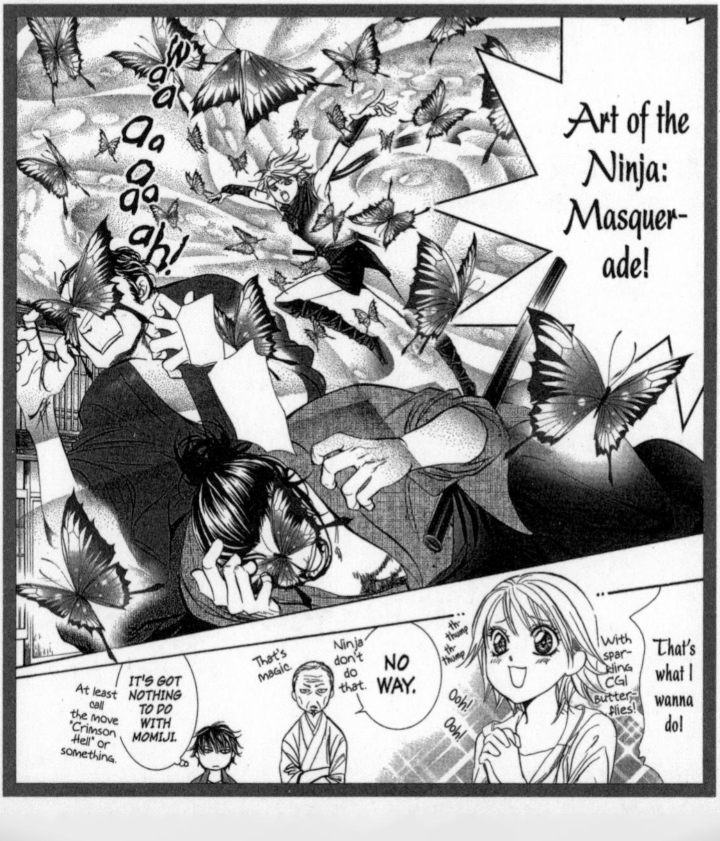
Art of the Ninja: Masquerade!
Waaaaaaaah!
That's what I wanna do!
With sparkling CGI butterflies!
th-thump th-thump
Ooh! Ooh!
NO WAY.
Ninja don't do that.
That's magic.
IT'S GOT NOTHING TO DO WITH MOMIJI.
At least call the move "Crimson Hell" or something.

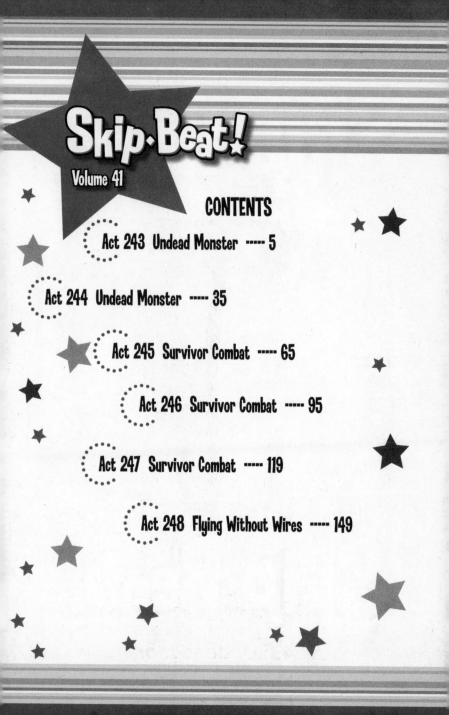

Skip·Beat!

Volume 41

CONTENTS

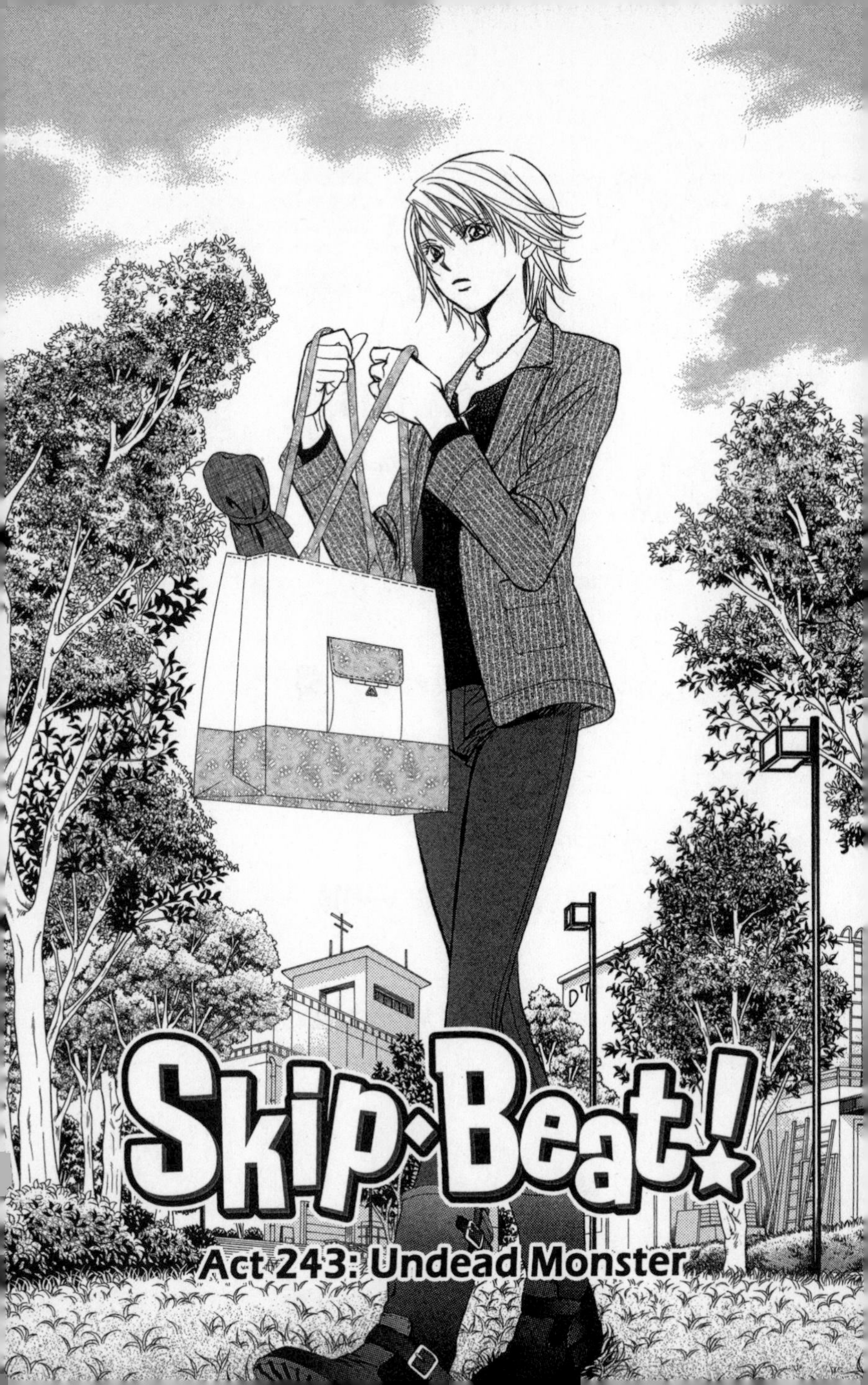
Skip·Beat!
Act 243: Undead Monster

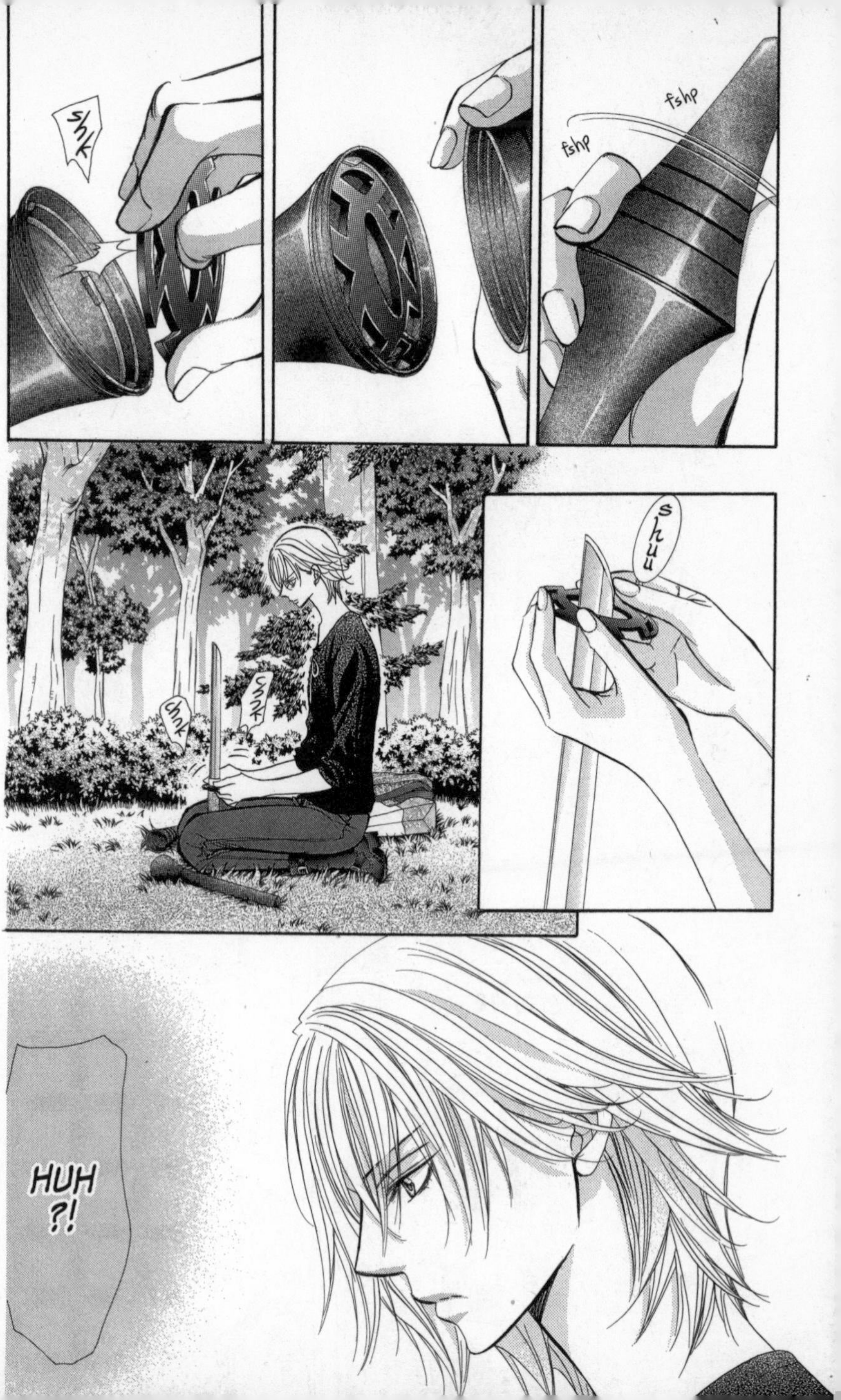
fshp
fshp
shk
shuu
chnk
chnk
HUH
?!

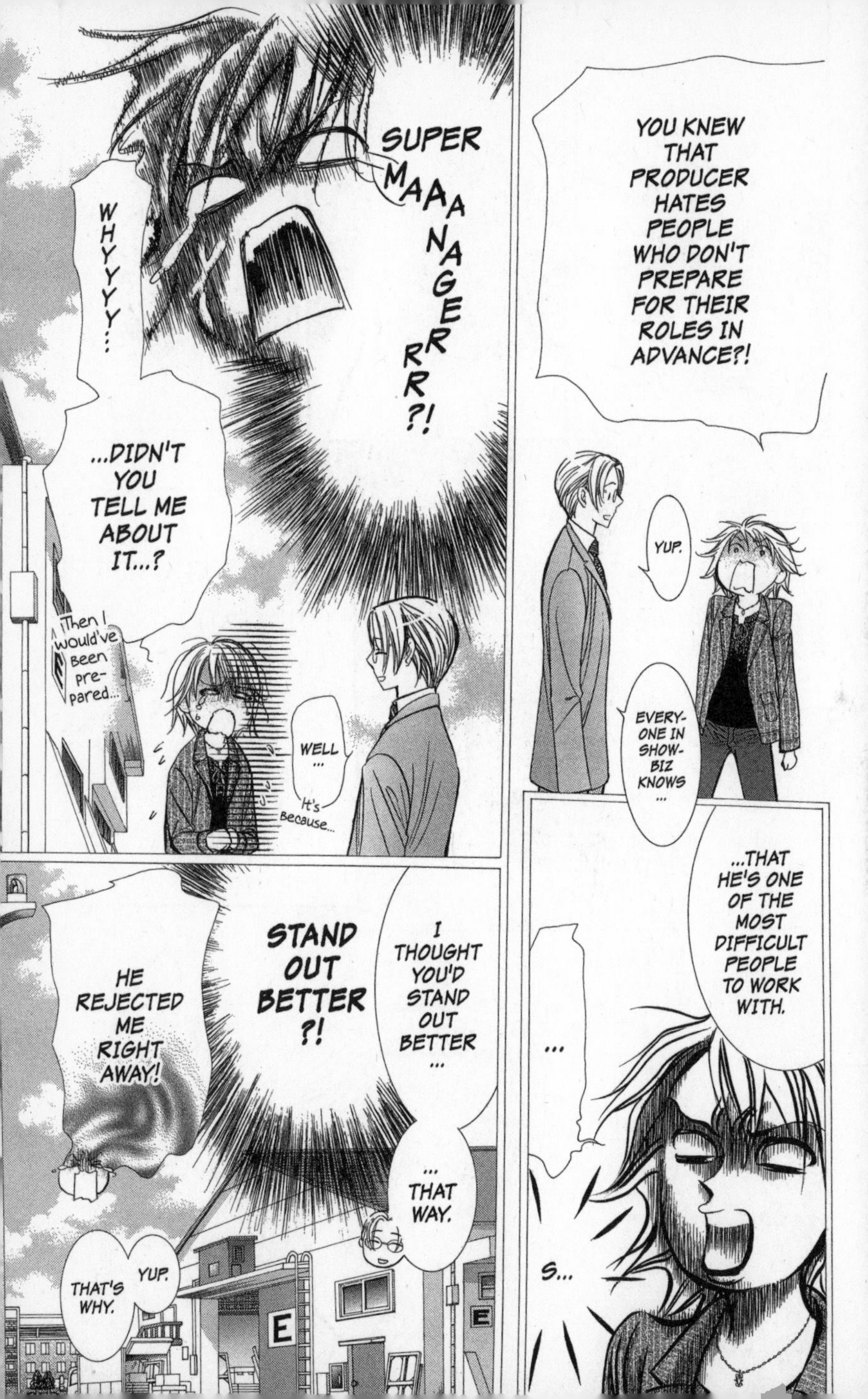
YOU KNEW THAT PRODUCER HATES PEOPLE WHO DON'T PREPARE FOR THEIR ROLES IN ADVANCE?!
YUP.
EVERYONE IN SHOWBIZ KNOWS...
...THAT HE'S ONE OF THE MOST DIFFICULT PEOPLE TO WORK WITH.
...
S...
SUPER MAAAANAGERRR?!
WHYYYY...
...DIDN'T YOU TELL ME ABOUT IT...?
Then I would've been prepared...
WELL...
It's because...
I THOUGHT YOU'D STAND OUT BETTER...
...THAT WAY.
STAND OUT BETTER?!
HE REJECTED ME RIGHT AWAY!
YUP.
THAT'S WHY.

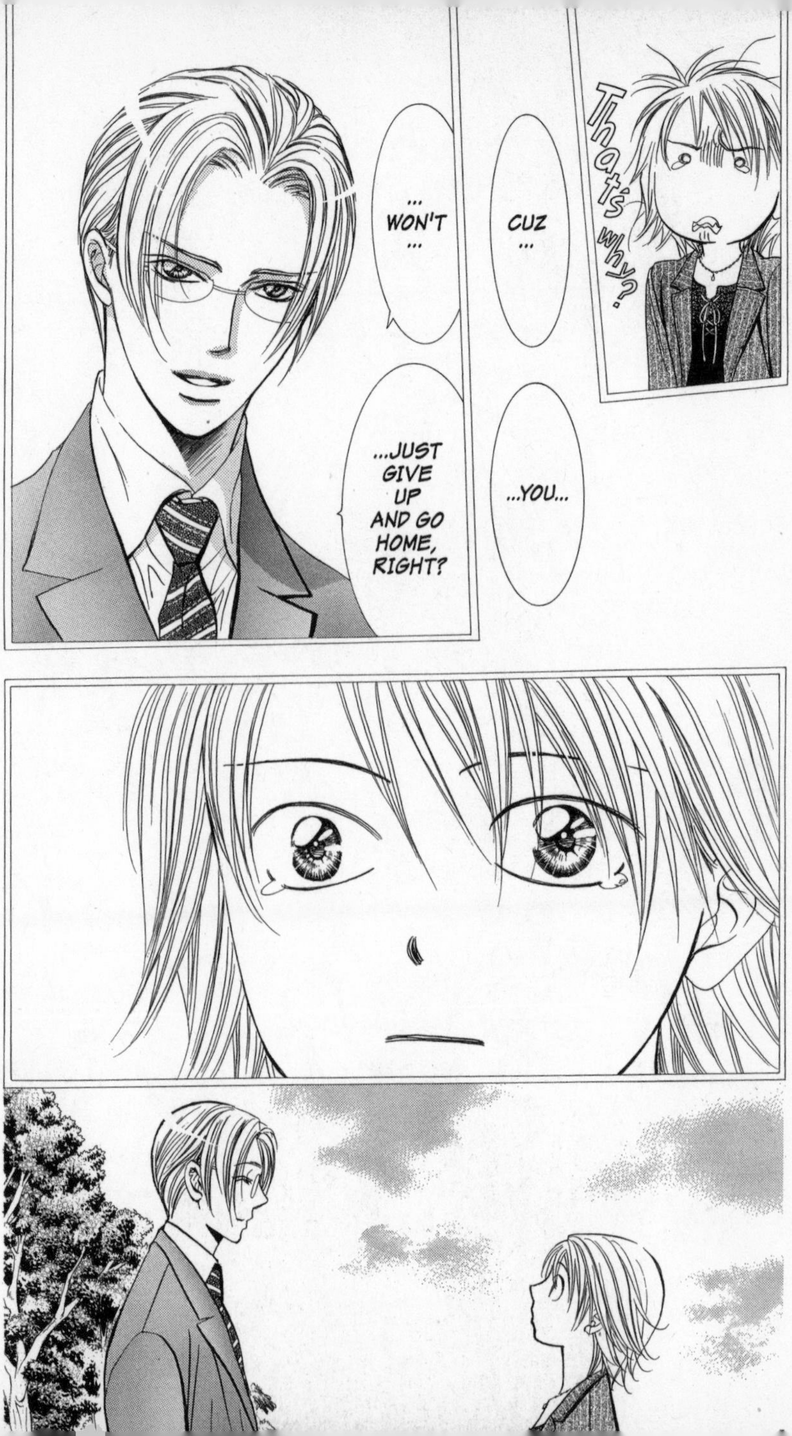
That's why?
CUZ ...
...YOU...
... WON'T ...
...JUST GIVE UP AND GO HOME, RIGHT?

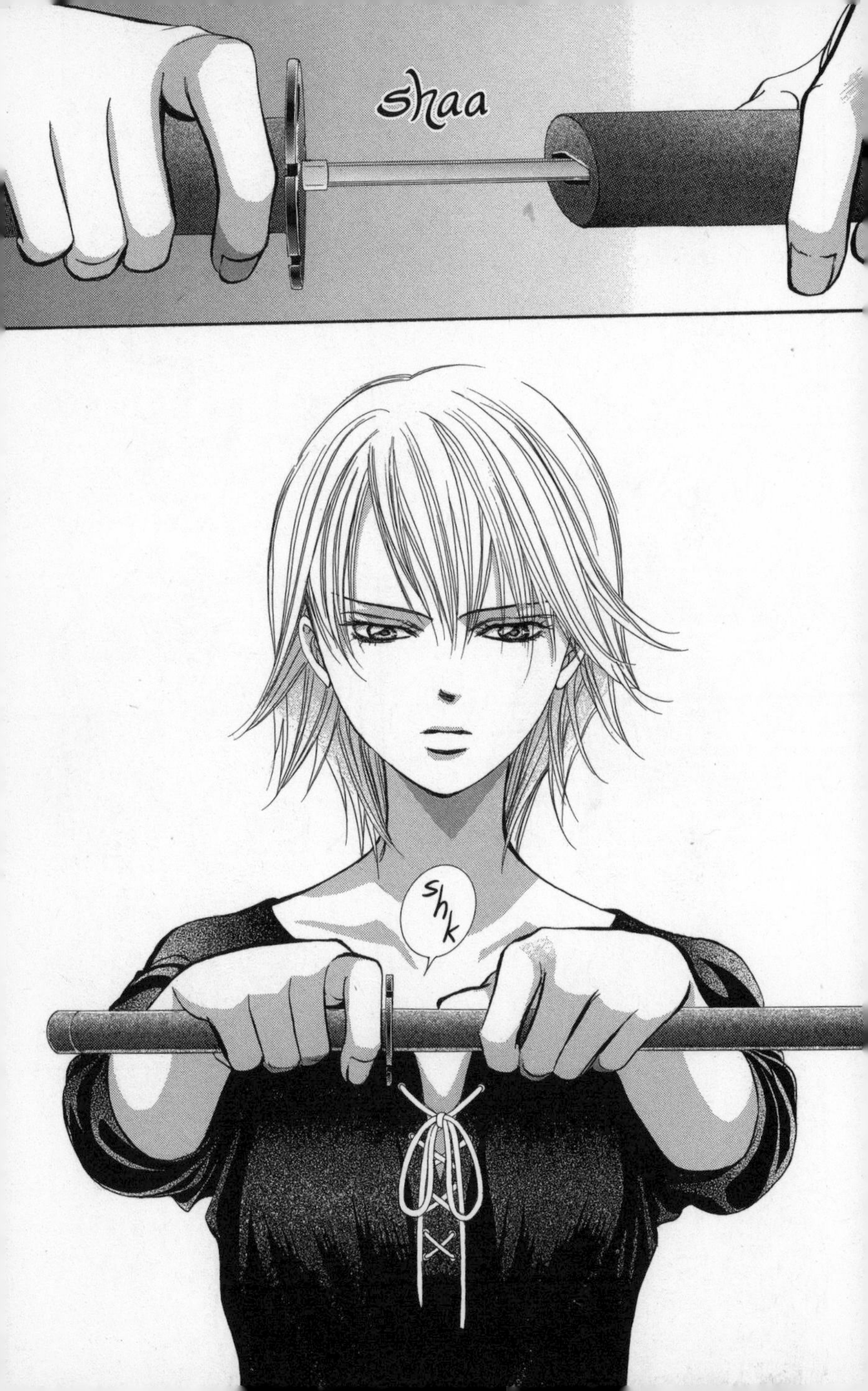
shaa
shk

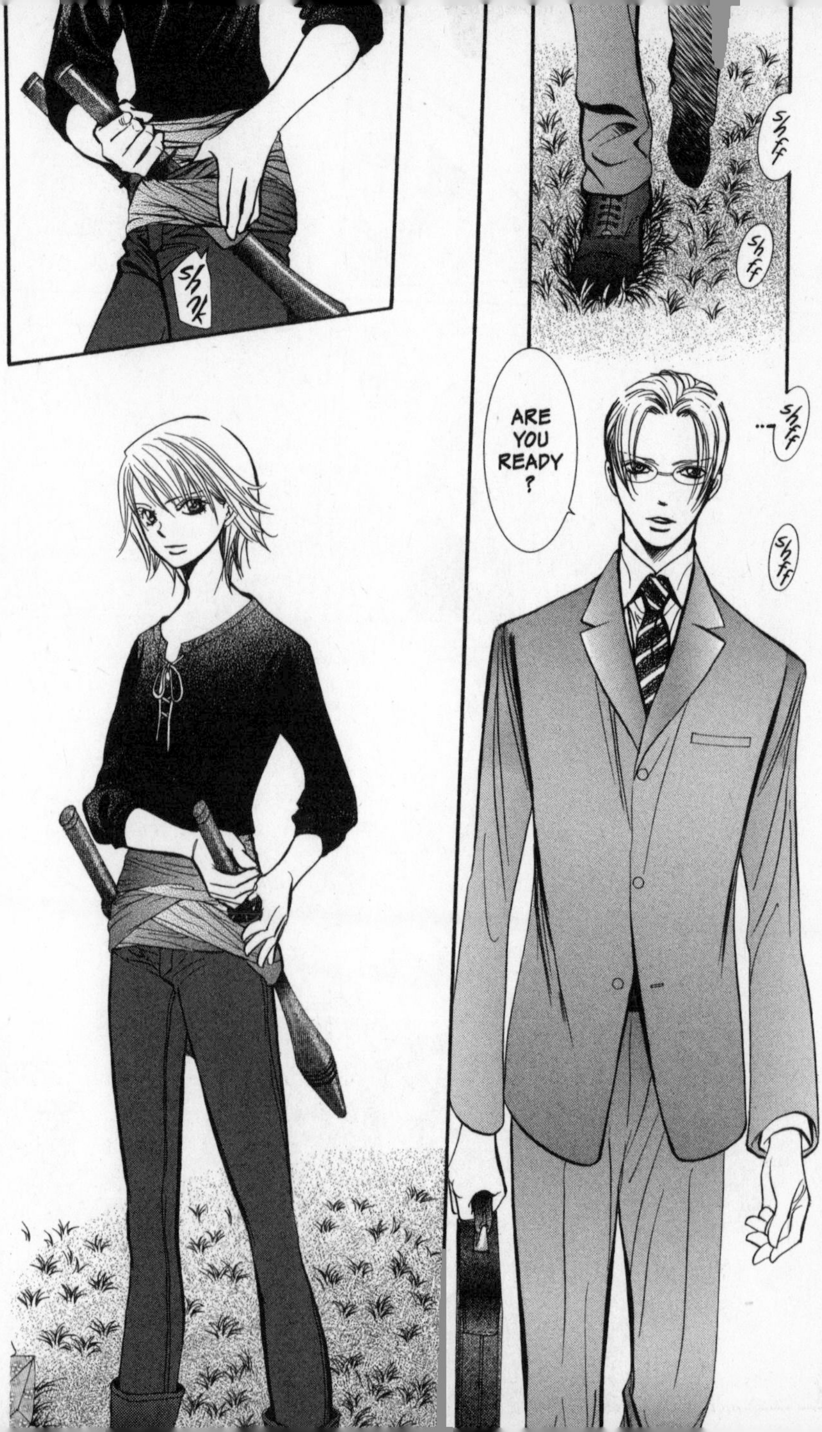
shff
shff
ARE YOU READY?
...
shff
shff
shnk

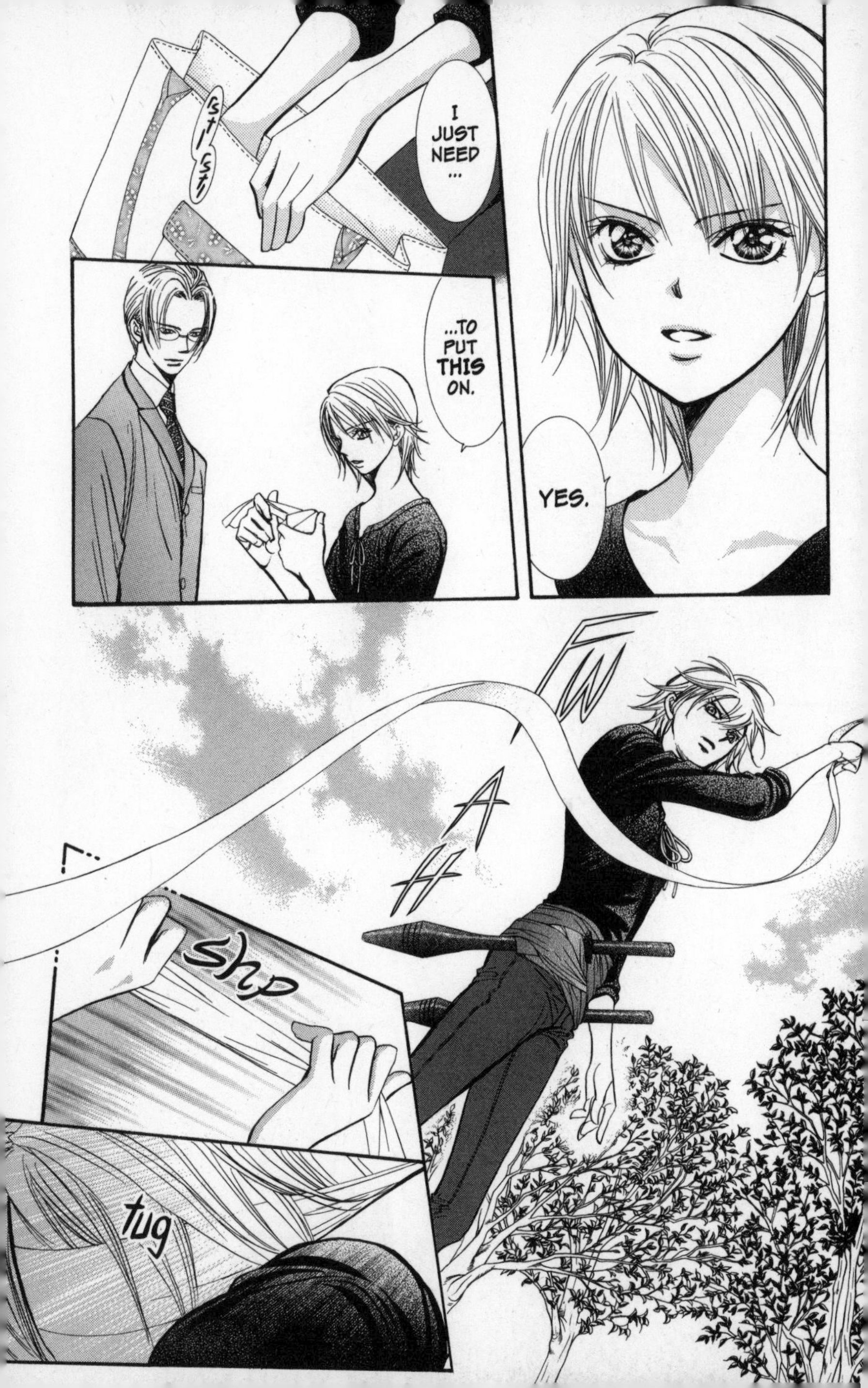
YES.
I JUST NEED ...
rstl rstl
...TO PUT THIS ON.
FWAH
shp
tug

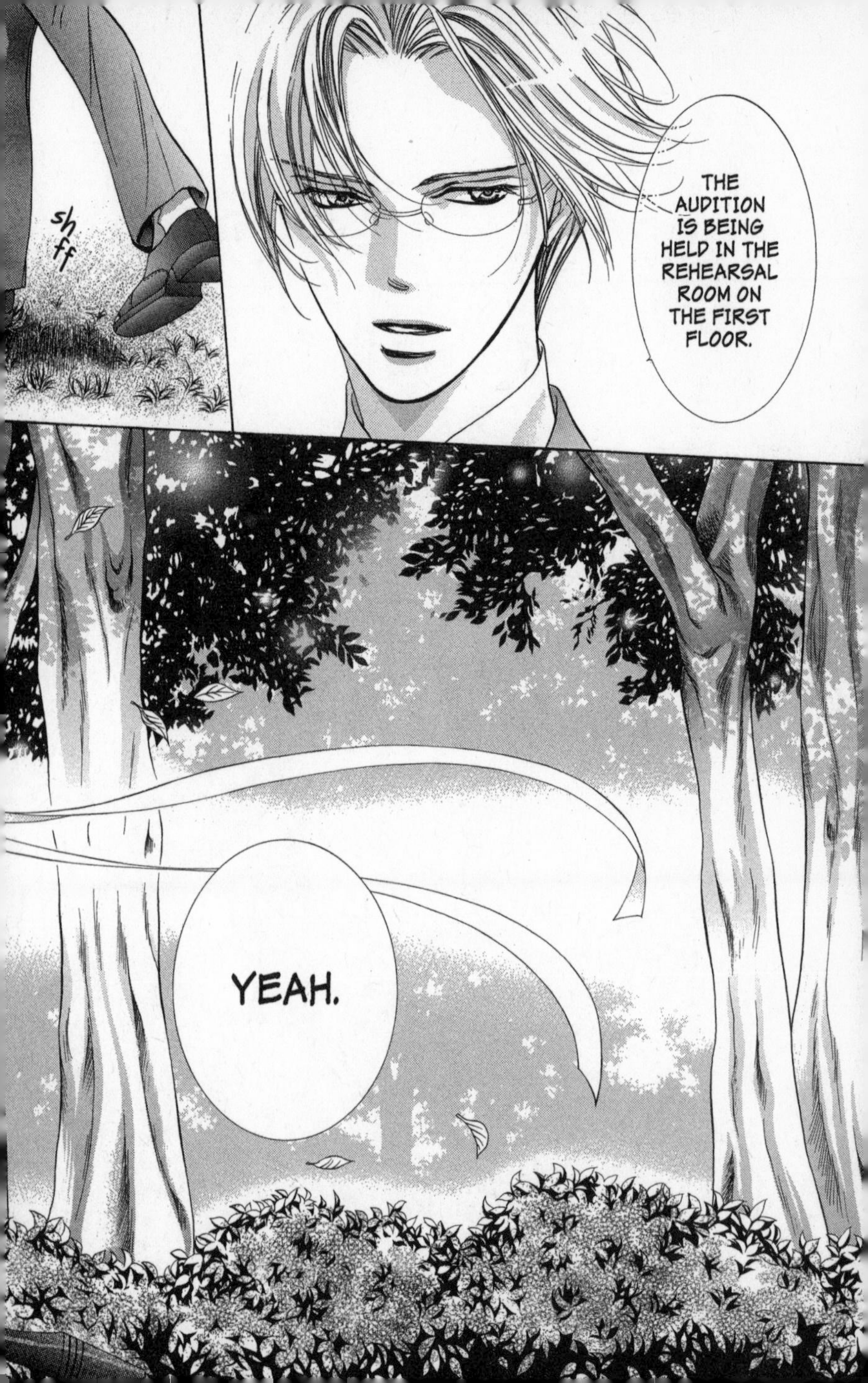
THE AUDITION IS BEING HELD IN THE REHEARSAL ROOM ON THE FIRST FLOOR.
shff
YEAH.

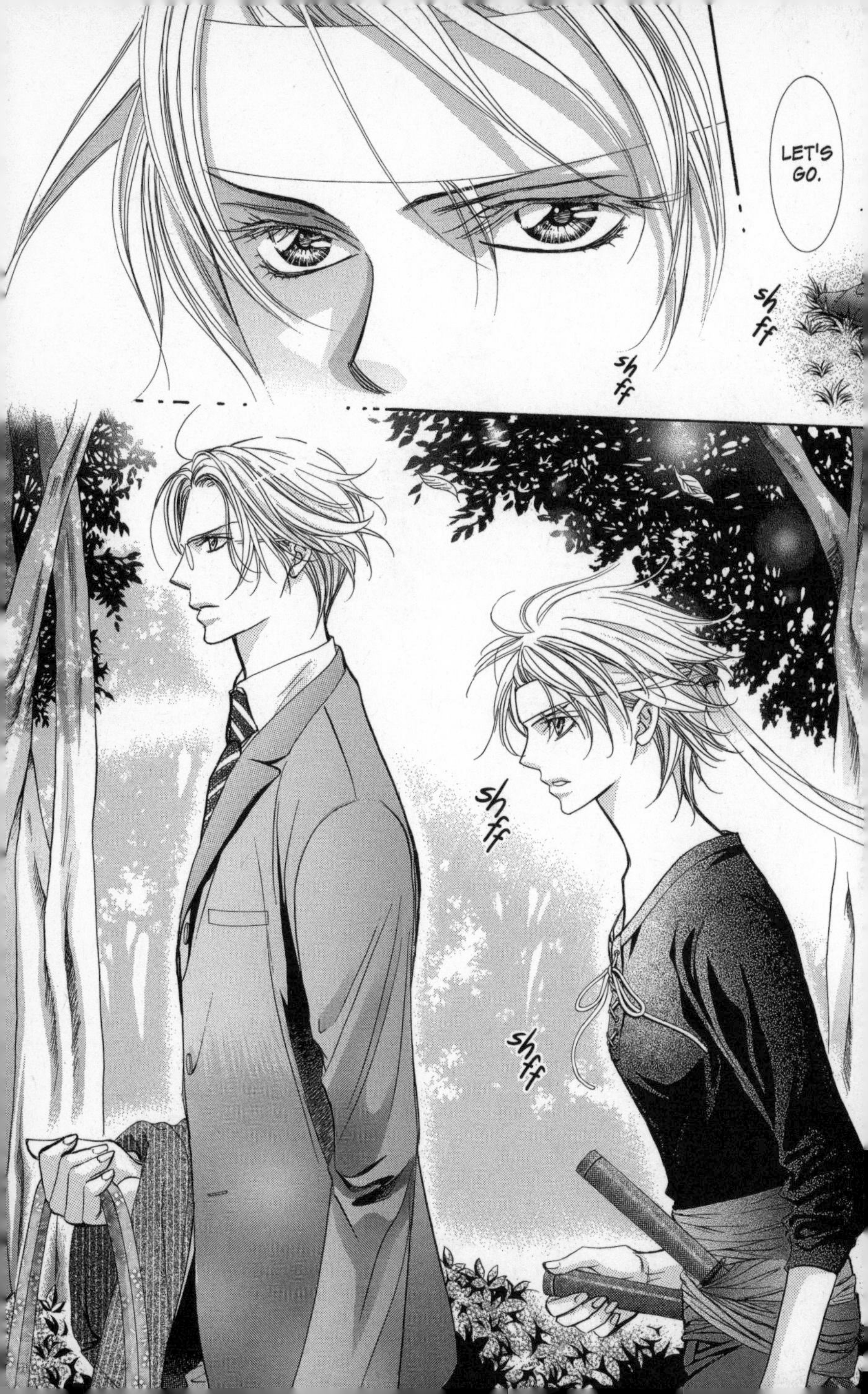
LET'S GO.
shff
shff
shff
shff

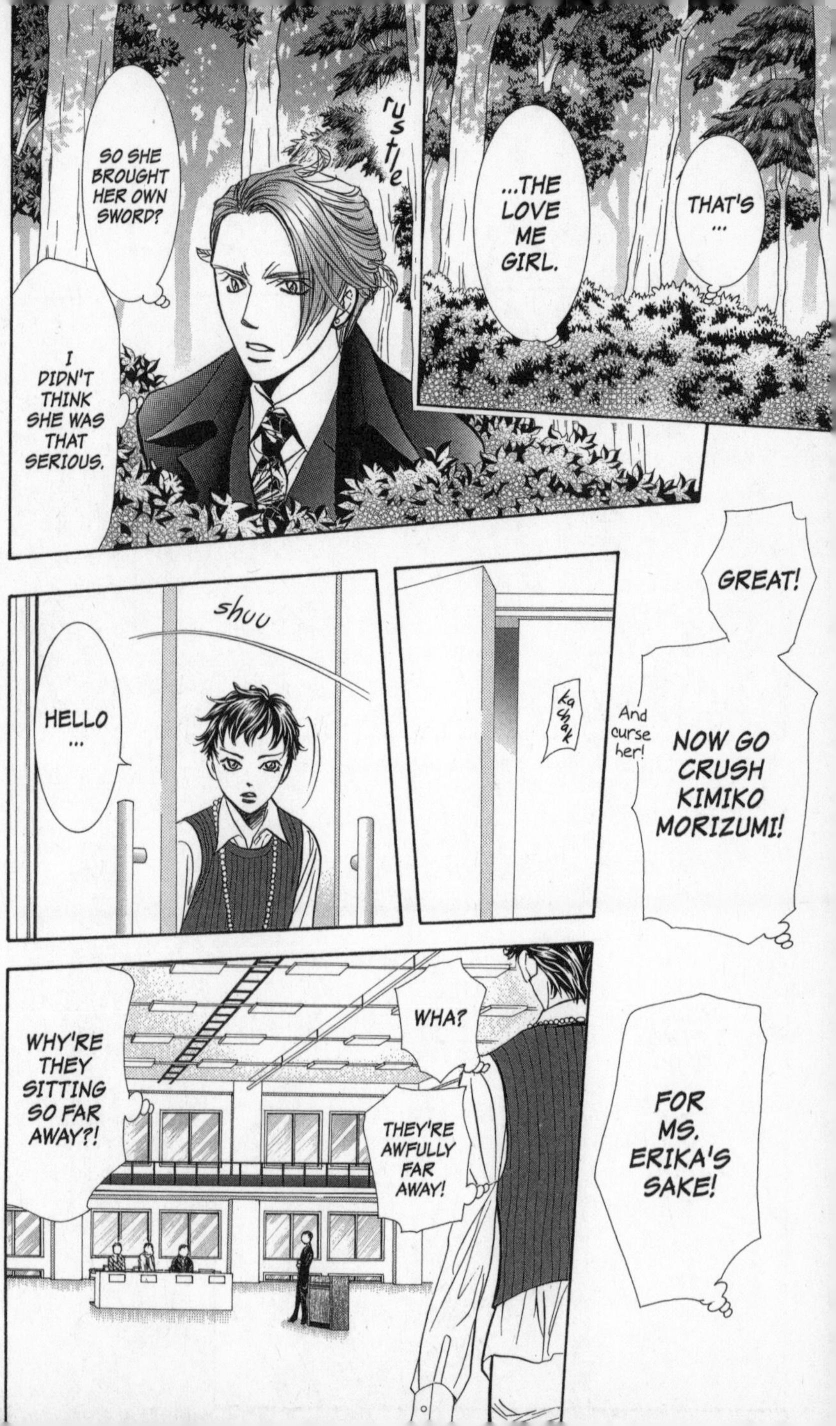
THAT'S ...
...THE LOVE ME GIRL.
rustle
SO SHE BROUGHT HER OWN SWORD?
I DIDN'T THINK SHE WAS THAT SERIOUS.
GREAT!
NOW GO CRUSH KIMIKO MORIZUMI!
And curse her!
ka chak
shuu
HELLO ...
FOR MS. ERIKA'S SAKE!
WHA?
THEY'RE AWFULLY FAR AWAY!
WHY'RE THEY SITTING SO FAR AWAY?!

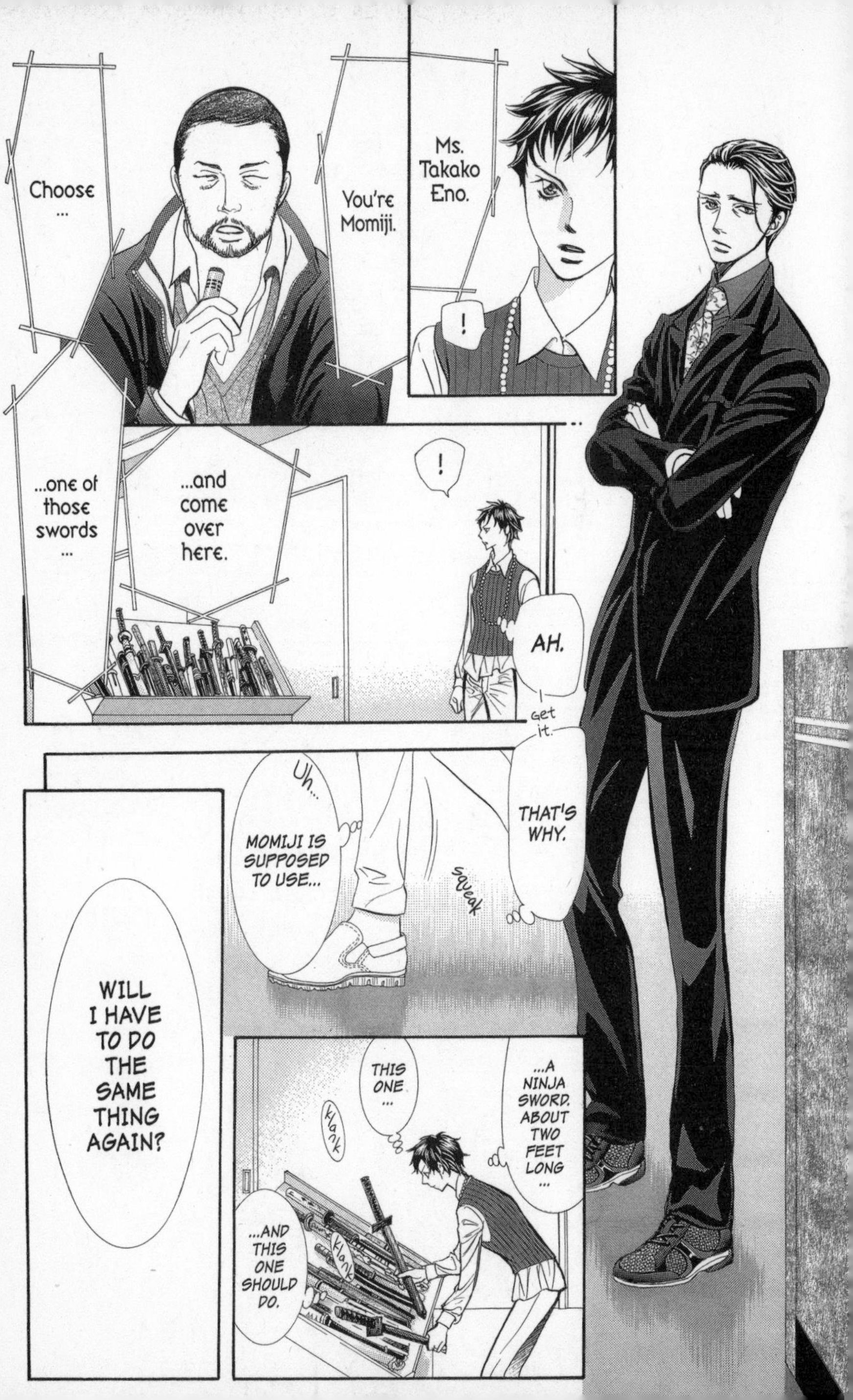
Ms. Takako Eno.
!
You're Momiji.
Choose ...
!
...one of those swords ...
...and come over here.
...
AH.
I get it.
THAT'S WHY.
Uh...
MOMIJI IS SUPPOSED TO USE...
squeak
...A NINJA SWORD. ABOUT TWO FEET LONG ...
THIS ONE ...
klank
klank
...AND THIS ONE SHOULD DO.
WILL I HAVE TO DO THE SAME THING AGAIN?

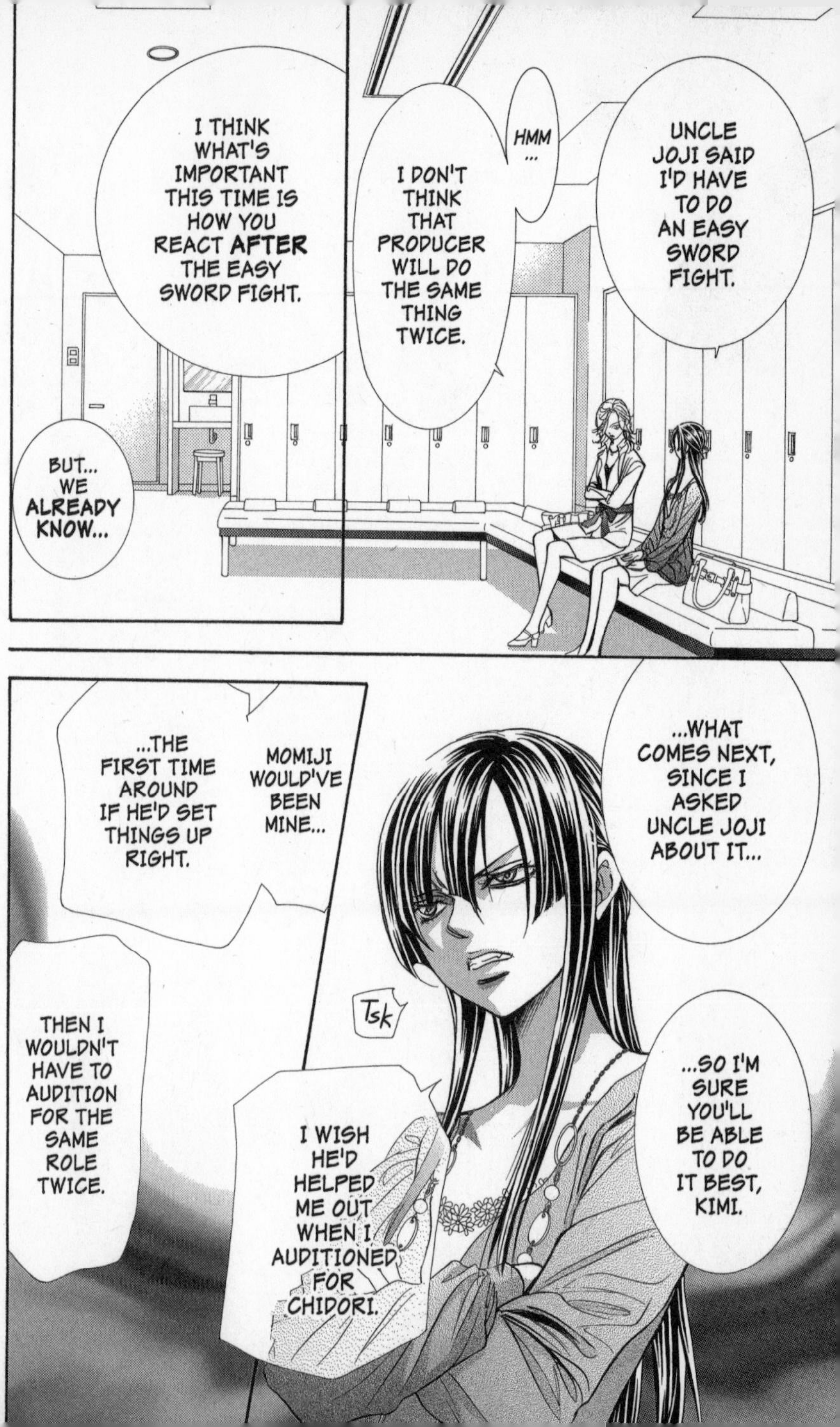
UNCLE JOJI SAID I'D HAVE TO DO AN EASY SWORD FIGHT.
HMM...
I DON'T THINK THAT PRODUCER WILL DO THE SAME THING TWICE.
I THINK WHAT'S IMPORTANT THIS TIME IS HOW YOU REACT **AFTER** THE EASY SWORD FIGHT.
BUT... WE ALREADY KNOW...
...WHAT COMES NEXT, SINCE I ASKED UNCLE JOJI ABOUT IT...
...SO I'M SURE YOU'LL BE ABLE TO DO IT BEST, KIMI.
Tsk
I WISH HE'D HELPED ME OUT WHEN I AUDITIONED FOR CHIDORI.
MOMIJI WOULD'VE BEEN MINE...
...THE FIRST TIME AROUND IF HE'D SET THINGS UP RIGHT.
THEN I WOULDN'T HAVE TO AUDITION FOR THE SAME ROLE TWICE.

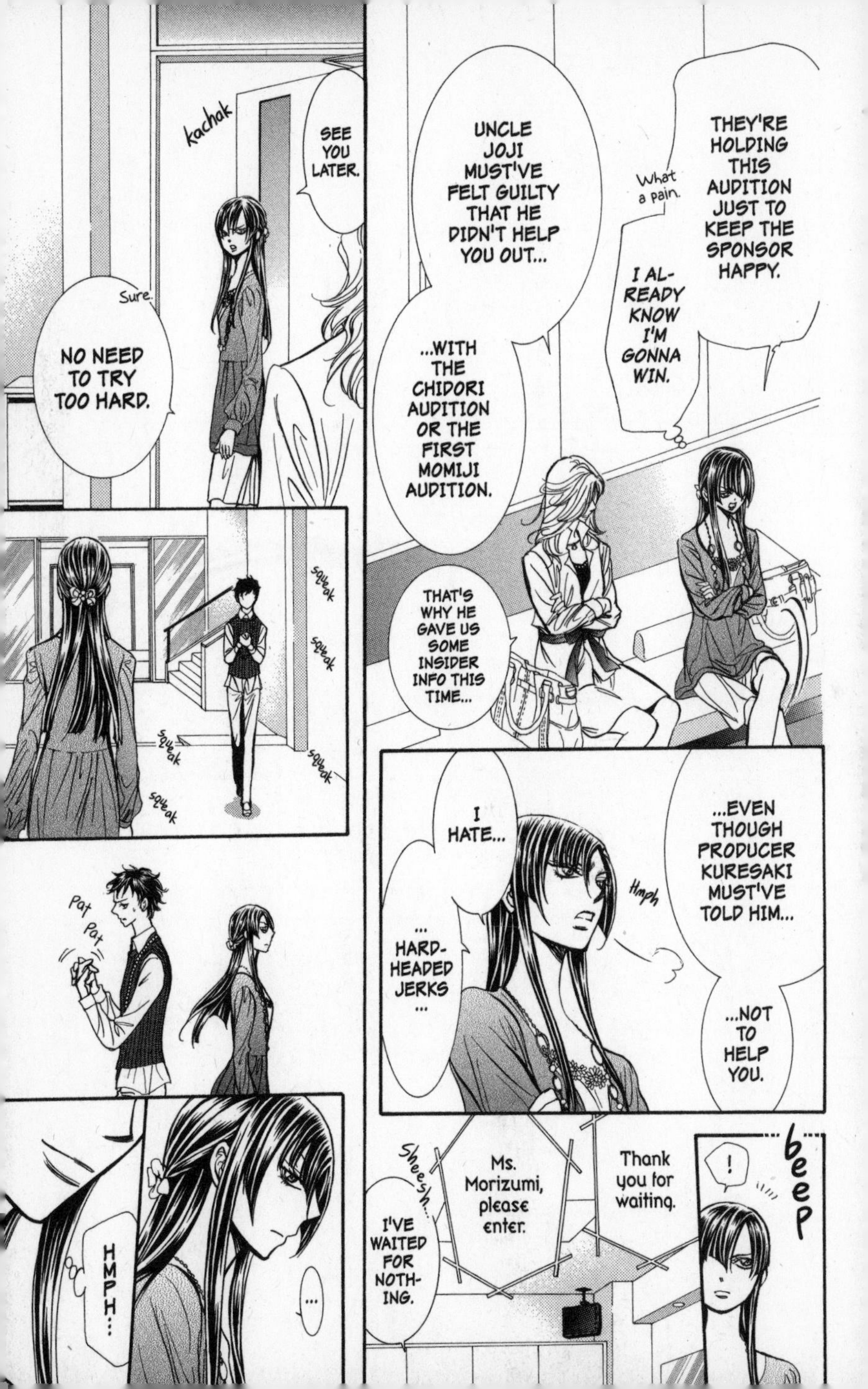
THEY'RE HOLDING THIS AUDITION JUST TO KEEP THE SPONSOR HAPPY.
What a pain.
I ALREADY KNOW I'M GONNA WIN.
UNCLE JOJI MUST'VE FELT GUILTY THAT HE DIDN'T HELP YOU OUT...
...WITH THE CHIDORI AUDITION OR THE FIRST MOMIJI AUDITION.
THAT'S WHY HE GAVE US SOME INSIDER INFO THIS TIME...
...EVEN THOUGH PRODUCER KURESAKI MUST'VE TOLD HIM...
...NOT TO HELP YOU.
Hmph
I HATE...
...HARD-HEADED JERKS...
beep
!
Thank you for waiting.
Ms. Morizumi, please enter.
Sheesh...
I'VE WAITED FOR NOTHING.
kachak
SEE YOU LATER.
Sure.
NO NEED TO TRY TOO HARD.
squeak
squeak
squeak
squeak
squeak
Pat Pat
HMPH...
...

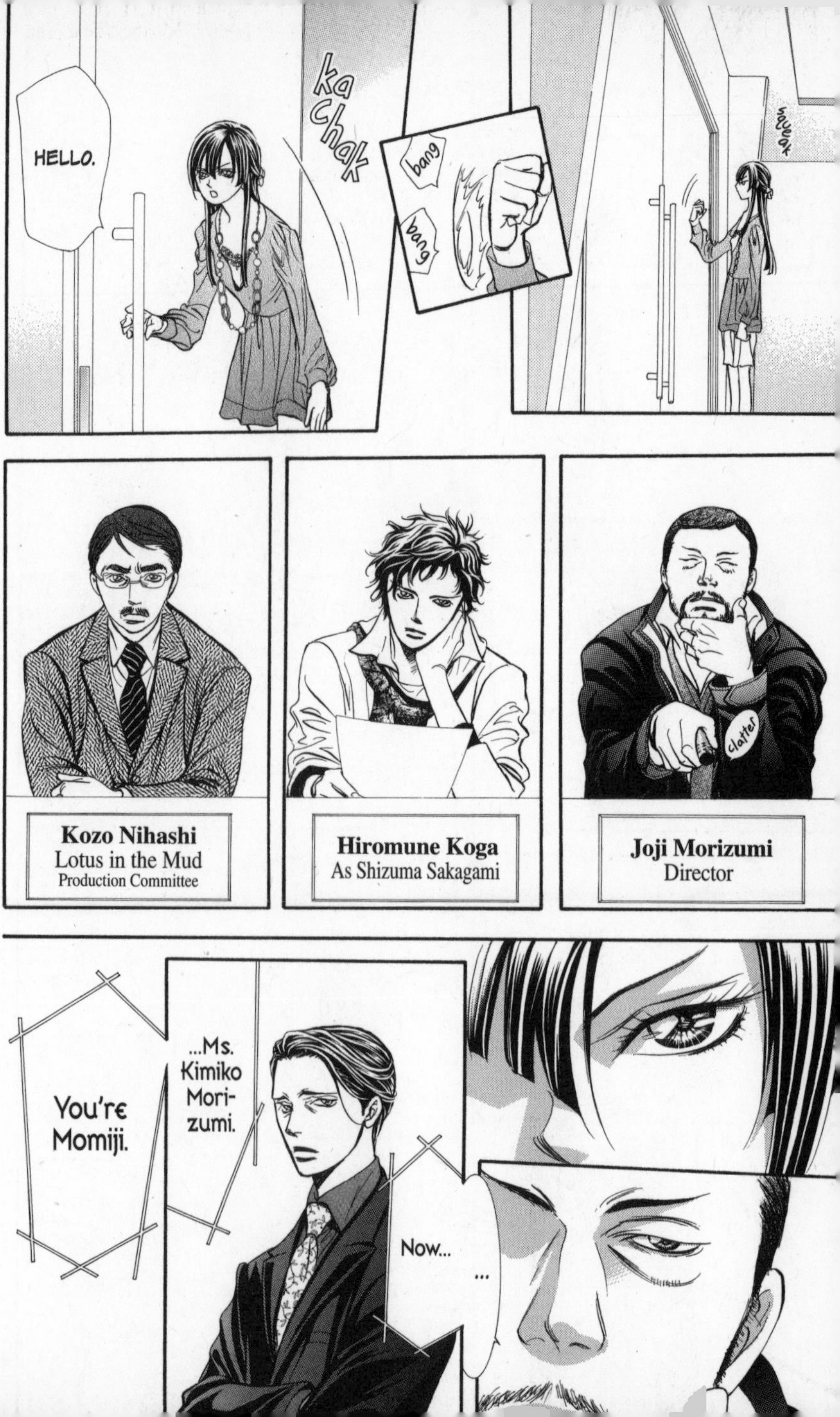
squeak
bang
bang
kachak
HELLO.
clatter
Joji Morizumi
Director
Hiromune Koga
As Shizuma Sakagami
Kozo Nihashi
Lotus in the Mud
Production Committee
Now...
...
...Ms. Kimiko Mori-zumi.
You're Momiji.

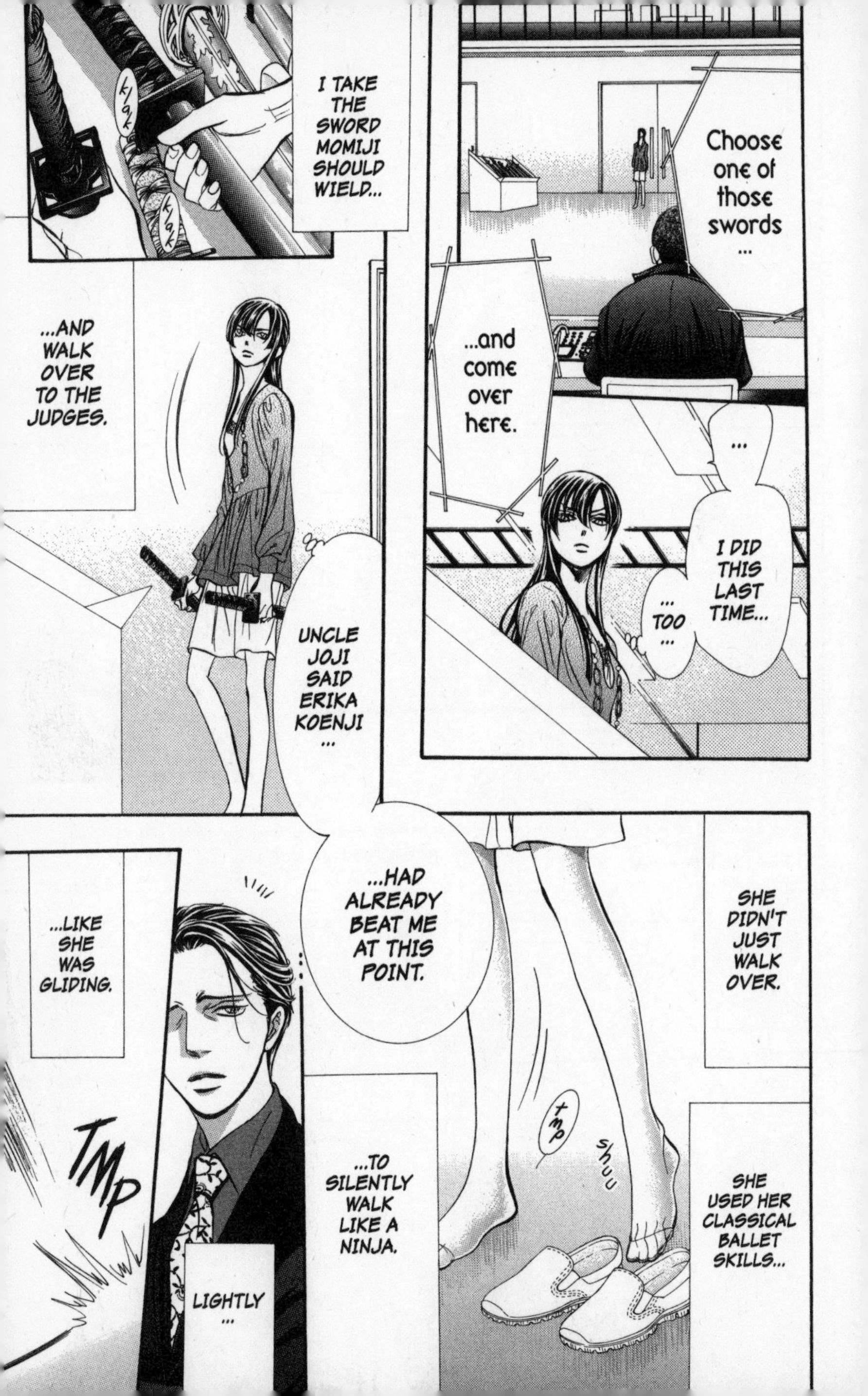
Choose one of those swords...
...and come over here.
...
I DID THIS LAST TIME...
...TOO...
klak
klak
I TAKE THE SWORD MOMIJI SHOULD WIELD...
...AND WALK OVER TO THE JUDGES.
UNCLE JOJI SAID ERIKA KOENJI...
...HAD ALREADY BEAT ME AT THIS POINT.
SHE DIDN'T JUST WALK OVER.
SHE USED HER CLASSICAL BALLET SKILLS...
tmp
shuu
...TO SILENTLY WALK LIKE A NINJA.
...LIKE SHE WAS GLIDING.
TMP
LIGHTLY...

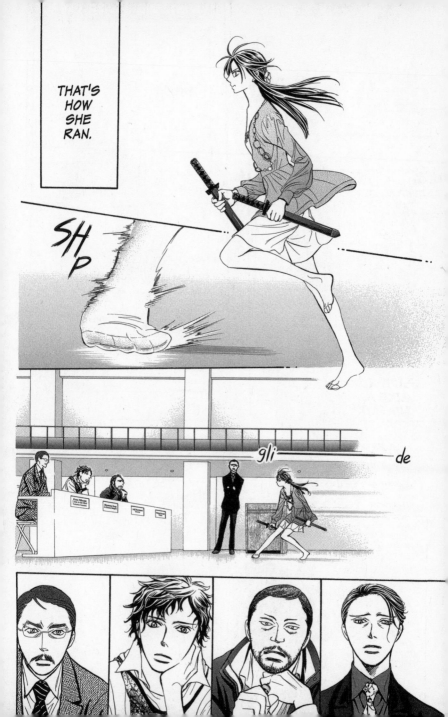

THAT'S HOW SHE RAN.

SH P

gli de

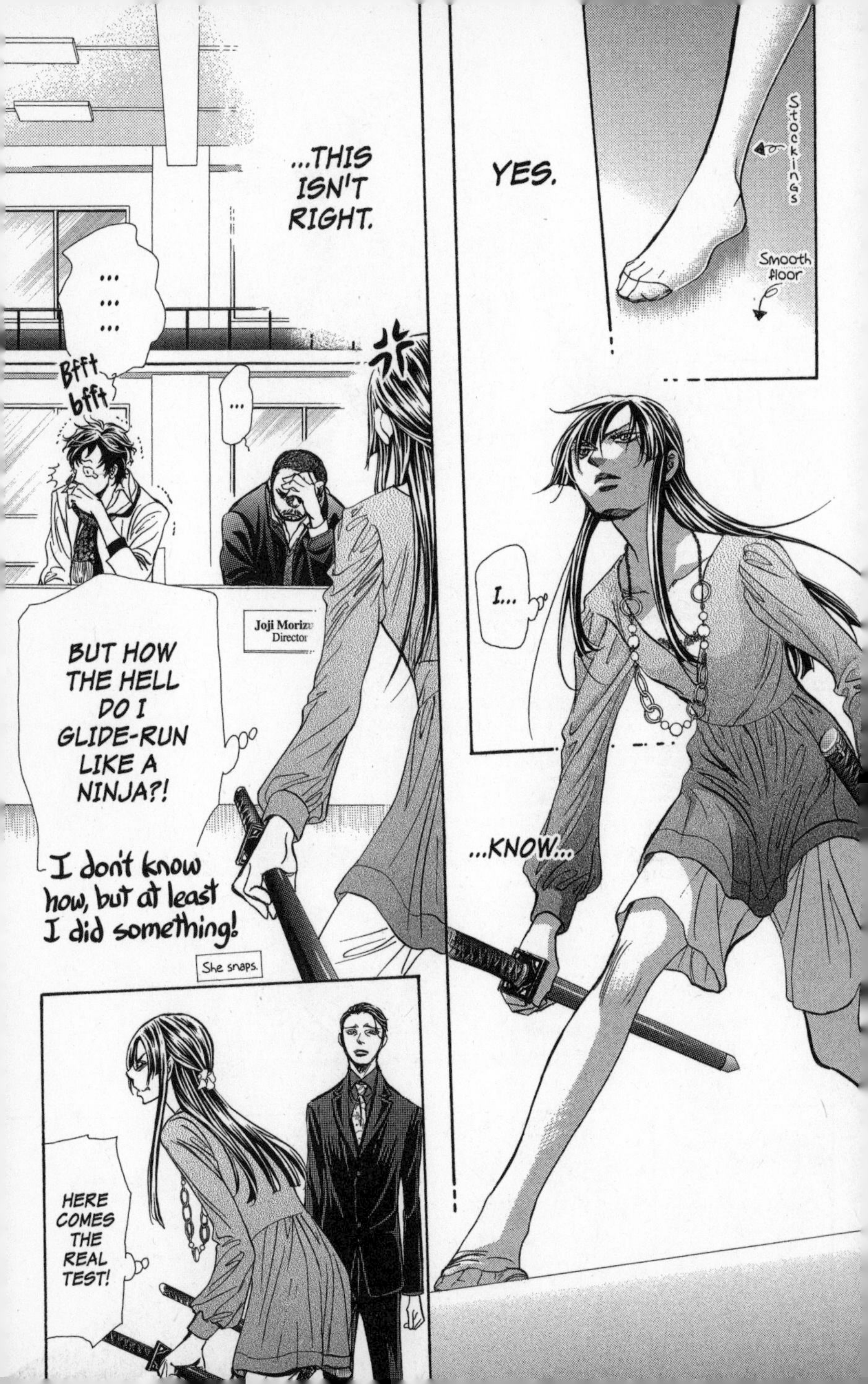
Stockings
Smooth floor
YES.
I...
...KNOW...
...THIS ISN'T RIGHT.
... ...
Bfft bfft
...
Joji Morizu Director
BUT HOW THE HELL DO I GLIDE-RUN LIKE A NINJA?!
I don't know how, but at least I did something!
She snaps.
HERE COMES THE REAL TEST!

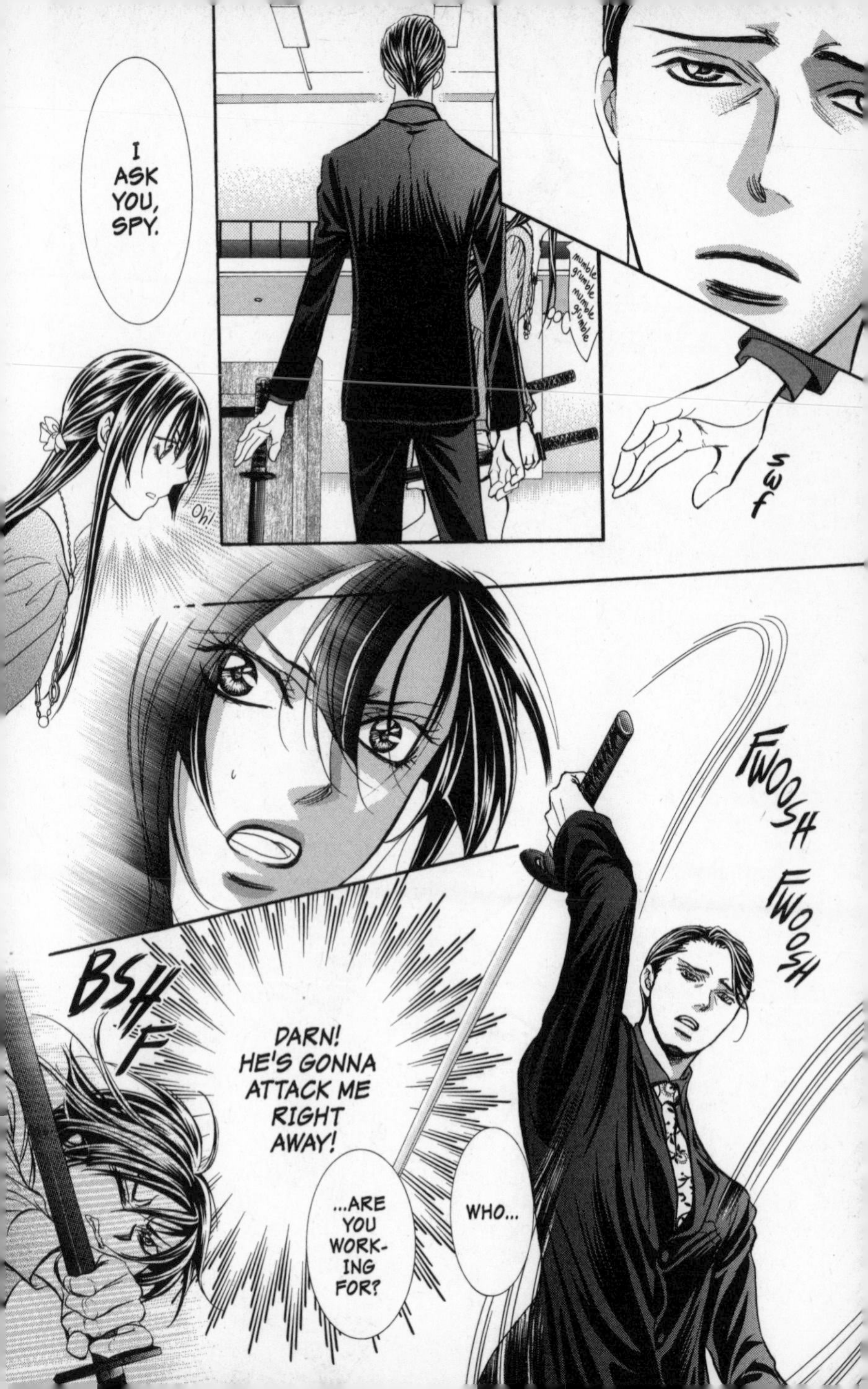
SWF
mumble grumble mumble grumble
I ASK YOU, SPY.
Oh!
FWOOSH FWOOSH
WHO...
...ARE YOU WORKING FOR?
DARN! HE'S GONNA ATTACK ME RIGHT AWAY!
BSHF

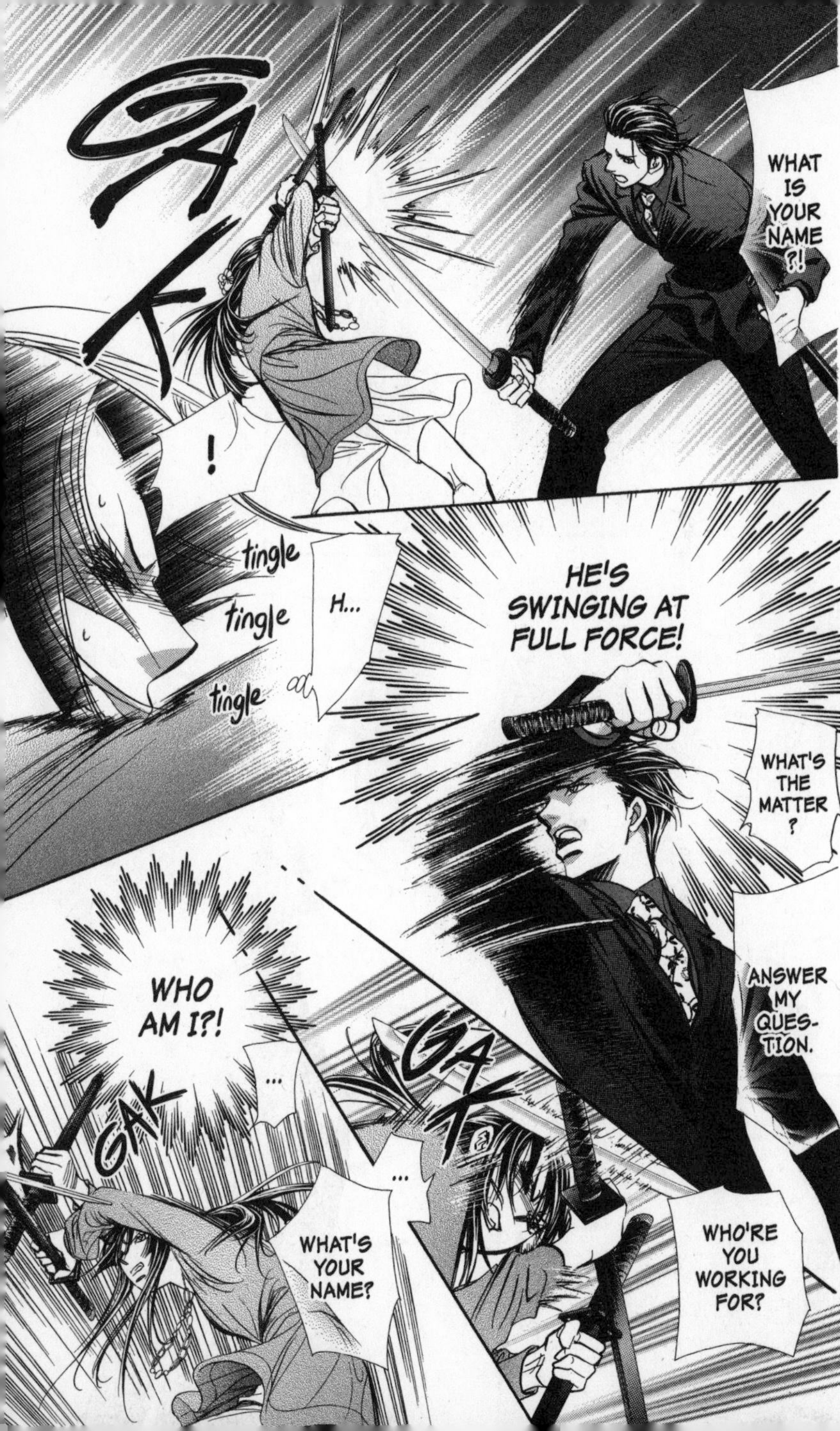
WHAT IS YOUR NAME?!
GAK
!
HE'S SWINGING AT FULL FORCE!
WHAT'S THE MATTER?
ANSWER MY QUESTION.
tingle
tingle
tingle
H...
GAK
...
WHO'RE YOU WORKING FOR?
WHO AM I?!
GAK
...
WHAT'S YOUR NAME?

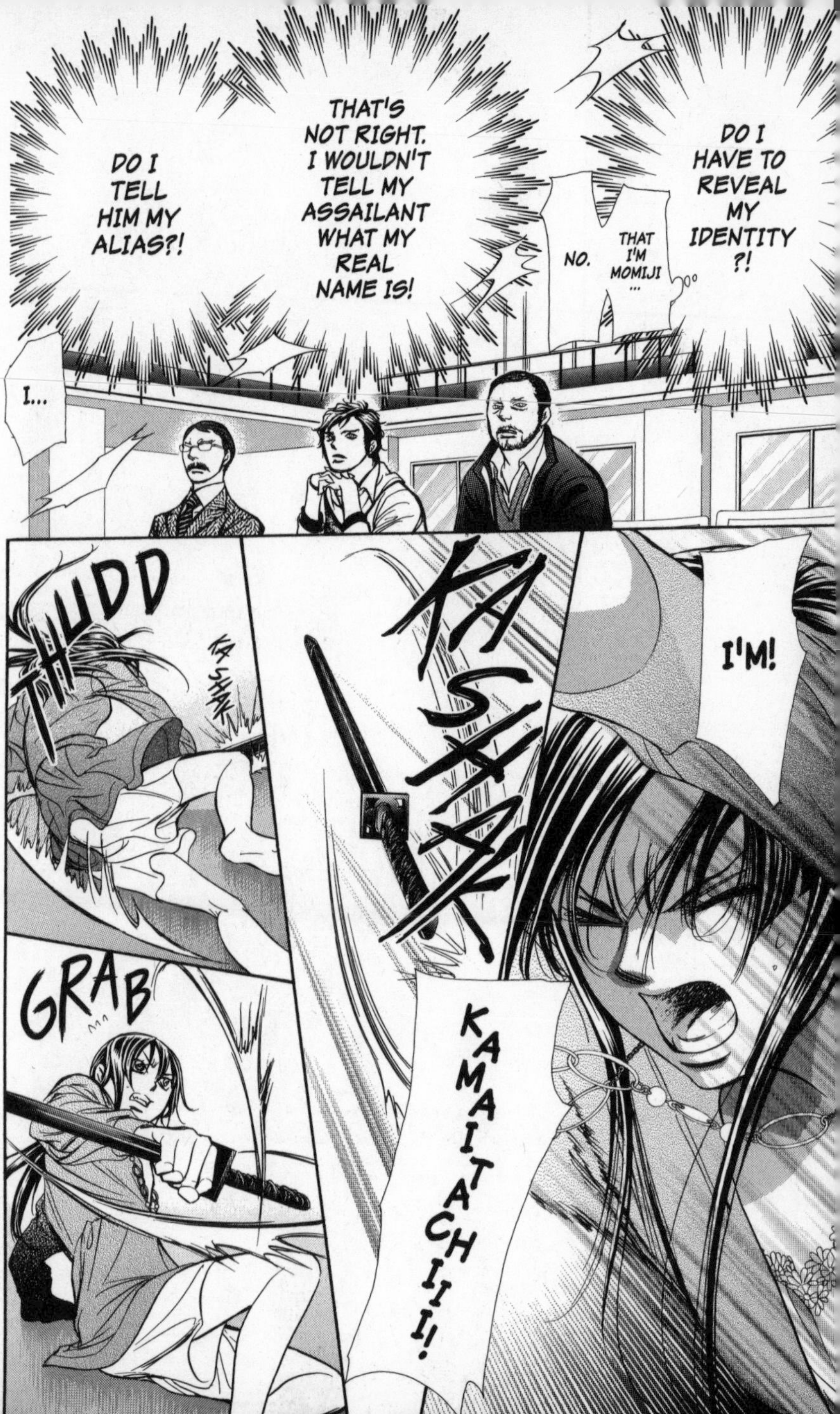
DO I HAVE TO REVEAL MY IDENTITY?!
THAT I'M MOMIJI...
NO.
THAT'S NOT RIGHT. I WOULDN'T TELL MY ASSAILANT WHAT MY REAL NAME IS!
DO I TELL HIM MY ALIAS?!
I...
I'M!
KAMAITACHIIII!
KA SHAK
THUDD
KA SHAK
GRAB

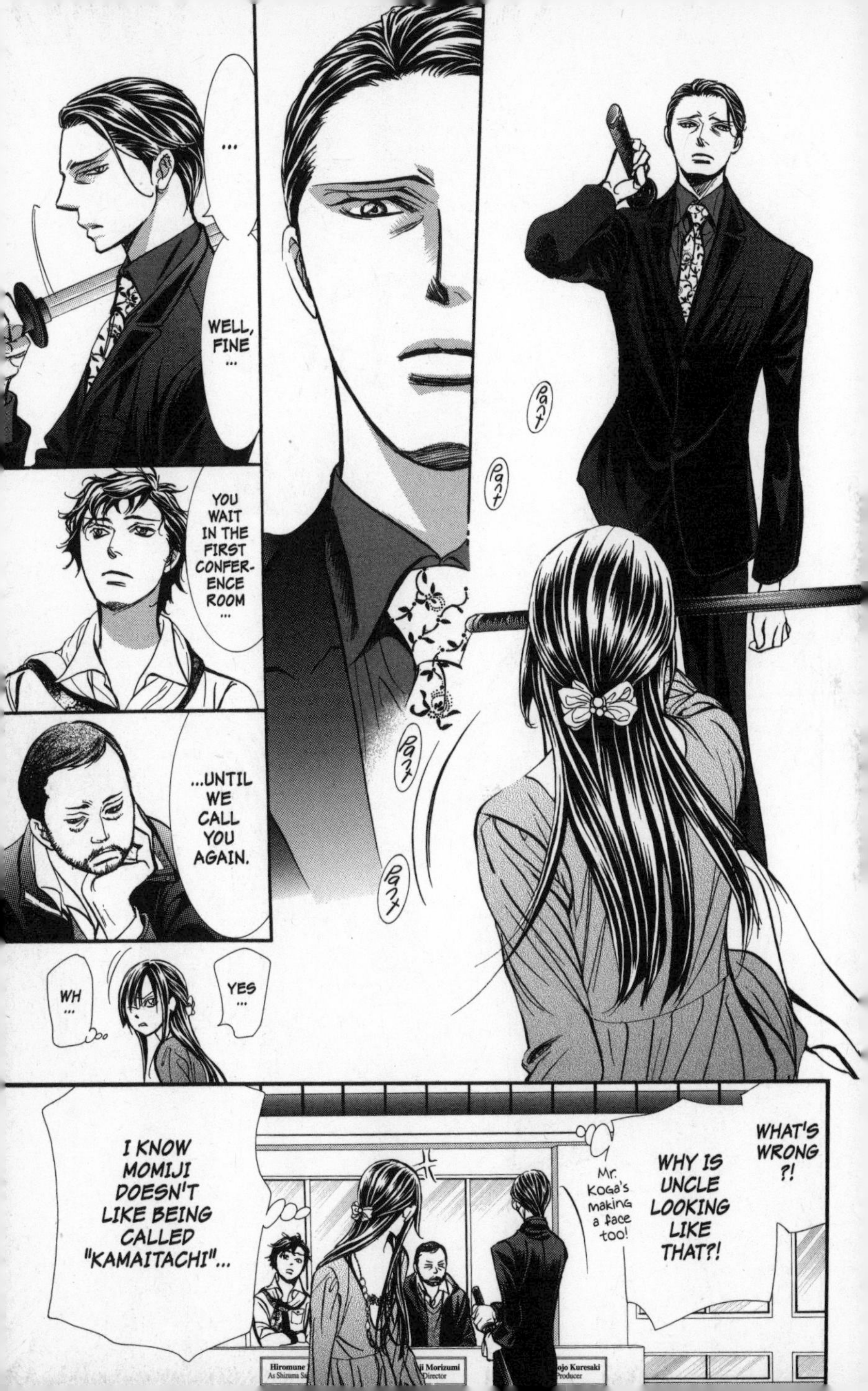
Pant
Pant
Pant
Pant
...
WELL, FINE ...
YOU WAIT IN THE FIRST CONFERENCE ROOM ...
...UNTIL WE CALL YOU AGAIN.
YES ...
WH ...
WHAT'S WRONG?!
WHY IS UNCLE LOOKING LIKE THAT?!
Mr. Koga's making a face too!
I KNOW MOMIJI DOESN'T LIKE BEING CALLED "KAMAITACHI"...

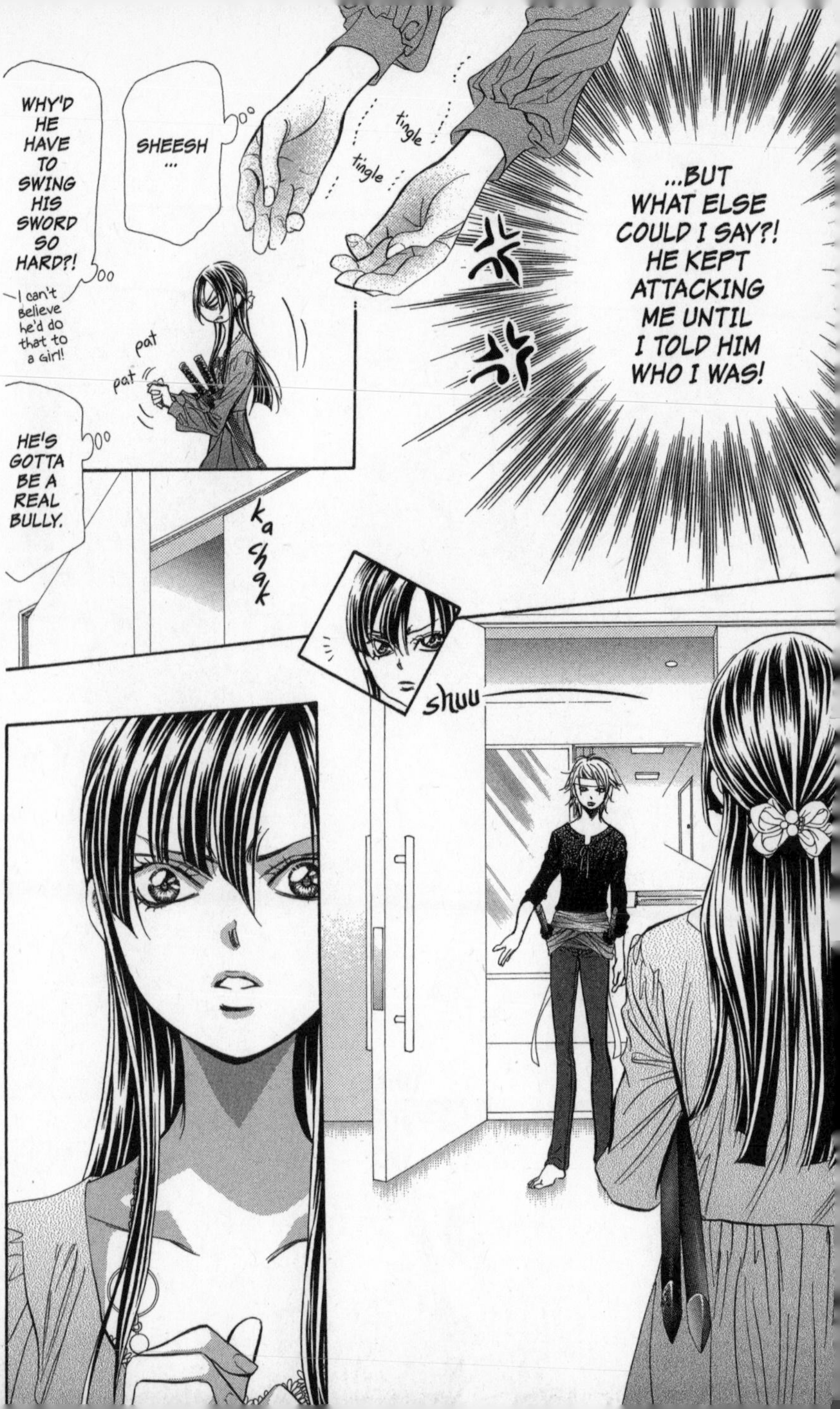

...BUT WHAT ELSE COULD I SAY?! HE KEPT ATTACKING ME UNTIL I TOLD HIM WHO I WAS!
tingle
tingle
SHEESH ...
WHY'D HE HAVE TO SWING HIS SWORD SO HARD?!
I can't believe he'd do that to a girl!
pat
pat
HE'S GOTTA BE A REAL BULLY.
ka chak
shuu

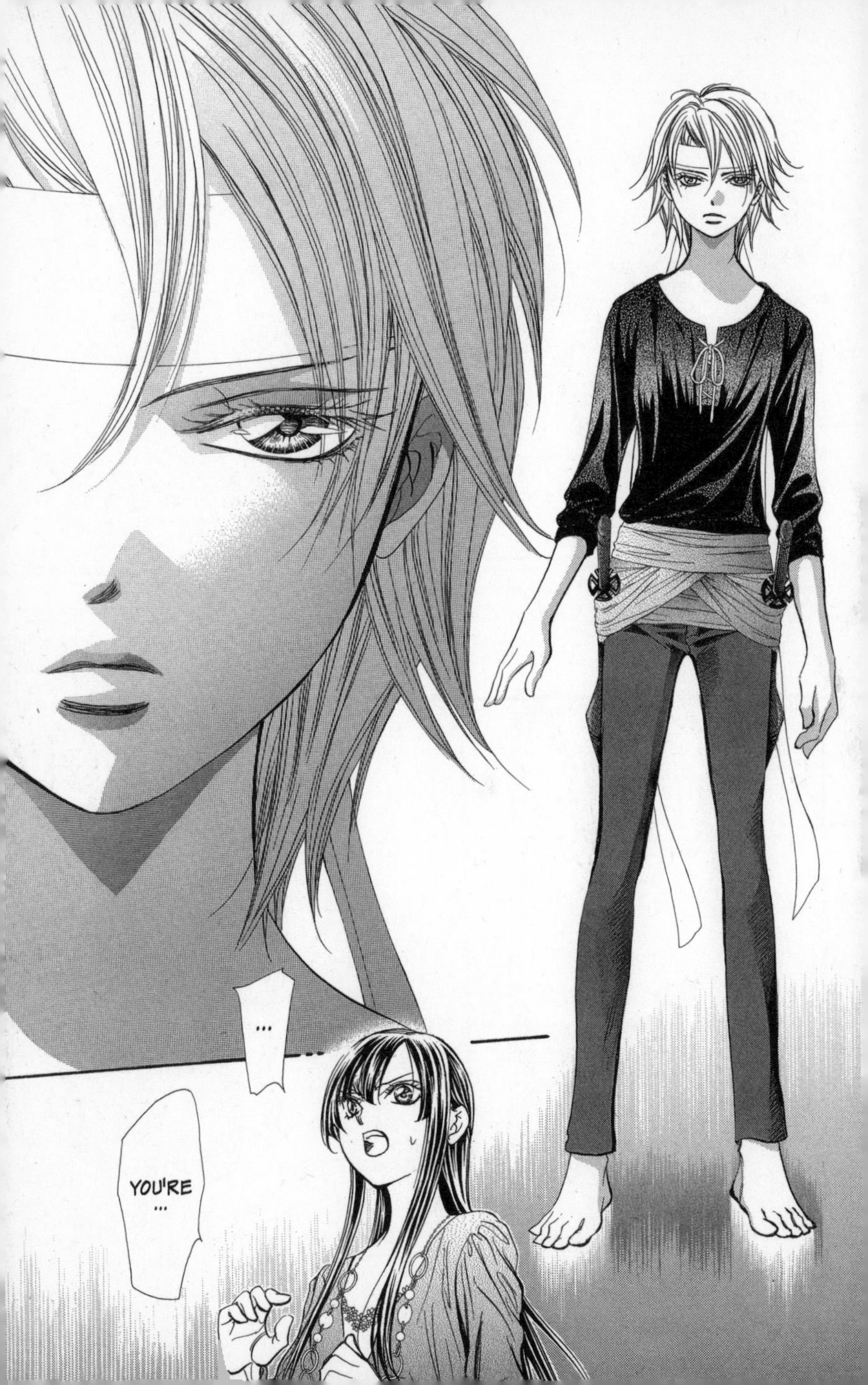
...
YOU'RE
...

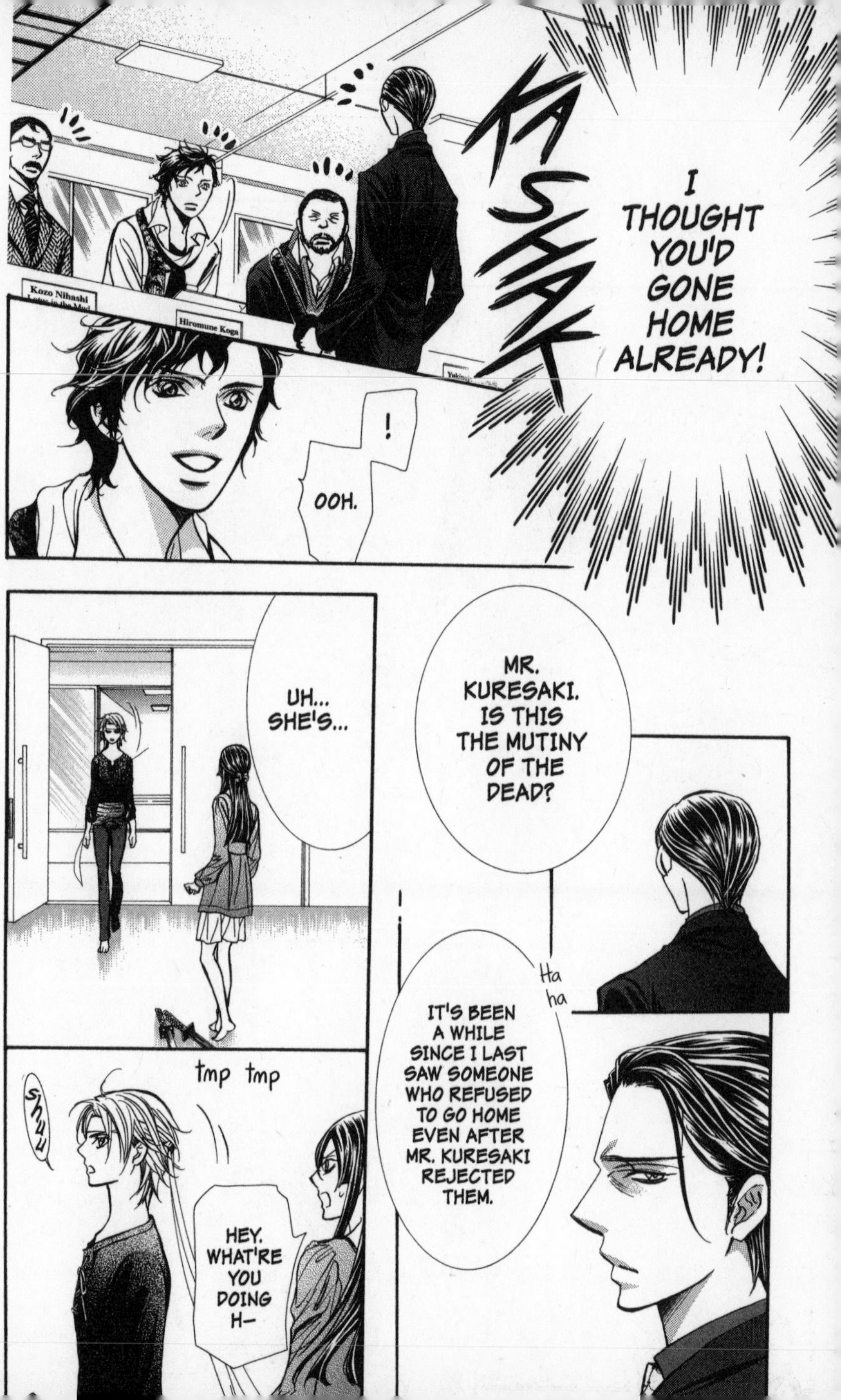
KA SHAK
I THOUGHT YOU'D GONE HOME ALREADY!
Kozo Nihashi
Hiromune Koga
!
OOH.
MR. KURESAKI. IS THIS THE MUTINY OF THE DEAD?
UH... SHE'S...
Ha ha
IT'S BEEN A WHILE SINCE I LAST SAW SOMEONE WHO REFUSED TO GO HOME EVEN AFTER MR. KURESAKI REJECTED THEM.
tmp tmp
shuu
HEY. WHAT'RE YOU DOING H—

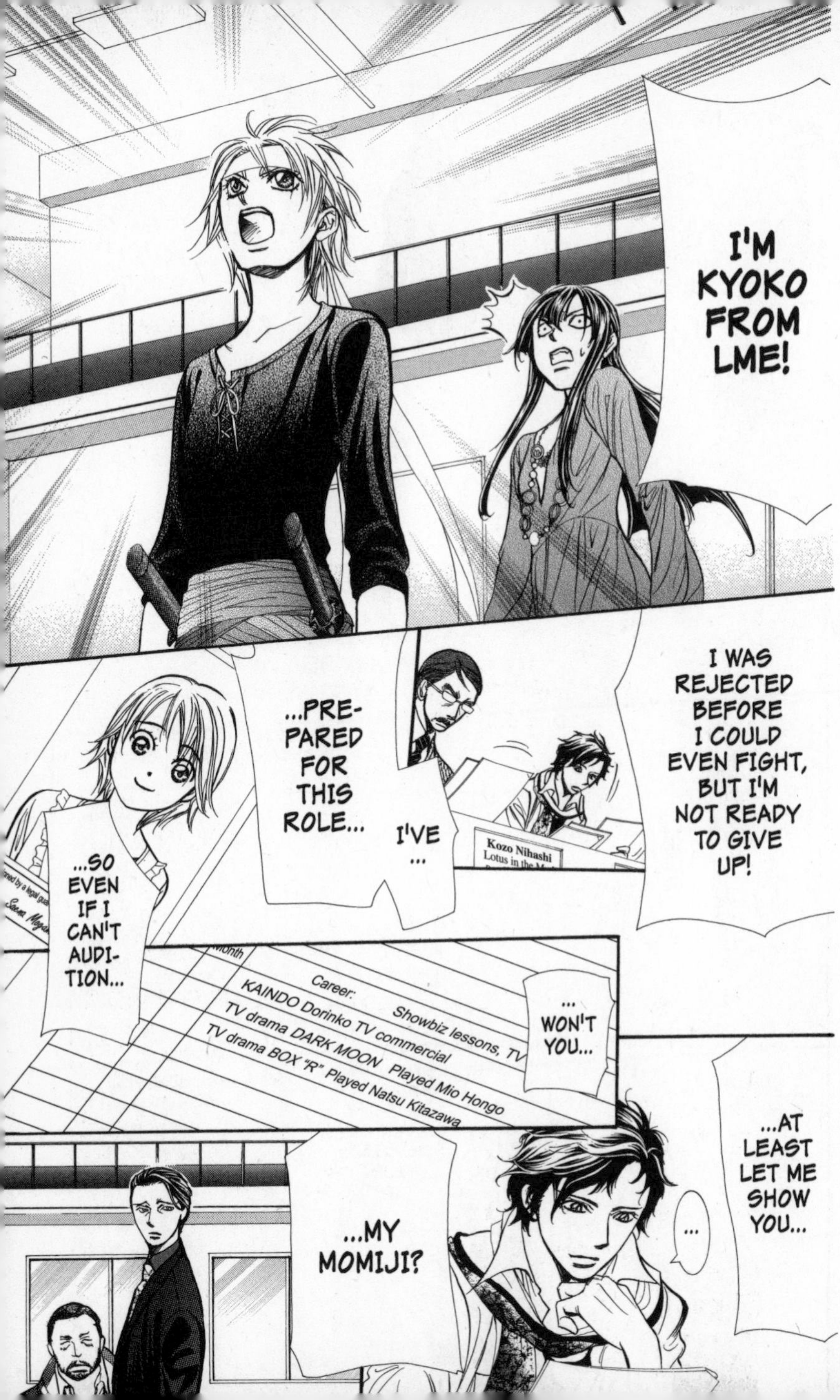
I'M KYOKO FROM LME!
I WAS REJECTED BEFORE I COULD EVEN FIGHT, BUT I'M NOT READY TO GIVE UP!
Kozo Nihashi
I'VE ...
...PRE-PARED FOR THIS ROLE...
...SO EVEN IF I CAN'T AUDI-TION...
Month
Career: Showbiz lessons, TV
KAINDO Dorinko TV commercial
TV drama DARK MOON Played Mio Hongo
TV drama BOX "R" Played Natsu Kitazawa
... WON'T YOU...
...AT LEAST LET ME SHOW YOU...
...
...MY MOMIJI?

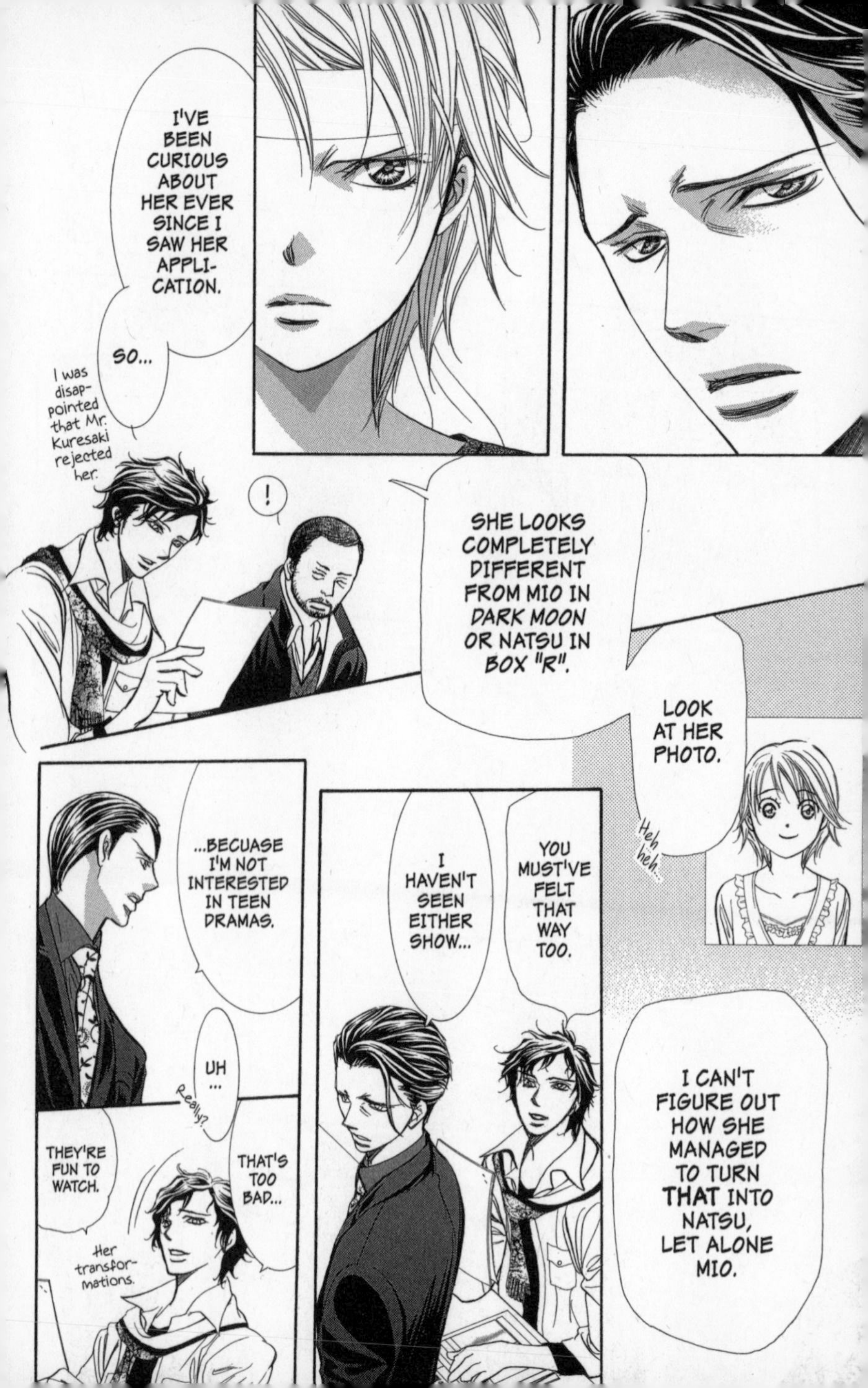

I'VE BEEN CURIOUS ABOUT HER EVER SINCE I SAW HER APPLICATION.
SO...
I was disappointed that Mr. Kuresaki rejected her.
SHE LOOKS COMPLETELY DIFFERENT FROM MIO IN DARK MOON OR NATSU IN BOX "R".
!
LOOK AT HER PHOTO.
Heh heh...
I CAN'T FIGURE OUT HOW SHE MANAGED TO TURN THAT INTO NATSU, LET ALONE MIO.
YOU MUST'VE FELT THAT WAY TOO.
I HAVEN'T SEEN EITHER SHOW...
...BECUASE I'M NOT INTERESTED IN TEEN DRAMAS.
UH...
Really?
THAT'S TOO BAD...
THEY'RE FUN TO WATCH.
Her transformations.

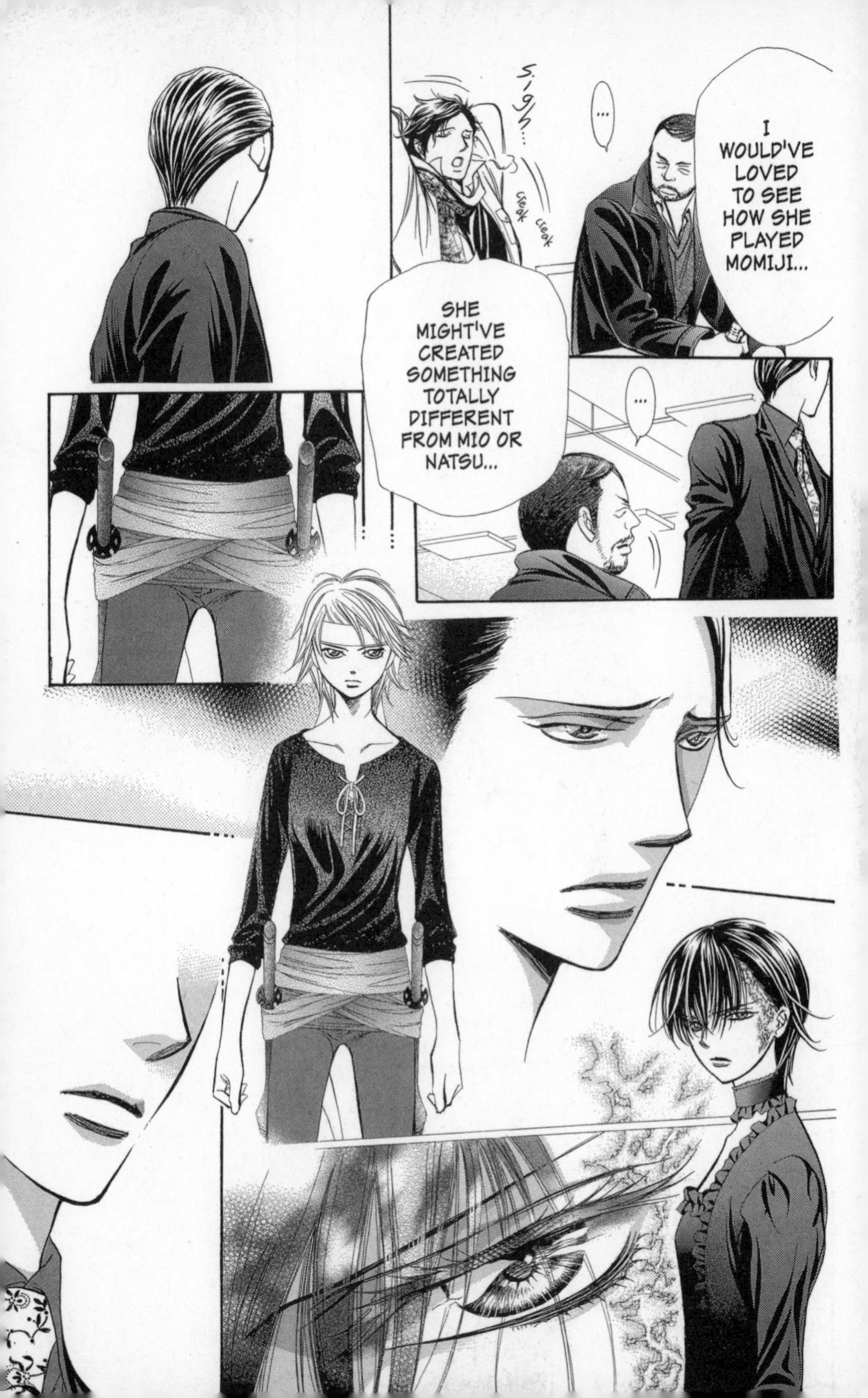
I WOULD'VE LOVED TO SEE HOW SHE PLAYED MOMIJI...
...
sigh...
creak
creak
SHE MIGHT'VE CREATED SOMETHING TOTALLY DIFFERENT FROM MIO OR NATSU...
...

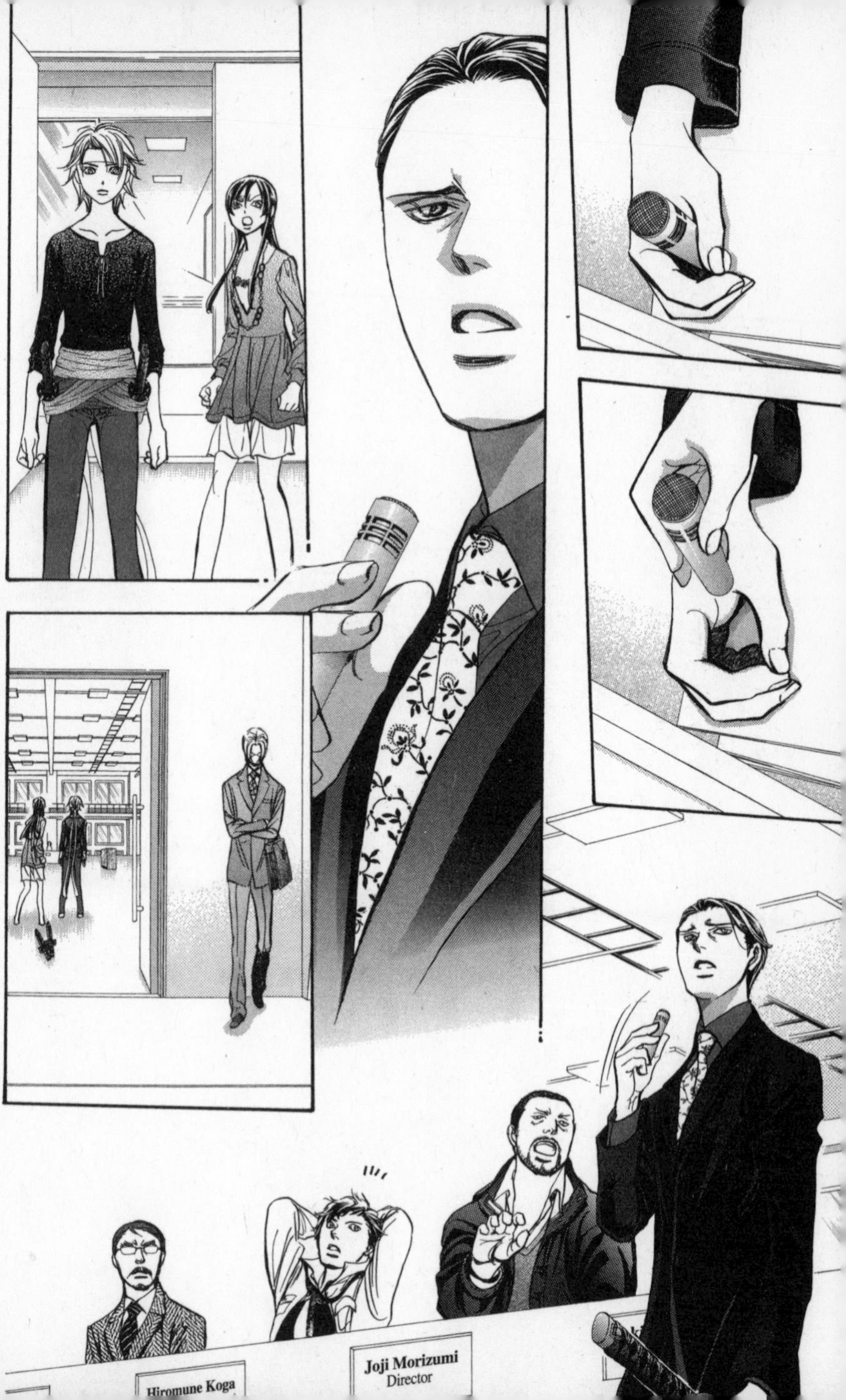
Joji Morizumi
Director
Hiromune Koga

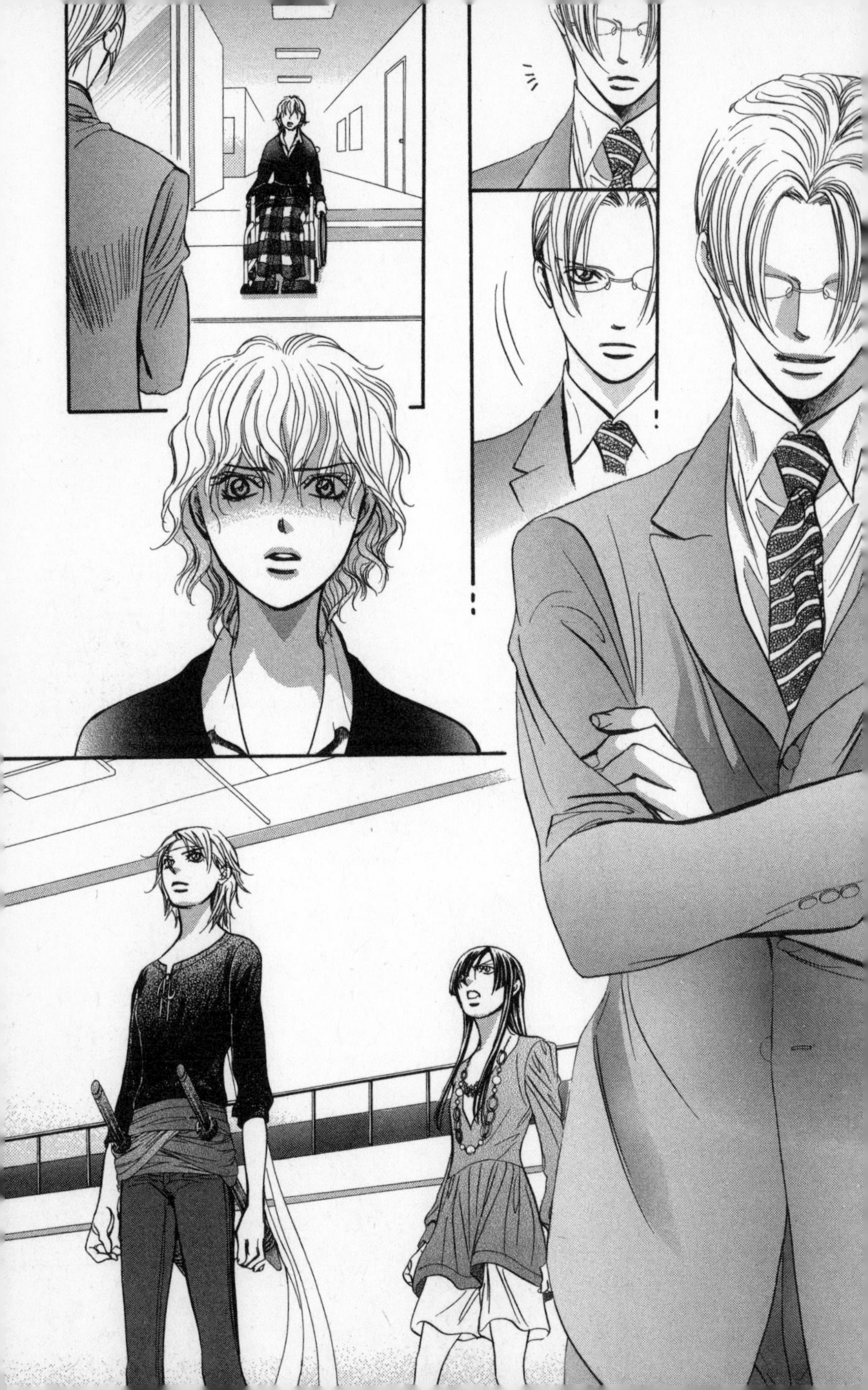

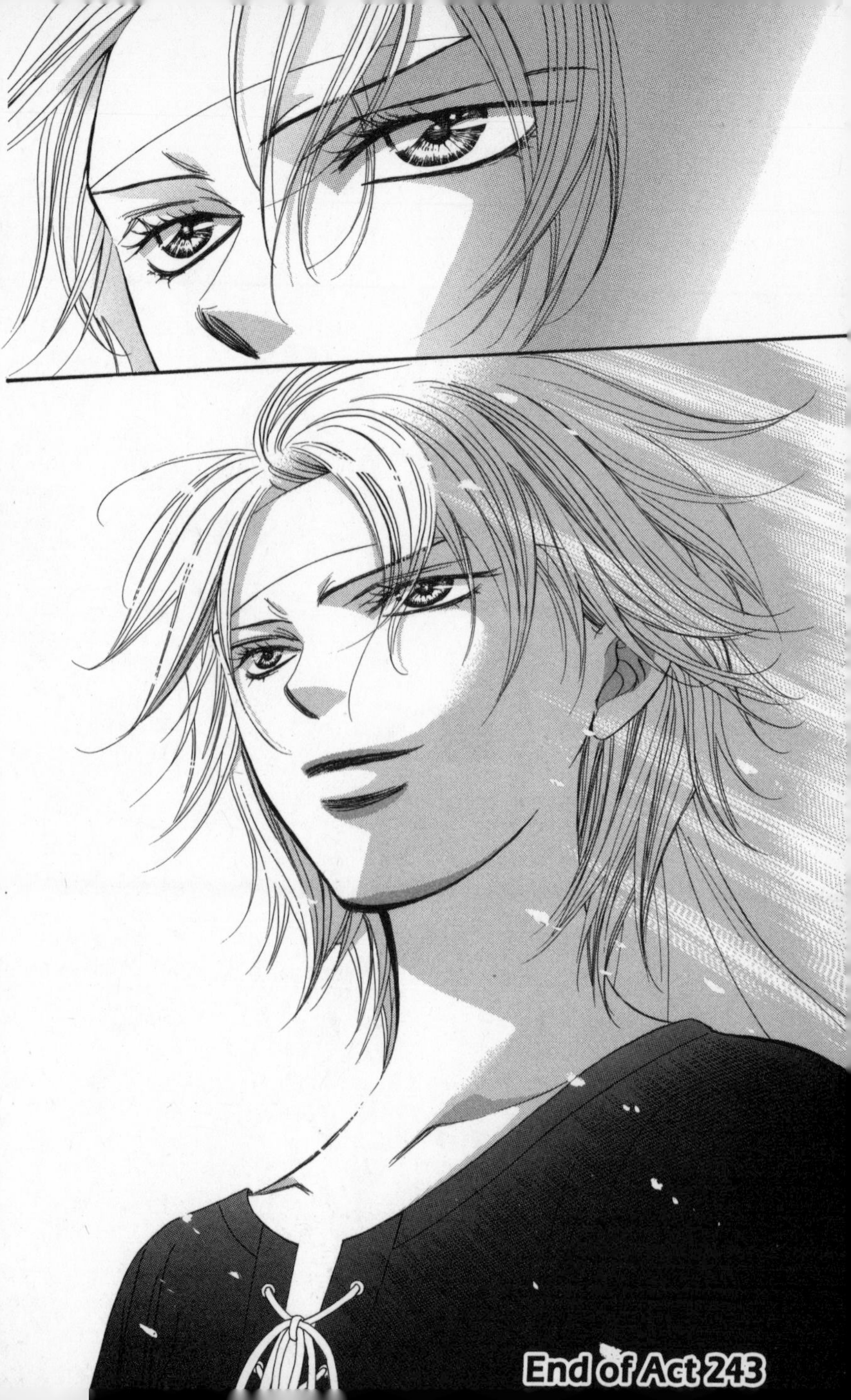
End of Act 243

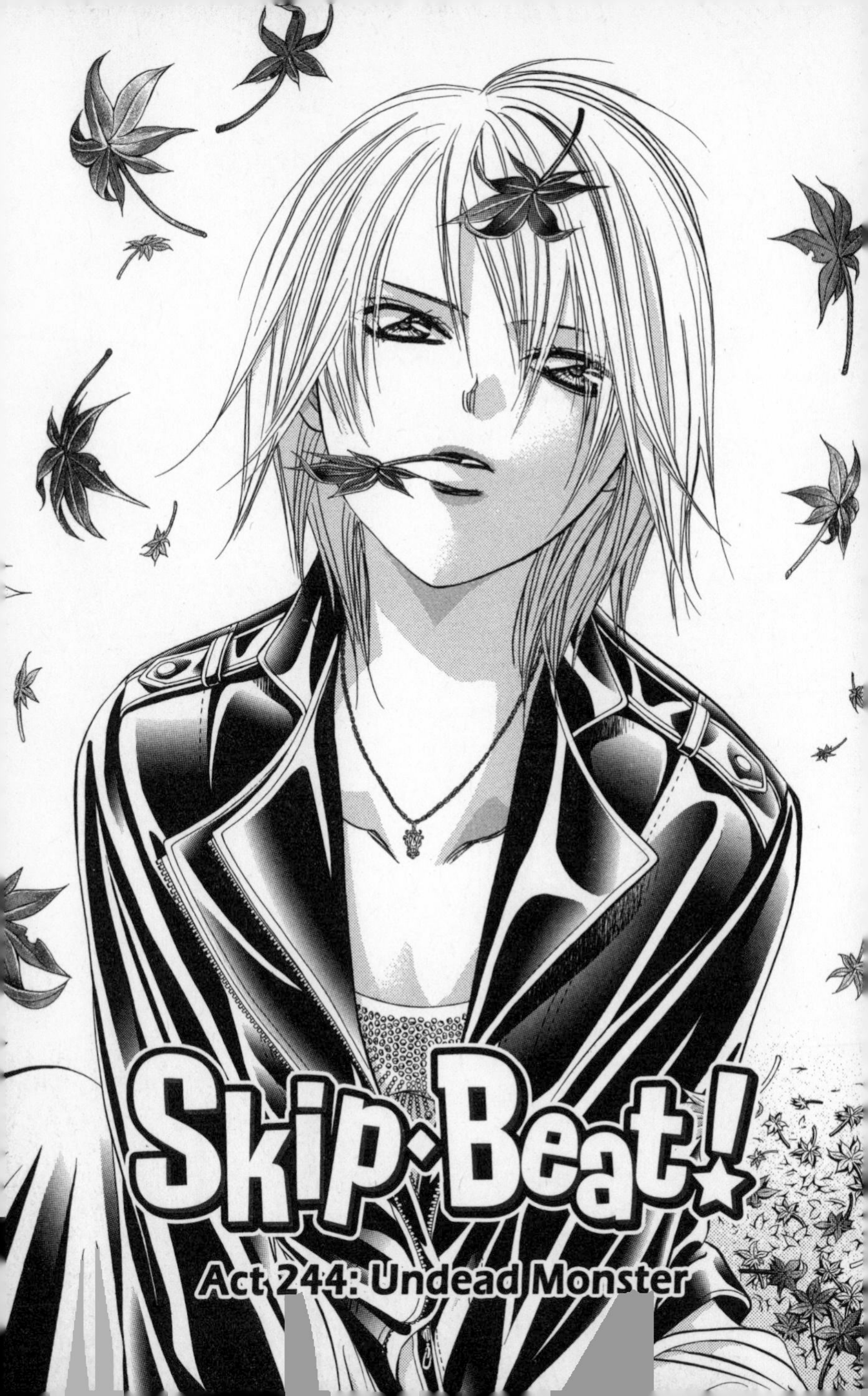
Skip·Beat!
Act 244: Undead Monster

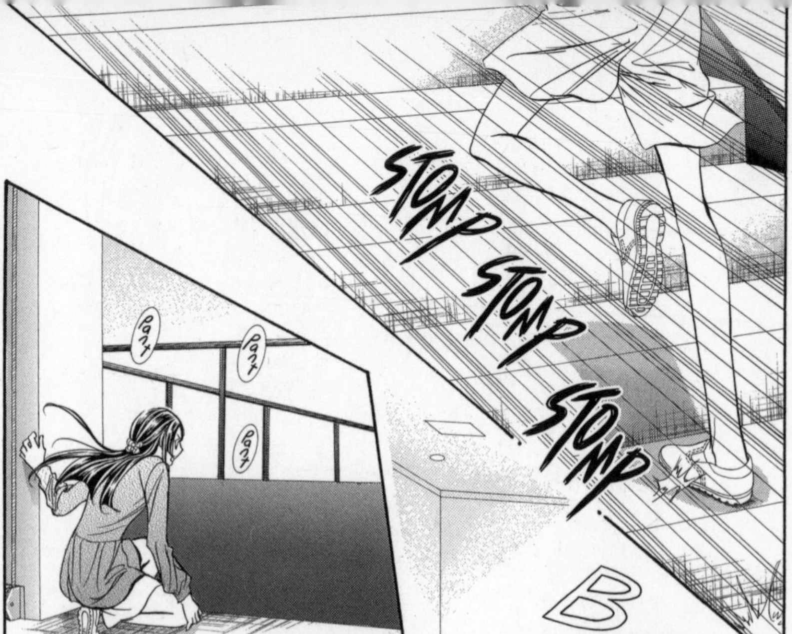
STOMP
STOMP
STOMP
pant
pant
pant
BAM
pant
pant

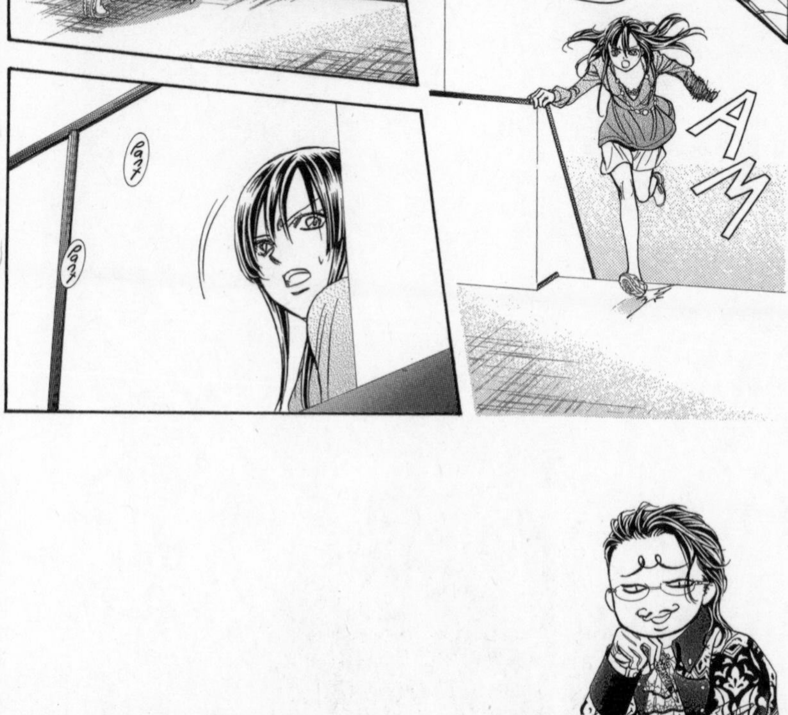

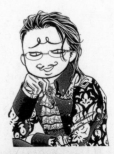

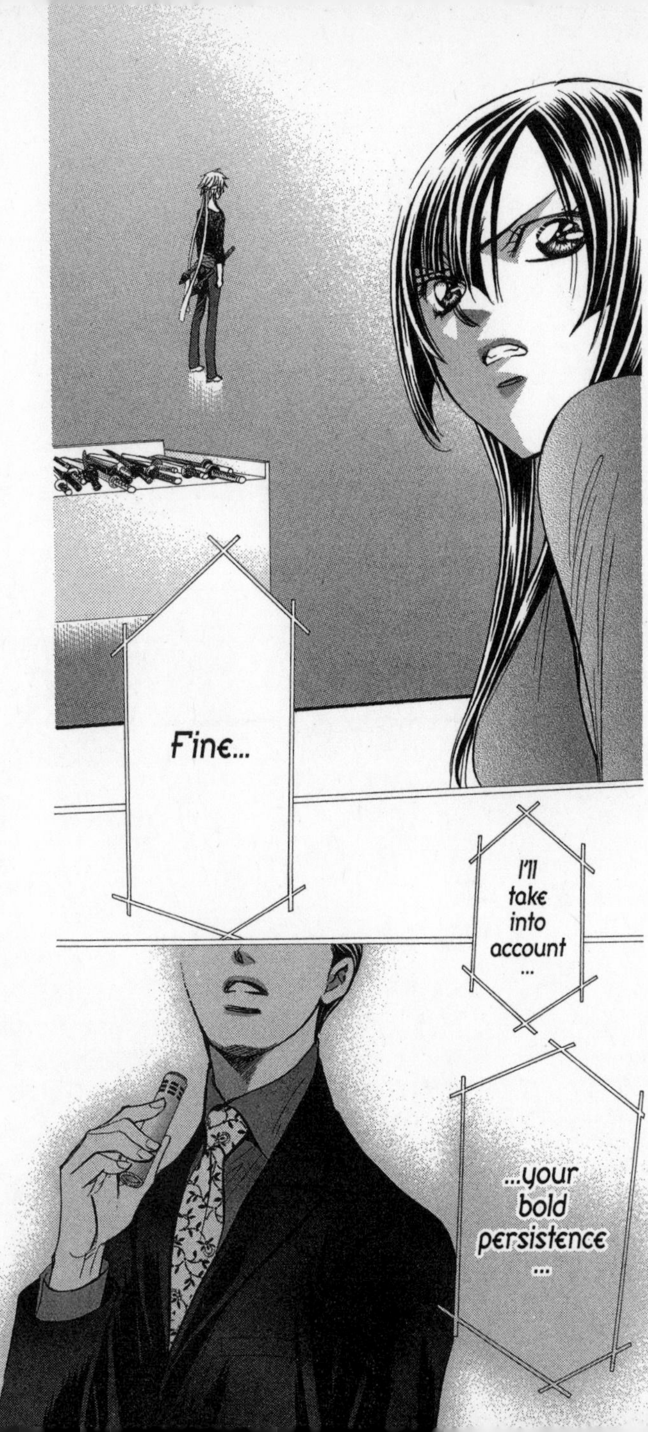
Fine...
I'll take into account ...
...your bold persistence ...

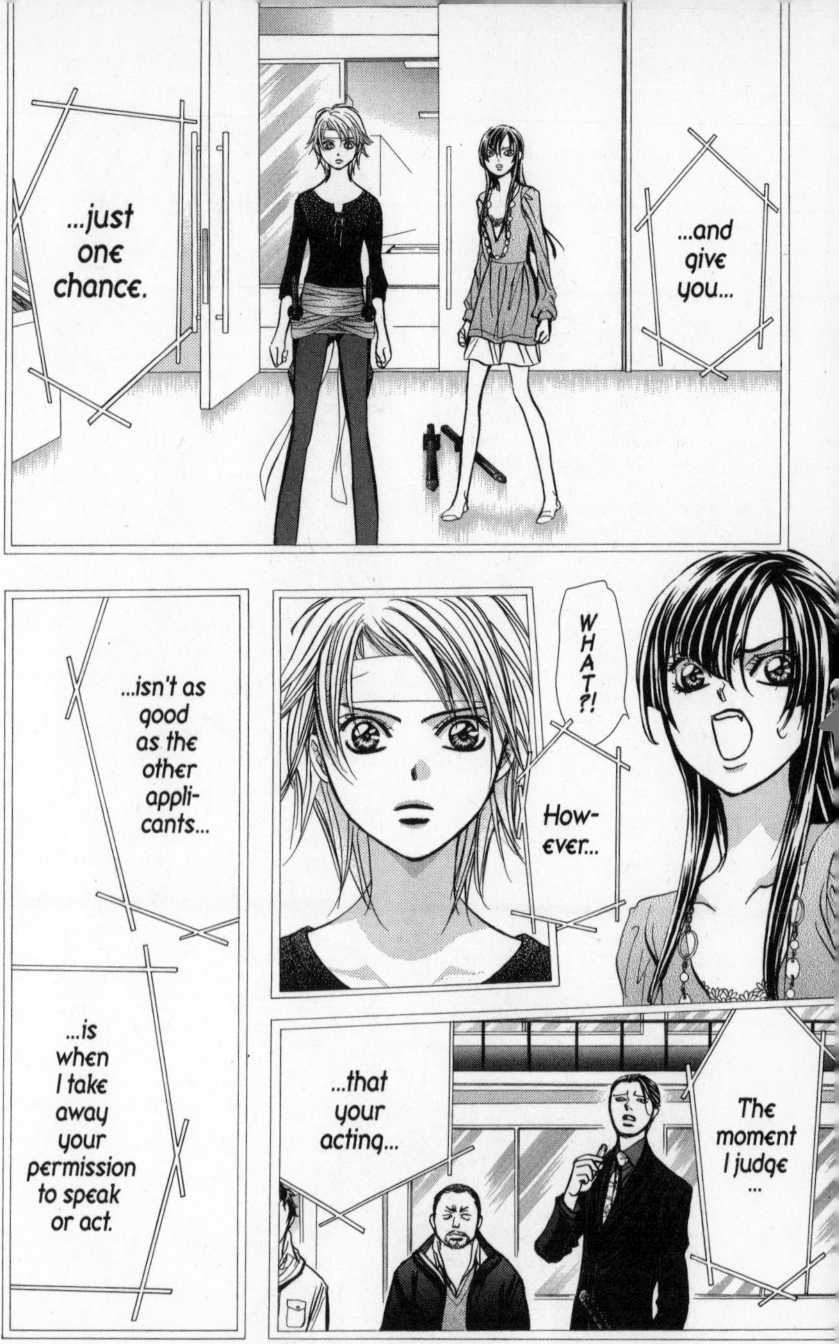
...and give you...
...just one chance.
WHAT?!
However...
The moment I judge...
...that your acting...
...isn't as good as the other applicants...
...is when I take away your permission to speak or act.

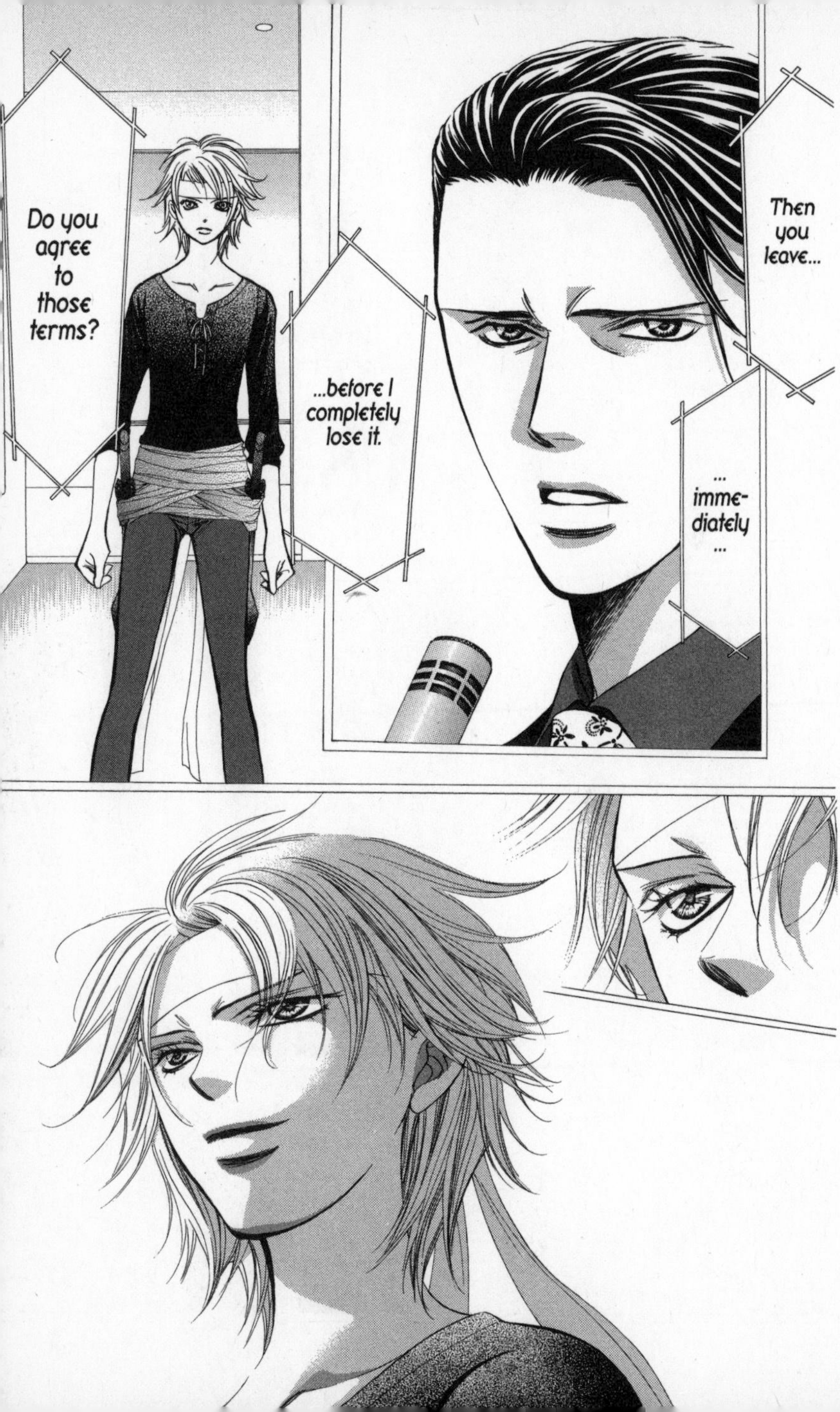
Then you leave...
...immediately...
...before I completely lose it.
Do you agree to those terms?

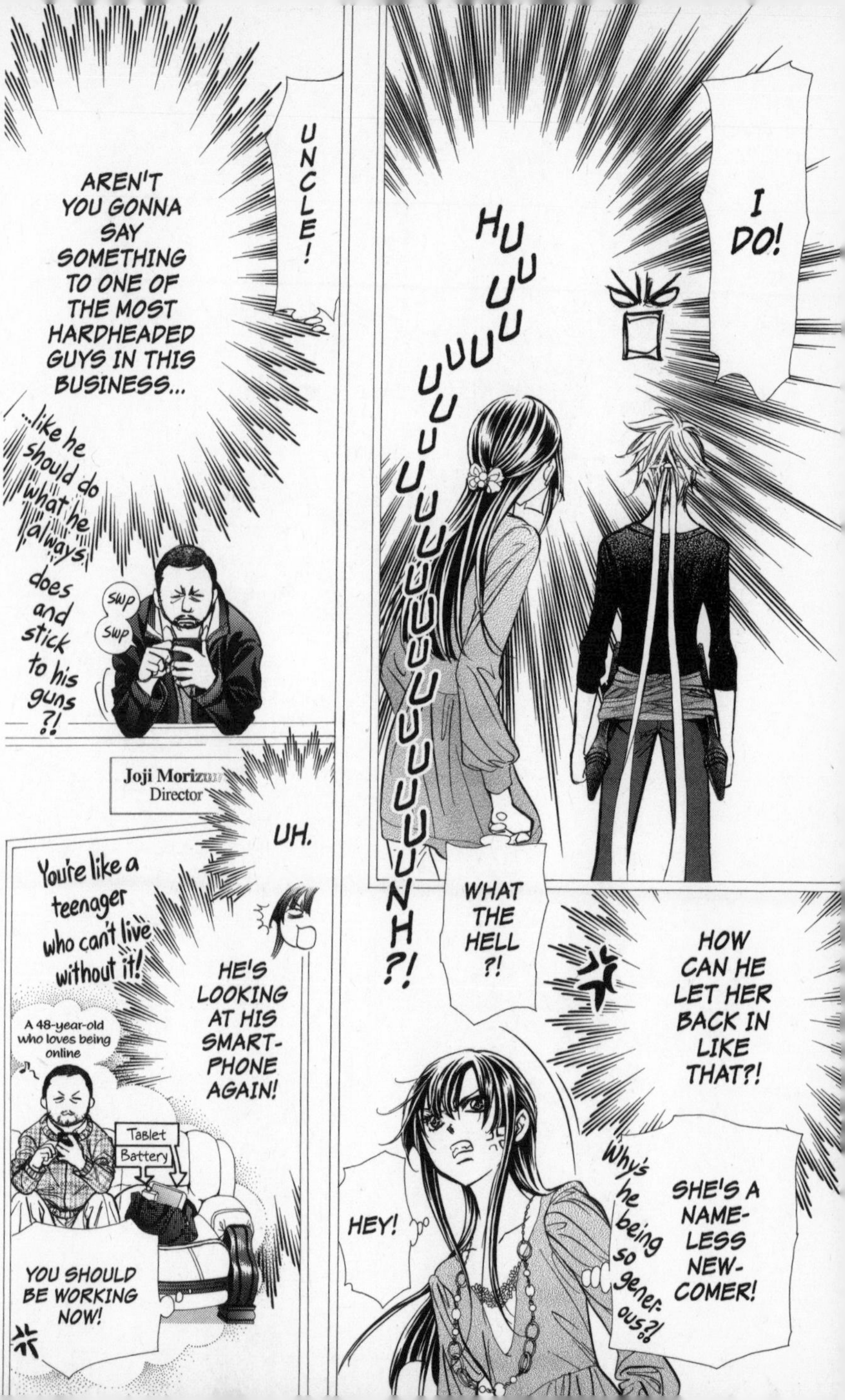
I DO!
HUUUUUUUUUUUUUUUUUUUUUNH?!
WHAT THE HELL?!
HOW CAN HE LET HER BACK IN LIKE THAT?!
SHE'S A NAMELESS NEWCOMER!
Why's he being so generous?!
HEY!
UNCLE!
AREN'T YOU GONNA SAY SOMETHING TO ONE OF THE MOST HARDHEADED GUYS IN THIS BUSINESS...
...like he should do what he always does and stick to his guns?!
swp
swp
Joji Morizu
Director
UH.
You're like a teenager who can't live without it!
HE'S LOOKING AT HIS SMARTPHONE AGAIN!
A 48-year-old who loves being online
Tablet
Battery
YOU SHOULD BE WORKING NOW!

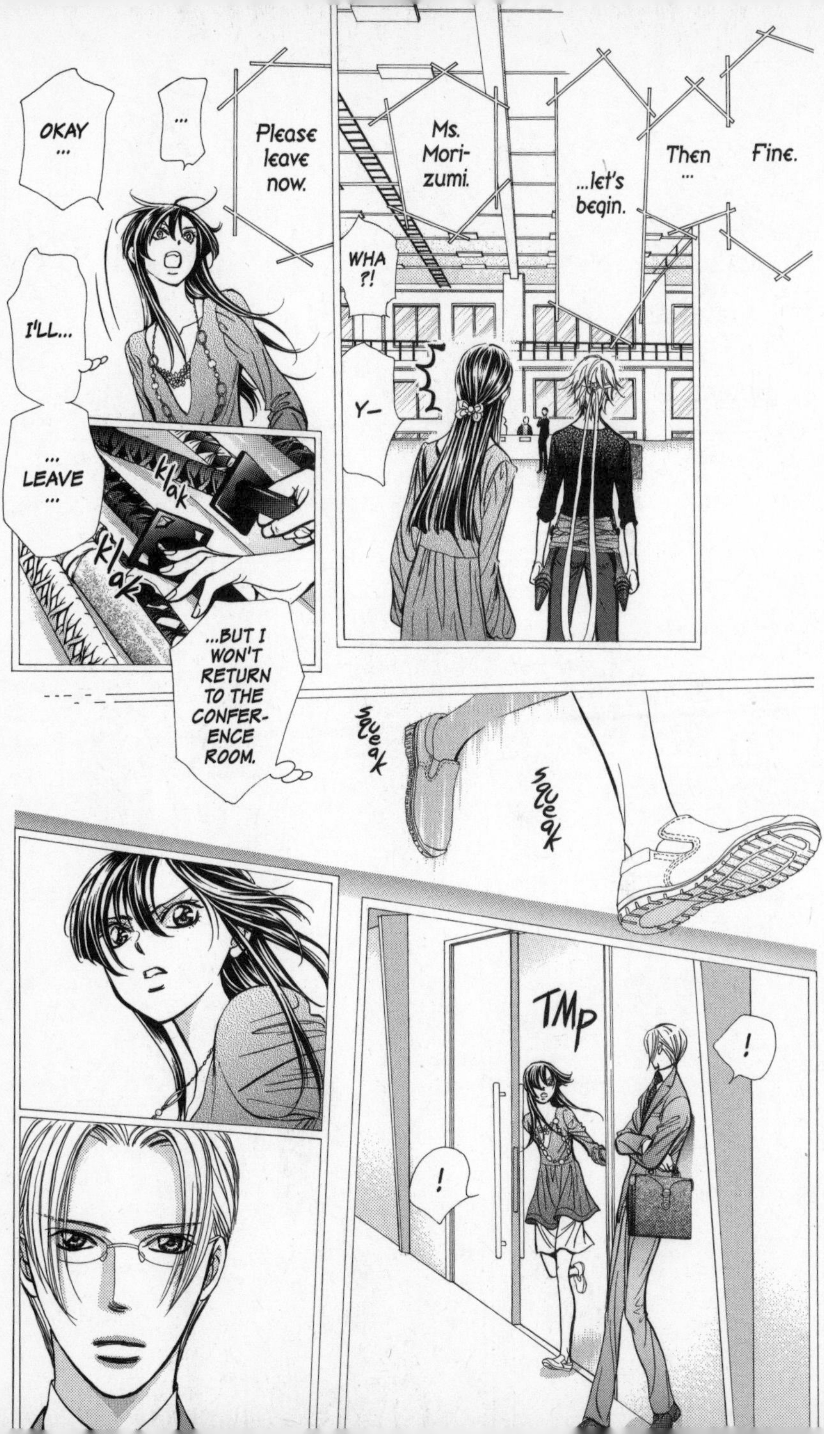
Fine.
Then...
...let's begin.
Ms. Morizumi.
Please leave now.
WHA?!
Y-
...
OKAY...
I'LL...
...LEAVE...
klak
klak
...BUT I WON'T RETURN TO THE CONFERENCE ROOM.
squeak
squeak
TMP
!
!

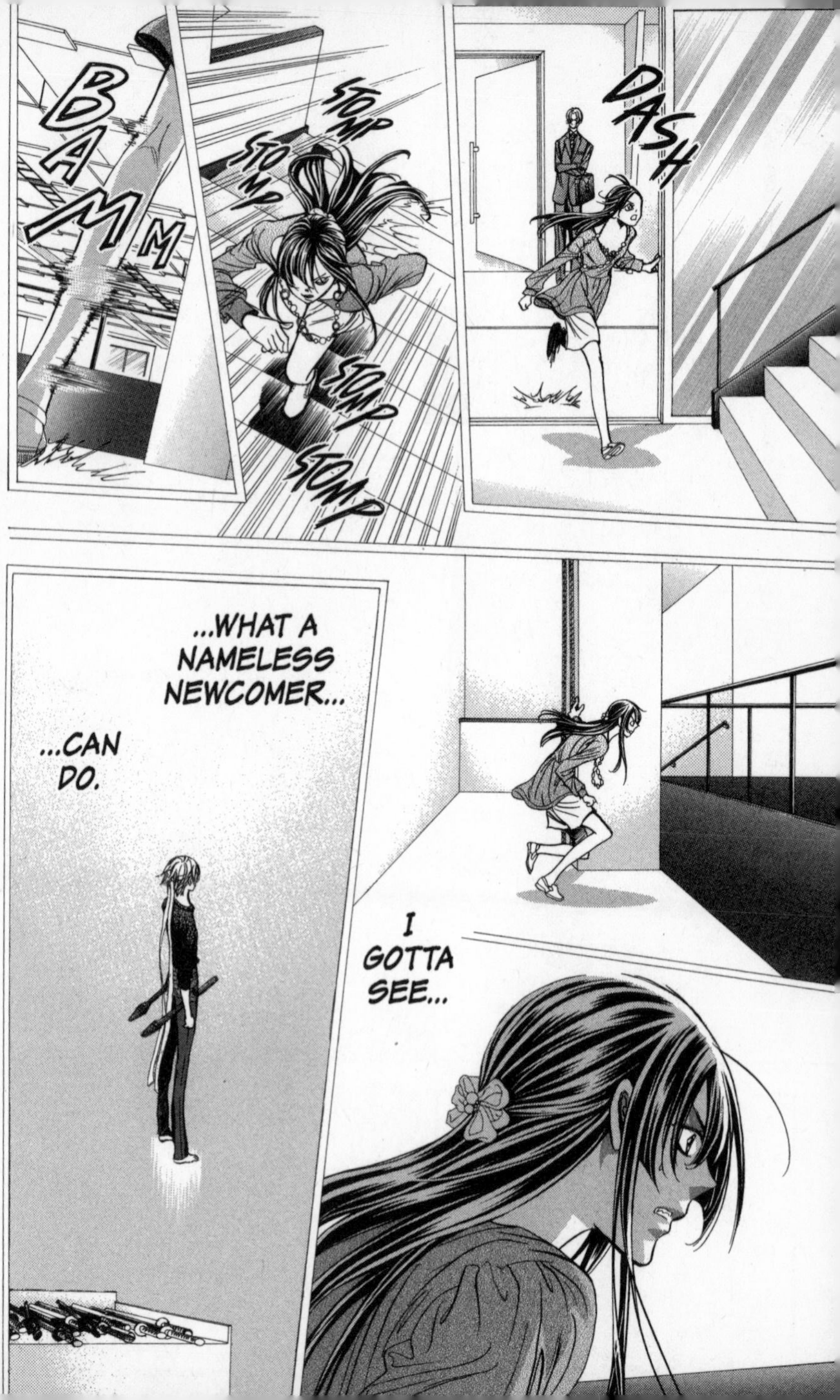
DASH
STOMP STOMP
STOMP STOMP
BAMMM
I GOTTA SEE...
...WHAT A NAMELESS NEWCOMER...
...CAN DO.

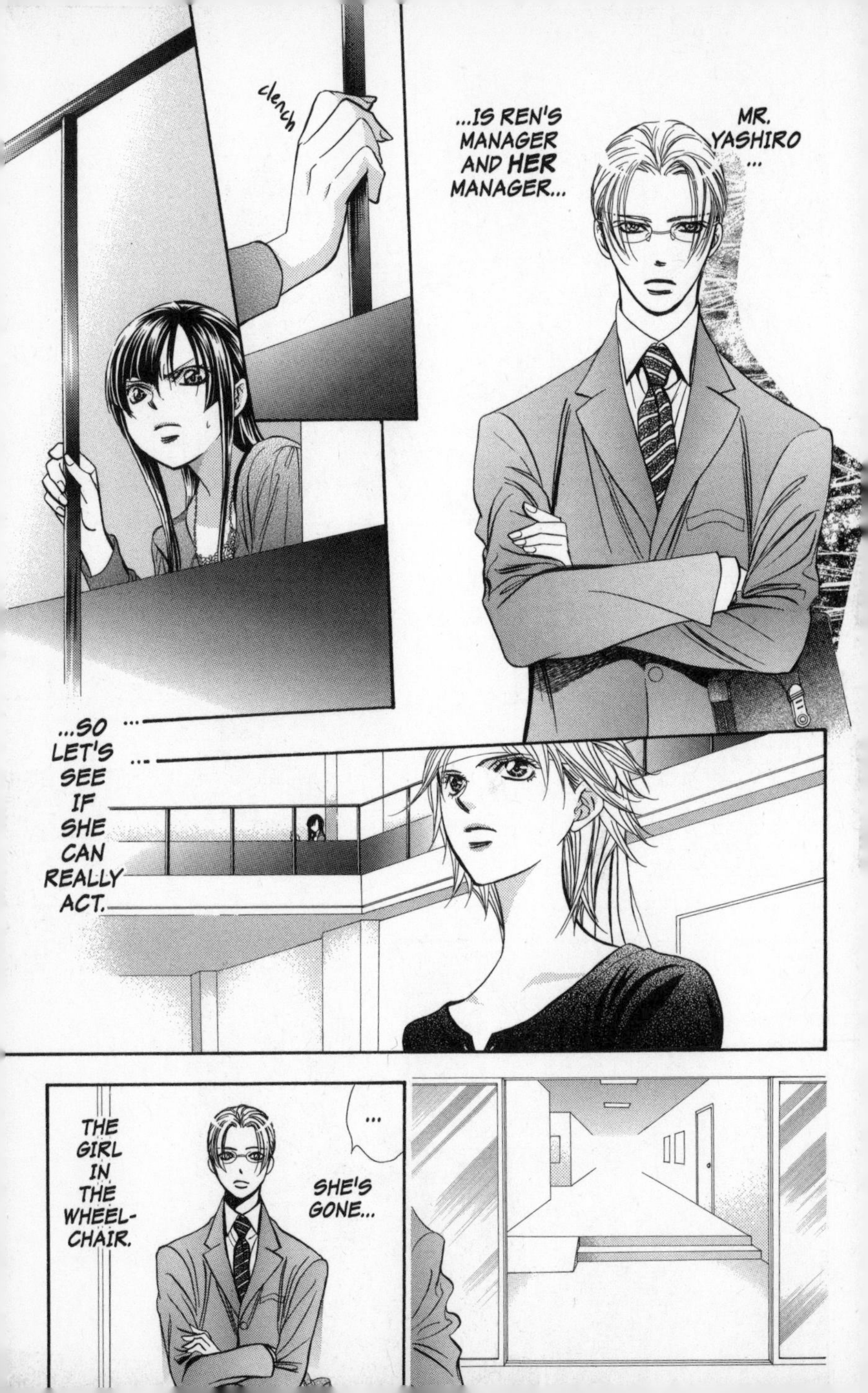
MR. YASHIRO...
...IS REN'S MANAGER AND **HER** MANAGER...
clench
...SO LET'S SEE IF SHE CAN REALLY ACT.
...
SHE'S GONE...
THE GIRL IN THE WHEEL-CHAIR.

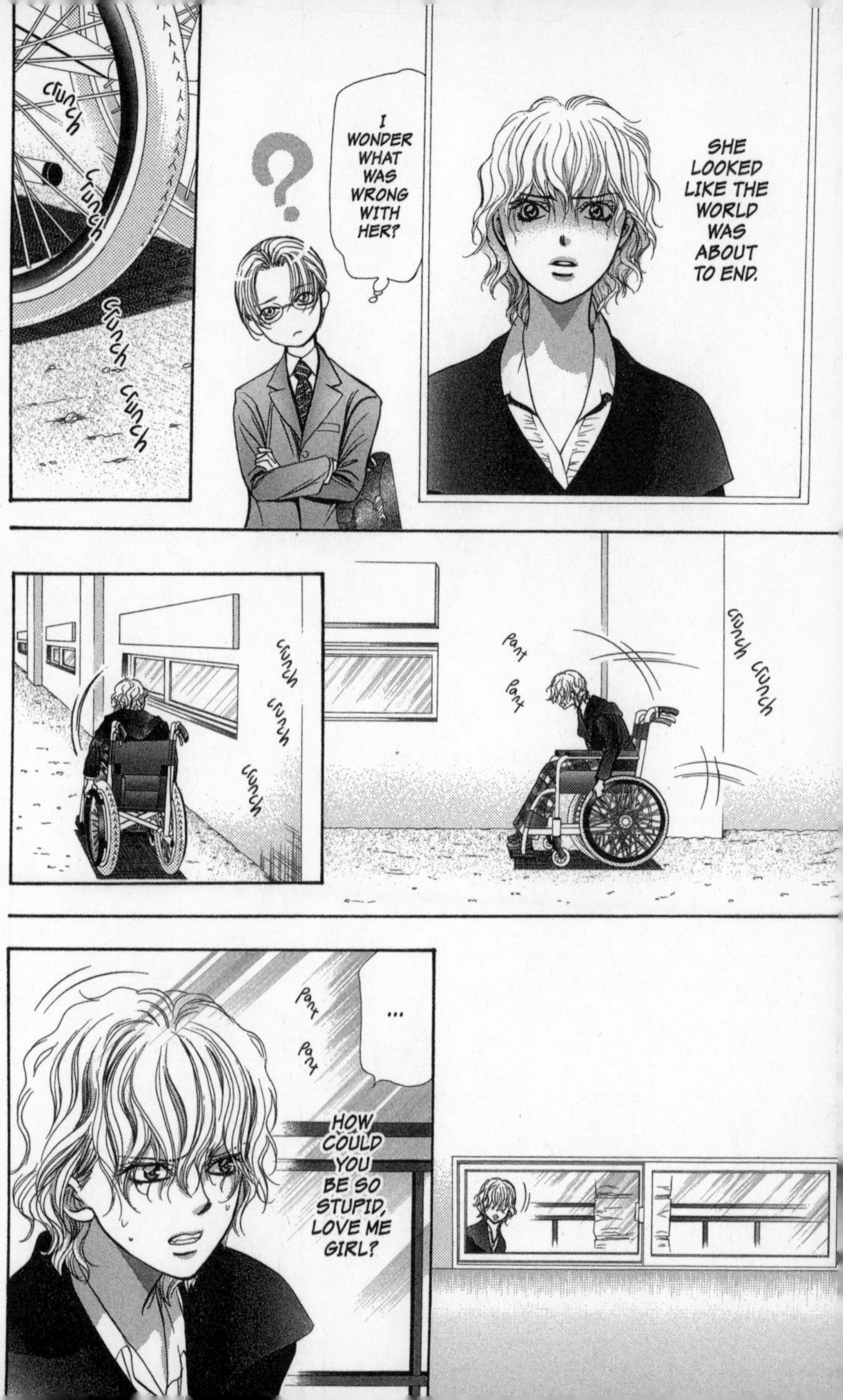
SHE LOOKED LIKE THE WORLD WAS ABOUT TO END.
I WONDER WHAT WAS WRONG WITH HER?
crunch
crunch
crunch
crunch
crunch crunch
pant
pant
crunch
crunch
crunch
crunch
pant
pant
...
HOW COULD YOU BE SO STUPID, LOVE ME GIRL?

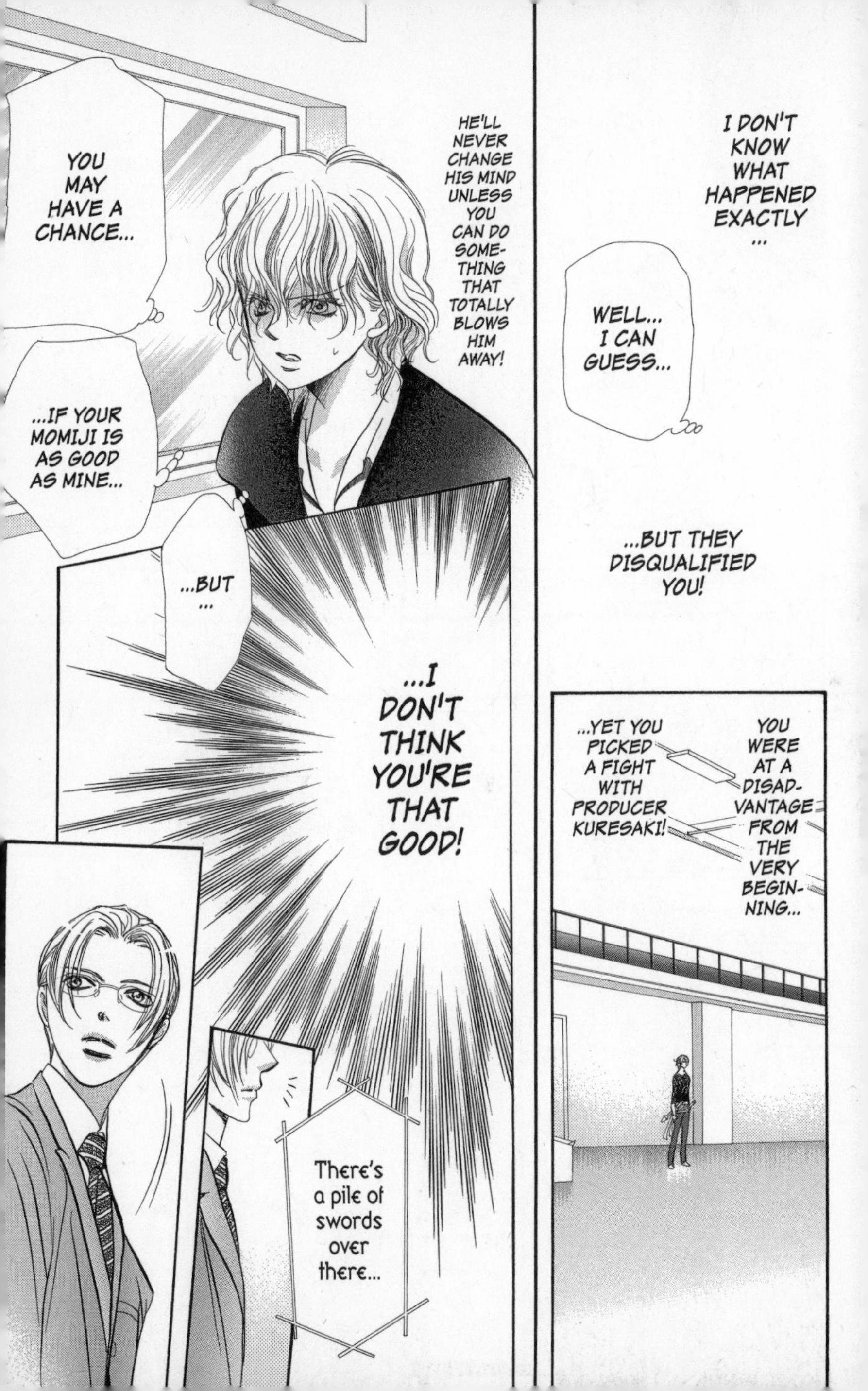
I DON'T KNOW WHAT HAPPENED EXACTLY...
WELL... I CAN GUESS...
...BUT THEY DISQUALIFIED YOU!
YOU WERE AT A DISADVANTAGE FROM THE VERY BEGINNING...
...YET YOU PICKED A FIGHT WITH PRODUCER KURESAKI!
HE'LL NEVER CHANGE HIS MIND UNLESS YOU CAN DO SOMETHING THAT TOTALLY BLOWS HIM AWAY!
YOU MAY HAVE A CHANCE...
...IF YOUR MOMIJI IS AS GOOD AS MINE...
...BUT ...
...I DON'T THINK YOU'RE THAT GOOD!
There's a pile of swords over there...

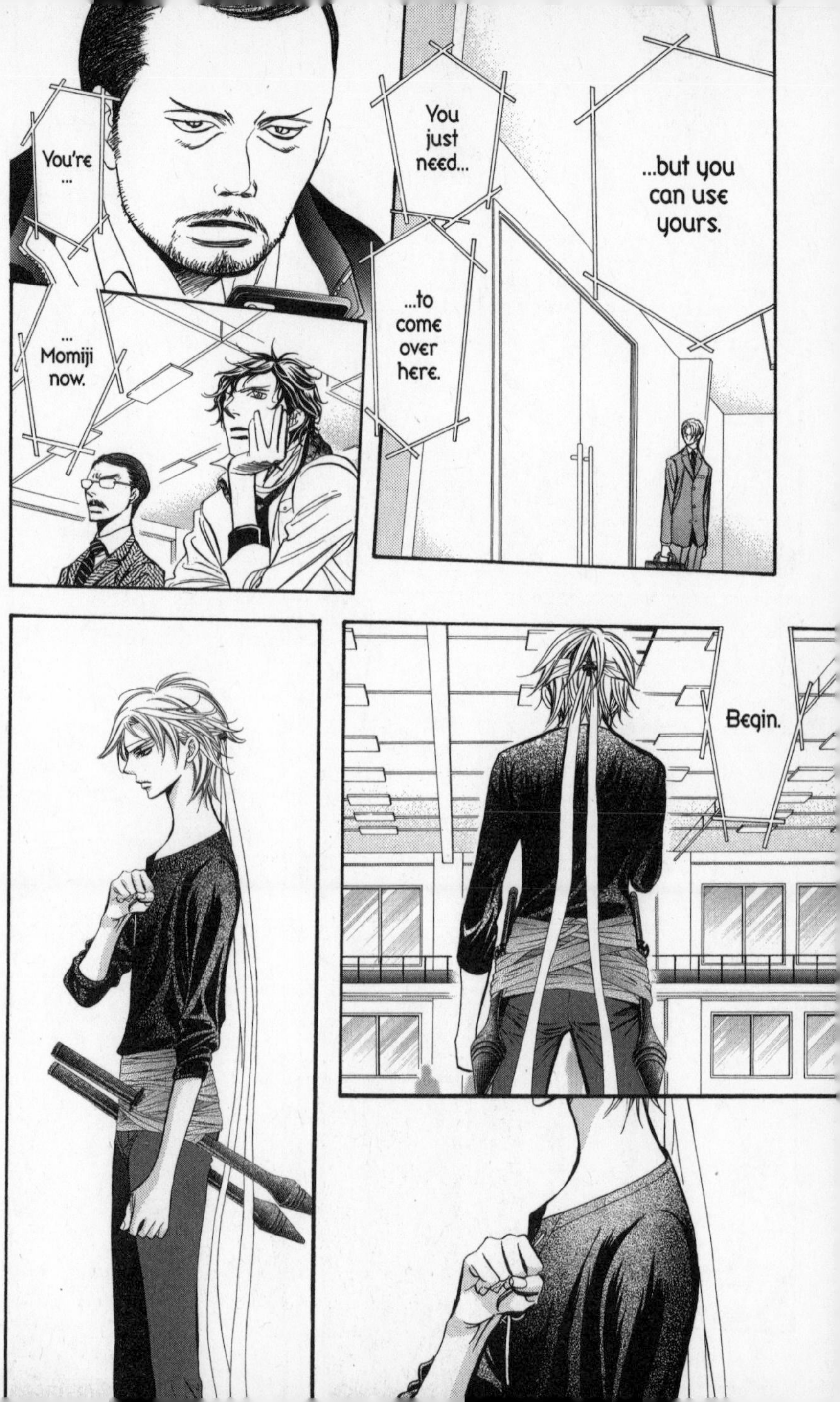
...but you can use yours.
You just need...
...to come over here.
You're ...
... Momiji now.
Begin.

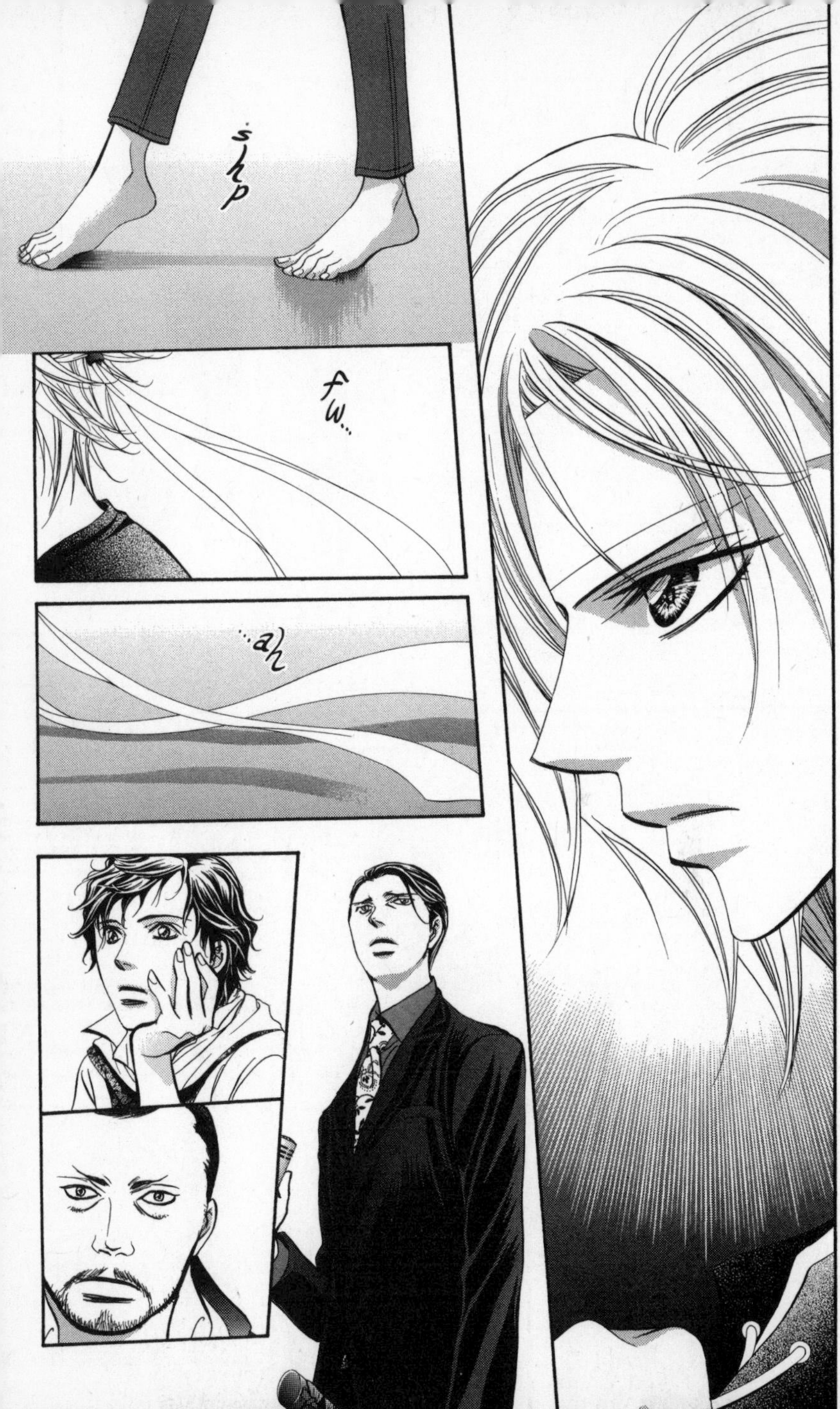
shp
fw...
...ah

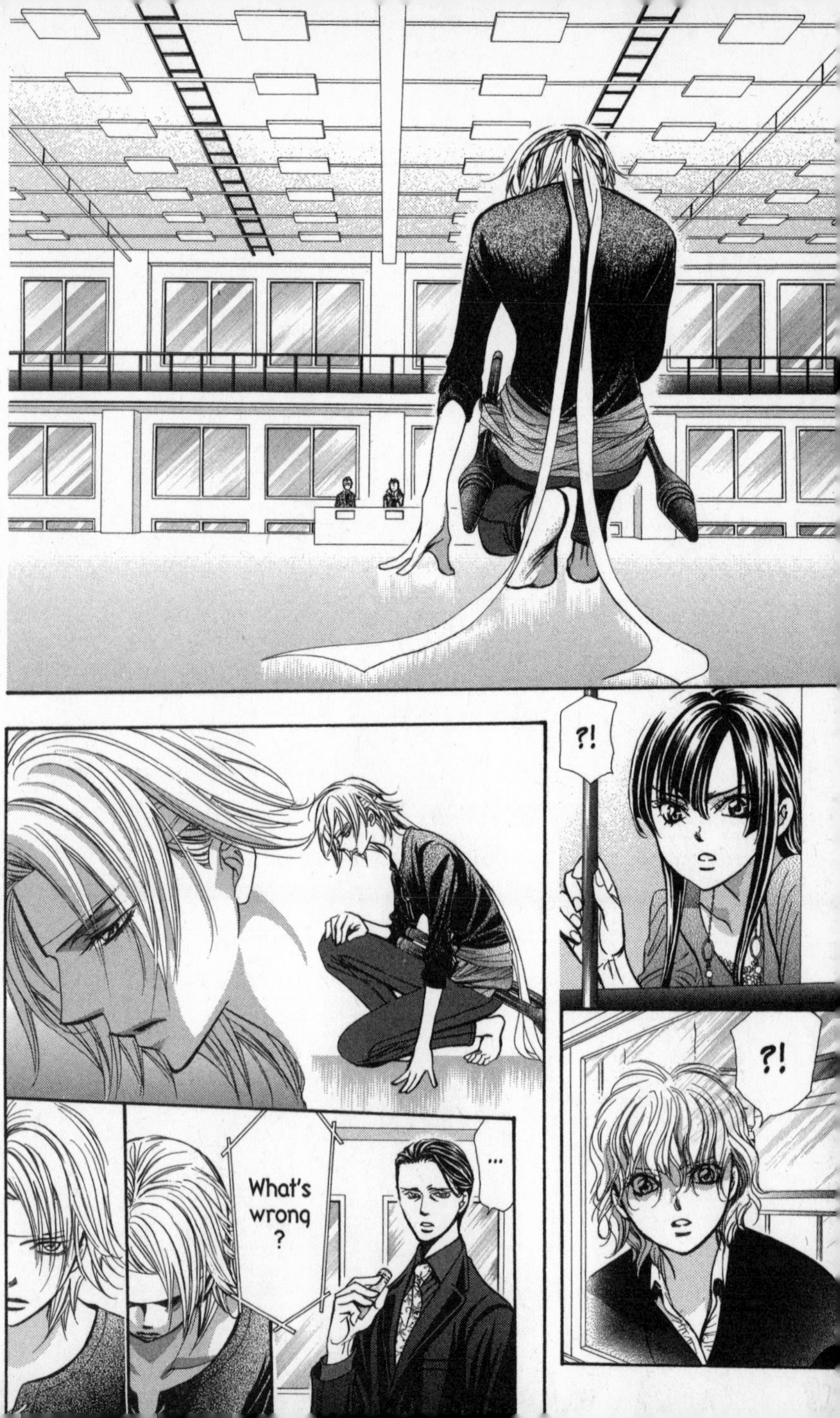
?!
?!
...
What's wrong ?

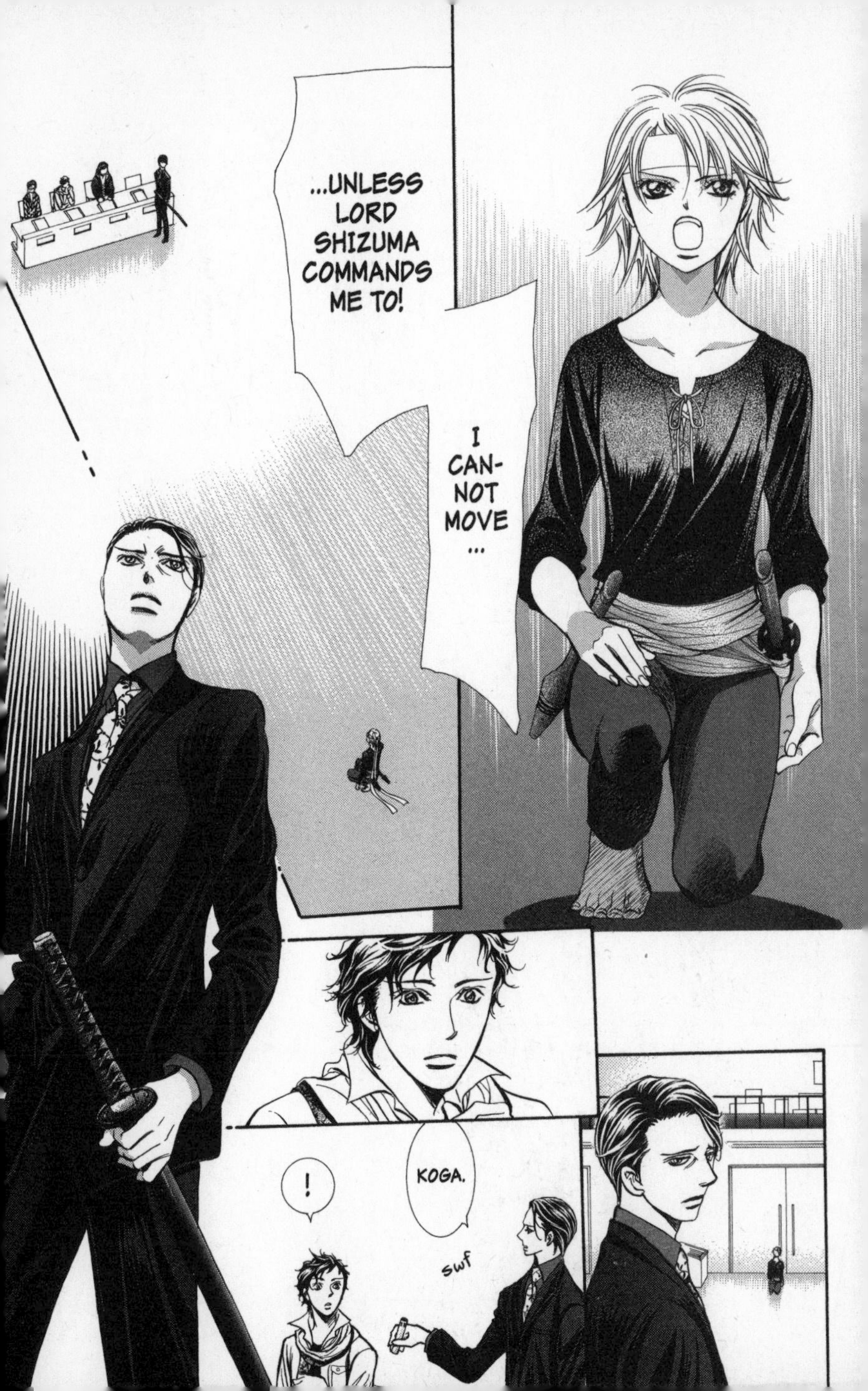
...UNLESS LORD SHIZUMA COMMANDS ME TO!
I CAN-NOT MOVE ...
KOGA.
swf
!

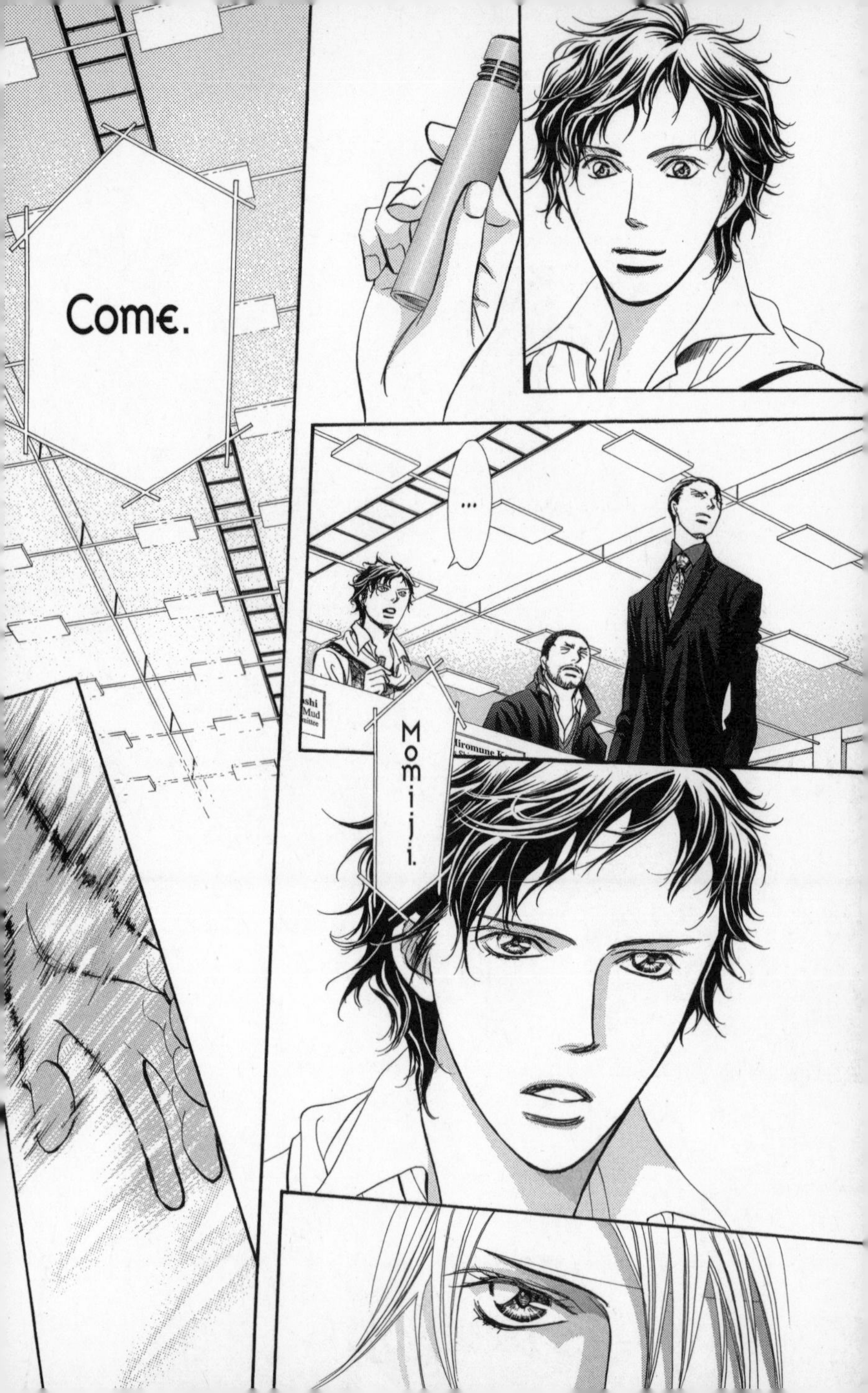
Come.
...
Momiji.

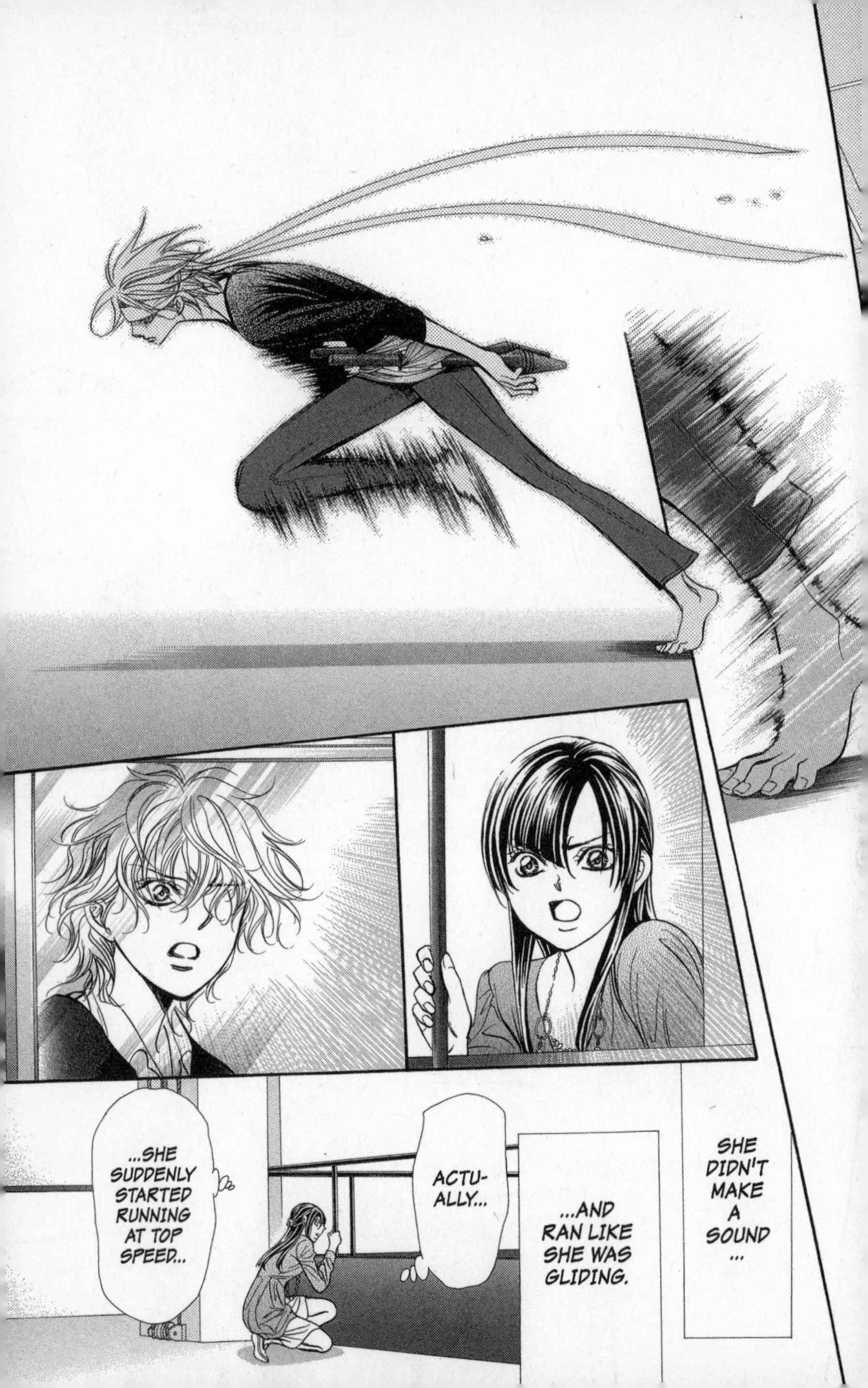
SHE DIDN'T MAKE A SOUND ...
...AND RAN LIKE SHE WAS GLIDING.
ACTU-ALLY...
...SHE SUDDENLY STARTED RUNNING AT TOP SPEED...

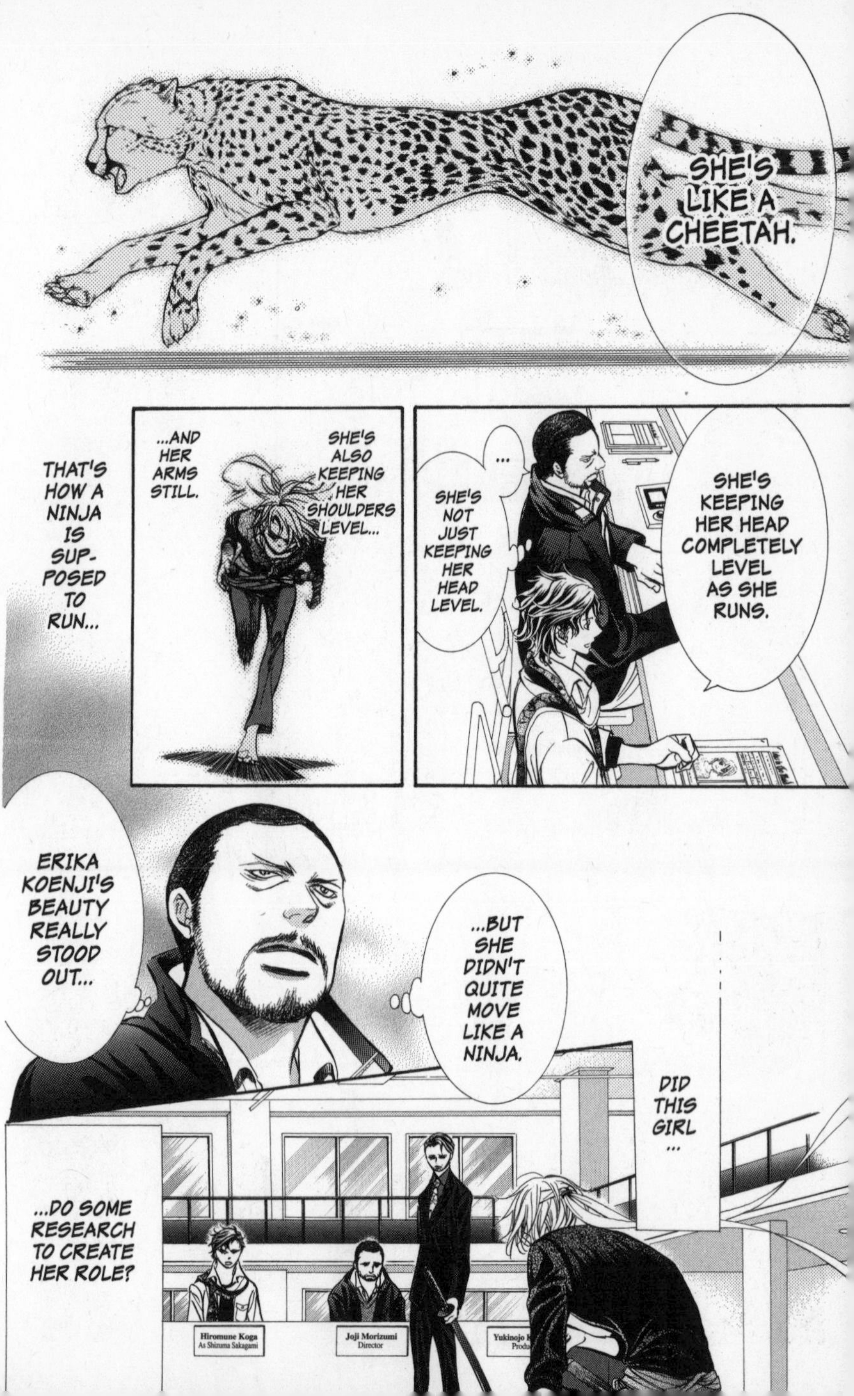
SHE'S LIKE A CHEETAH.
SHE'S KEEPING HER HEAD COMPLETELY LEVEL AS SHE RUNS.
...
SHE'S NOT JUST KEEPING HER HEAD LEVEL.
SHE'S ALSO KEEPING HER SHOULDERS LEVEL...
...AND HER ARMS STILL.
THAT'S HOW A NINJA IS SUP-POSED TO RUN...
ERIKA KOENJI'S BEAUTY REALLY STOOD OUT...
...BUT SHE DIDN'T QUITE MOVE LIKE A NINJA.
DID THIS GIRL...
...DO SOME RESEARCH TO CREATE HER ROLE?
Joji Morizumi
Director
Hiromune Koga
As Shizuma Sakagami

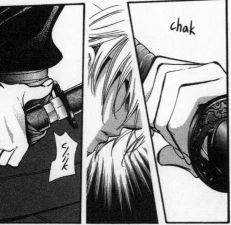

Joji Morizumi
Director

chak

Joji Morizumi
Director

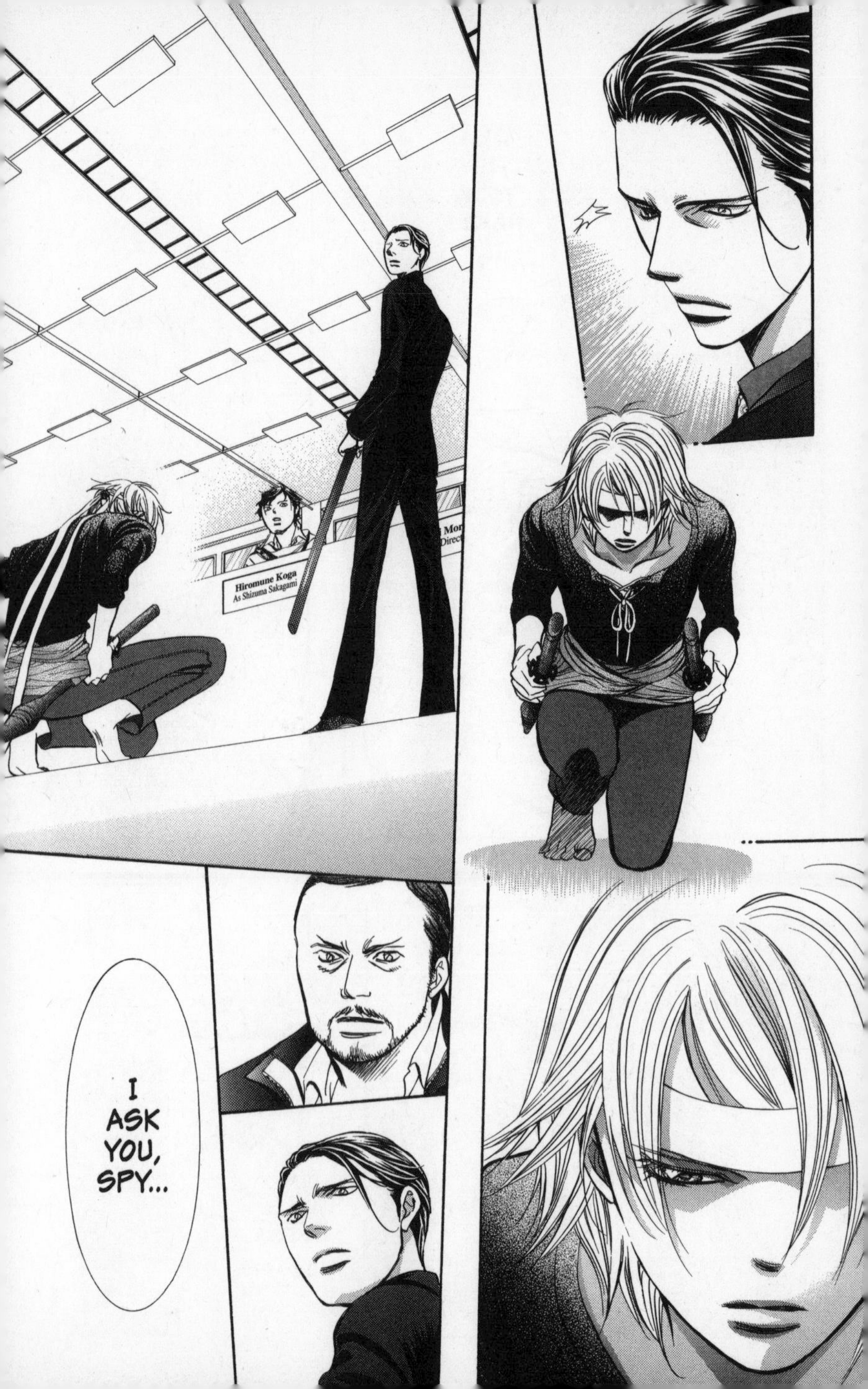
Hiromune Koga
As Shizuma Sakagami
I ASK YOU, SPY...

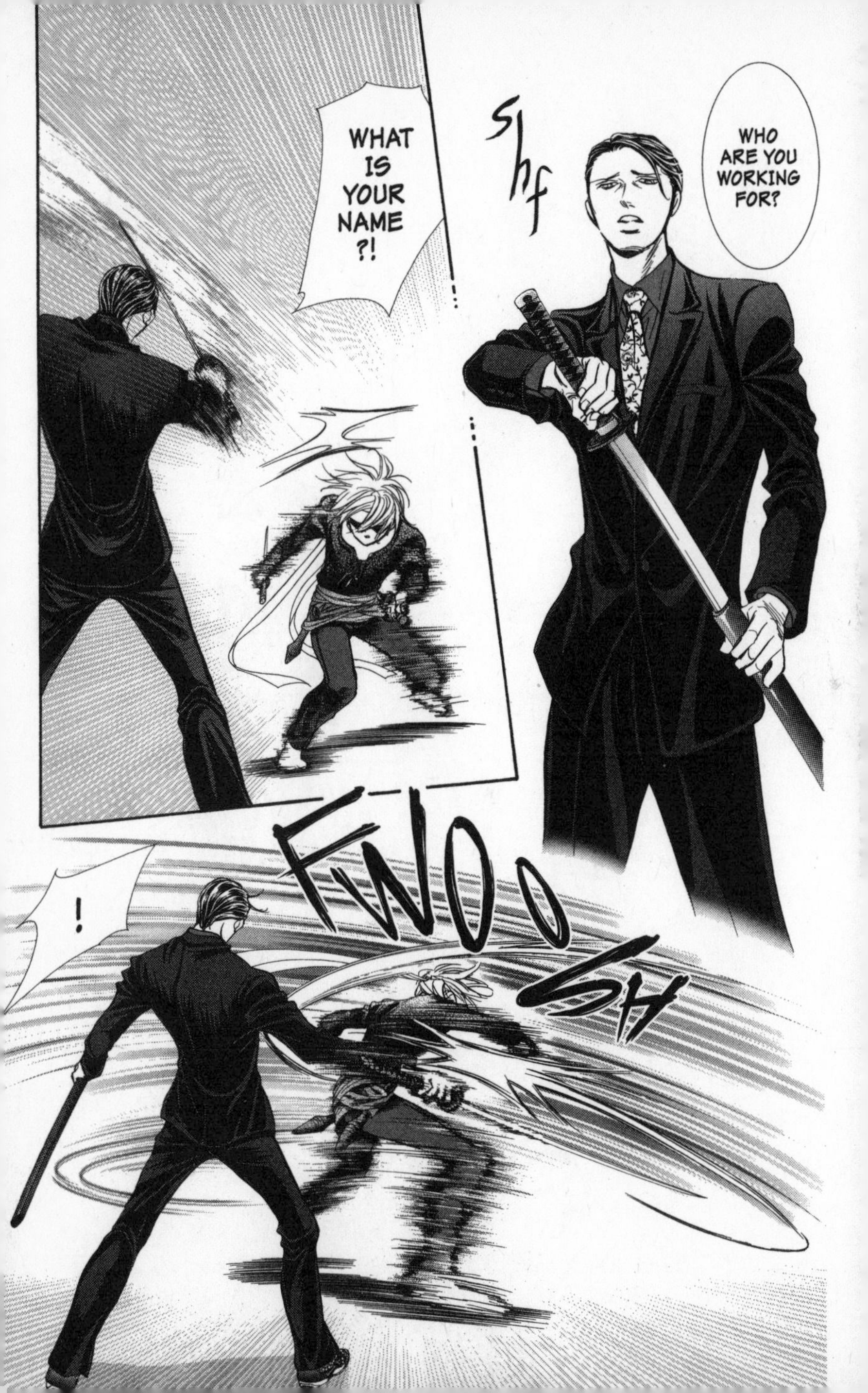
WHO ARE YOU WORKING FOR?
SHF
WHAT IS YOUR NAME?!
!
FWOOSH

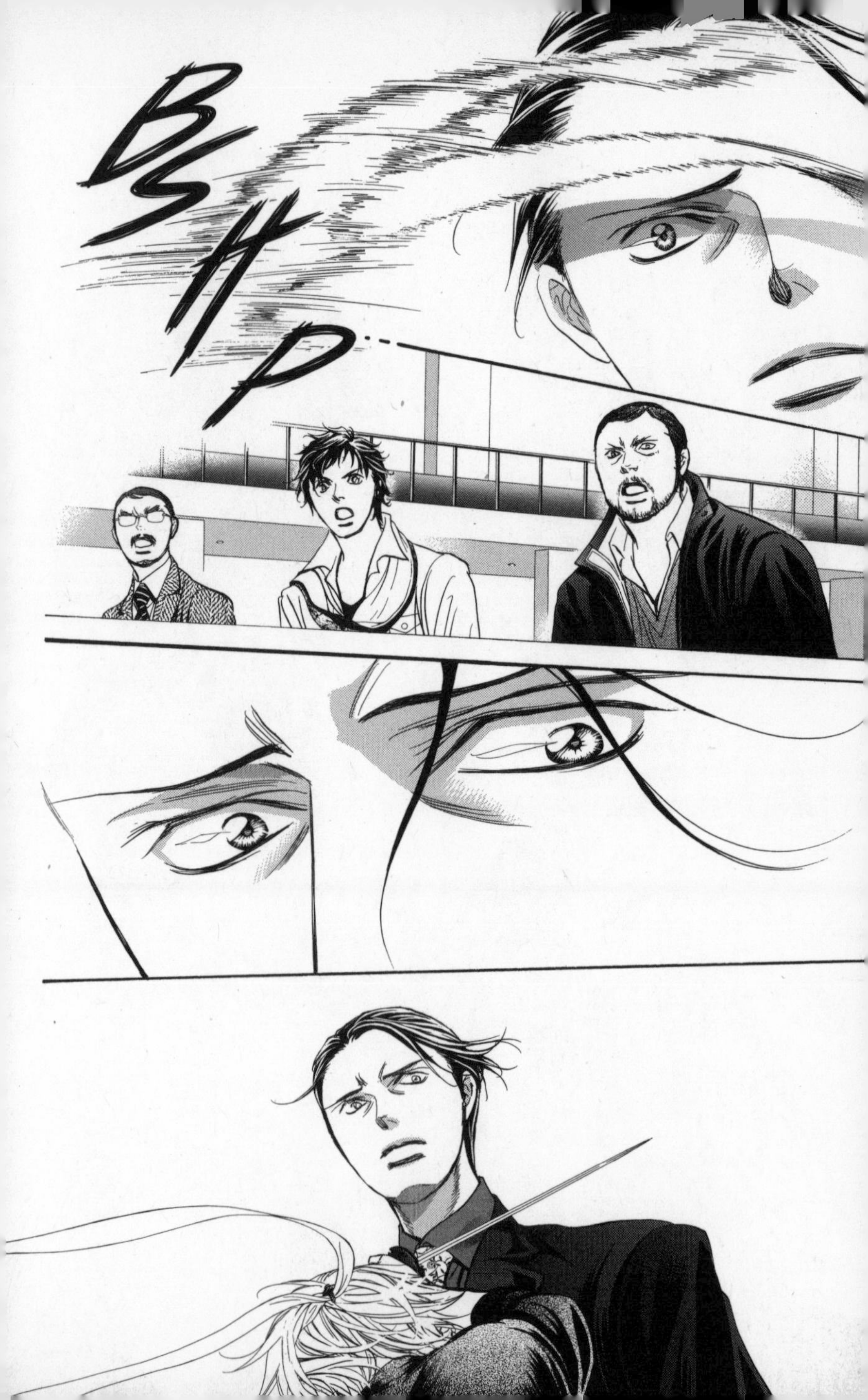
BSHP

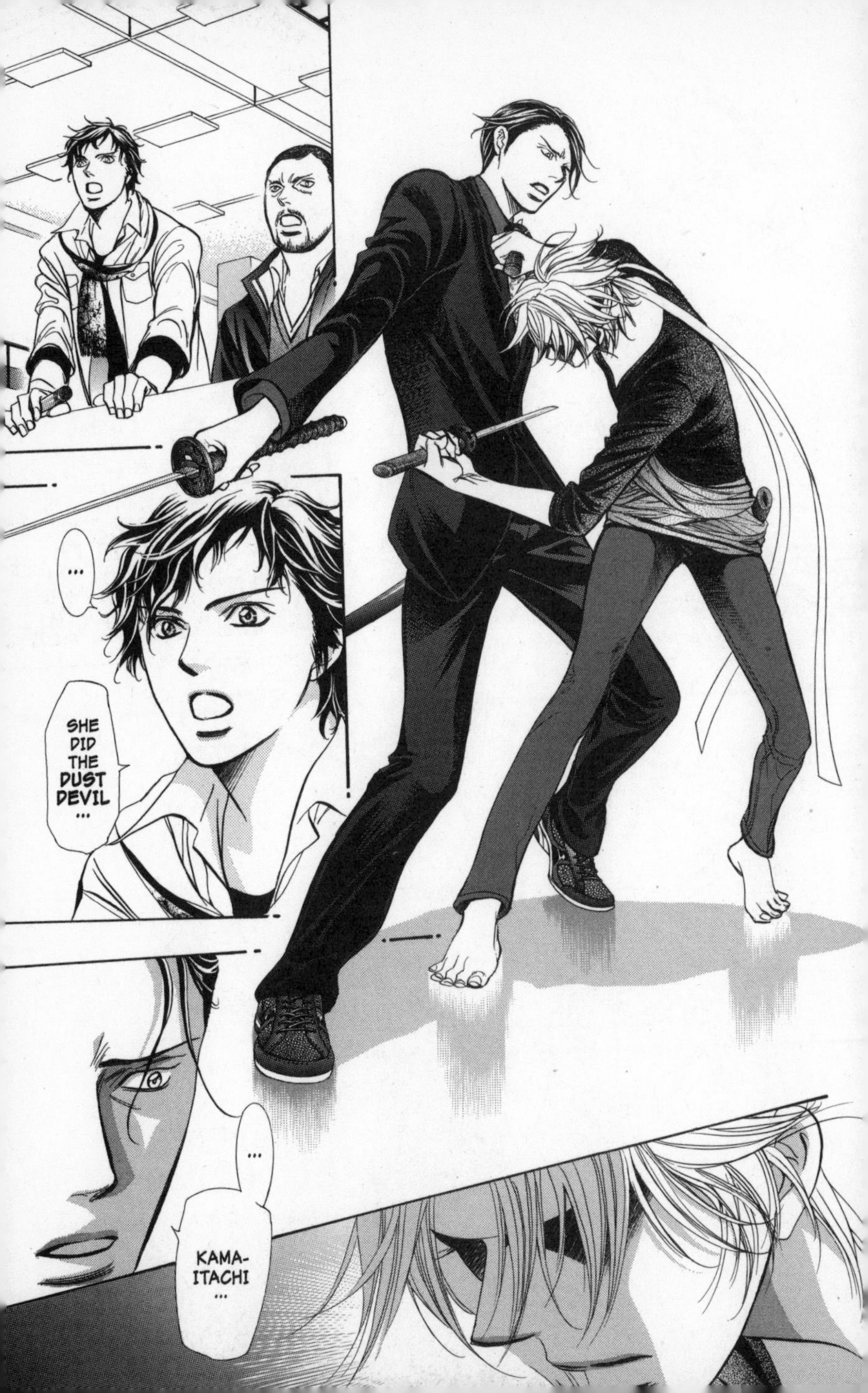
...
SHE DID THE DUST DEVIL ...
...
KAMA-ITACHI ...

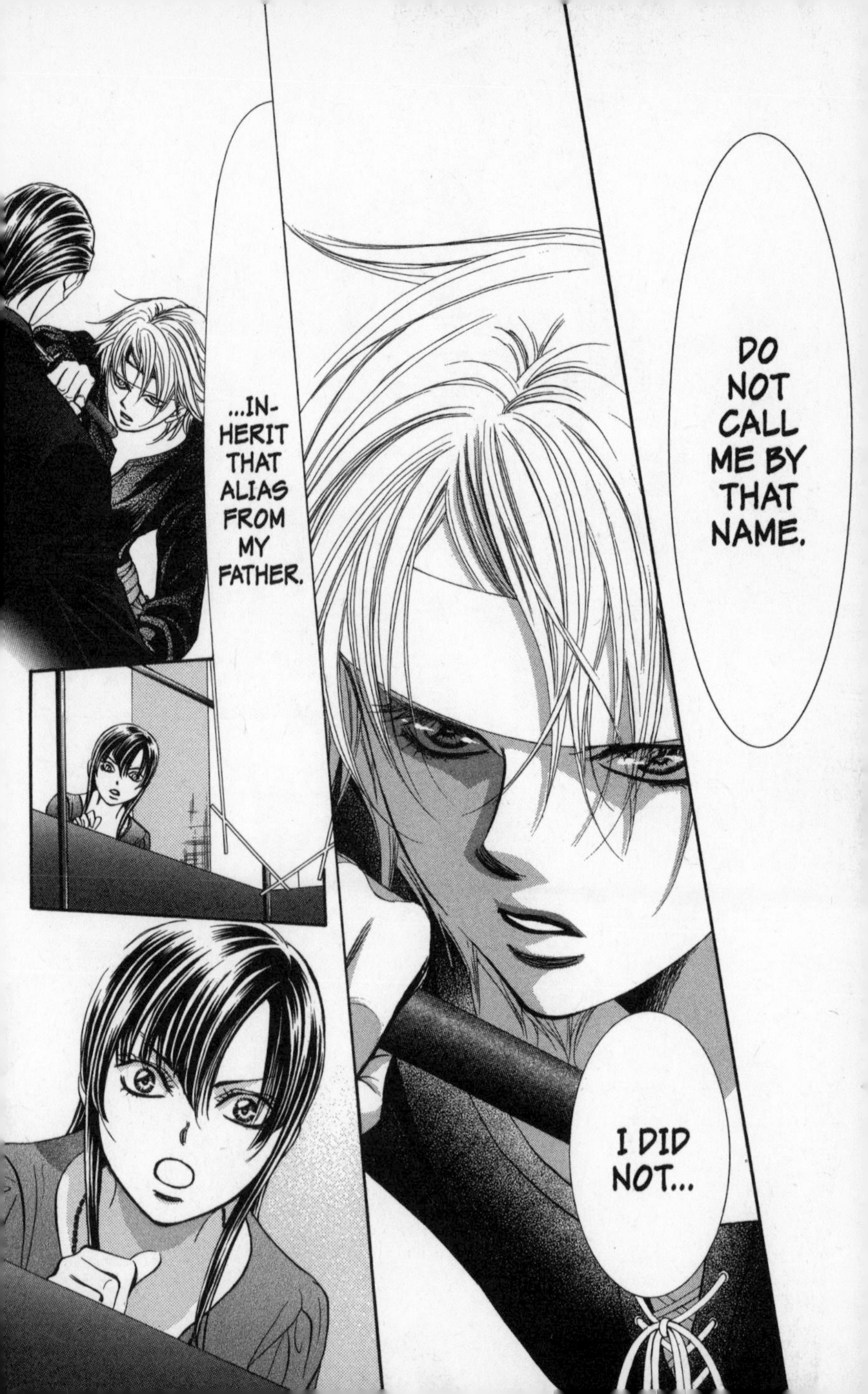

DO NOT CALL ME BY THAT NAME.
I DID NOT...
...IN-HERIT THAT ALIAS FROM MY FATHER.

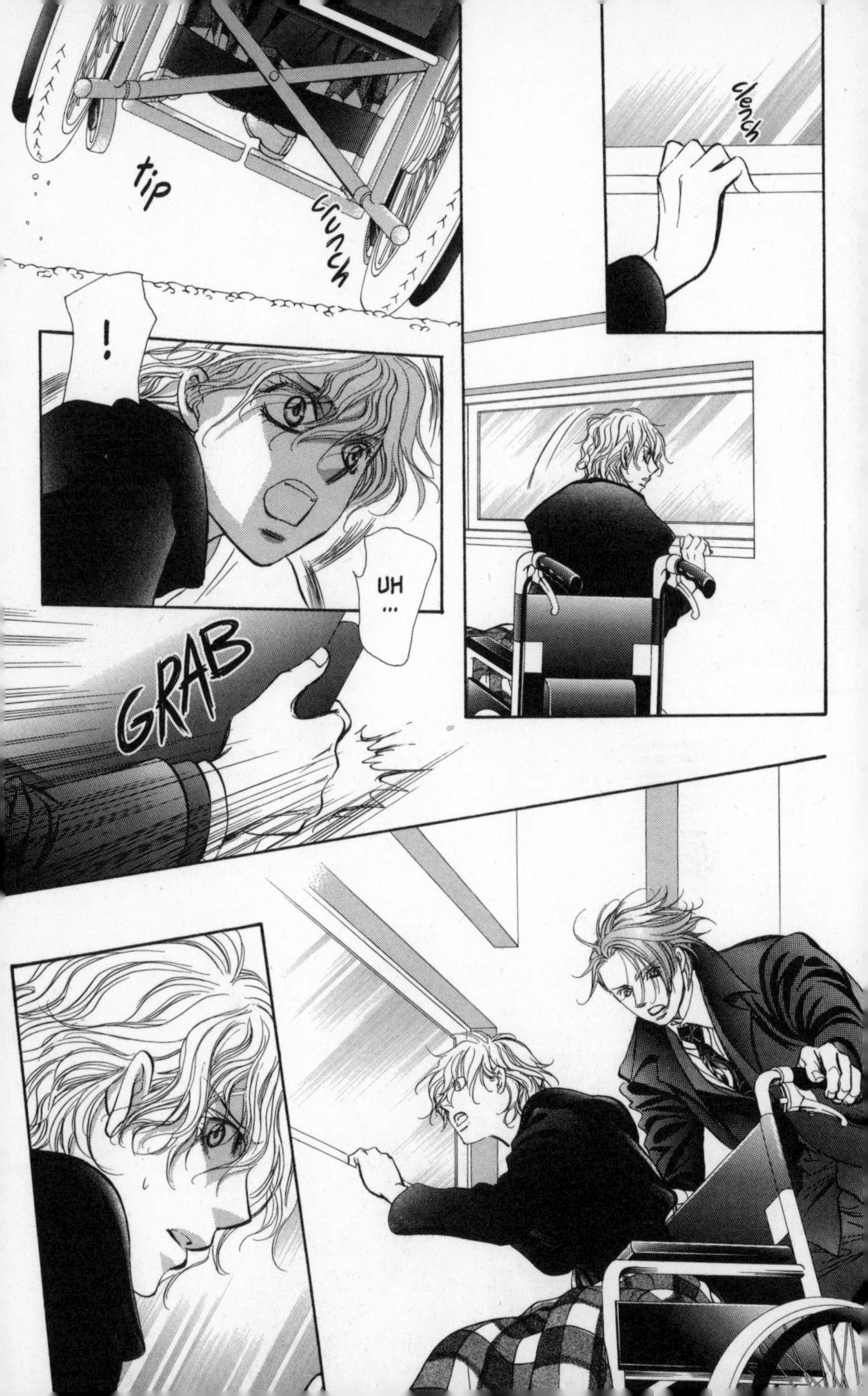
clench
tip
crunch
!
UH ...
GRAB

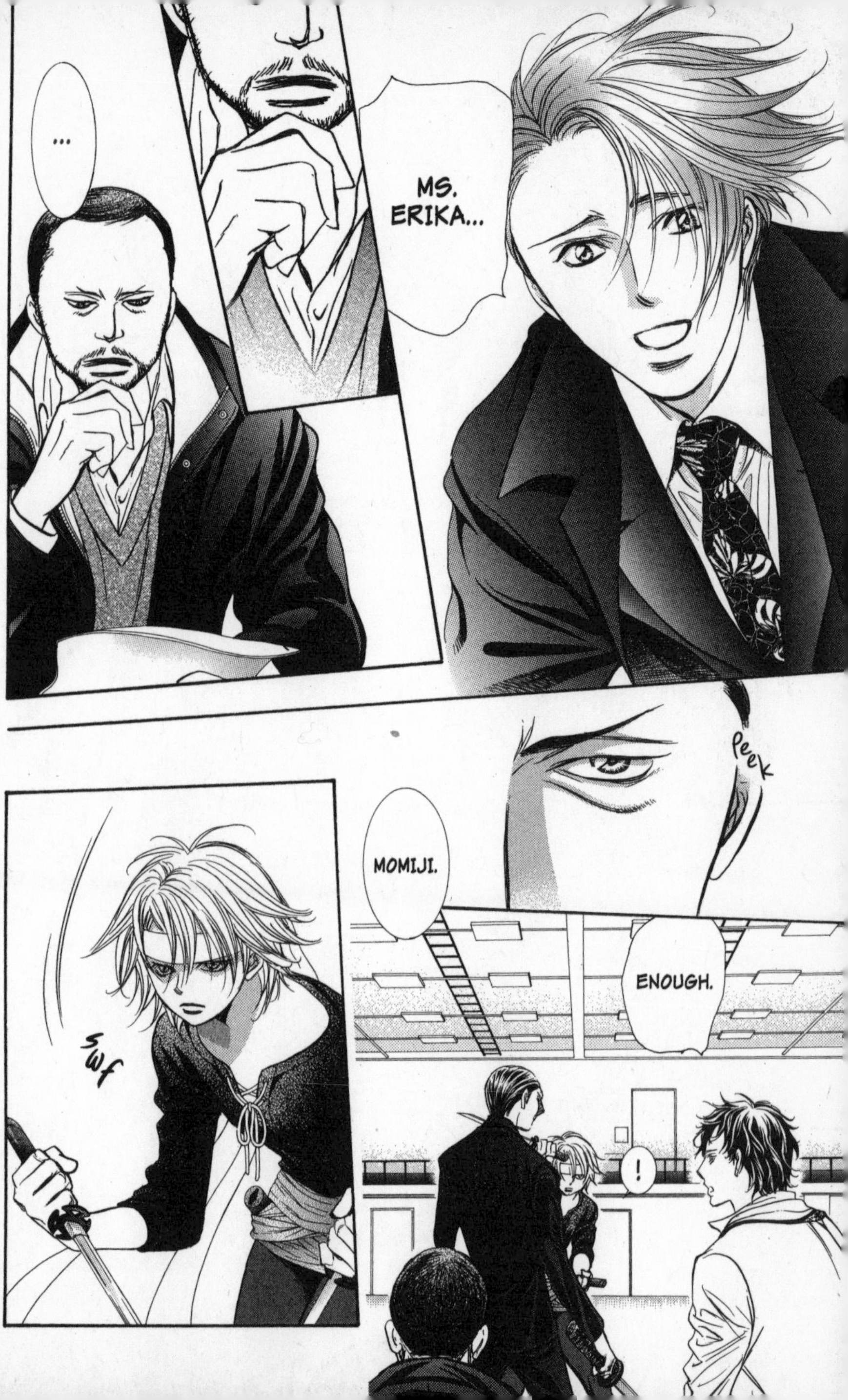
MS. ERIKA...
...
Peek
MOMIJI.
ENOUGH.
!
swf

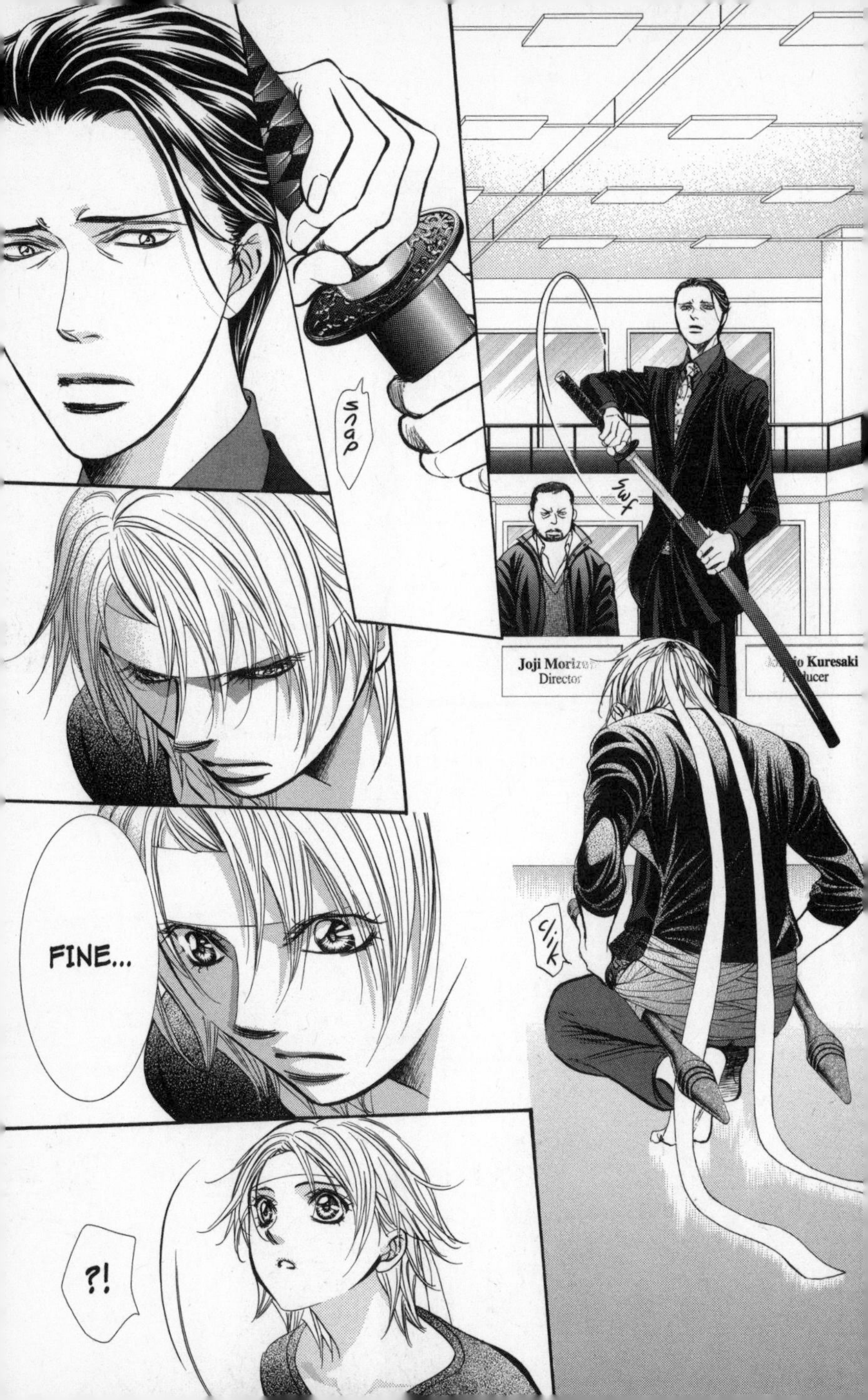
swf
Joji Morizo
Director
Kuresaki
clik
snap
FINE...
?!

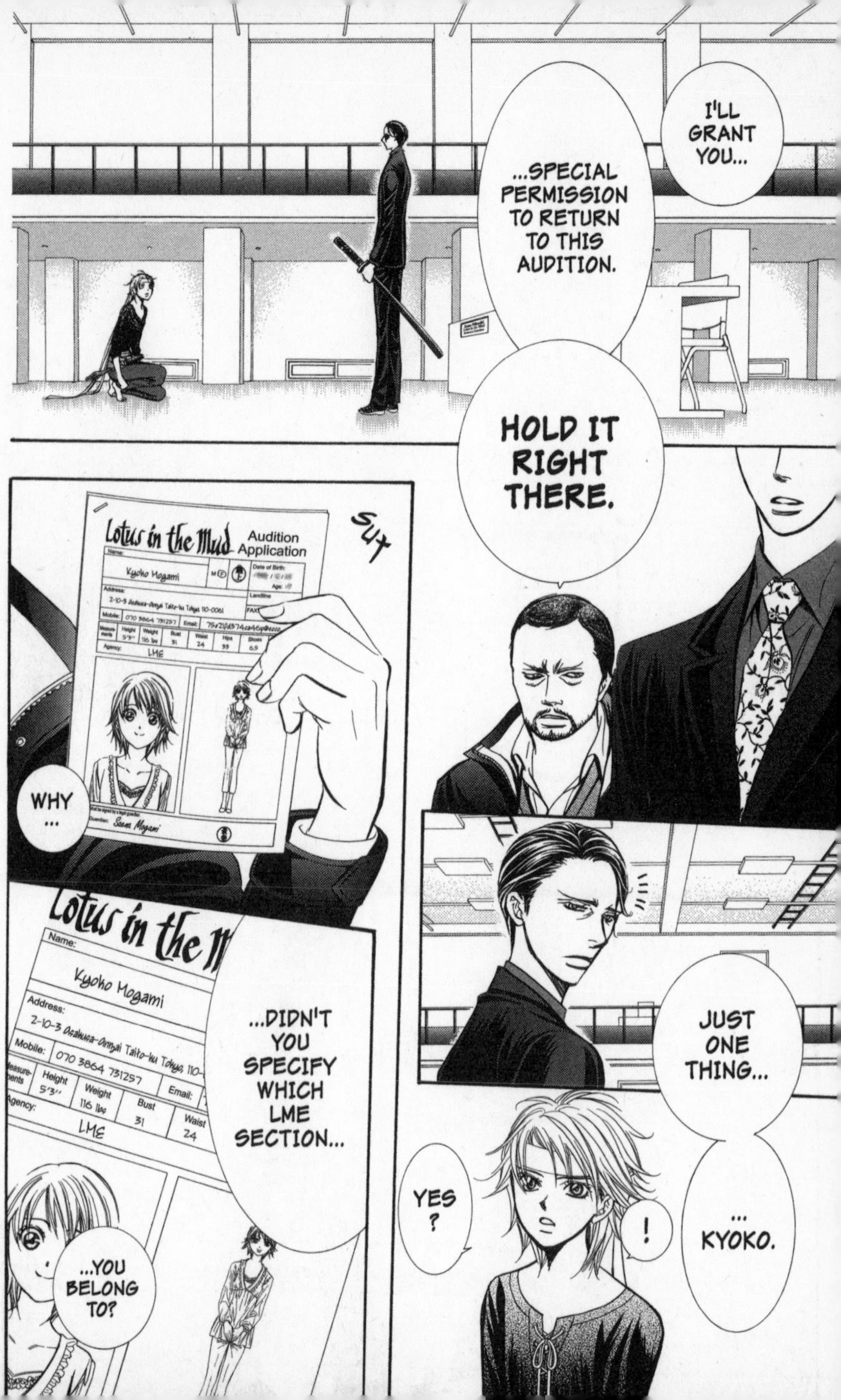

I'LL GRANT YOU...
...SPECIAL PERMISSION TO RETURN TO THIS AUDITION.
HOLD IT RIGHT THERE.
JUST ONE THING...
...KYOKO.
!
YES?
SUT
Lotus in the Mud Audition Application
Name:
Kyoko Mogami
Address:
2-10-3 Asakusa-Onnyai Taito-ku Tokyo 110-0061
Mobile: 070 3864 731257
Height 5'3'' Weight 116 lbs Bust 31 Waist 24 Hips 33 Shoes 6.5
Agency: LME
Guardian: Saena Mogami
WHY...
...DIDN'T YOU SPECIFY WHICH LME SECTION...
...YOU BELONG TO?

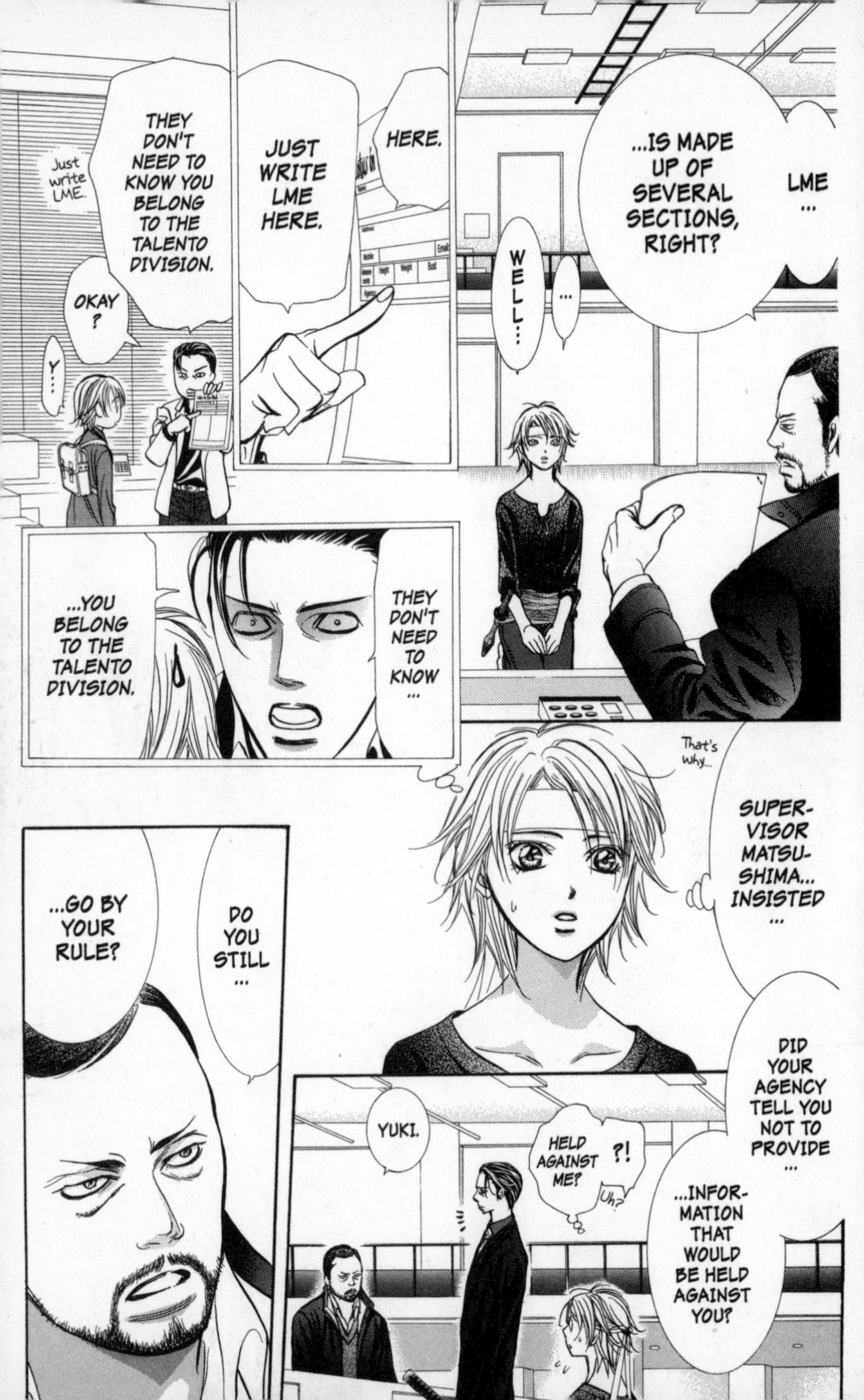
LME...
...IS MADE UP OF SEVERAL SECTIONS, RIGHT?
...
WELL...
HERE.
JUST WRITE LME HERE.
THEY DON'T NEED TO KNOW YOU BELONG TO THE TALENTO DIVISION.
Just write LME.
OKAY?
Y...
THEY DON'T NEED TO KNOW...
...YOU BELONG TO THE TALENTO DIVISION.
That's why...
SUPERVISOR MATSUSHIMA... INSISTED...
DID YOUR AGENCY TELL YOU NOT TO PROVIDE...
...INFORMATION THAT WOULD BE HELD AGAINST YOU?
HELD AGAINST ME?
?!
Uh?
YUKI.
DO YOU STILL...
...GO BY YOUR RULE?

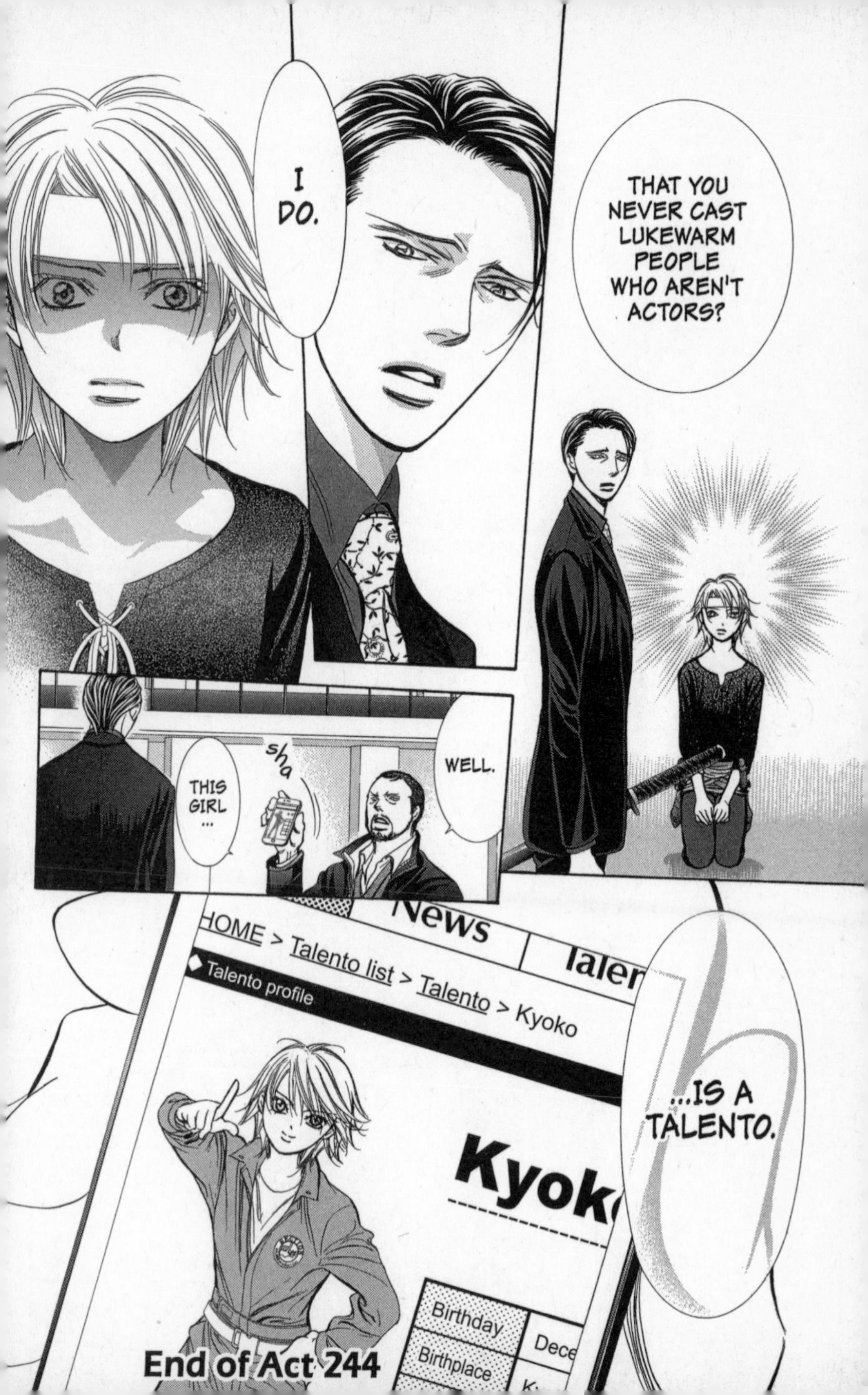
THAT YOU NEVER CAST LUKEWARM PEOPLE WHO AREN'T ACTORS?
I DO.
WELL.
sha
THIS GIRL ...
...IS A TALENTO.
News
HOME > Talento list > Talento > Kyoko
Talento profile
Birthday
Birthplace
End of Act 244

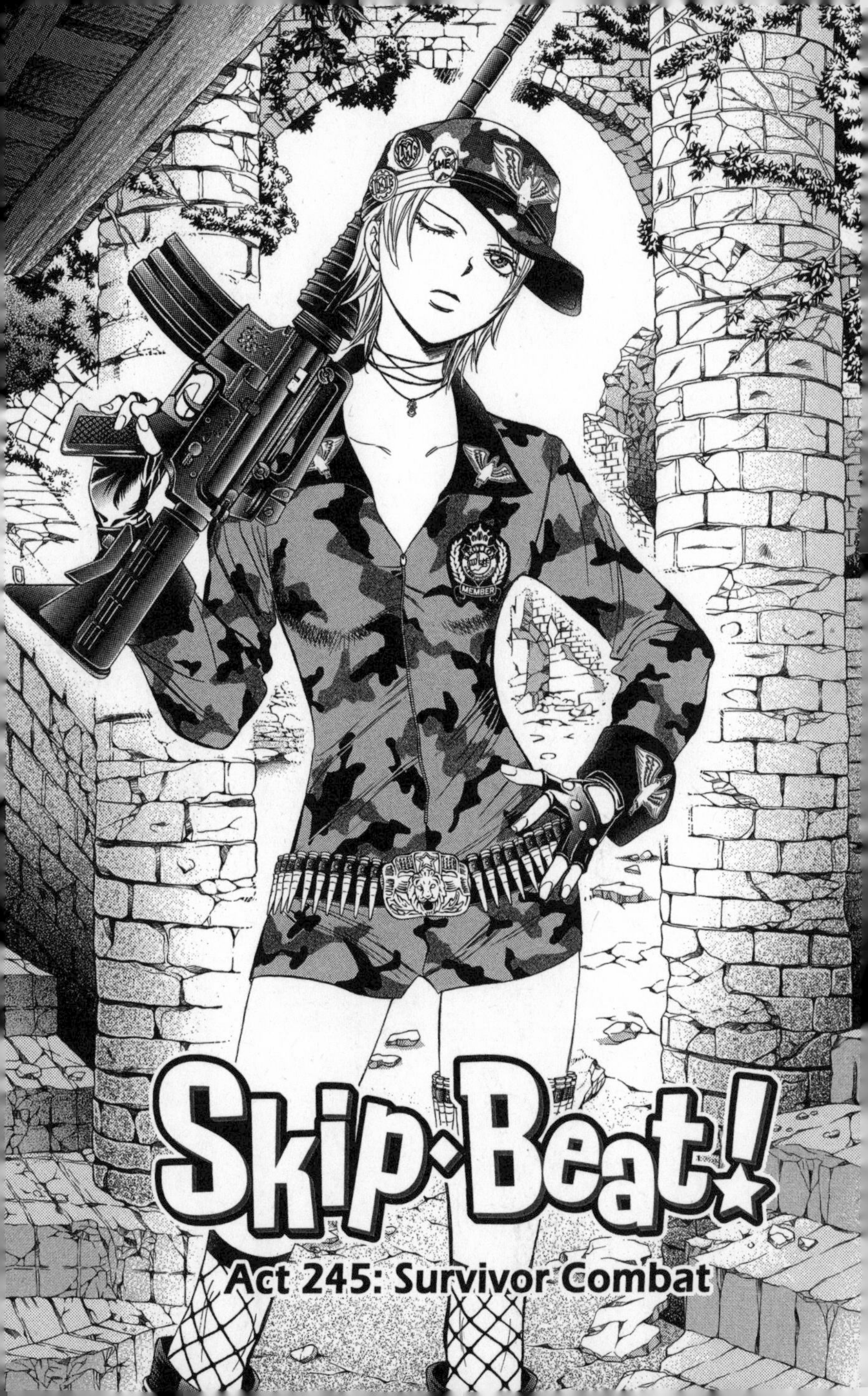
Skip·Beat!
Act 245: Survivor Combat

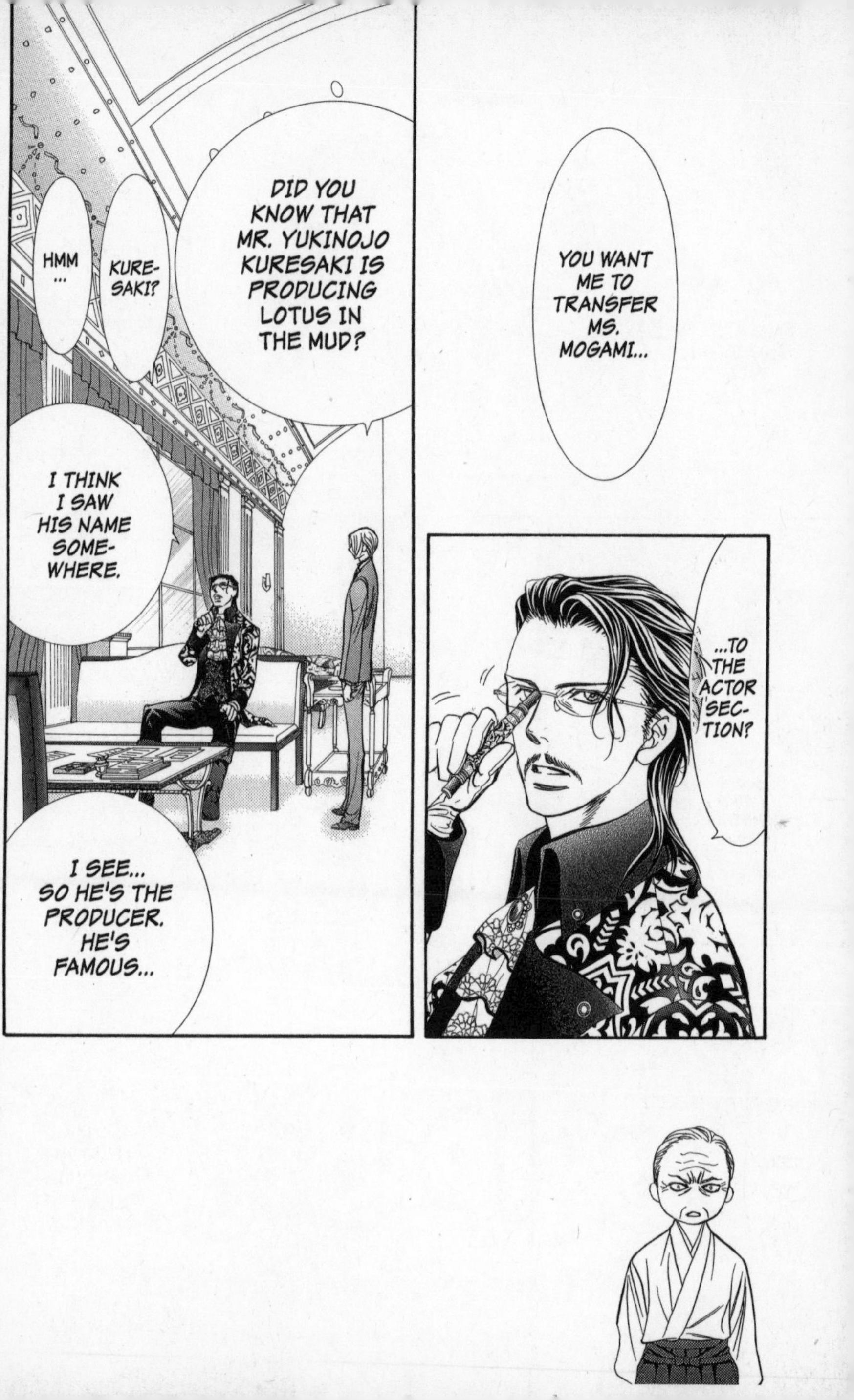
YOU WANT ME TO TRANSFER MS. MOGAMI...
...TO THE ACTOR SECTION?
DID YOU KNOW THAT MR. YUKINOJO KURESAKI IS PRODUCING LOTUS IN THE MUD?
KURE-SAKI?
HMM ...
I THINK I SAW HIS NAME SOME-WHERE.
I SEE... SO HE'S THE PRODUCER. HE'S FAMOUS...

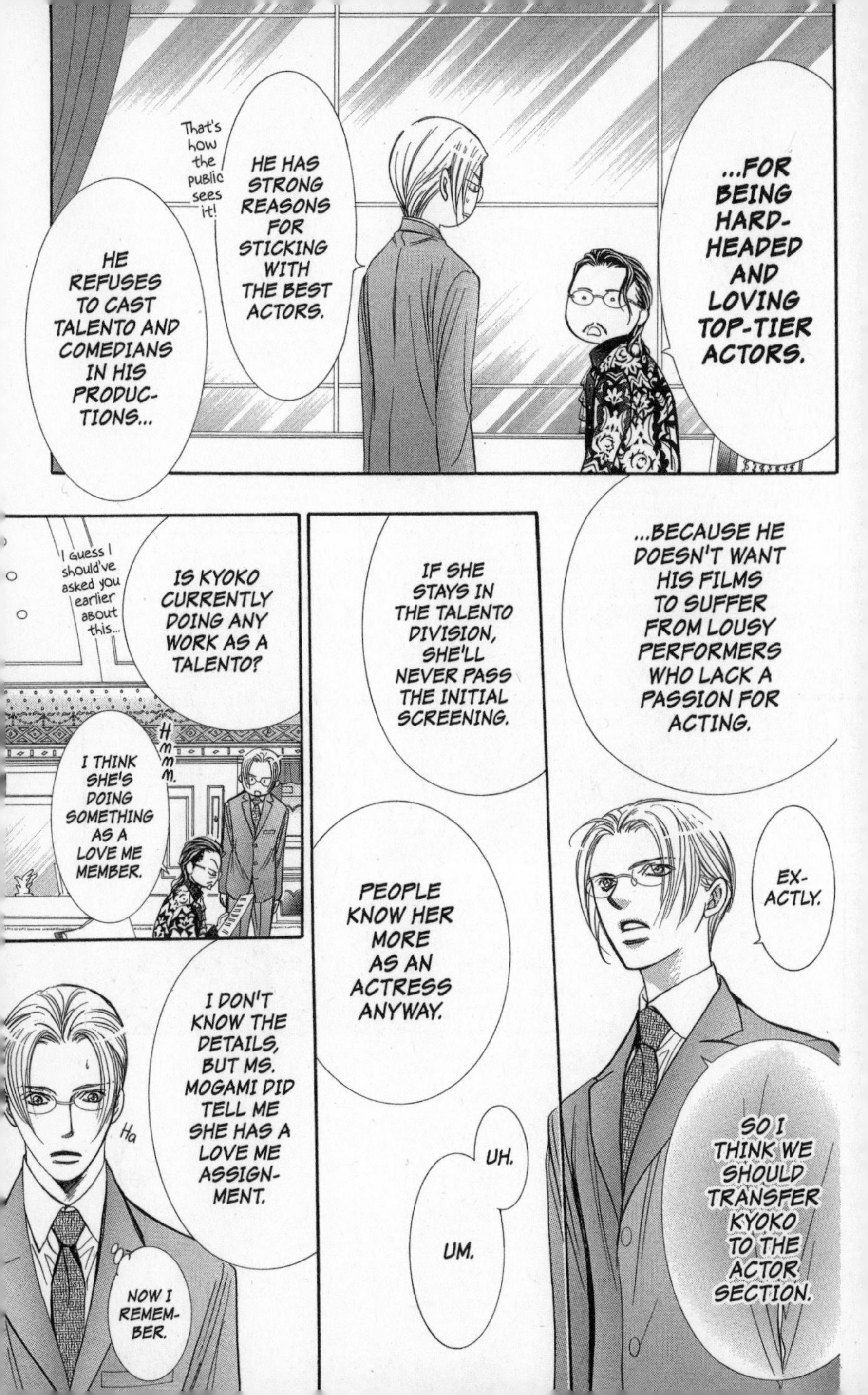
...FOR BEING HARD-HEADED AND LOVING TOP-TIER ACTORS.
HE HAS STRONG REASONS FOR STICKING WITH THE BEST ACTORS.
That's how the public sees it!
HE REFUSES TO CAST TALENTO AND COMEDIANS IN HIS PRODUCTIONS...
...BECAUSE HE DOESN'T WANT HIS FILMS TO SUFFER FROM LOUSY PERFORMERS WHO LACK A PASSION FOR ACTING.
EX-ACTLY.
SO I THINK WE SHOULD TRANSFER KYOKO TO THE ACTOR SECTION.
IF SHE STAYS IN THE TALENTO DIVISION, SHE'LL NEVER PASS THE INITIAL SCREENING.
PEOPLE KNOW HER MORE AS AN ACTRESS ANYWAY.
UH.
UM.
IS KYOKO CURRENTLY DOING ANY WORK AS A TALENTO?
I guess I should've asked you earlier about this...
Hmmm.
I THINK SHE'S DOING SOMETHING AS A LOVE ME MEMBER.
I DON'T KNOW THE DETAILS, BUT MS. MOGAMI DID TELL ME SHE HAS A LOVE ME ASSIGNMENT.
Ha
NOW I REMEMBER.

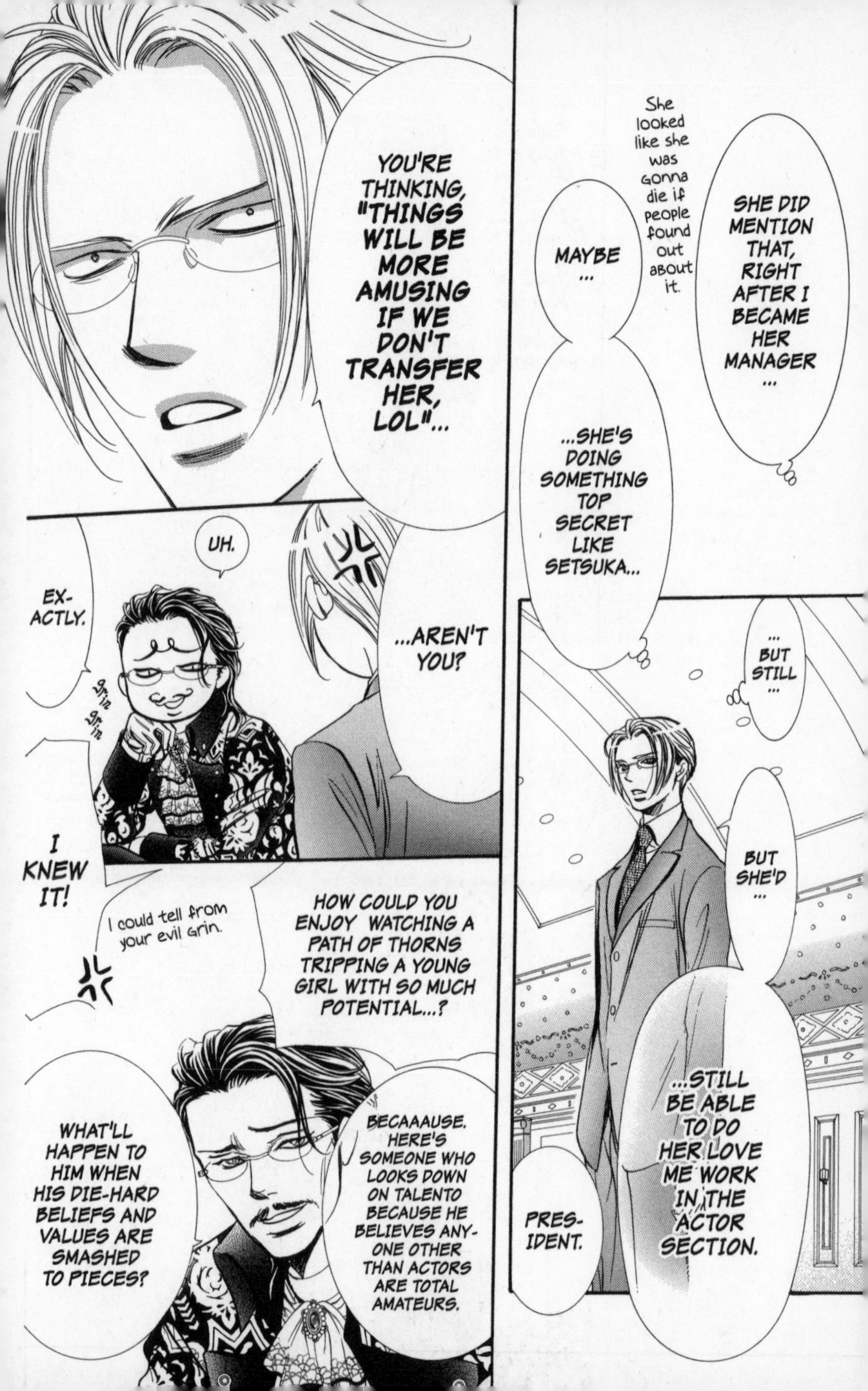
SHE DID MENTION THAT, RIGHT AFTER I BECAME HER MANAGER...
She looked like she was gonna die if people found out about it.
MAYBE...
...SHE'S DOING SOMETHING TOP SECRET LIKE SETSUKA...
... BUT STILL ...
BUT SHE'D ...
...STILL BE ABLE TO DO HER LOVE ME WORK IN THE ACTOR SECTION.
PRES-IDENT.
YOU'RE THINKING, "THINGS WILL BE MORE AMUSING IF WE DON'T TRANSFER HER, LOL"...
...AREN'T YOU?
UH.
EX-ACTLY.
grin grin
I KNEW IT!
HOW COULD YOU ENJOY WATCHING A PATH OF THORNS TRIPPING A YOUNG GIRL WITH SO MUCH POTENTIAL...?
I could tell from your evil Grin.
BECAAAUSE. HERE'S SOMEONE WHO LOOKS DOWN ON TALENTO BECAUSE HE BELIEVES ANY-ONE OTHER THAN ACTORS ARE TOTAL AMATEURS.
WHAT'LL HAPPEN TO HIM WHEN HIS DIE-HARD BELIEFS AND VALUES ARE SMASHED TO PIECES?

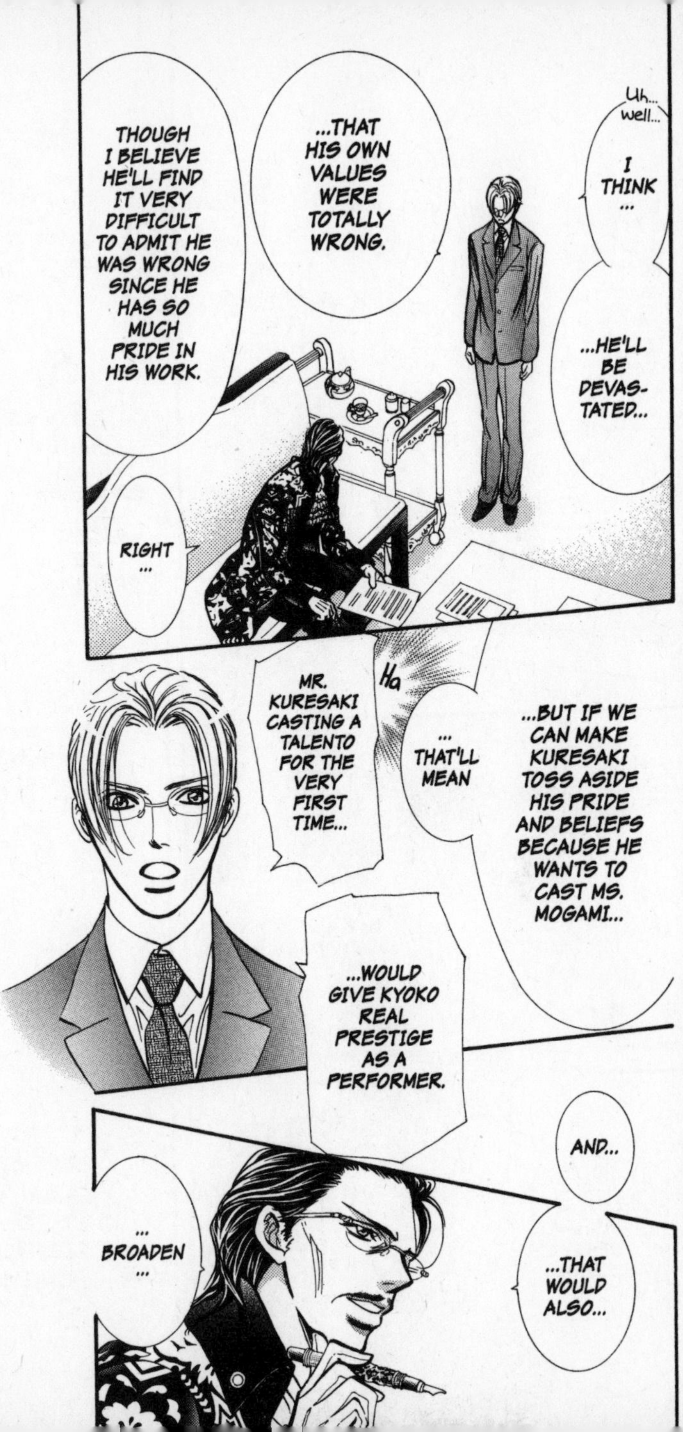
Uh... well...
I THINK...
...HE'LL BE DEVASTATED...
...THAT HIS OWN VALUES WERE TOTALLY WRONG.
THOUGH I BELIEVE HE'LL FIND IT VERY DIFFICULT TO ADMIT HE WAS WRONG SINCE HE HAS SO MUCH PRIDE IN HIS WORK.
RIGHT...
Ha
...BUT IF WE CAN MAKE KURESAKI TOSS ASIDE HIS PRIDE AND BELIEFS BECAUSE HE WANTS TO CAST MS. MOGAMI...
...THAT'LL MEAN
MR. KURESAKI CASTING A TALENTO FOR THE VERY FIRST TIME...
...WOULD GIVE KYOKO REAL PRESTIGE AS A PERFORMER.
AND...
...THAT WOULD ALSO...
...BROADEN...

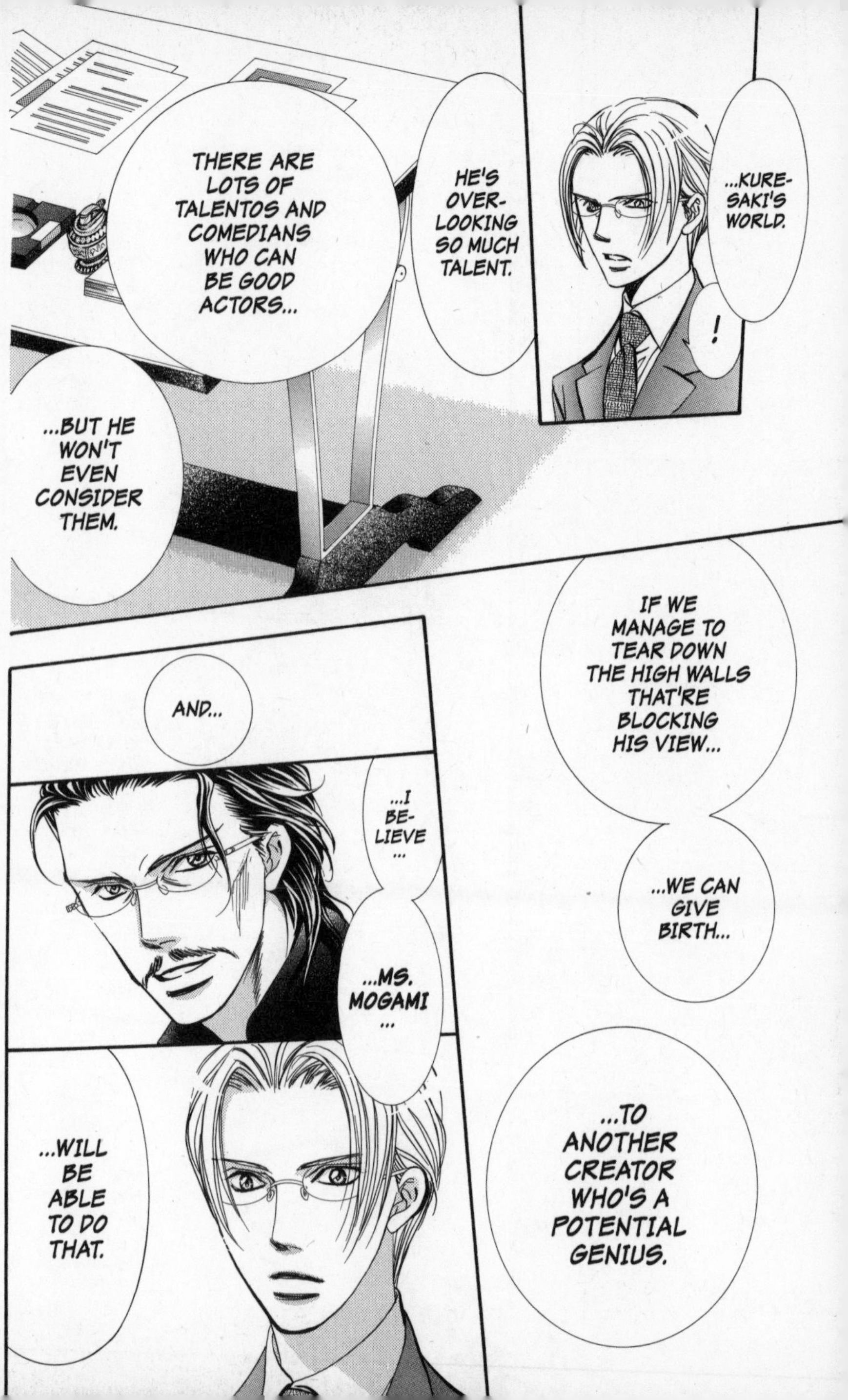

...KURE-SAKI'S WORLD.
!
HE'S OVER-LOOKING SO MUCH TALENT.
THERE ARE LOTS OF TALENTOS AND COMEDIANS WHO CAN BE GOOD ACTORS...
...BUT HE WON'T EVEN CONSIDER THEM.
IF WE MANAGE TO TEAR DOWN THE HIGH WALLS THAT'RE BLOCKING HIS VIEW...
...WE CAN GIVE BIRTH...
...TO ANOTHER CREATOR WHO'S A POTENTIAL GENIUS.
AND...
...I BE-LIEVE...
...MS. MOGAMI...
...WILL BE ABLE TO DO THAT.

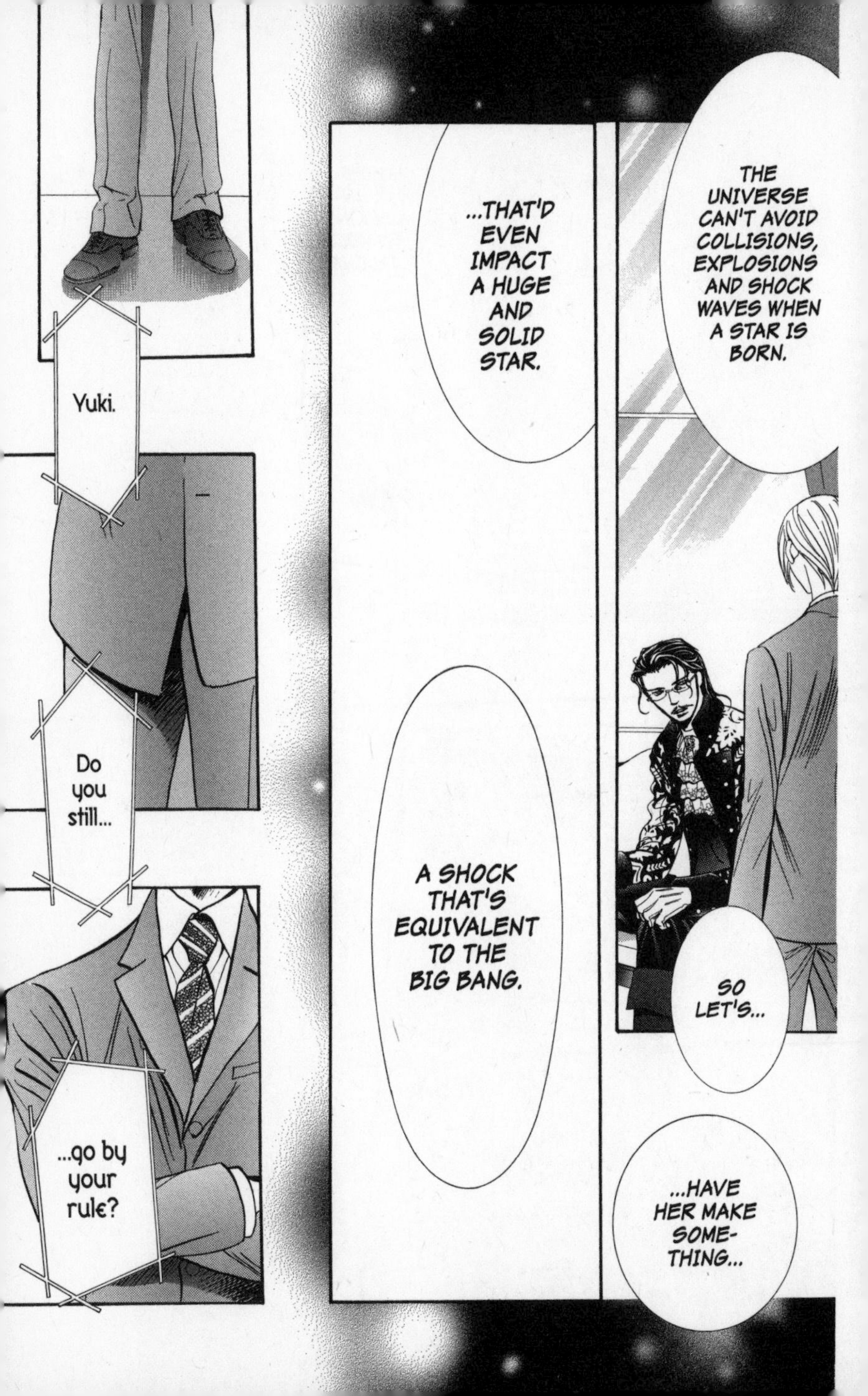
THE UNIVERSE CAN'T AVOID COLLISIONS, EXPLOSIONS AND SHOCK WAVES WHEN A STAR IS BORN.
...THAT'D EVEN IMPACT A HUGE AND SOLID STAR.
A SHOCK THAT'S EQUIVALENT TO THE BIG BANG.
SO LET'S...
...HAVE HER MAKE SOME-THING...
Yuki.
Do you still...
...go by your rule?

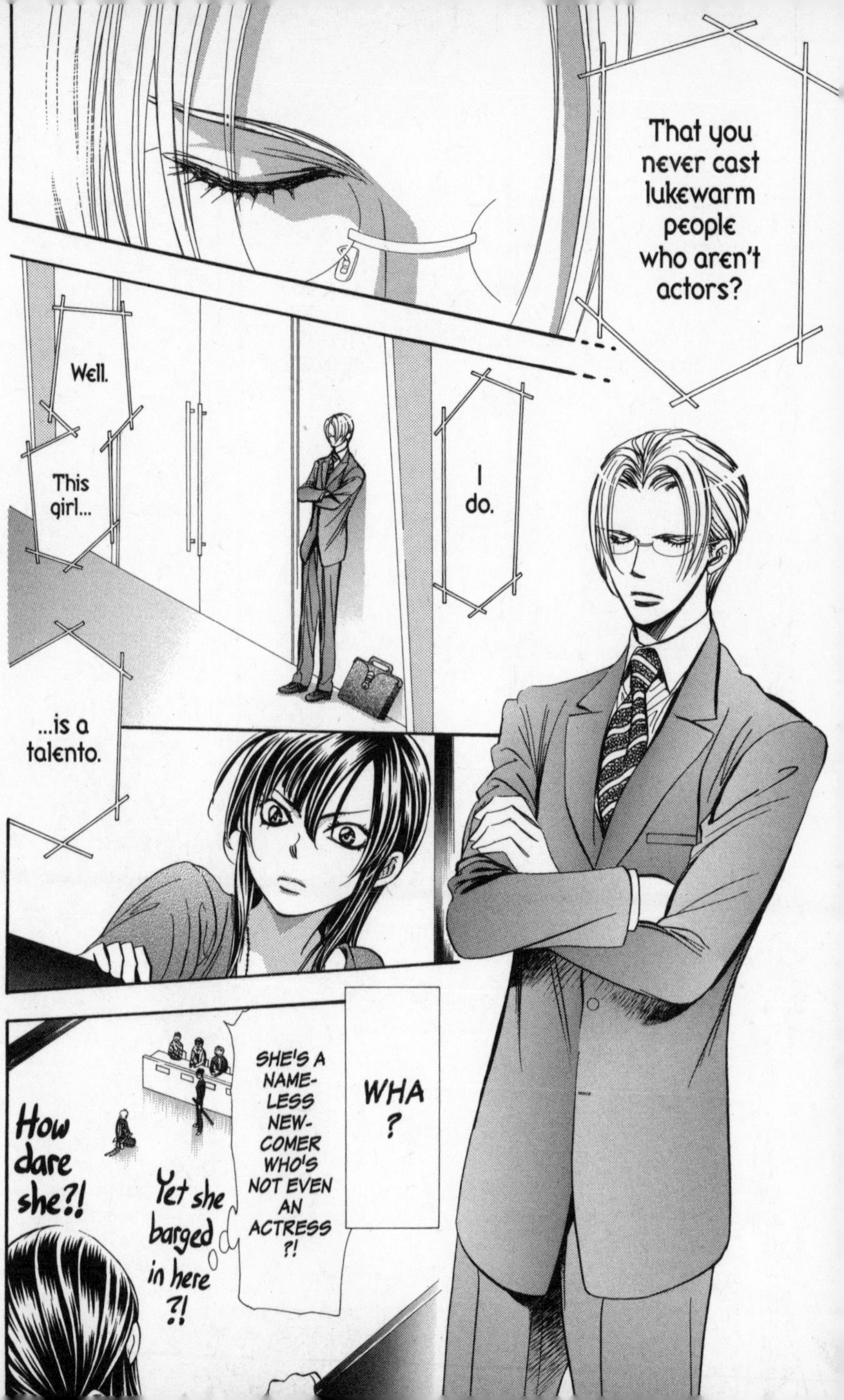
That you never cast lukewarm people who aren't actors?
I do.
Well.
This girl...
...is a talento.
WHA?
SHE'S A NAMELESS NEWCOMER WHO'S NOT EVEN AN ACTRESS?!
Yet she barged in here?!
How dare she?!

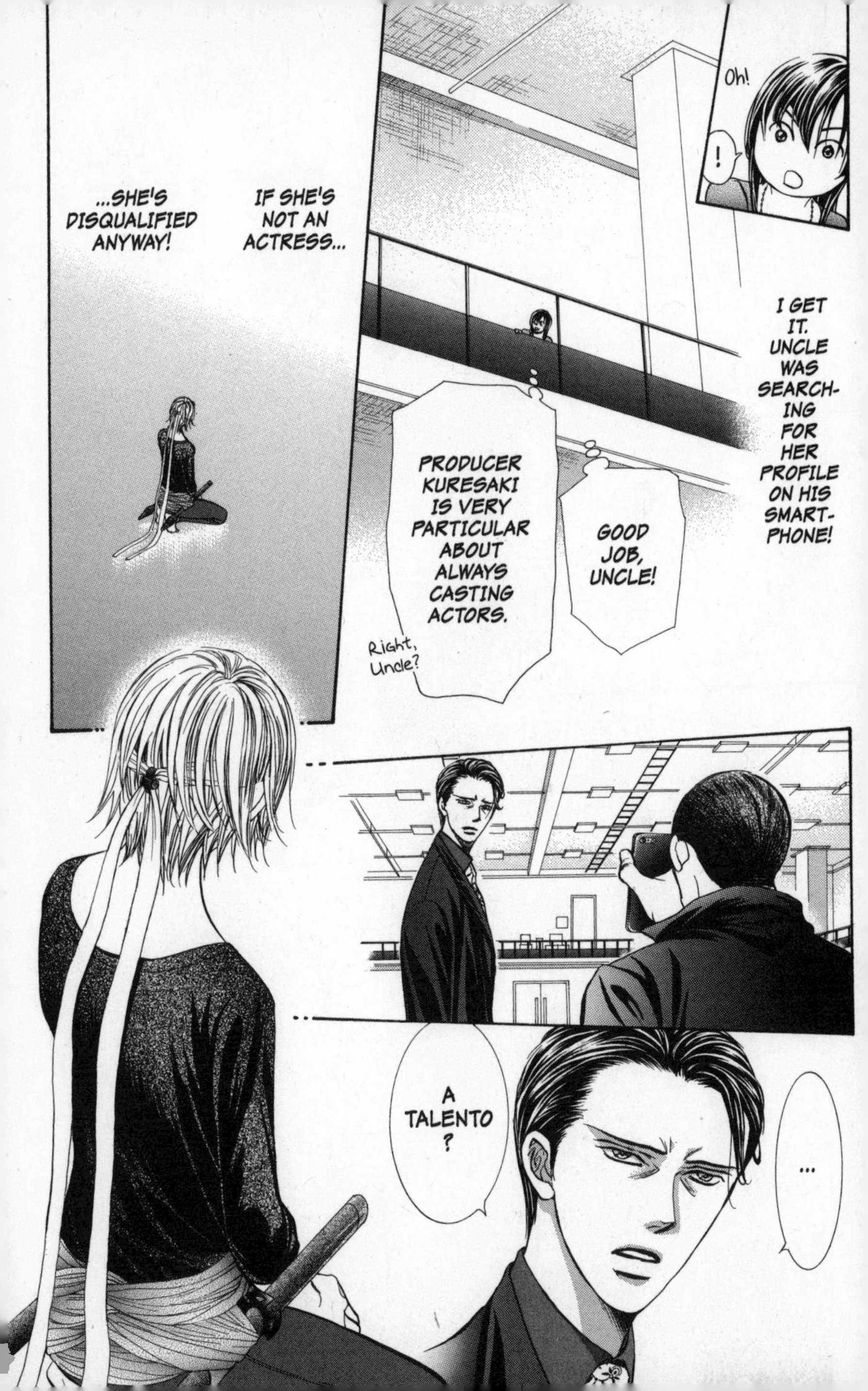
Oh!
!
I GET IT. UNCLE WAS SEARCHING FOR HER PROFILE ON HIS SMARTPHONE!
GOOD JOB, UNCLE!
PRODUCER KURESAKI IS VERY PARTICULAR ABOUT ALWAYS CASTING ACTORS.
Right, Uncle?
IF SHE'S NOT AN ACTRESS...
...SHE'S DISQUALIFIED ANYWAY!
...
A TALENTO?

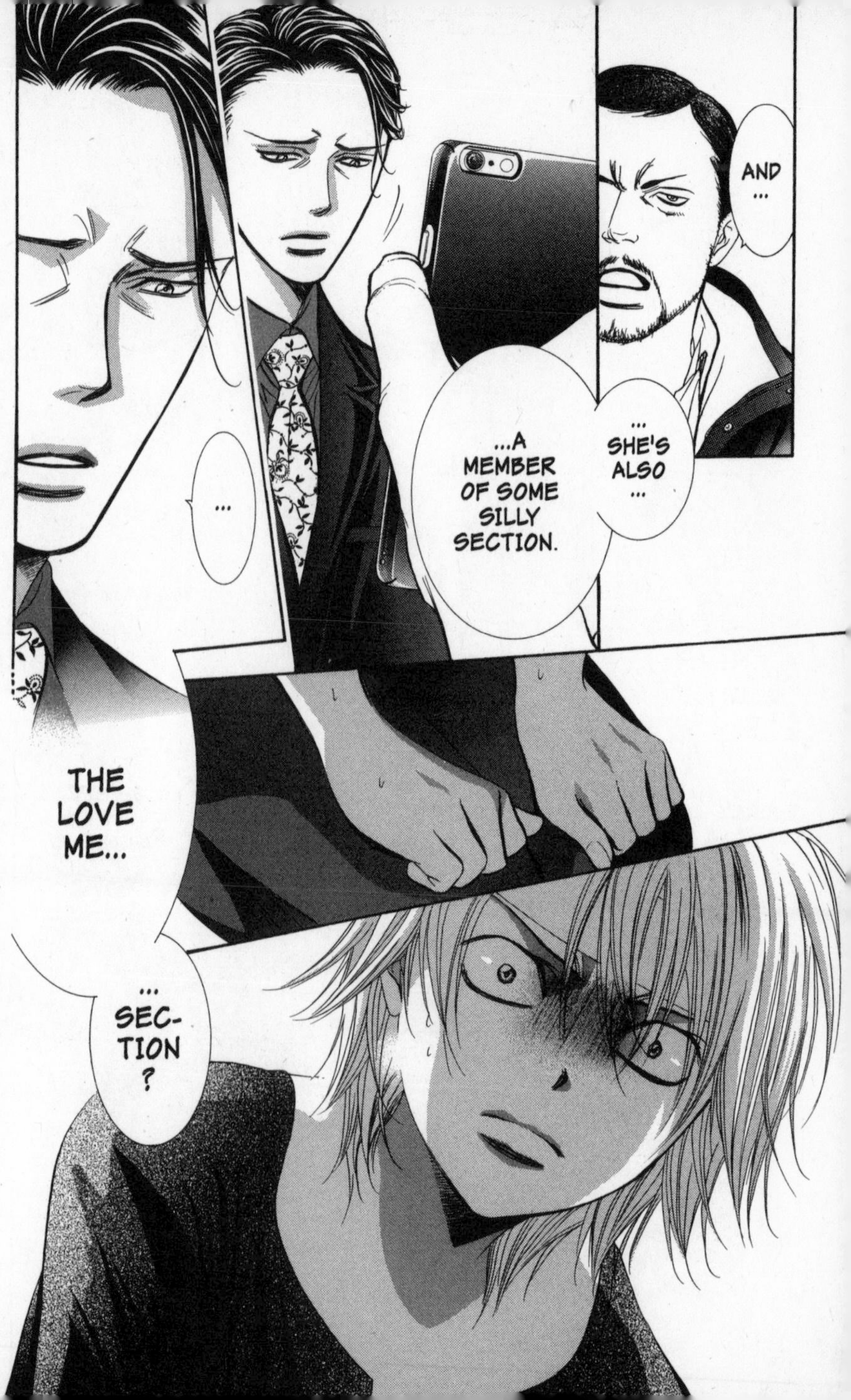
AND ...
... SHE'S ALSO ...
...A MEMBER OF SOME SILLY SECTION.
...
THE LOVE ME...
... SEC-TION ?

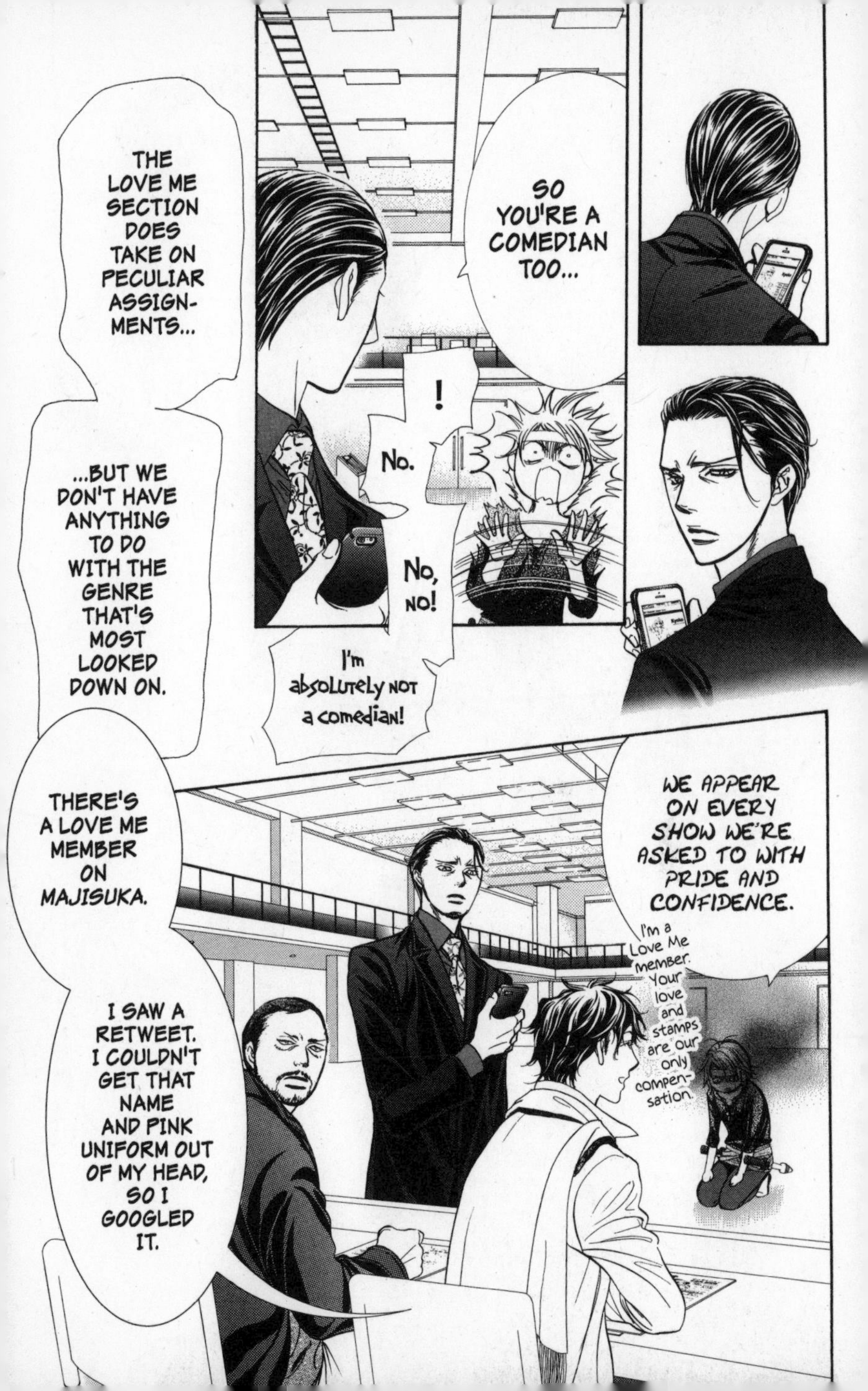
SO YOU'RE A COMEDIAN TOO...
!
No.
No, no!
I'm absolutely not a comedian!
THE LOVE ME SECTION DOES TAKE ON PECULIAR ASSIGNMENTS...
...BUT WE DON'T HAVE ANYTHING TO DO WITH THE GENRE THAT'S MOST LOOKED DOWN ON.
WE APPEAR ON EVERY SHOW WE'RE ASKED TO WITH PRIDE AND CONFIDENCE.
I'm a Love Me member. Your love and stamps are our only compensation.
THERE'S A LOVE ME MEMBER ON MAJISUKA.
I SAW A RETWEET. I COULDN'T GET THAT NAME AND PINK UNIFORM OUT OF MY HEAD, SO I GOOGLED IT.

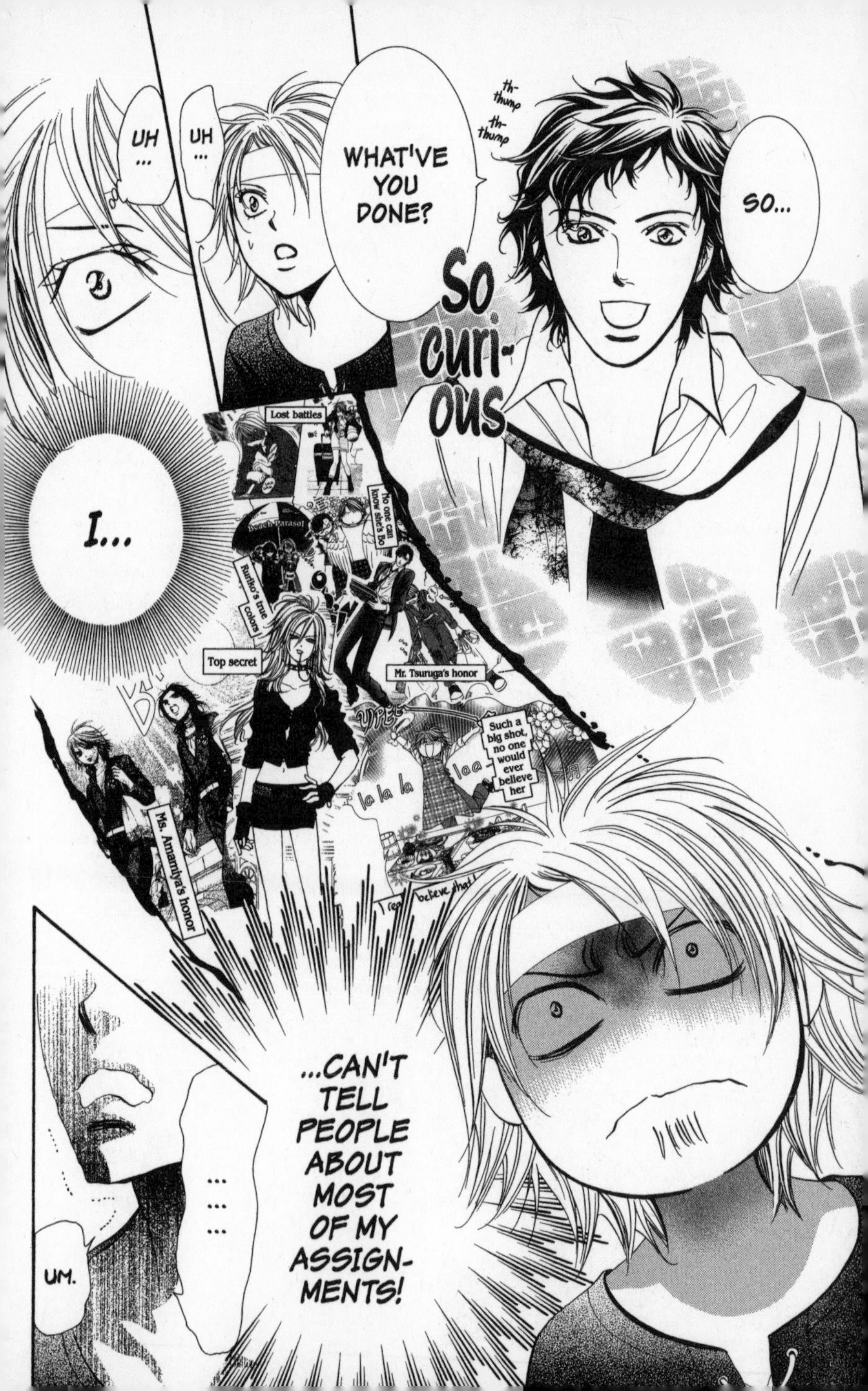
th-thump th-thump
SO...
So curious
WHAT'VE YOU DONE?
UH ...
UH ...
I...
Lost battles
No one can know she's Bo
Beach Parasol
Ruriko's true colors
Mr. Tsuruga's honor
Top secret
Such a big shot, no one would ever believe her
la la la
laa
Ms. Amamiya's honor
...CAN'T TELL PEOPLE ABOUT MOST OF MY ASSIGNMENTS!
...
...
...
UM.

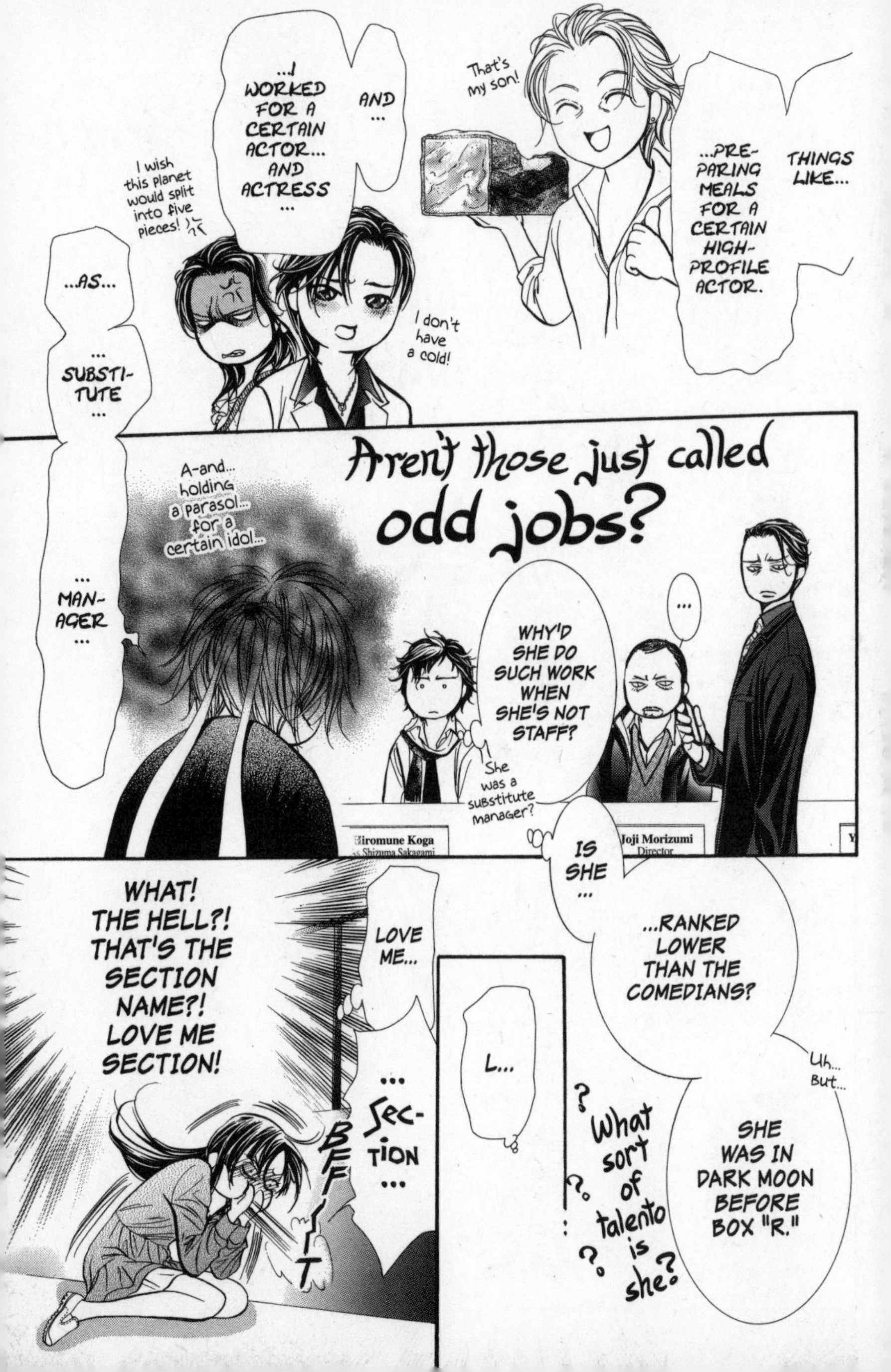
That's my son!
THINGS LIKE...
...PRE-PARING MEALS FOR A CERTAIN HIGH-PROFILE ACTOR.
AND ...
...I WORKED FOR A CERTAIN ACTOR... AND ACTRESS ...
I wish this planet would split into five pieces!
I don't have a cold!
...AS...
... SUBSTI-TUTE ...
Aren't those just called odd jobs?
...
WHY'D SHE DO SUCH WORK WHEN SHE'S NOT STAFF?
She was a substitute manager?
Joji Morizumi
Director
Hiromune Koga
as Shizuma Sakagami
A-and... holding a parasol... for a certain idol...
... MAN-AGER ...
IS SHE ...
...RANKED LOWER THAN THE COMEDIANS?
Uh... But...
SHE WAS IN DARK MOON BEFORE BOX "R."
What sort of talento is she?
L...
LOVE ME...
... SEC-TION ...
BFFT
WHAT! THE HELL?! THAT'S THE SECTION NAME?! LOVE ME SECTION!

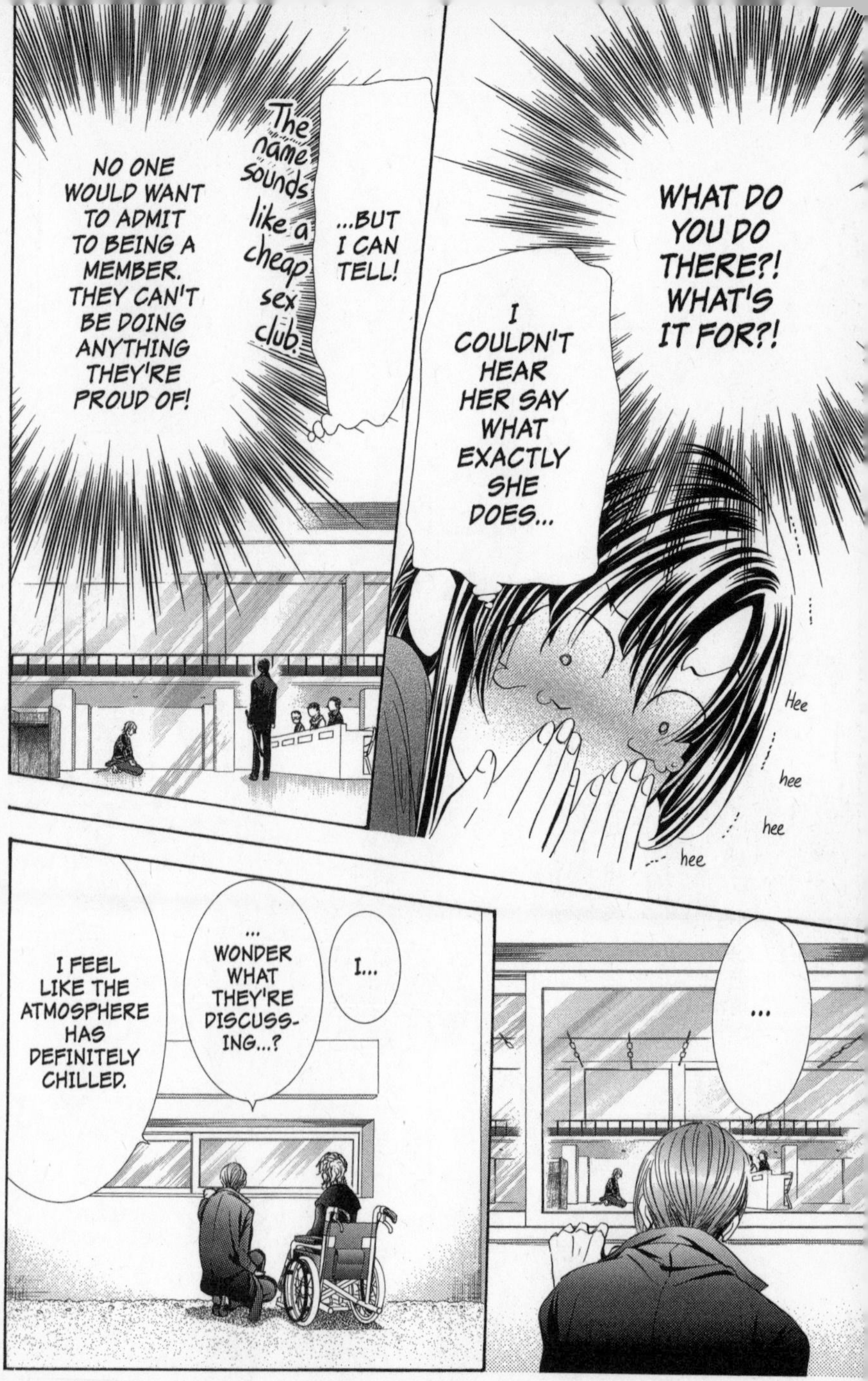
WHAT DO YOU DO THERE?! WHAT'S IT FOR?!
I COULDN'T HEAR HER SAY WHAT EXACTLY SHE DOES...
Hee hee hee hee
...BUT I CAN TELL!
The name sounds like a cheap sex club.
NO ONE WOULD WANT TO ADMIT TO BEING A MEMBER. THEY CAN'T BE DOING ANYTHING THEY'RE PROUD OF!
...
I...
... WONDER WHAT THEY'RE DISCUSS-ING...?
I FEEL LIKE THE ATMOSPHERE HAS DEFINITELY CHILLED.

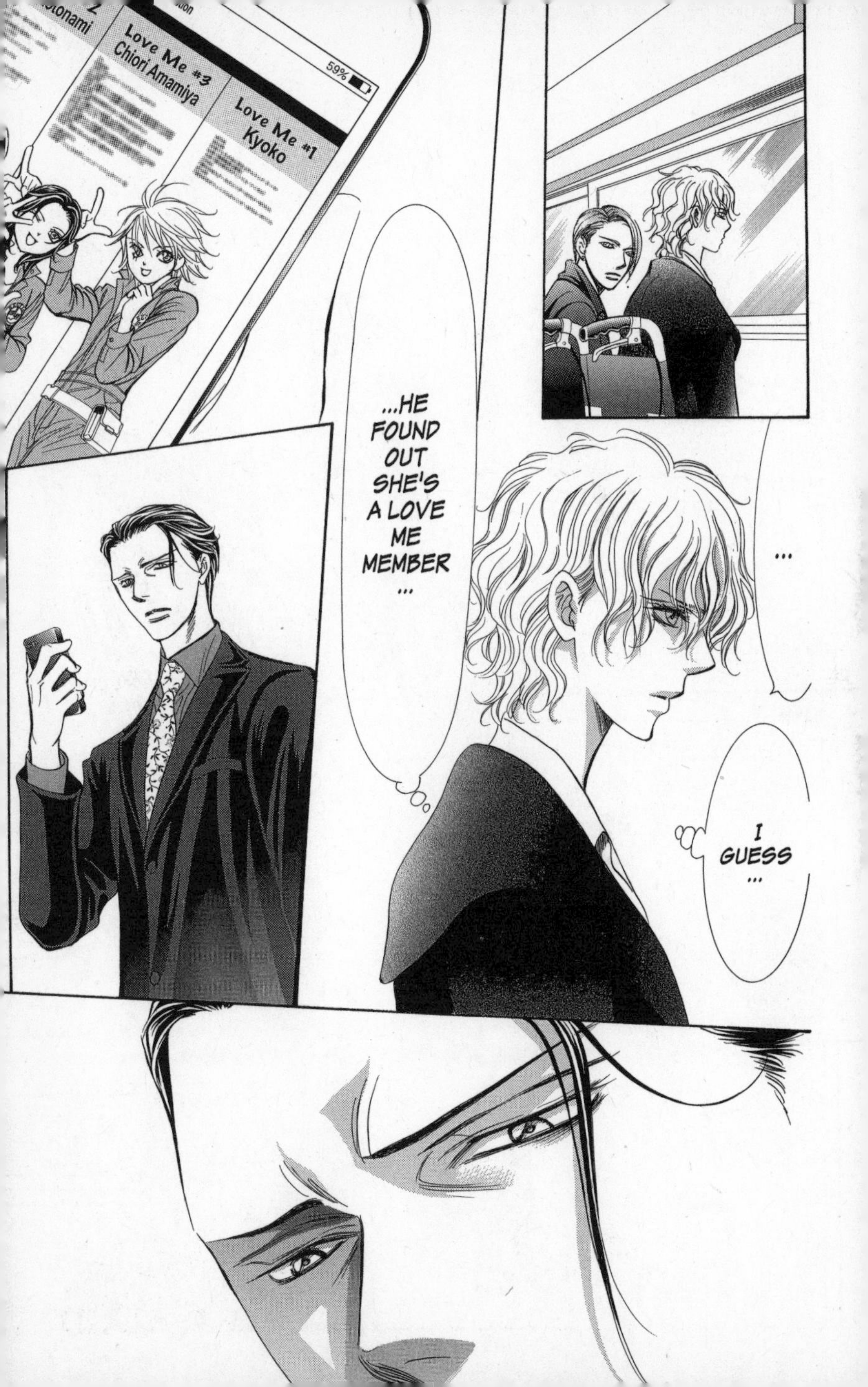
59%
Love Me #1
Kyoko
Love Me #3
Chiori Amamiya
...HE FOUND OUT SHE'S A LOVE ME MEMBER ...
...
I GUESS ...

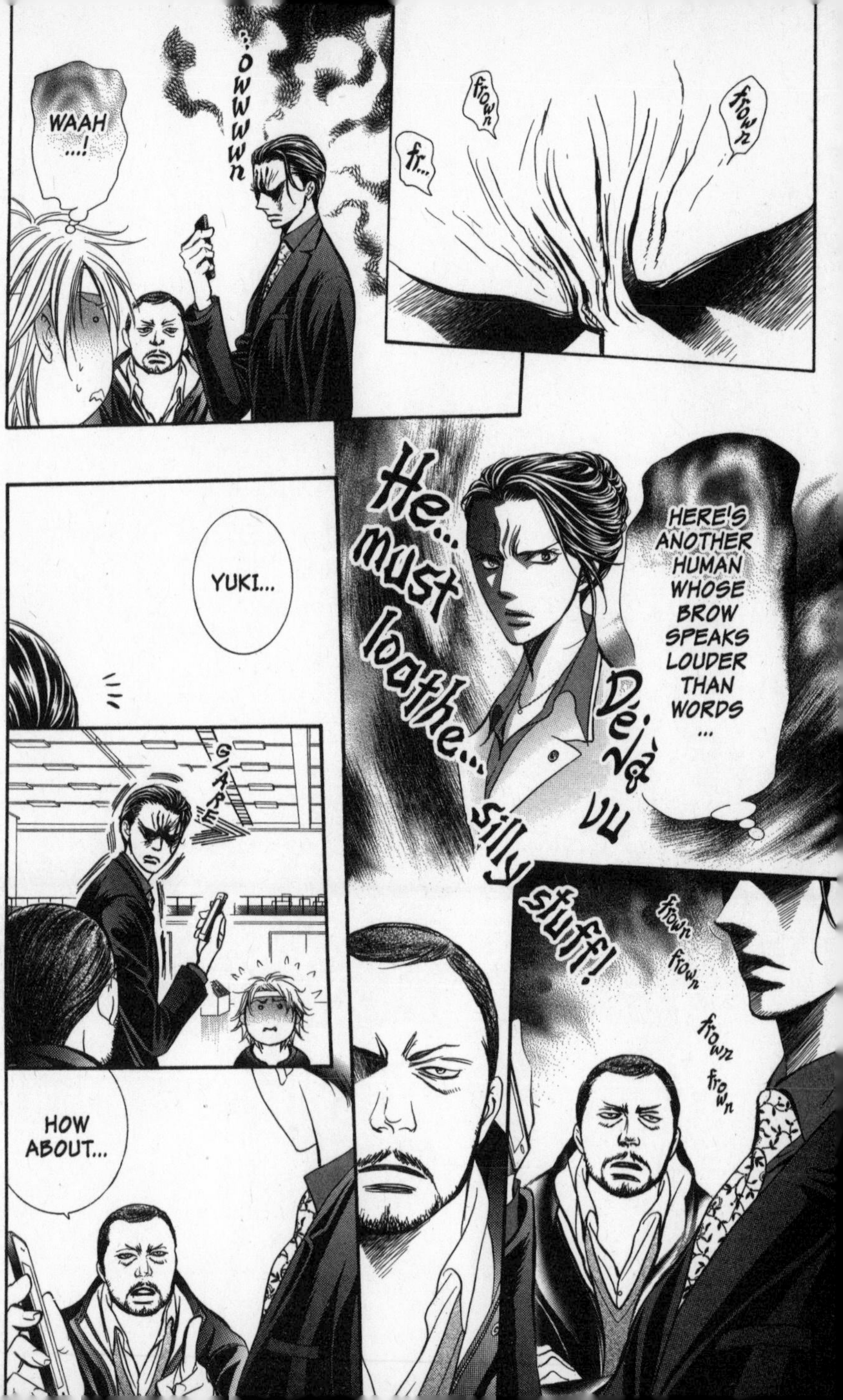
frown
frown
fr...
...OWWWWn
WAAH ...!
HERE'S ANOTHER HUMAN WHOSE BROW SPEAKS LOUDER THAN WORDS...
Déjà vu
He... must loathe... silly stuff!
YUKI...
GLARE
frown
frown
frown
frown
HOW ABOUT...

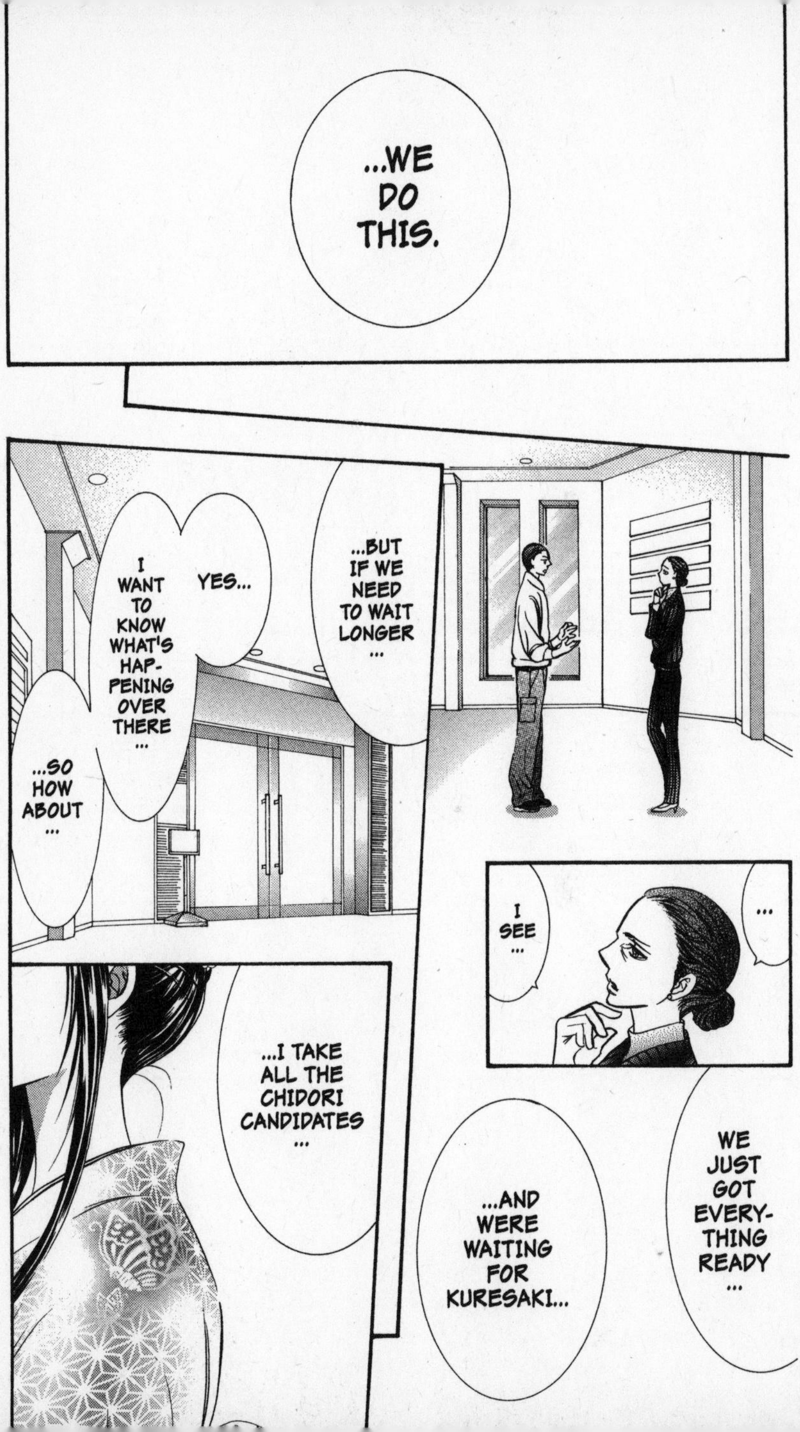
...WE DO THIS.
...BUT IF WE NEED TO WAIT LONGER ...
YES...
I WANT TO KNOW WHAT'S HAP-PENING OVER THERE ...
...SO HOW ABOUT ...
...
I SEE ...
WE JUST GOT EVERY-THING READY ...
...AND WERE WAITING FOR KURESAKI...
...I TAKE ALL THE CHIDORI CANDIDATES ...

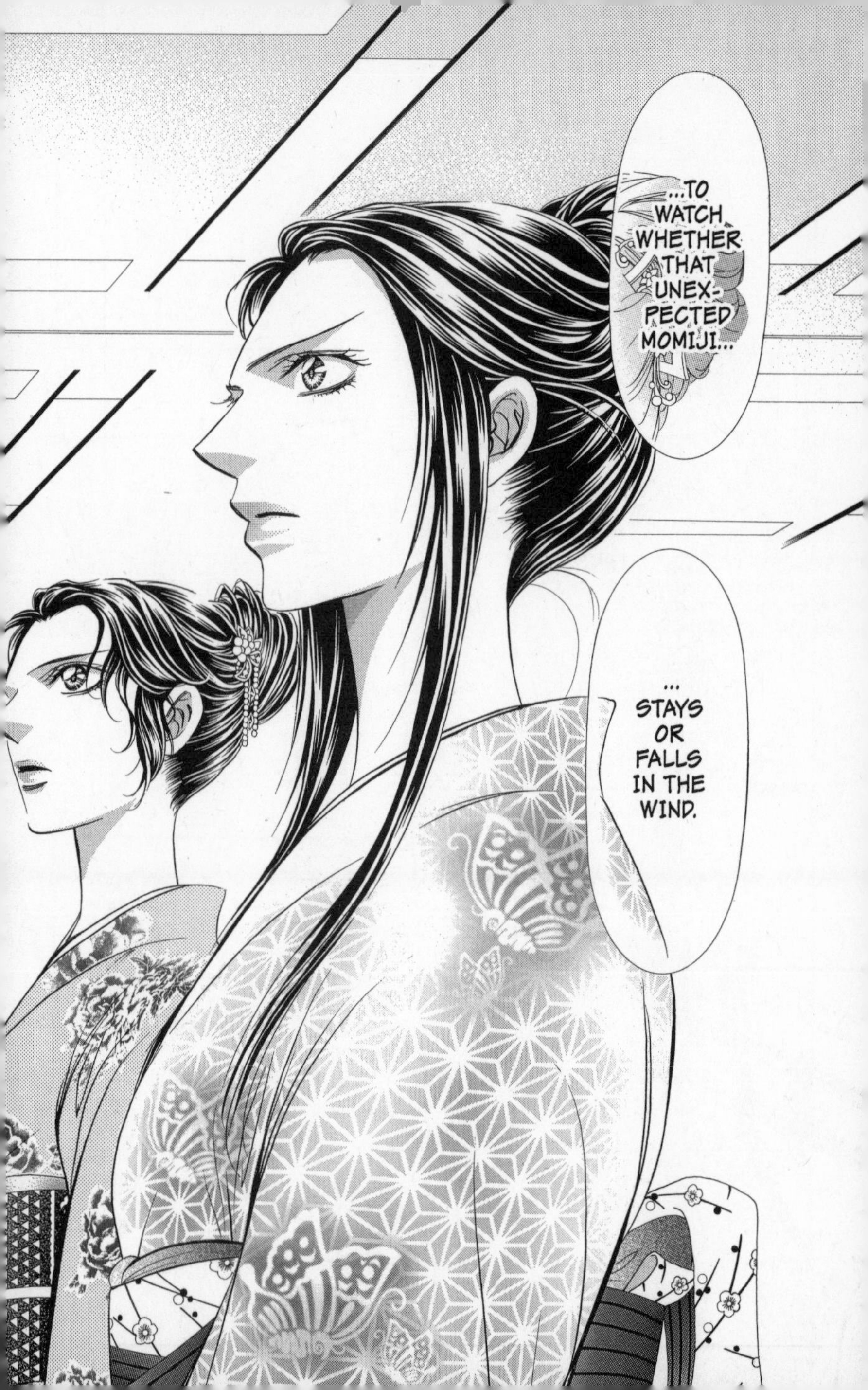
...TO WATCH WHETHER THAT UNEX-PECTED MOMIJI...
... STAYS OR FALLS IN THE WIND.

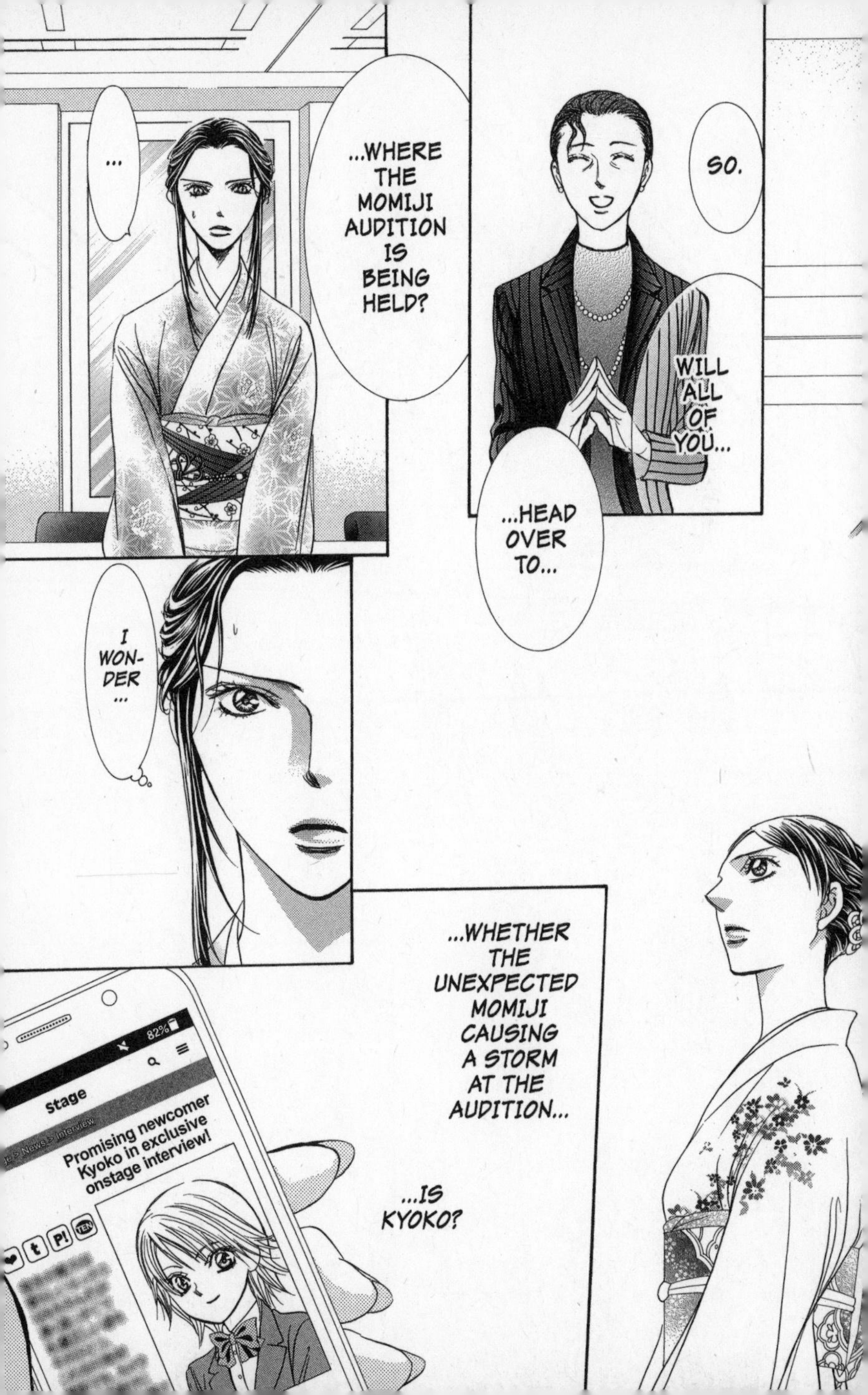
SO.
WILL ALL OF YOU...
...HEAD OVER TO...
...WHERE THE MOMIJI AUDITION IS BEING HELD?
...
I WONDER...
...WHETHER THE UNEXPECTED MOMIJI CAUSING A STORM AT THE AUDITION...
...IS KYOKO?
82%
Stage
News > Interview
Promising newcomer Kyoko in exclusive onstage interview!

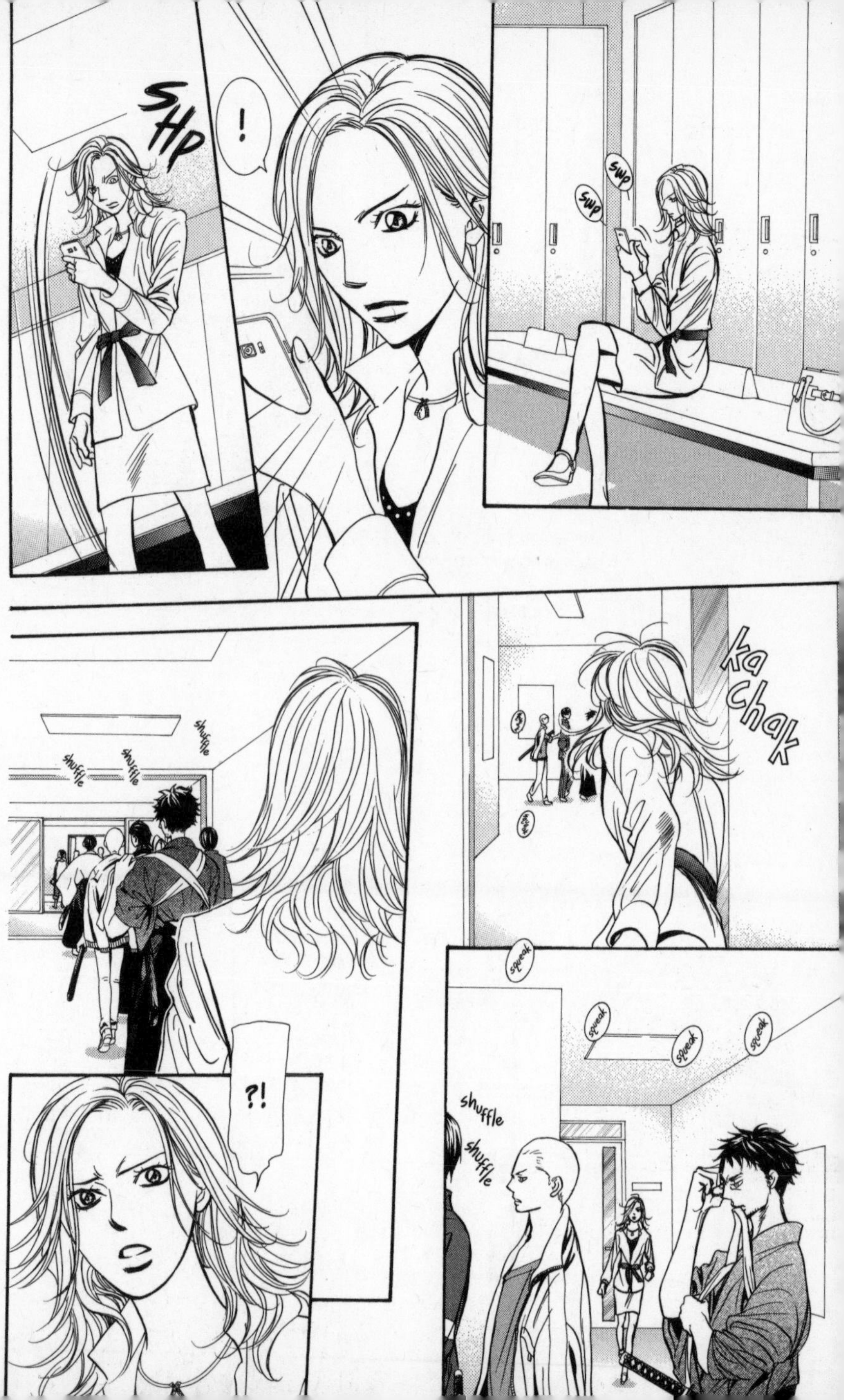
swp
swp
!
SHP
ka chak
shuffle
shuffle
shuffle
squeak
squeak
squeak
squeak
shuffle
shuffle
?!

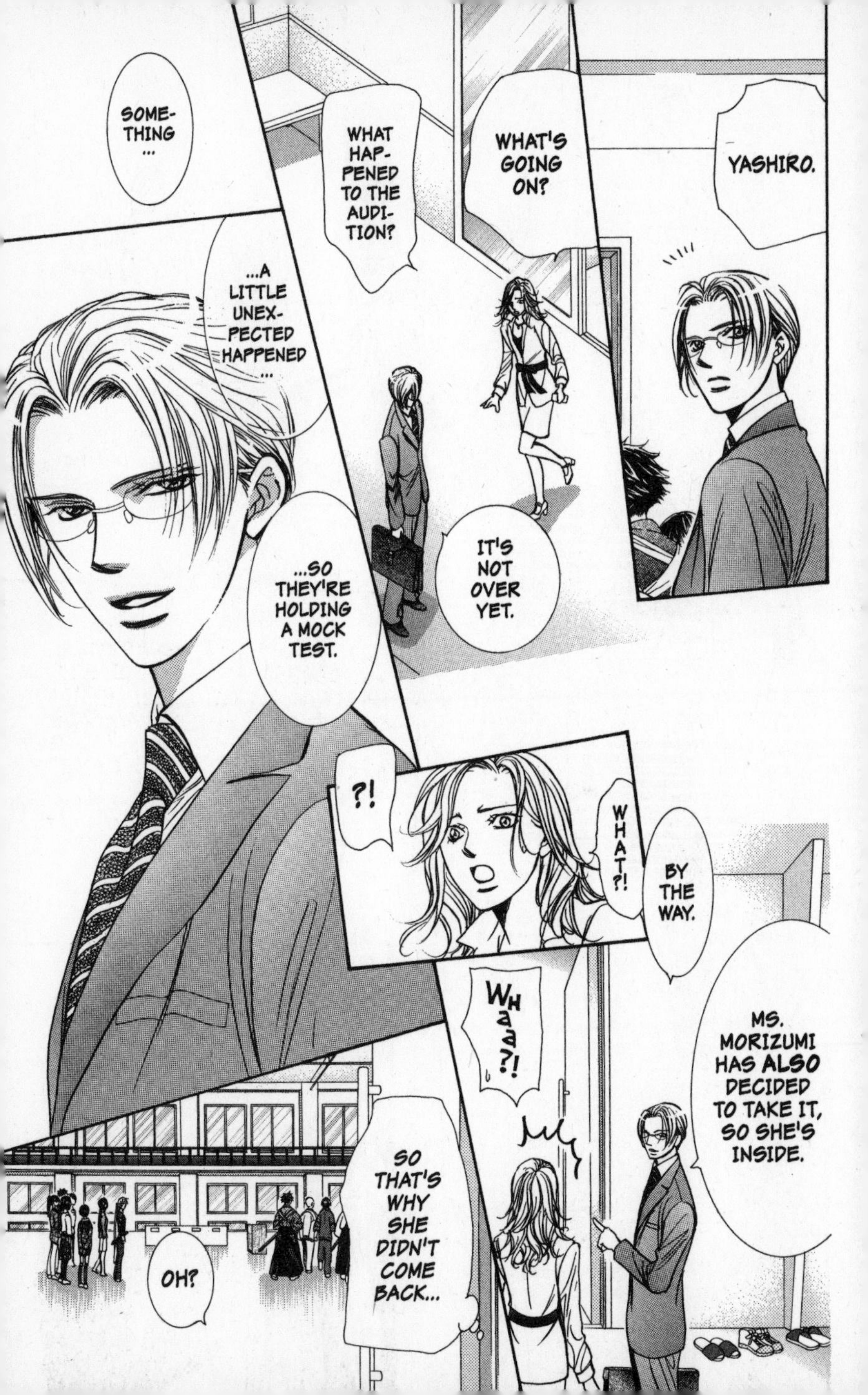

YASHIRO.
WHAT'S GOING ON?
WHAT HAPPENED TO THE AUDITION?
IT'S NOT OVER YET.
SOMETHING...
...A LITTLE UNEXPECTED HAPPENED...
...SO THEY'RE HOLDING A MOCK TEST.
WHAT?!
?!
BY THE WAY.
MS. MORIZUMI HAS ALSO DECIDED TO TAKE IT, SO SHE'S INSIDE.
Whaaa?!
SO THAT'S WHY SHE DIDN'T COME BACK...
OH?

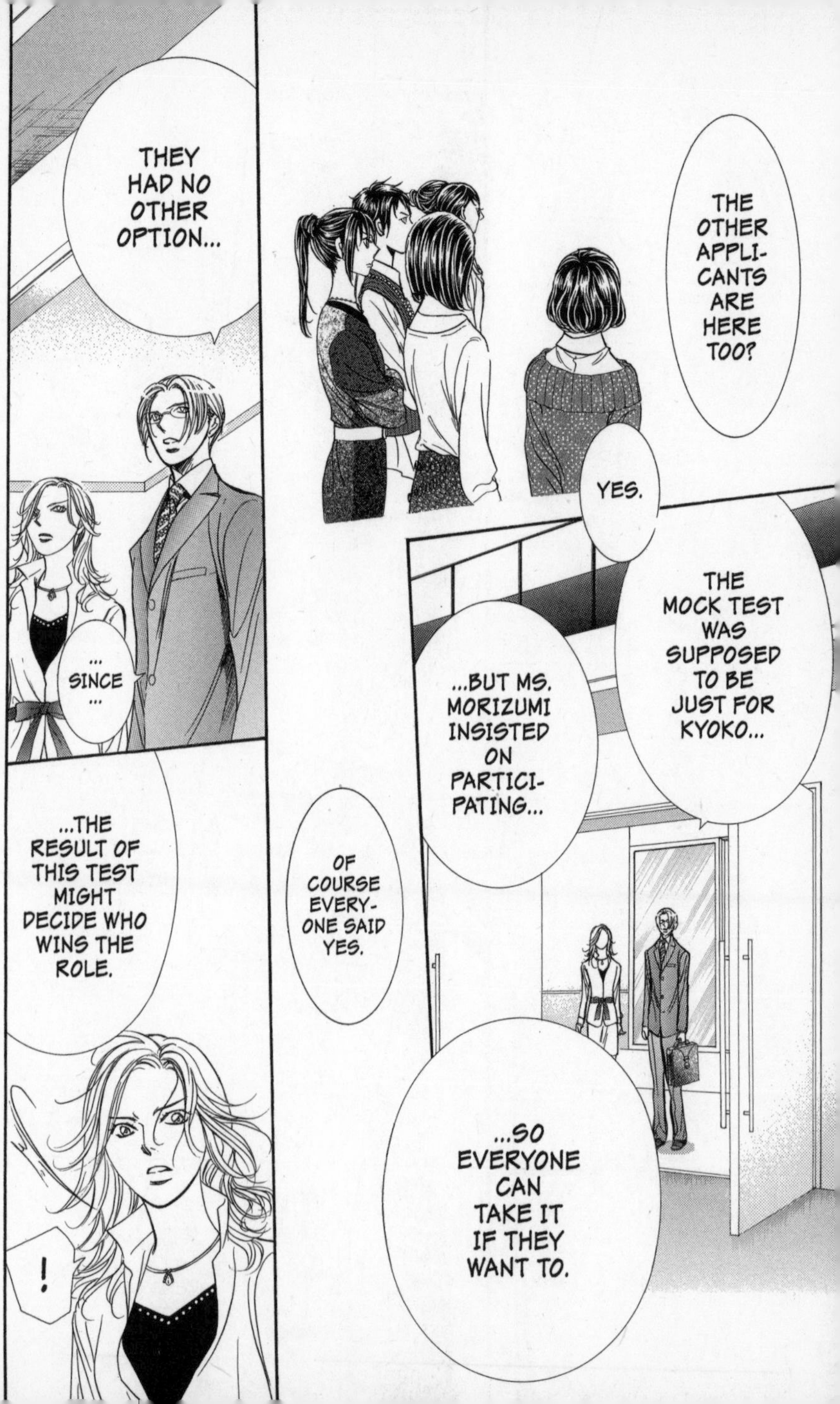
THE OTHER APPLICANTS ARE HERE TOO?
YES.
THE MOCK TEST WAS SUPPOSED TO BE JUST FOR KYOKO...
...BUT MS. MORIZUMI INSISTED ON PARTICIPATING...
OF COURSE EVERYONE SAID YES.
...SO EVERYONE CAN TAKE IT IF THEY WANT TO.
THEY HAD NO OTHER OPTION...
...SINCE...
...THE RESULT OF THIS TEST MIGHT DECIDE WHO WINS THE ROLE.
!

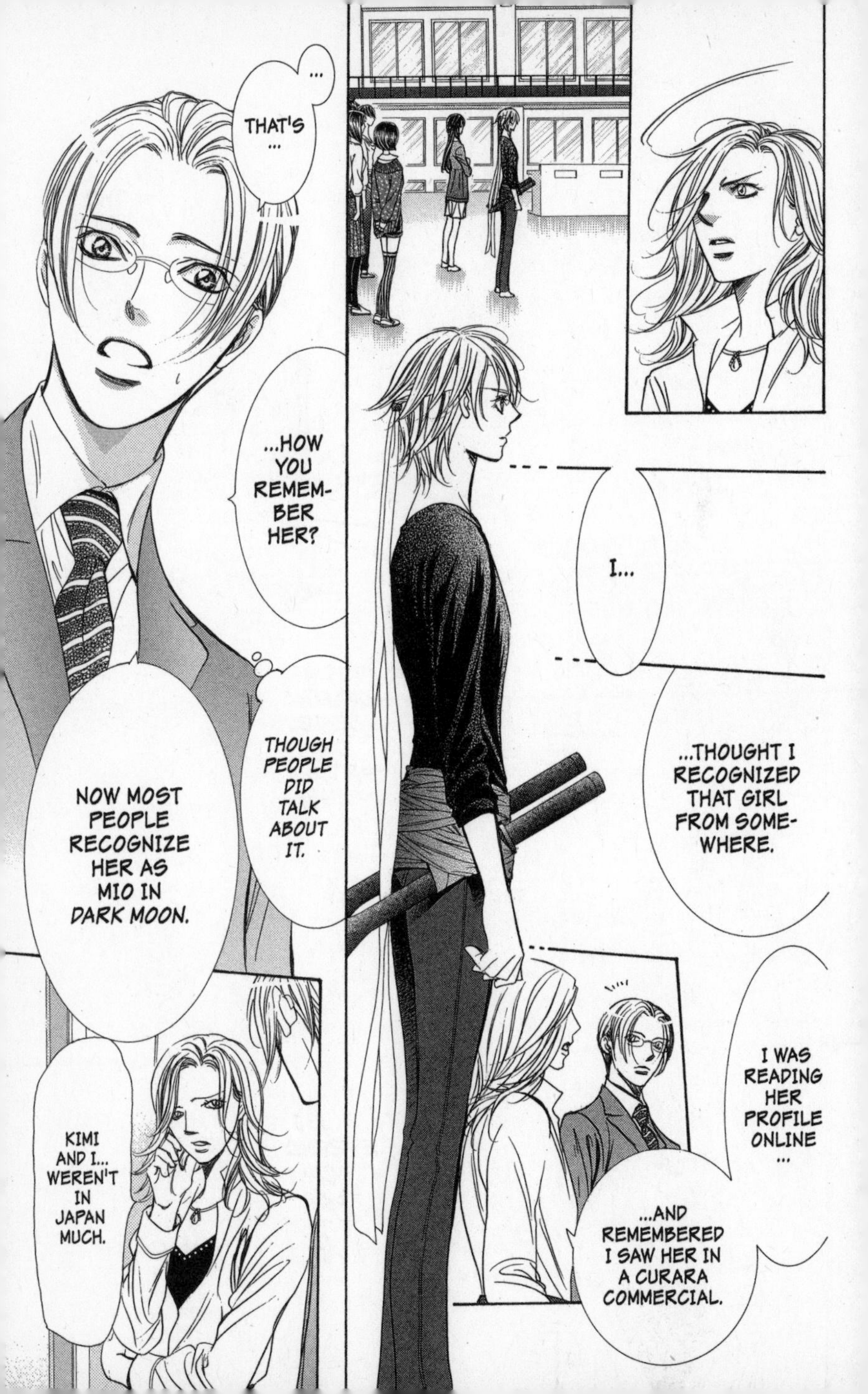
I...
...THOUGHT I RECOGNIZED THAT GIRL FROM SOME-WHERE.
I WAS READING HER PROFILE ONLINE ...
...AND REMEMBERED I SAW HER IN A CURARA COMMERCIAL.
... THAT'S ...
...HOW YOU REMEM-BER HER?
THOUGH PEOPLE DID TALK ABOUT IT.
NOW MOST PEOPLE RECOGNIZE HER AS MIO IN DARK MOON.
KIMI AND I... WEREN'T IN JAPAN MUCH.

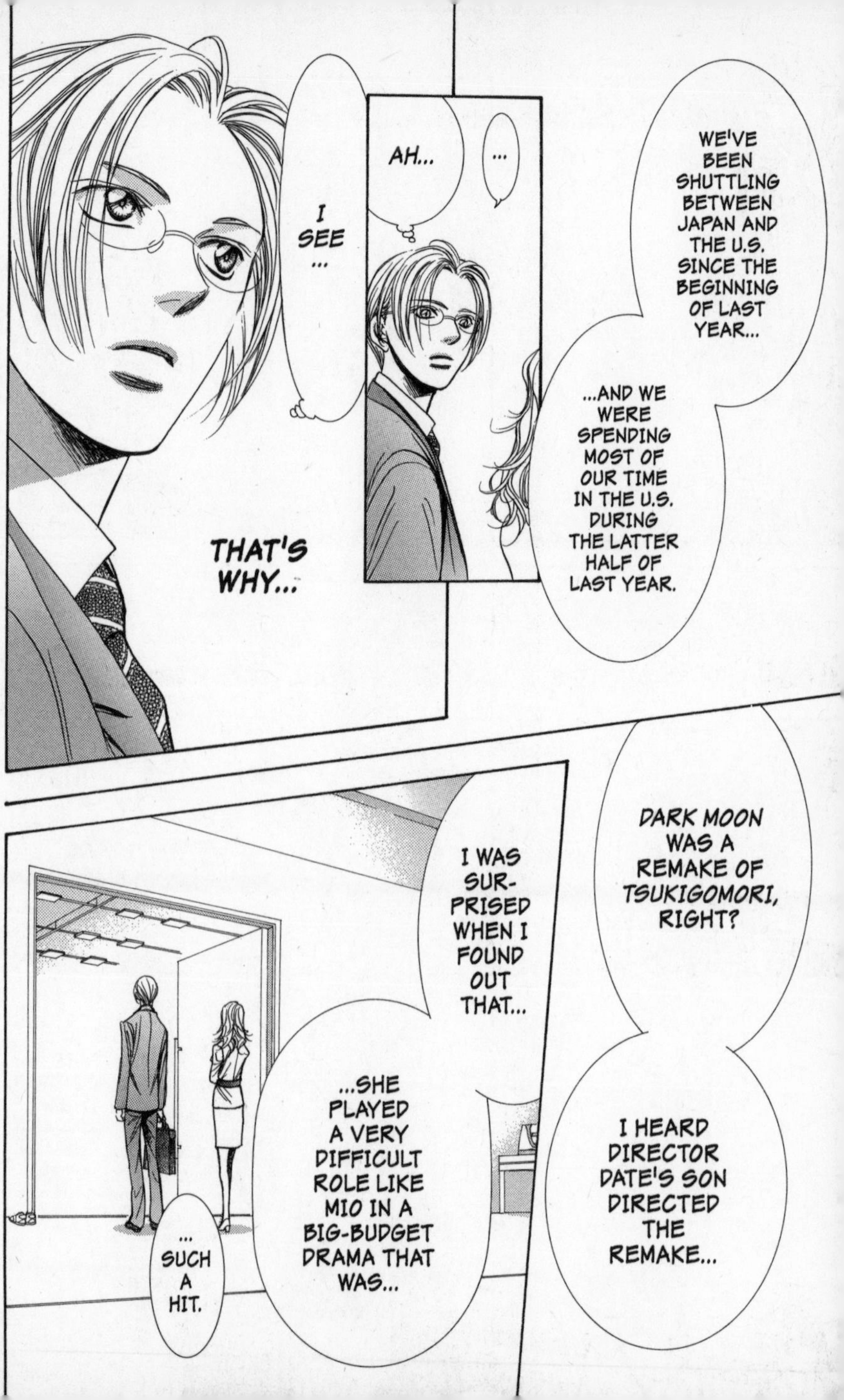
WE'VE BEEN SHUTTLING BETWEEN JAPAN AND THE U.S. SINCE THE BEGINNING OF LAST YEAR...
...AND WE WERE SPENDING MOST OF OUR TIME IN THE U.S. DURING THE LATTER HALF OF LAST YEAR.
...
AH...
I SEE...
THAT'S WHY...
DARK MOON WAS A REMAKE OF TSUKIGOMORI, RIGHT?
I HEARD DIRECTOR DATE'S SON DIRECTED THE REMAKE...
I WAS SUR-PRISED WHEN I FOUND OUT THAT...
...SHE PLAYED A VERY DIFFICULT ROLE LIKE MIO IN A BIG-BUDGET DRAMA THAT WAS...
...SUCH A HIT.

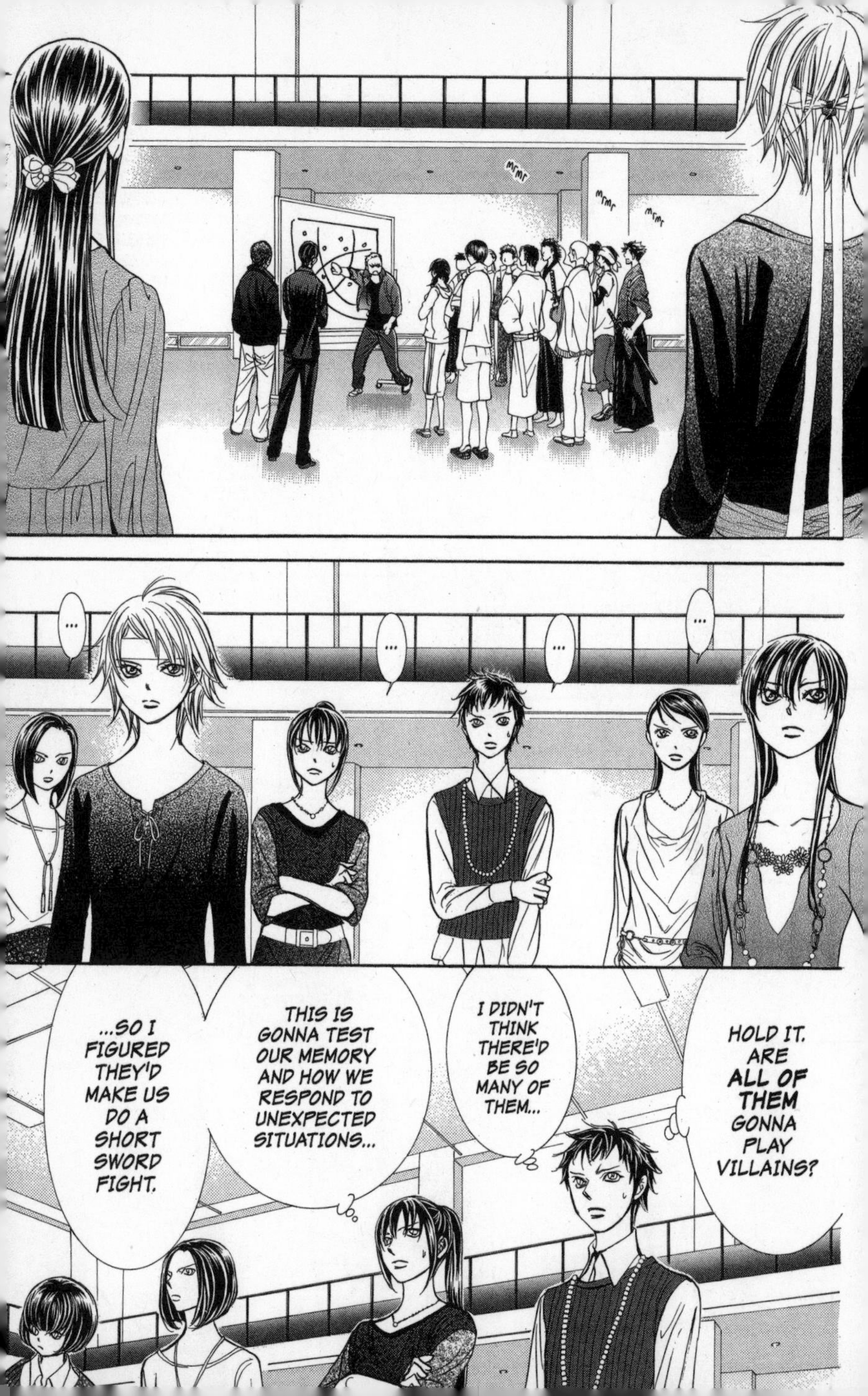
mrmr
mrmr
mrmr
...
...
...
...
HOLD IT. ARE ALL OF THEM GONNA PLAY VILLAINS?
I DIDN'T THINK THERE'D BE SO MANY OF THEM...
THIS IS GONNA TEST OUR MEMORY AND HOW WE RESPOND TO UNEXPECTED SITUATIONS...
...SO I FIGURED THEY'D MAKE US DO A SHORT SWORD FIGHT.

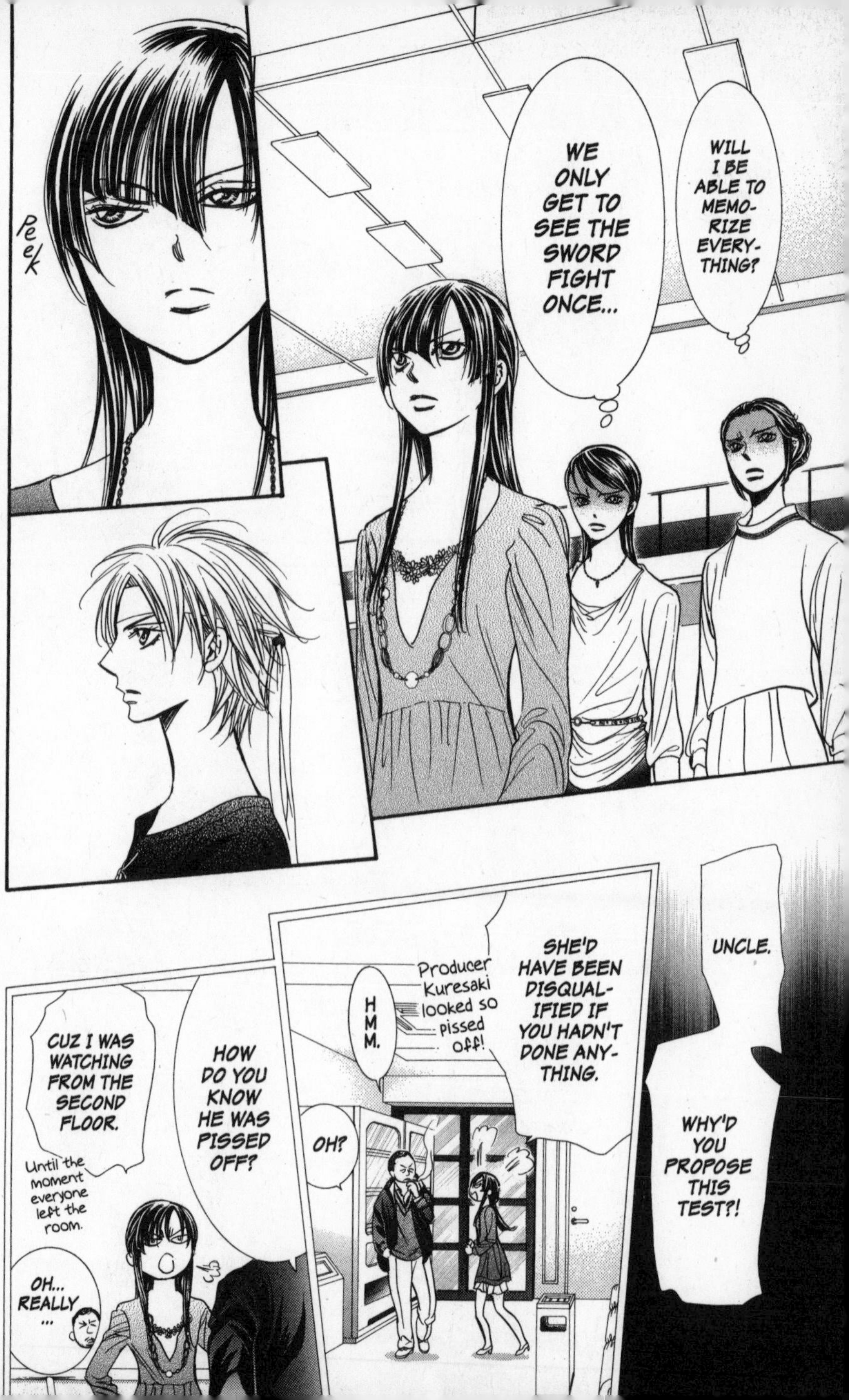
WILL I BE ABLE TO MEMORIZE EVERYTHING?
WE ONLY GET TO SEE THE SWORD FIGHT ONCE...
Peek
UNCLE.
WHY'D YOU PROPOSE THIS TEST?!
SHE'D HAVE BEEN DISQUALIFIED IF YOU HADN'T DONE ANYTHING.
Producer Kuresaki looked so pissed off!
HMM.
OH?
HOW DO YOU KNOW HE WAS PISSED OFF?
CUZ I WAS WATCHING FROM THE SECOND FLOOR.
Until the moment everyone left the room.
OH... REALLY ...

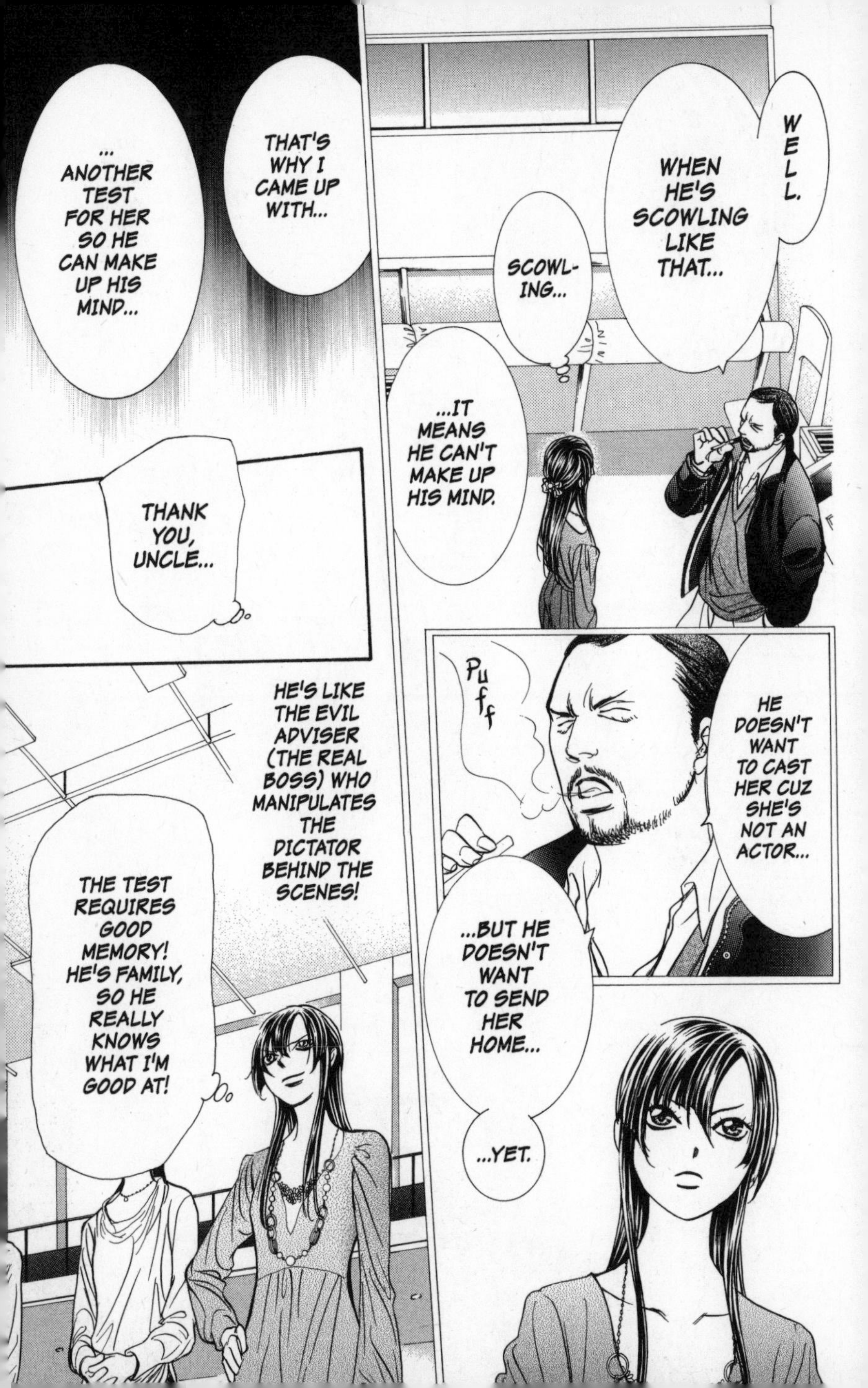
WELL.
WHEN HE'S SCOWLING LIKE THAT...
SCOWLING...
...IT MEANS HE CAN'T MAKE UP HIS MIND.
THAT'S WHY I CAME UP WITH...
...ANOTHER TEST FOR HER SO HE CAN MAKE UP HIS MIND...
THANK YOU, UNCLE...
PUFF
HE DOESN'T WANT TO CAST HER CUZ SHE'S NOT AN ACTOR...
...BUT HE DOESN'T WANT TO SEND HER HOME...
...YET.
HE'S LIKE THE EVIL ADVISER (THE REAL BOSS) WHO MANIPULATES THE DICTATOR BEHIND THE SCENES!
THE TEST REQUIRES GOOD MEMORY! HE'S FAMILY, SO HE REALLY KNOWS WHAT I'M GOOD AT!

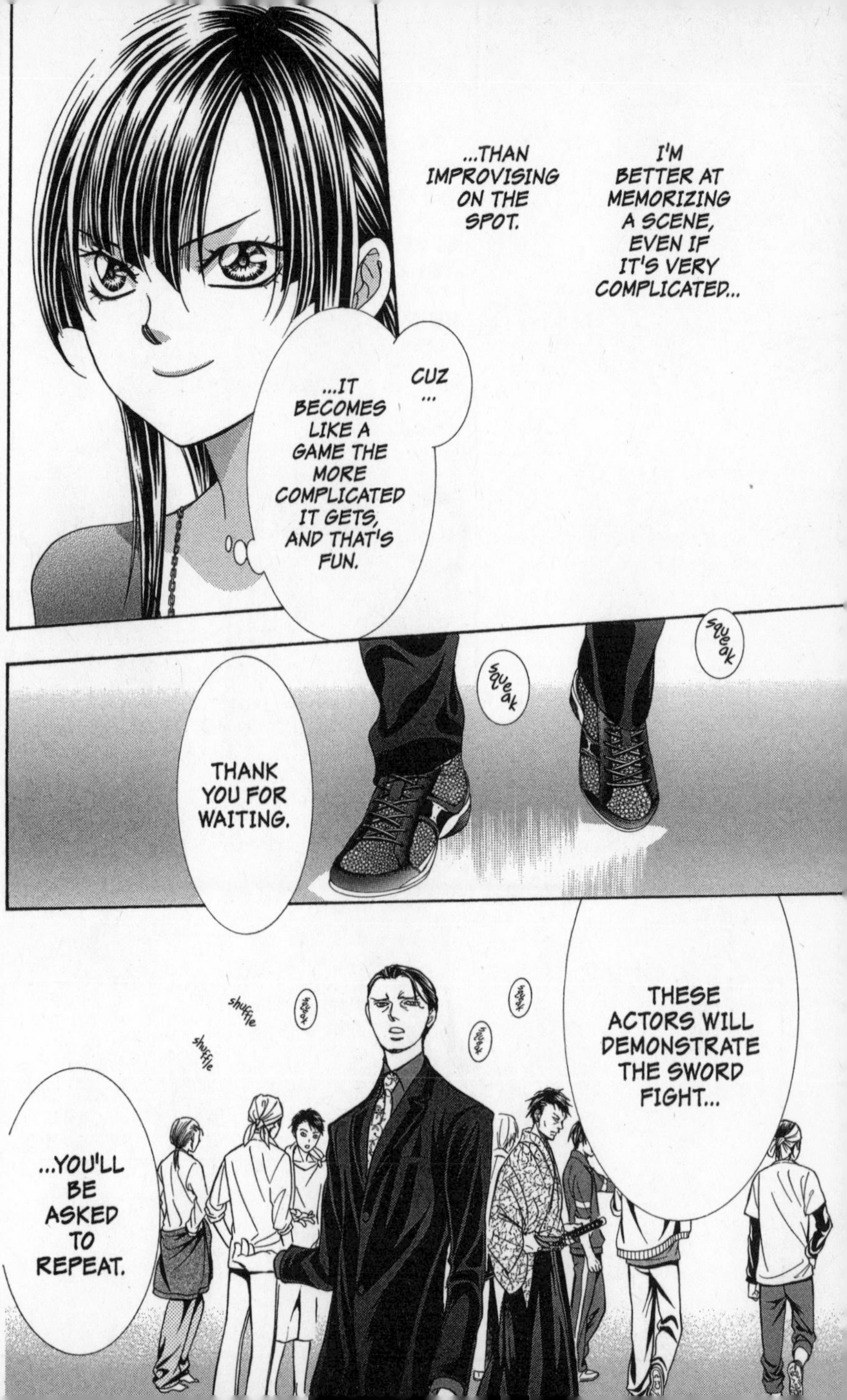
I'M BETTER AT MEMORIZING A SCENE, EVEN IF IT'S VERY COMPLICATED...
...THAN IMPROVISING ON THE SPOT.
CUZ ...
...IT BECOMES LIKE A GAME THE MORE COMPLICATED IT GETS, AND THAT'S FUN.
squeak
squeak
THANK YOU FOR WAITING.
THESE ACTORS WILL DEMONSTRATE THE SWORD FIGHT...
shuffle
shuffle
...YOU'LL BE ASKED TO REPEAT.

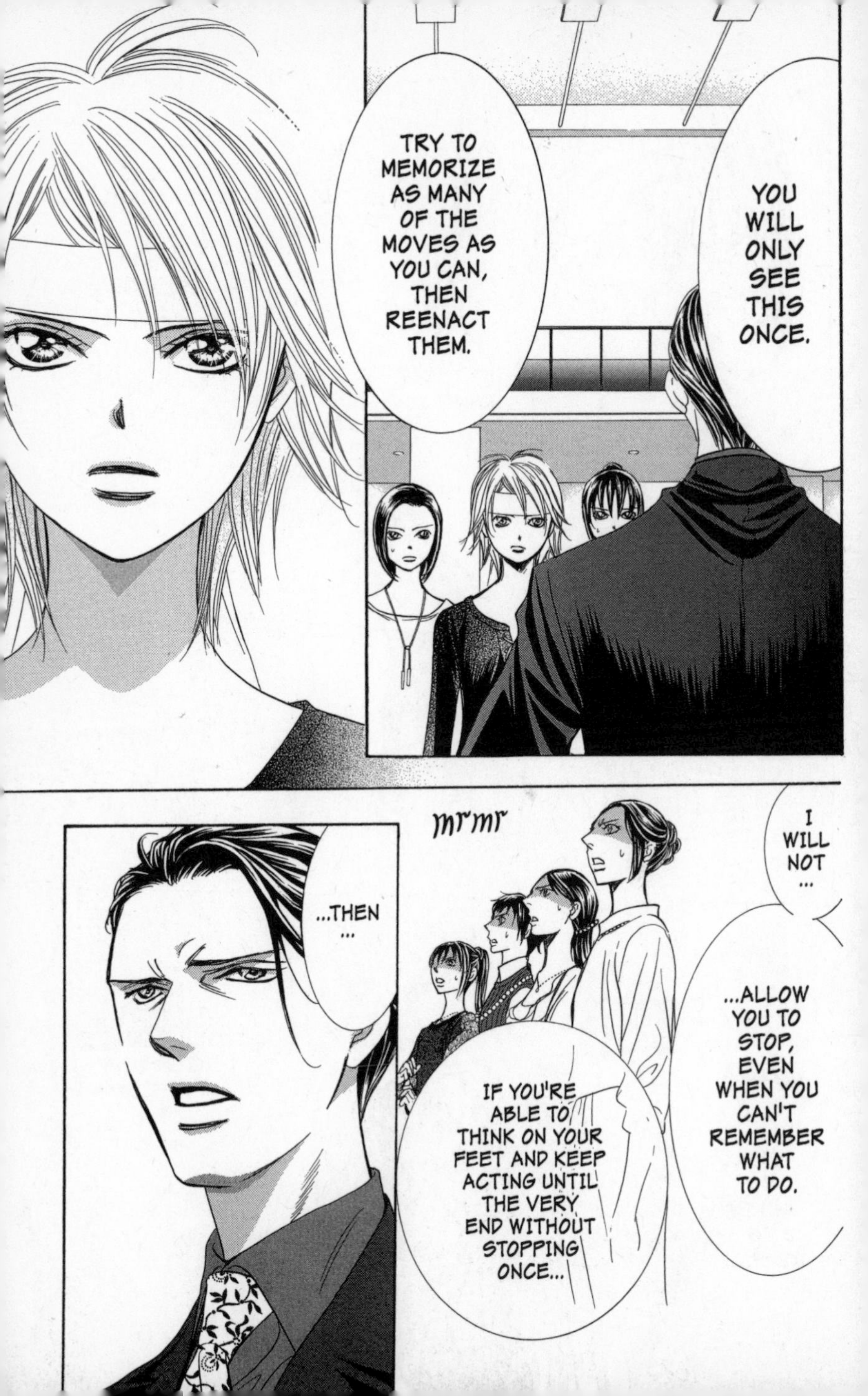
YOU WILL ONLY SEE THIS ONCE.
TRY TO MEMORIZE AS MANY OF THE MOVES AS YOU CAN, THEN REENACT THEM.
I WILL NOT ...
...ALLOW YOU TO STOP, EVEN WHEN YOU CAN'T REMEMBER WHAT TO DO.
mrmr
IF YOU'RE ABLE TO THINK ON YOUR FEET AND KEEP ACTING UNTIL THE VERY END WITHOUT STOPPING ONCE...
...THEN ...

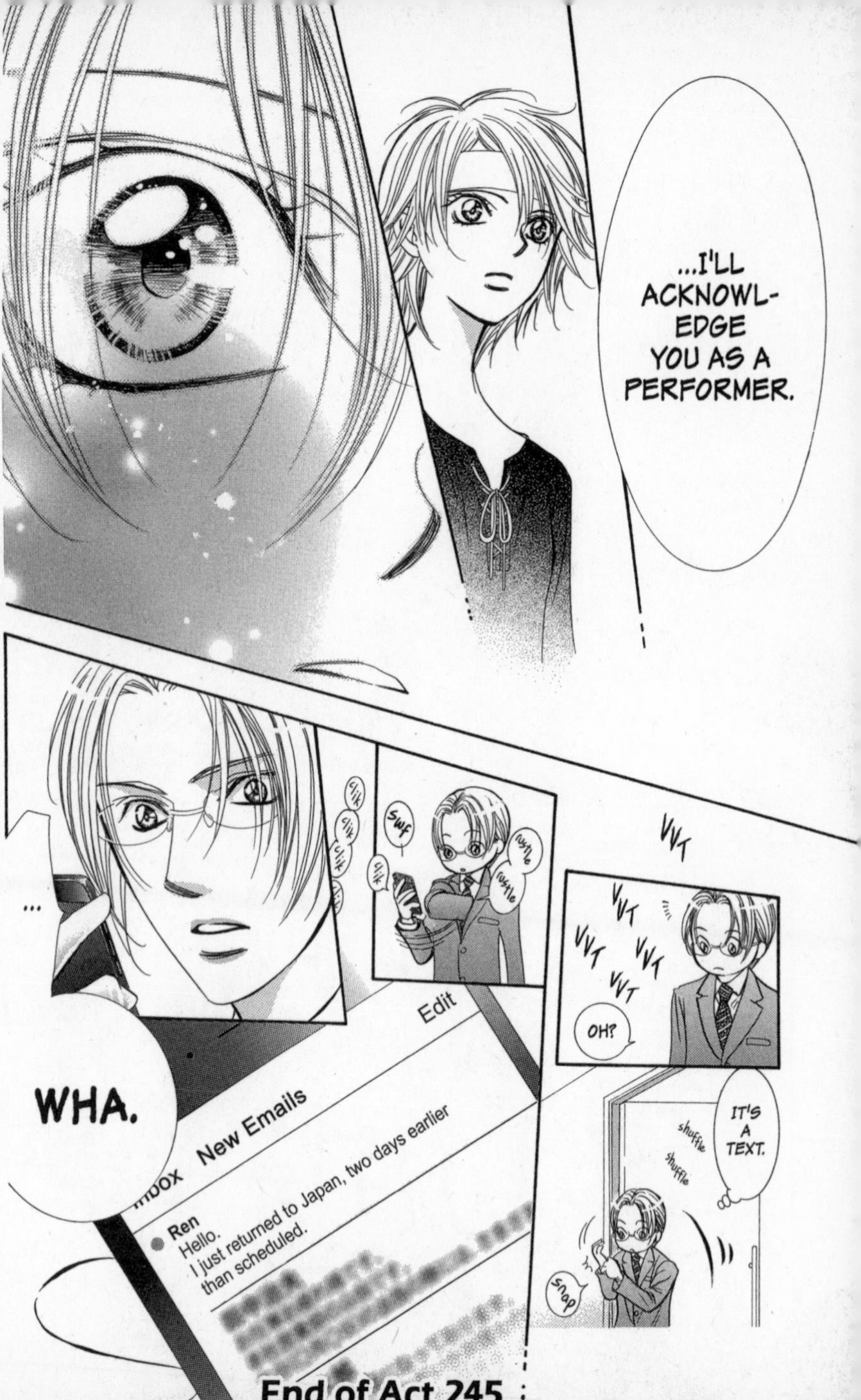
...I'LL ACKNOWL-EDGE YOU AS A PERFORMER.
VVT
VVT
VVT
VVT
VVT
OH?
swf
rustle
rustle
clik
clik
clik
clik
clik
...
shuffle
shuffle
IT'S A TEXT.
snap
Edit
New Emails
Ren
Hello.
I just returned to Japan, two days earlier than scheduled.
WHA.

End of Act 245

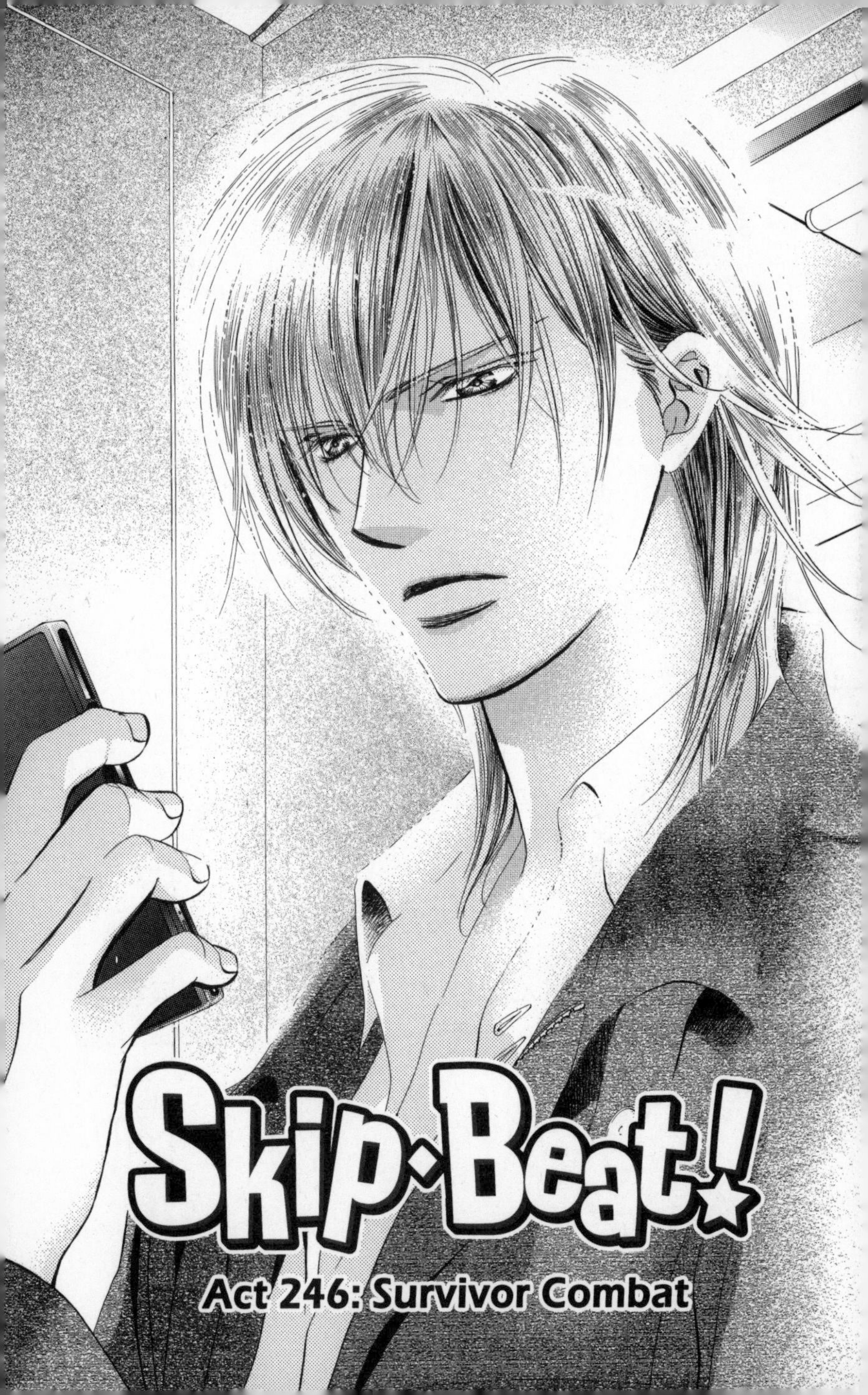
Skip·Beat!
Act 246: Survivor Combat

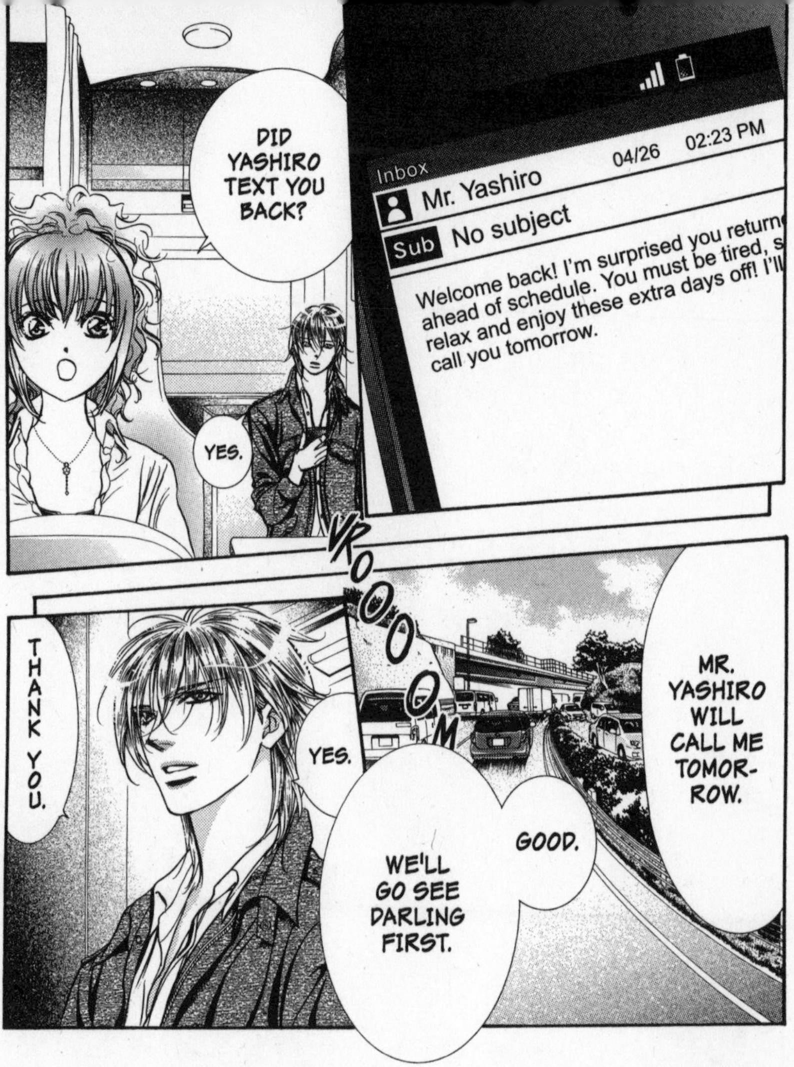
Inbox
04/26
02:23 PM
Mr. Yashiro
Sub
No subject
Welcome back! I'm surprised you returne ahead of schedule. You must be tired, s relax and enjoy these extra days off! I'll call you tomorrow.
DID YASHIRO TEXT YOU BACK?
YES.
VROOOOOM
MR. YASHIRO WILL CALL ME TOMOR-ROW.
GOOD.
WE'LL GO SEE DARLING FIRST.
YES.
THANK YOU.

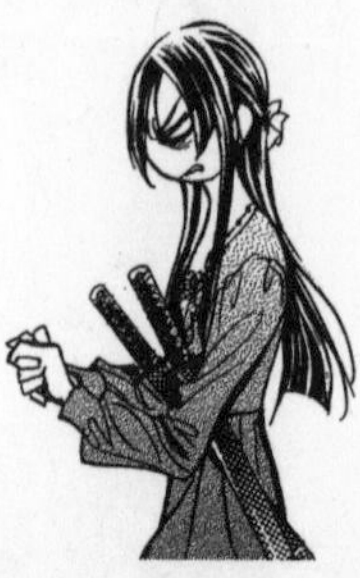

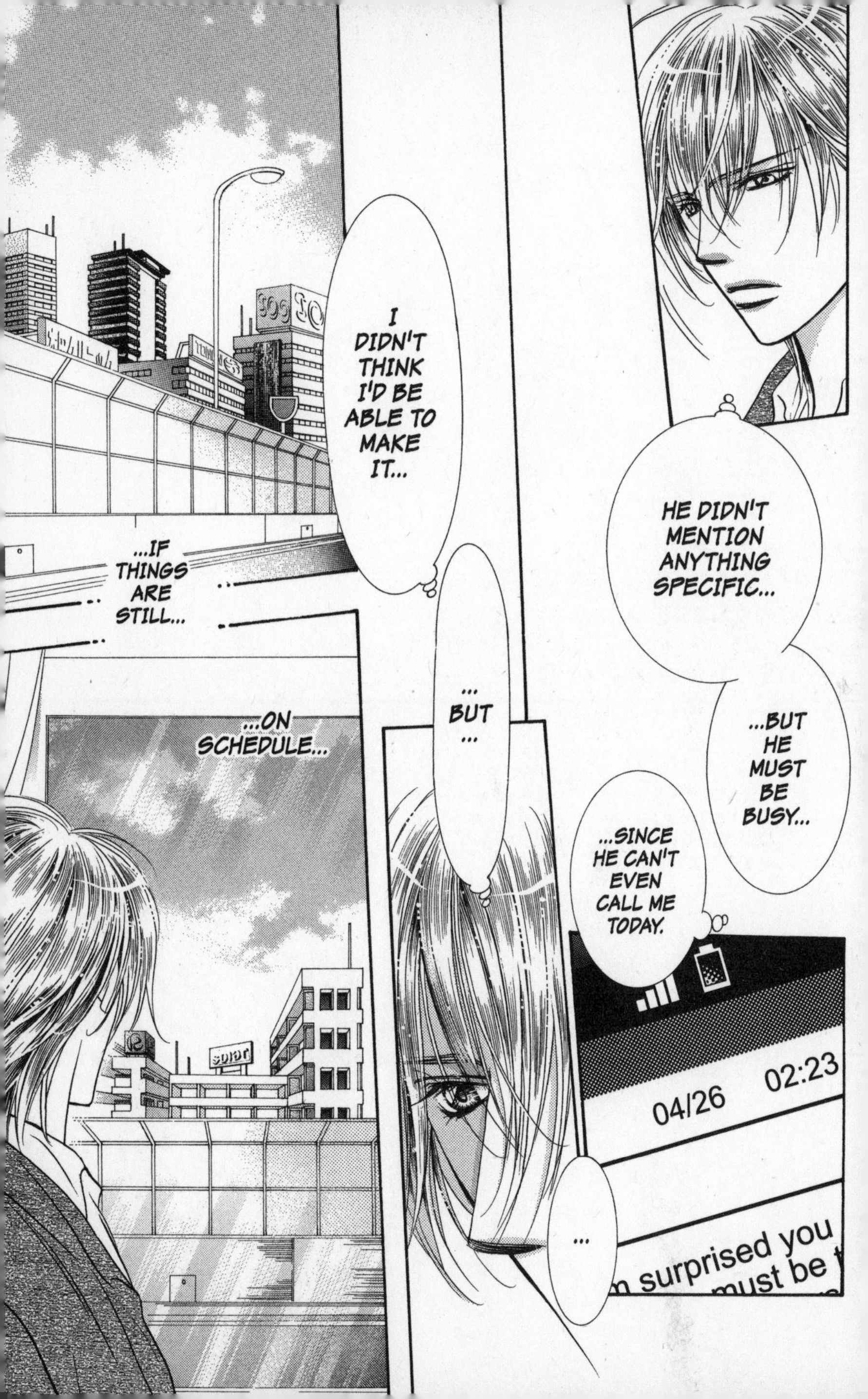
HE DIDN'T MENTION ANYTHING SPECIFIC...
...BUT HE MUST BE BUSY...
...SINCE HE CAN'T EVEN CALL ME TODAY.
04/26
02:23
surprised you
must be
...
I DIDN'T THINK I'D BE ABLE TO MAKE IT...
...BUT...
...IF THINGS ARE STILL...
...ON SCHEDULE...

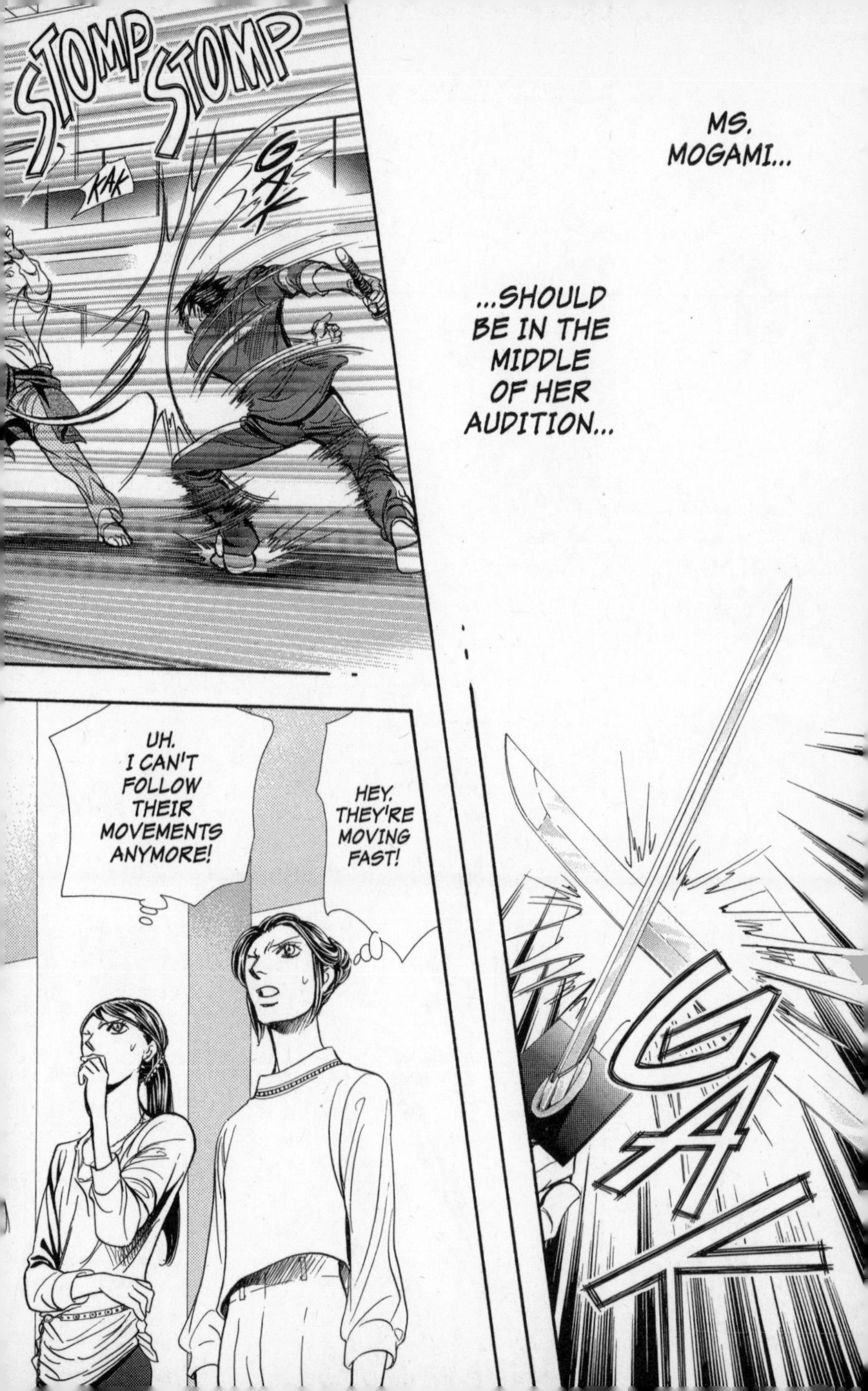
MS. MOGAMI...
...SHOULD BE IN THE MIDDLE OF HER AUDITION...
GAK
STOMP STOMP
GAK
KAK
HEY. THEY'RE MOVING FAST!
UH. I CAN'T FOLLOW THEIR MOVEMENTS ANYMORE!

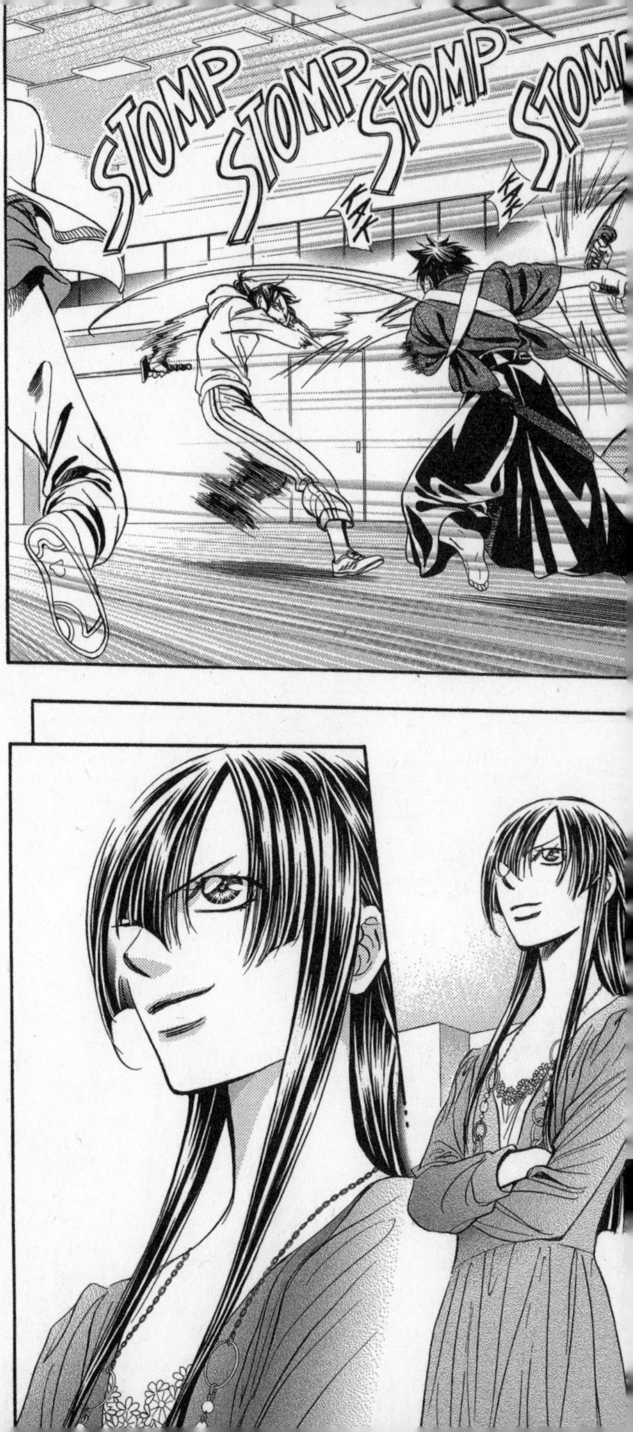
STOM
STOMP
STOMP
STOMP
KAK
KAK
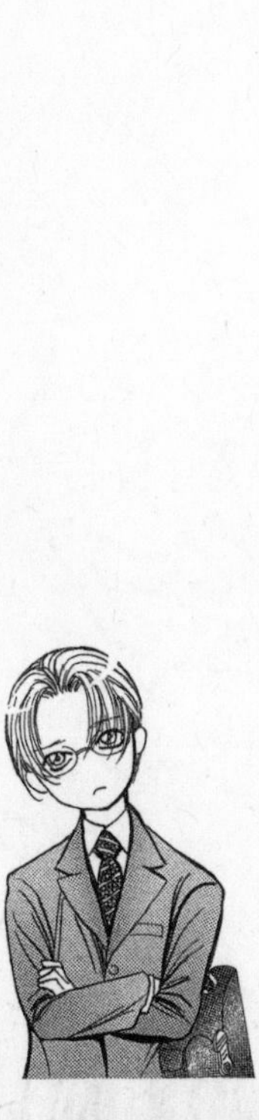

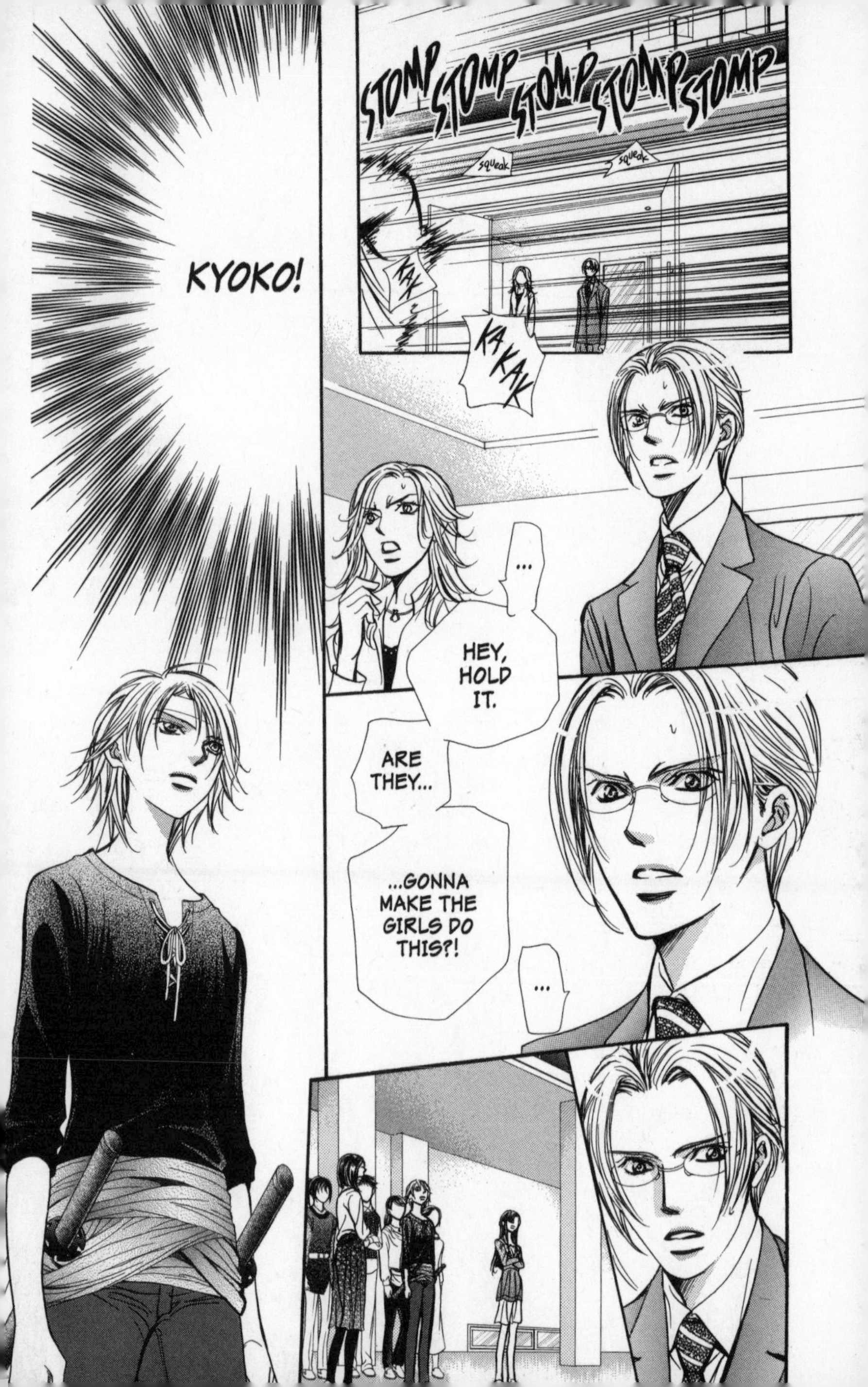
STOMP STOMP STOMP STOMP STOMP
squeak
squeak
KAK
KA KAK
...
HEY, HOLD IT.
ARE THEY...
...GONNA MAKE THE GIRLS DO THIS?!
...
KYOKO!

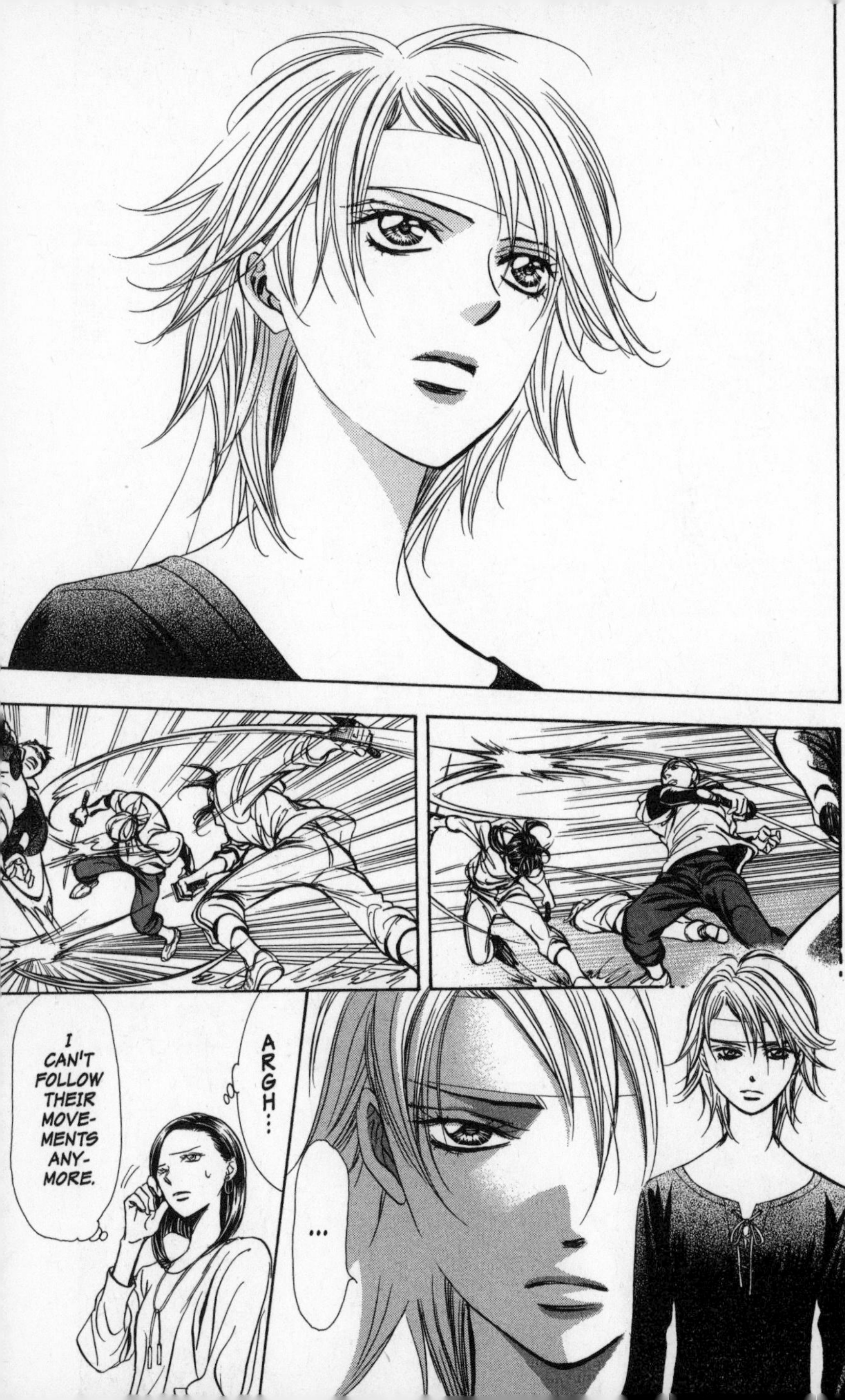
ARGH...
...
I CAN'T FOLLOW THEIR MOVEMENTS ANYMORE.

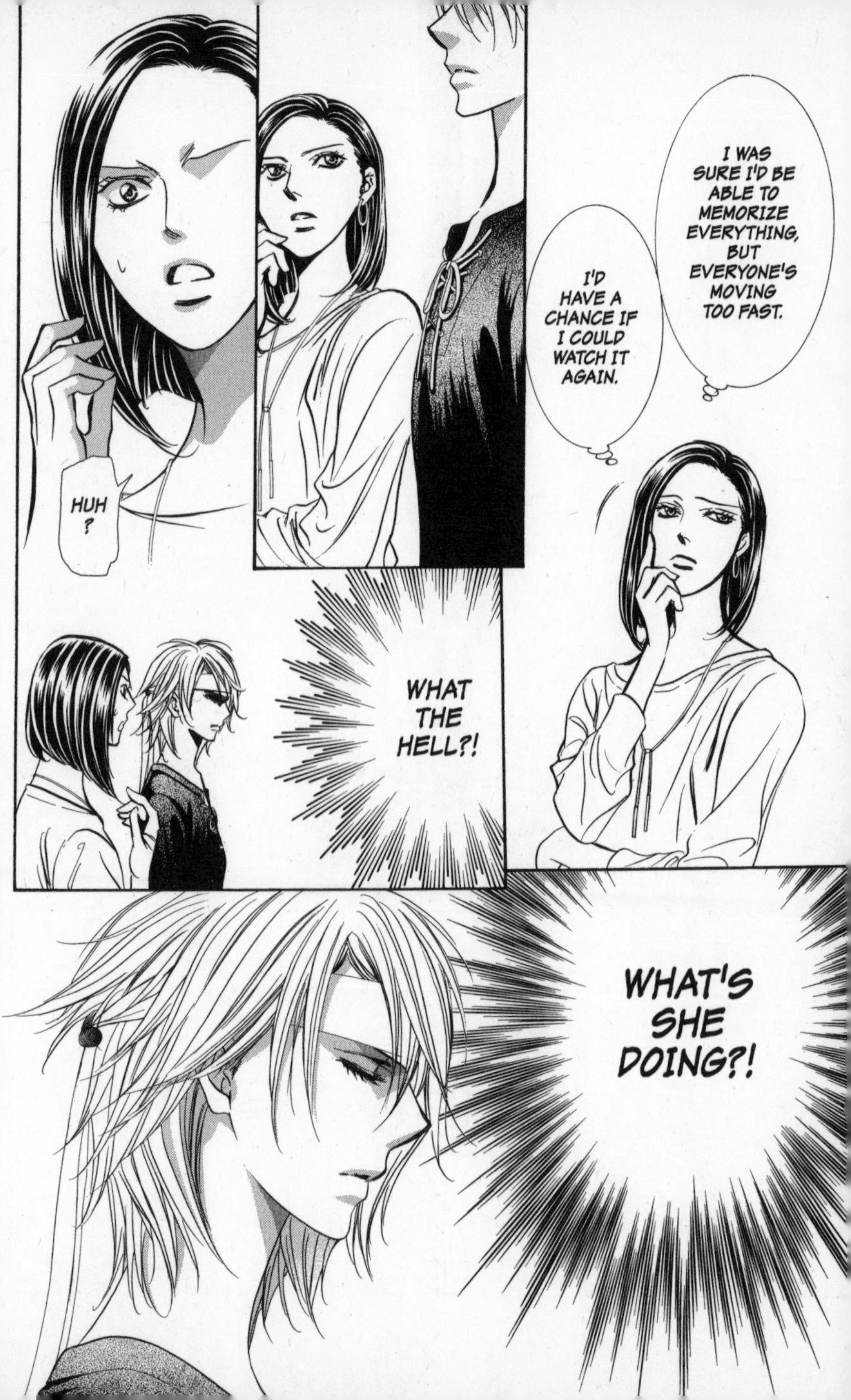
I WAS SURE I'D BE ABLE TO MEMORIZE EVERYTHING, BUT EVERYONE'S MOVING TOO FAST.
I'D HAVE A CHANCE IF I COULD WATCH IT AGAIN.
HUH?
WHAT THE HELL?!
WHAT'S SHE DOING?!

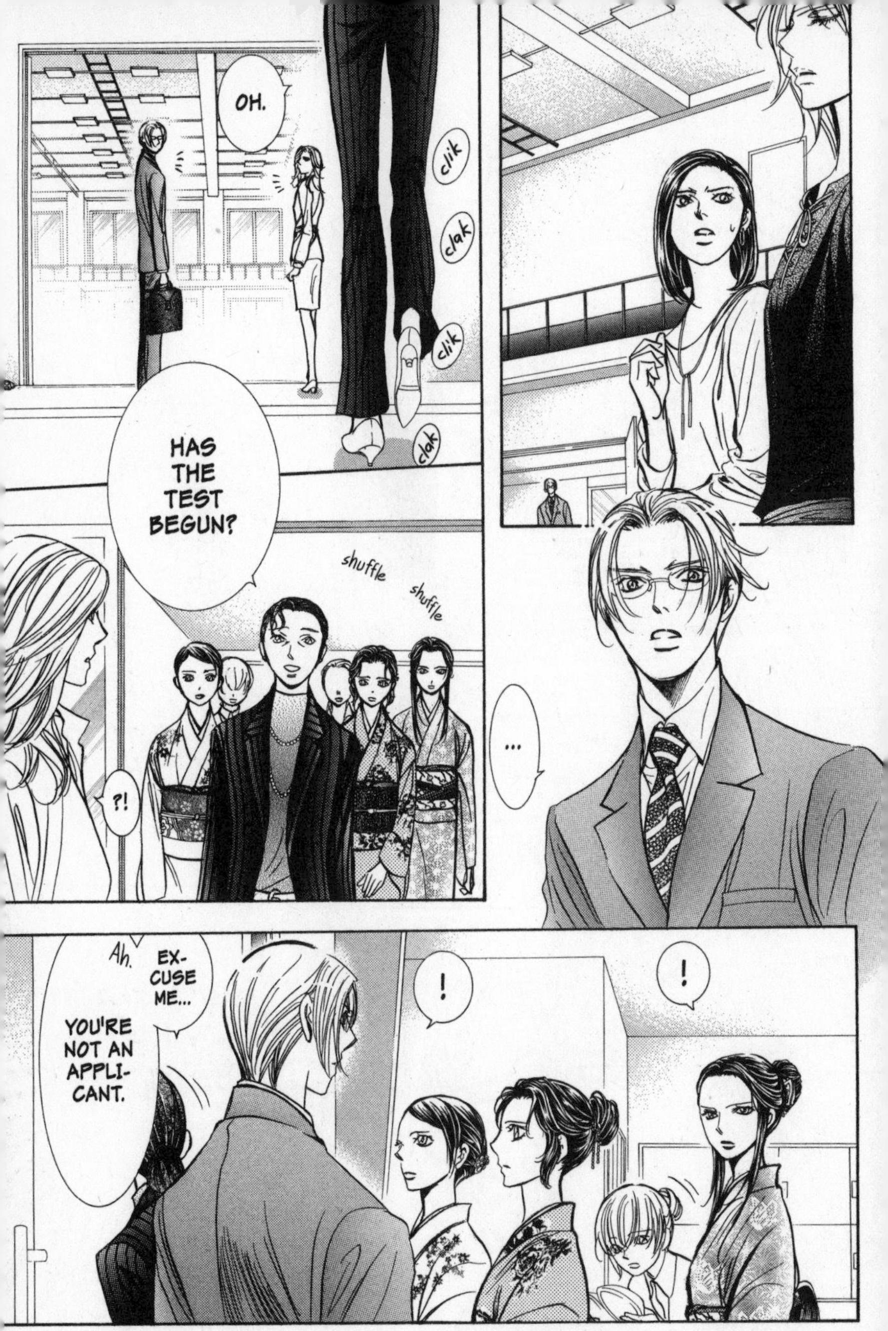
clik
clak
clik
clak
OH.
...
HAS THE TEST BEGUN?
shuffle
shuffle
?!
!
!
Ah.
EXCUSE ME...
YOU'RE NOT AN APPLICANT.

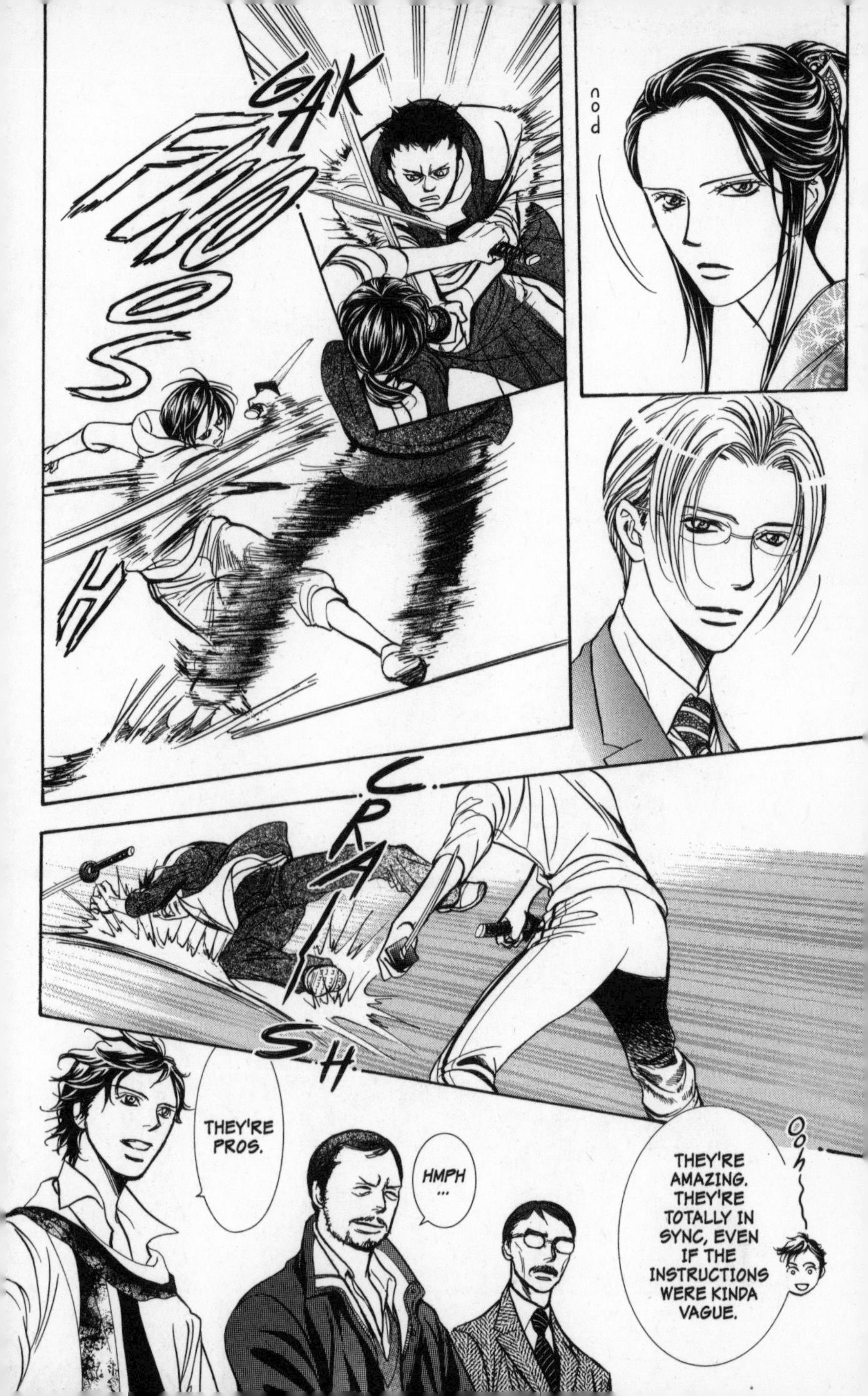
nod
GAK
FWOOSSH
CRASH
Ooh...
THEY'RE AMAZING. THEY'RE TOTALLY IN SYNC, EVEN IF THE INSTRUCTIONS WERE KINDA VAGUE.
HMPH...
THEY'RE PROS.

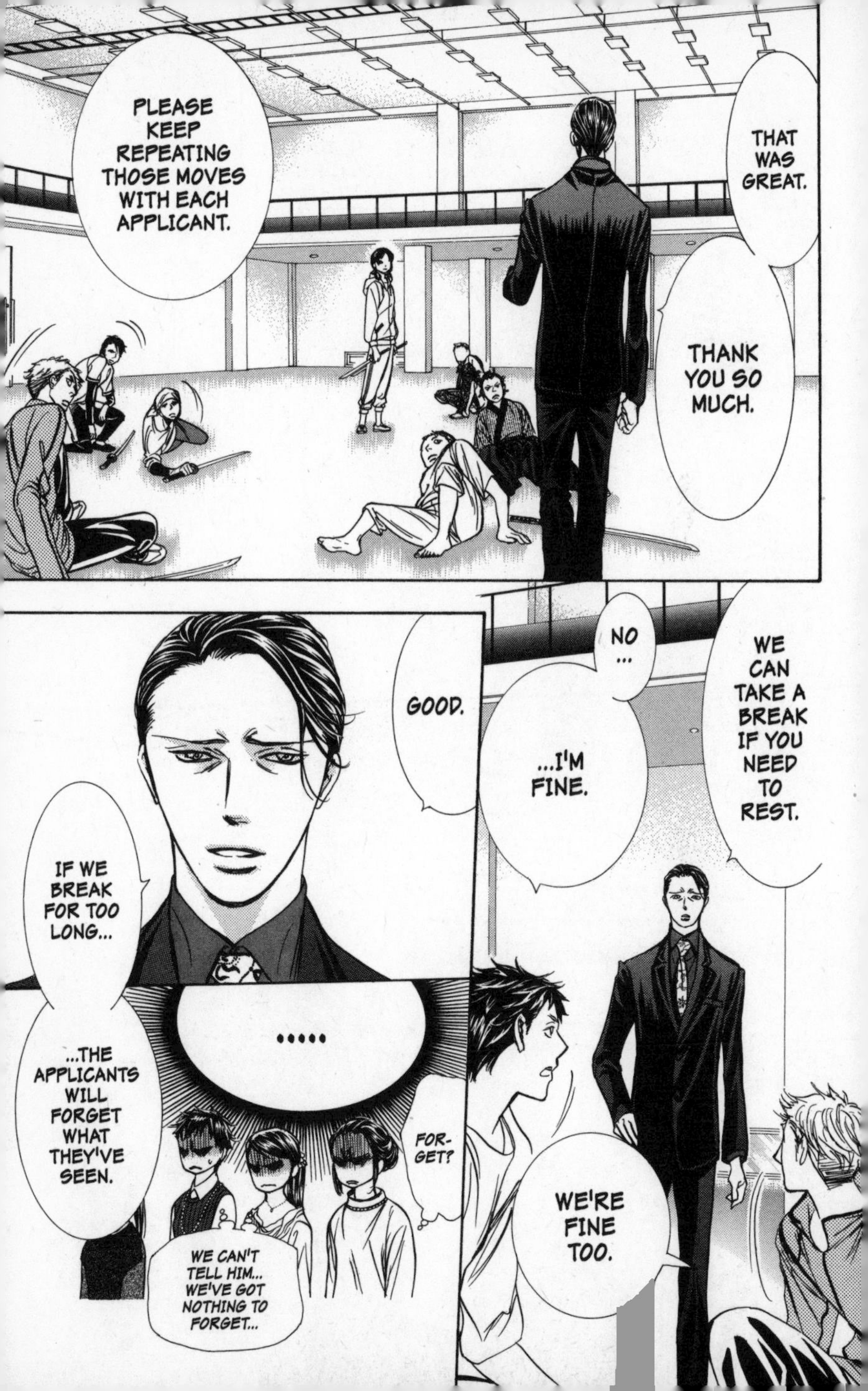
THAT WAS GREAT.
THANK YOU SO MUCH.
PLEASE KEEP REPEATING THOSE MOVES WITH EACH APPLICANT.
WE CAN TAKE A BREAK IF YOU NEED TO REST.
NO...
...I'M FINE.
WE'RE FINE TOO.
GOOD.
IF WE BREAK FOR TOO LONG...
...THE APPLICANTS WILL FORGET WHAT THEY'VE SEEN.
.....
FOR-GET?
WE CAN'T TELL HIM... WE'VE GOT NOTHING TO FORGET...

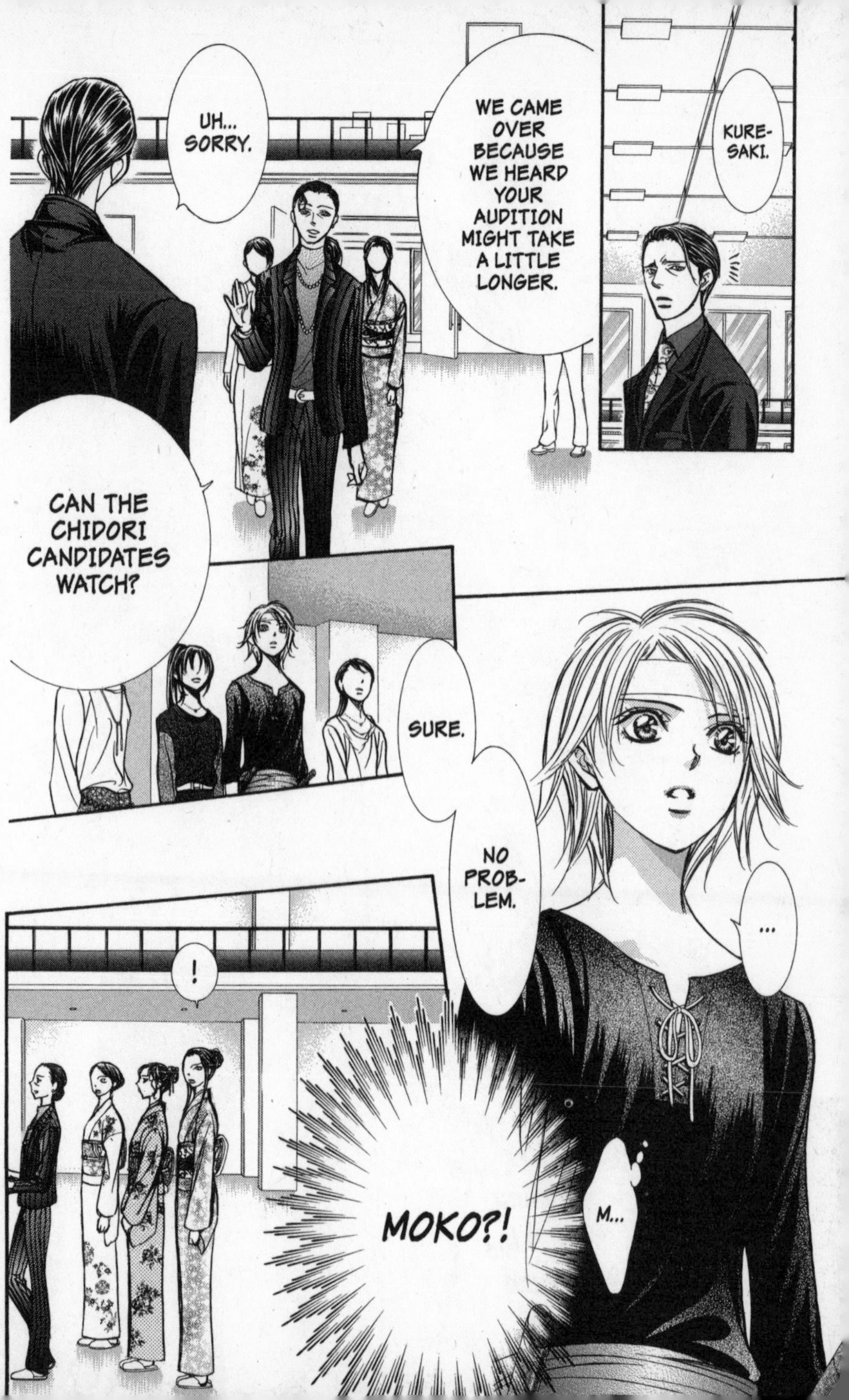
KURE-SAKI.
WE CAME OVER BECAUSE WE HEARD YOUR AUDITION MIGHT TAKE A LITTLE LONGER.
UH... SORRY.
CAN THE CHIDORI CANDIDATES WATCH?
SURE.
NO PROBLEM.
...
!
M...
MOKO?!

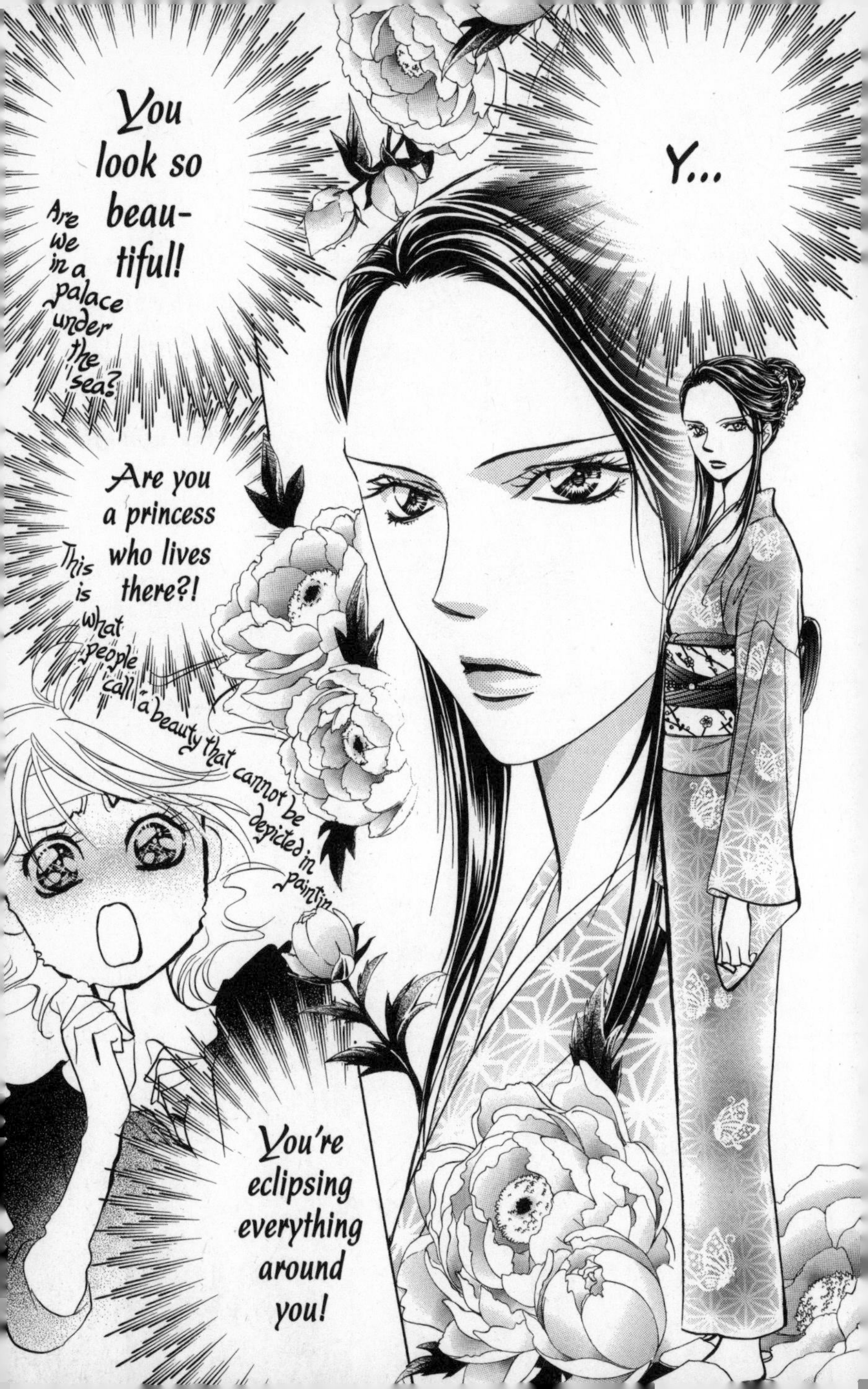
Y...
You look so beau-tiful!
Are we in a palace under the sea?
Are you a princess who lives there?!
This is what people call a beauty that cannot be depicted in paintin
You're eclipsing everything around you!

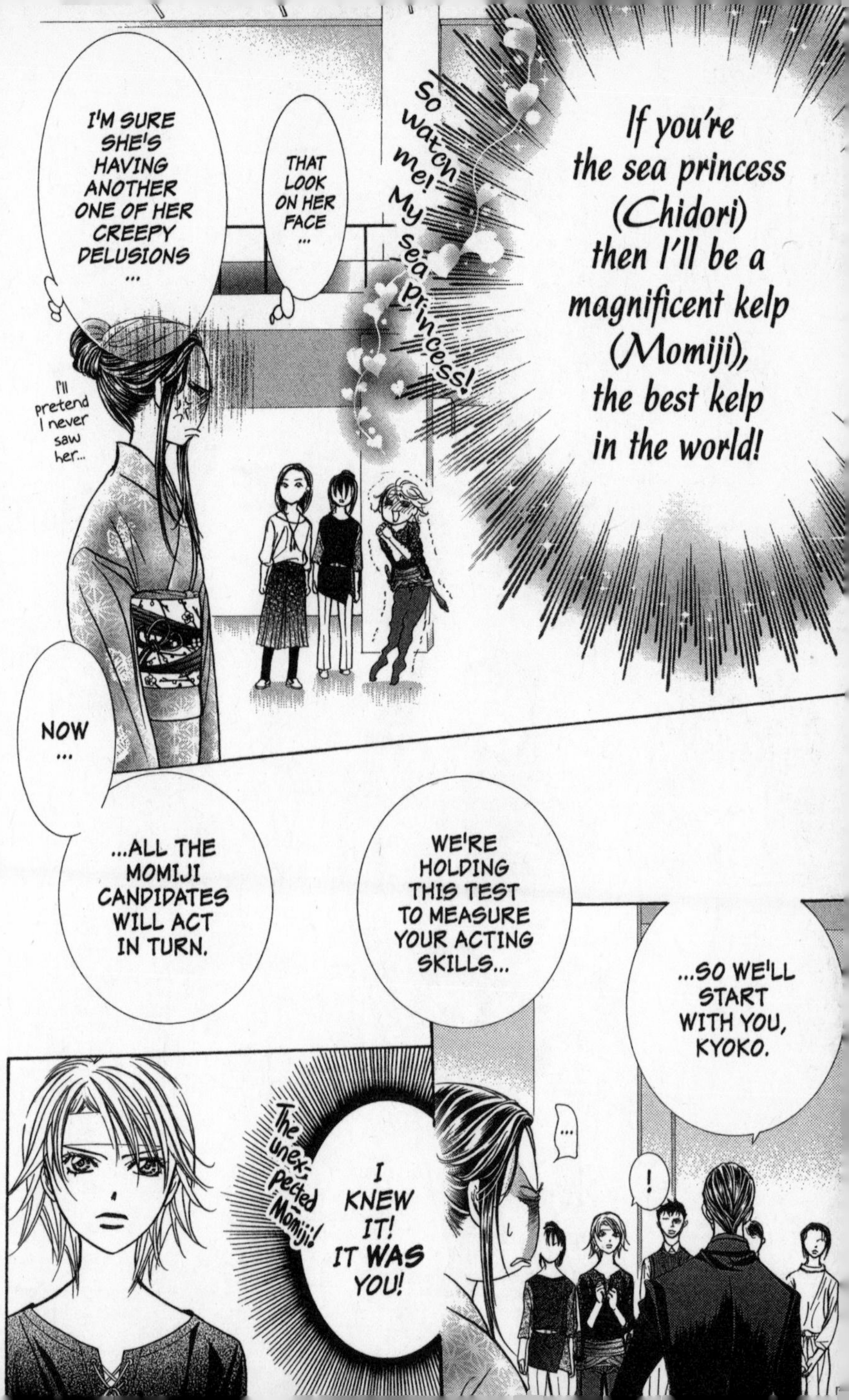
If you're the sea princess (Chidori) then I'll be a magnificent kelp (Momiji), the best kelp in the world!
So watch me! My sea princess!
THAT LOOK ON HER FACE ...
I'M SURE SHE'S HAVING ANOTHER ONE OF HER CREEPY DELUSIONS ...
I'll pretend I never saw her...
NOW ...
...SO WE'LL START WITH YOU, KYOKO.
WE'RE HOLDING THIS TEST TO MEASURE YOUR ACTING SKILLS...
...ALL THE MOMIJI CANDIDATES WILL ACT IN TURN.
!
...
I KNEW IT! IT WAS YOU!
The unexpected Momiji!

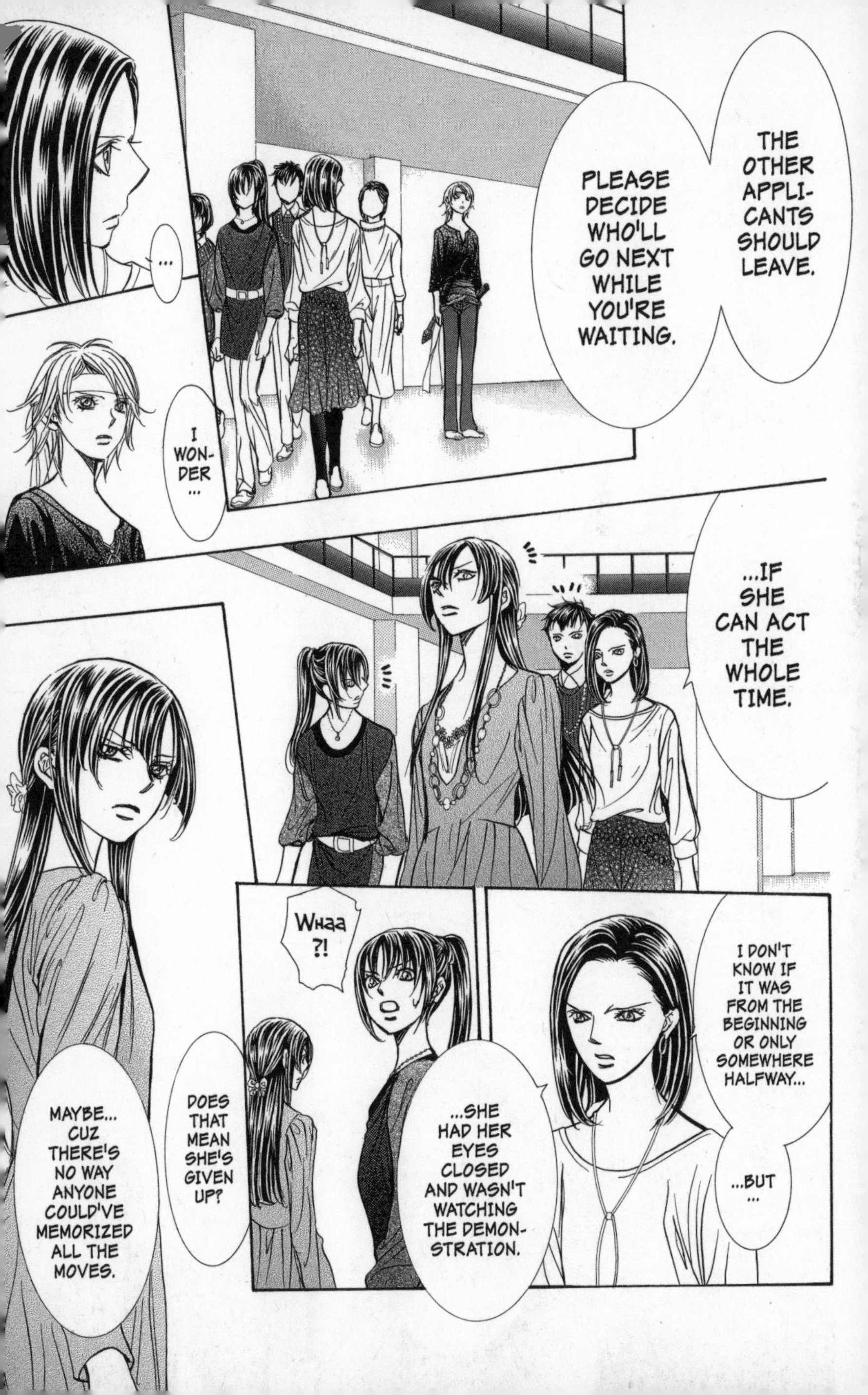
THE OTHER APPLICANTS SHOULD LEAVE.
PLEASE DECIDE WHO'LL GO NEXT WHILE YOU'RE WAITING.
...
I WONDER...
...IF SHE CAN ACT THE WHOLE TIME.
I DON'T KNOW IF IT WAS FROM THE BEGINNING OR ONLY SOMEWHERE HALFWAY...
...BUT...
Whaa?!
...SHE HAD HER EYES CLOSED AND WASN'T WATCHING THE DEMONSTRATION.
DOES THAT MEAN SHE'S GIVEN UP?
MAYBE... CUZ THERE'S NO WAY ANYONE COULD'VE MEMORIZED ALL THE MOVES.

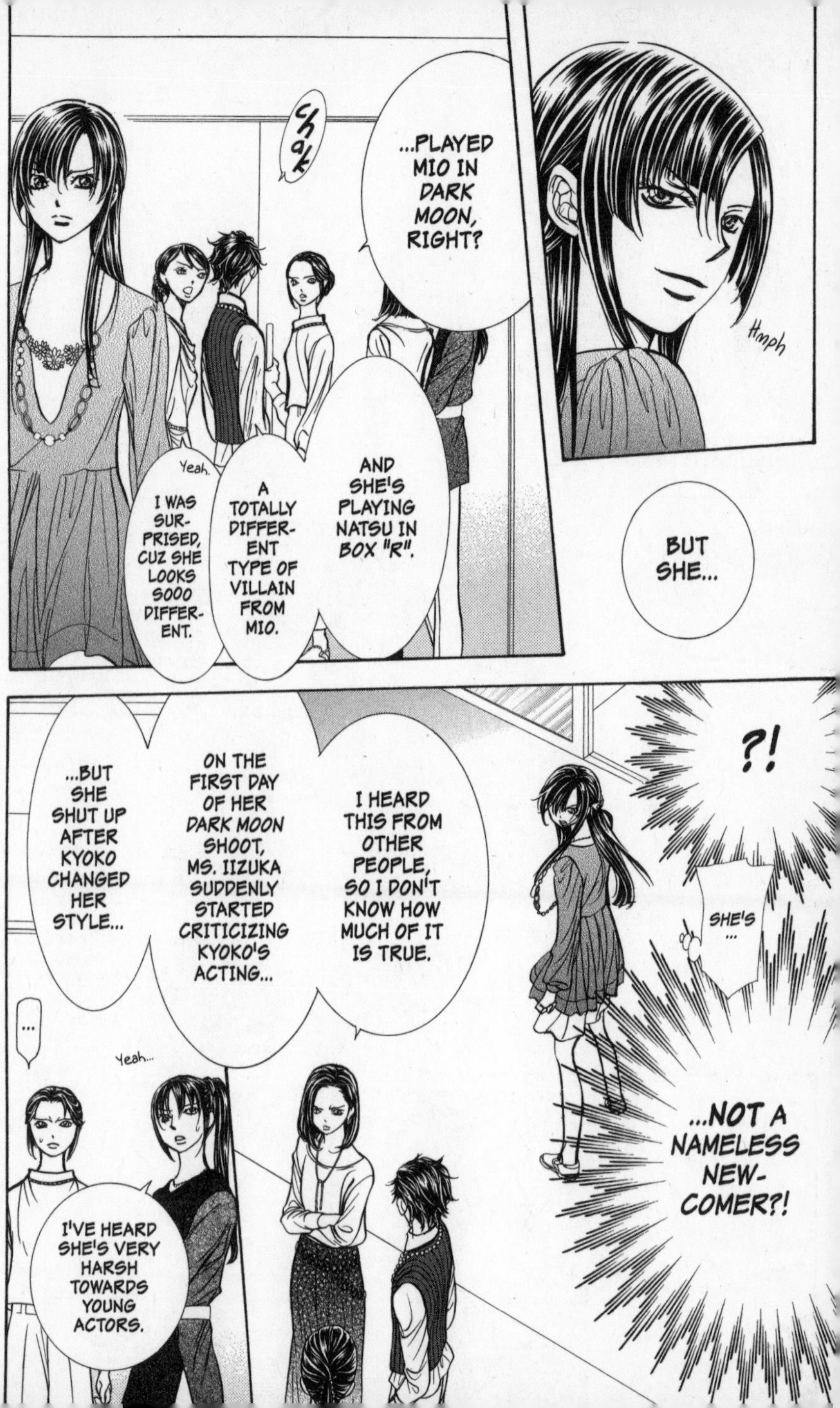
Hmph
BUT SHE...
...PLAYED MIO IN DARK MOON, RIGHT?
Chak
AND SHE'S PLAYING NATSU IN BOX "R".
A TOTALLY DIFFER-ENT TYPE OF VILLAIN FROM MIO.
Yeah.
I WAS SUR-PRISED, CUZ SHE LOOKS SOOO DIFFER-ENT.
?!
SHE'S ...
...NOT A NAMELESS NEW-COMER?!
I HEARD THIS FROM OTHER PEOPLE, SO I DON'T KNOW HOW MUCH OF IT IS TRUE.
ON THE FIRST DAY OF HER DARK MOON SHOOT, MS. IIZUKA SUDDENLY STARTED CRITICIZING KYOKO'S ACTING...
...BUT SHE SHUT UP AFTER KYOKO CHANGED HER STYLE...
...
Yeah...
I'VE HEARD SHE'S VERY HARSH TOWARDS YOUNG ACTORS.

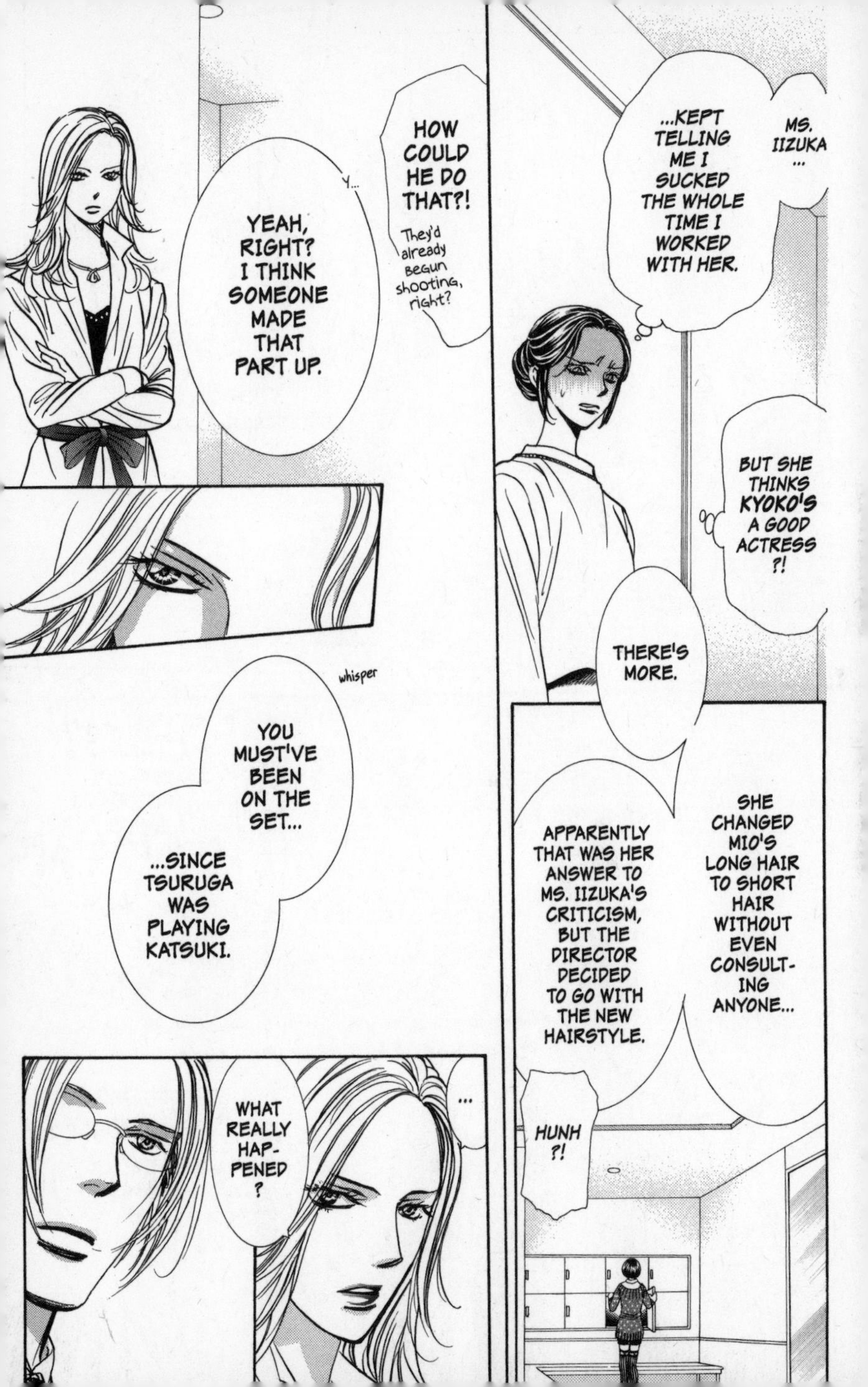
MS. IIZUKA...
...KEPT TELLING ME I SUCKED THE WHOLE TIME I WORKED WITH HER.
BUT SHE THINKS KYOKO'S A GOOD ACTRESS?!
THERE'S MORE.
SHE CHANGED MIO'S LONG HAIR TO SHORT HAIR WITHOUT EVEN CONSULT-ING ANYONE...
APPARENTLY THAT WAS HER ANSWER TO MS. IIZUKA'S CRITICISM, BUT THE DIRECTOR DECIDED TO GO WITH THE NEW HAIRSTYLE.
HUNH?!
HOW COULD HE DO THAT?!
They'd already begun shooting, right?
Y...
YEAH, RIGHT? I THINK SOMEONE MADE THAT PART UP.
whisper
YOU MUST'VE BEEN ON THE SET...
...SINCE TSURUGA WAS PLAYING KATSUKI.
...
WHAT REALLY HAP-PENED?

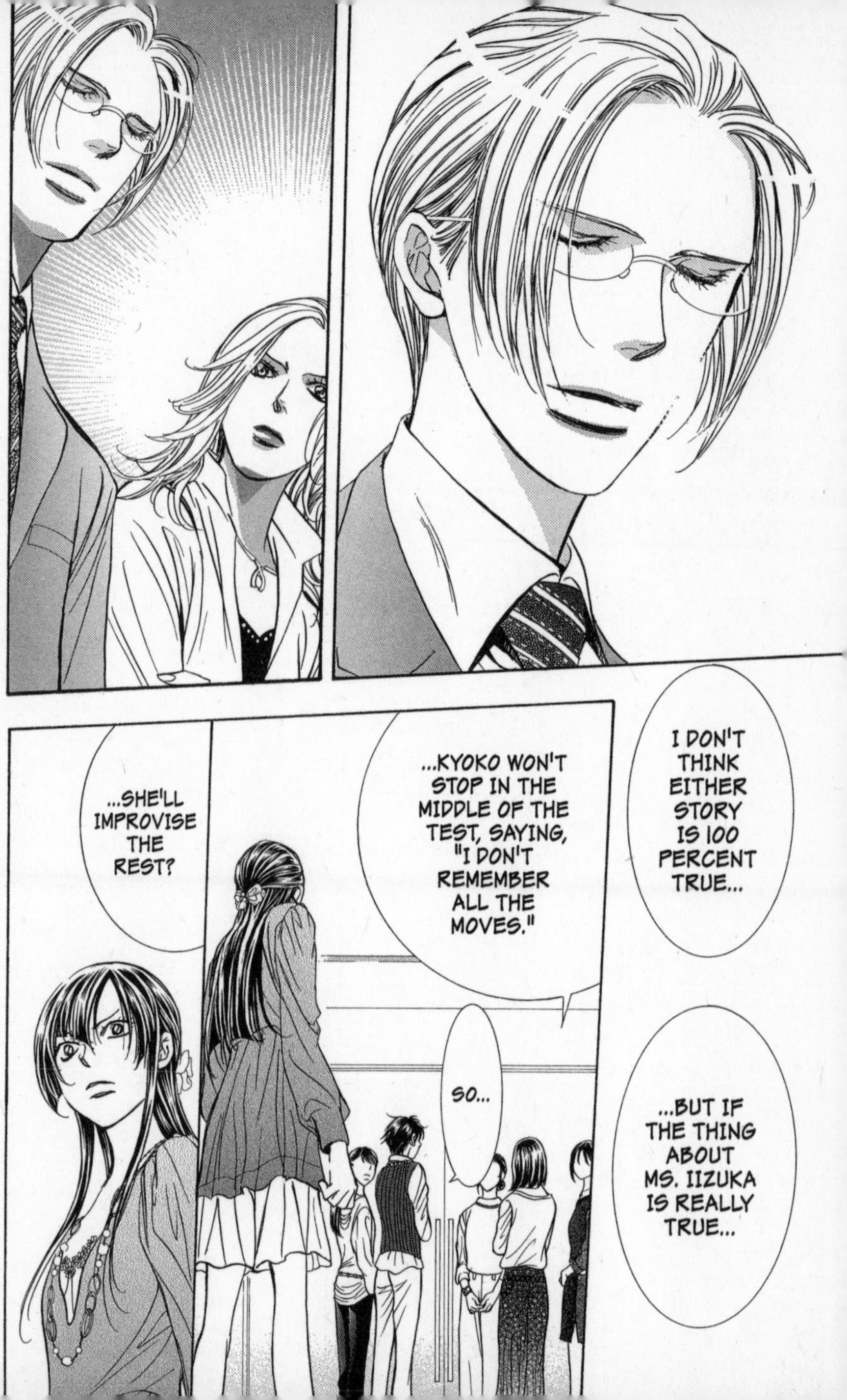
I DON'T THINK EITHER STORY IS 100 PERCENT TRUE...
...BUT IF THE THING ABOUT MS. IIZUKA IS REALLY TRUE...
...KYOKO WON'T STOP IN THE MIDDLE OF THE TEST, SAYING, "I DON'T REMEMBER ALL THE MOVES."
SO...
...SHE'LL IMPROVISE THE REST?

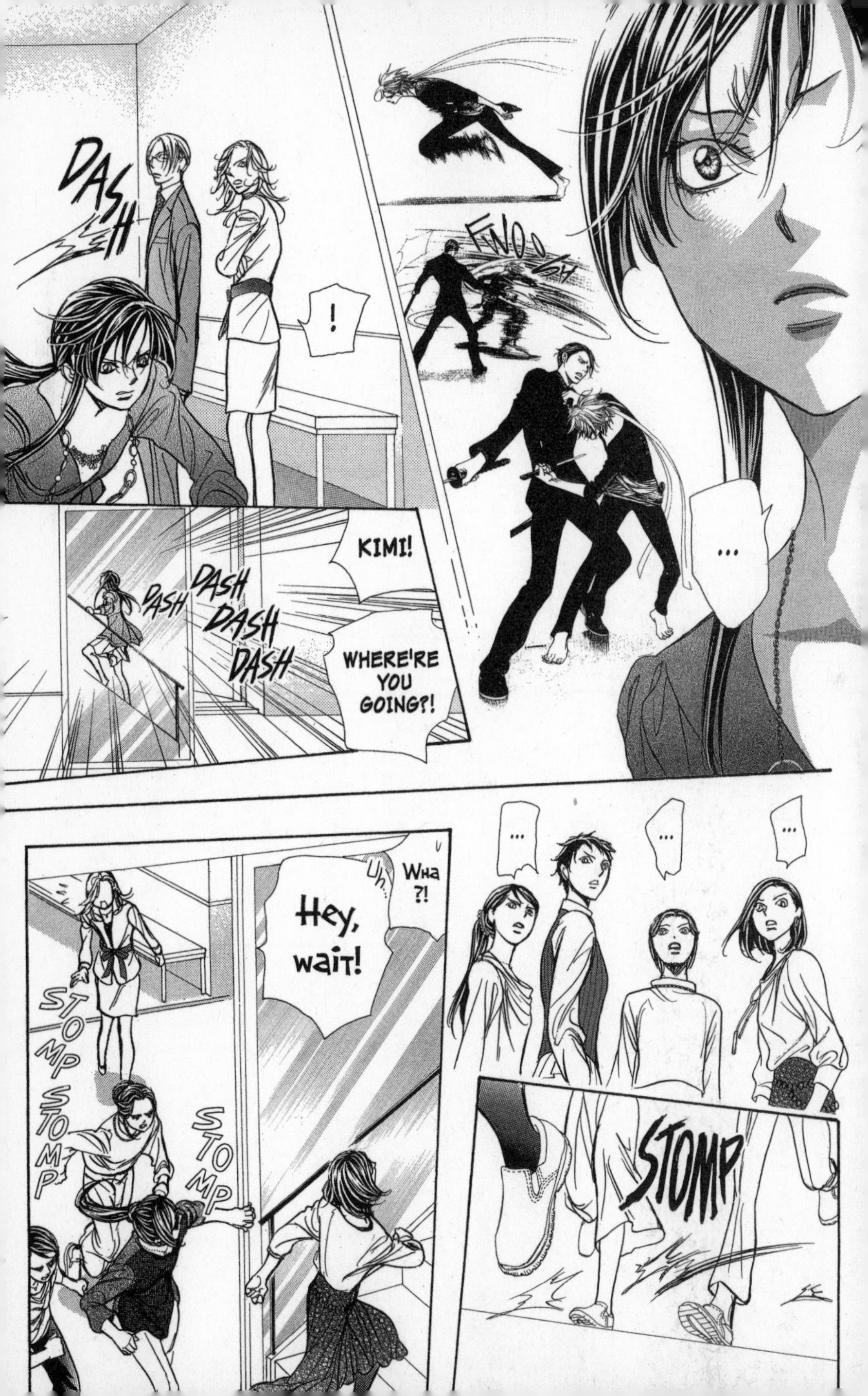
...
FWOOSH
DASH
!
KIMI!
WHERE'RE YOU GOING?!
DASH DASH DASH DASH
...
...
...
STOMP
Wha ?!
Uh...
Hey, wait!
STOMP
STOMP
STOMP

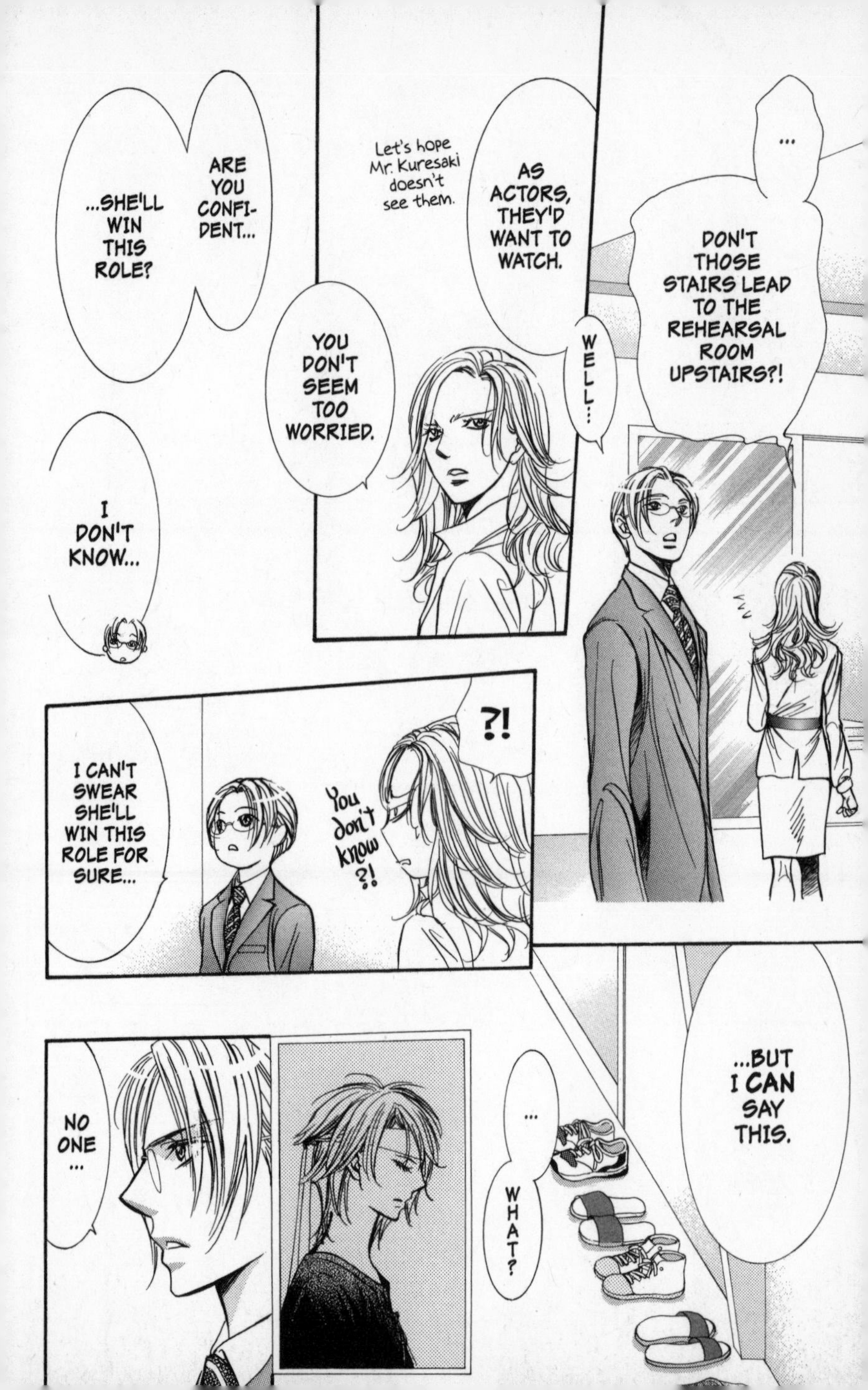
...
DON'T THOSE STAIRS LEAD TO THE REHEARSAL ROOM UPSTAIRS?!
WELL...
AS ACTORS, THEY'D WANT TO WATCH.
Let's hope Mr. Kuresaki doesn't see them.
YOU DON'T SEEM TOO WORRIED.
ARE YOU CONFIDENT...
...SHE'LL WIN THIS ROLE?
I DON'T KNOW...
?!
You don't know?!
I CAN'T SWEAR SHE'LL WIN THIS ROLE FOR SURE...
...BUT I CAN SAY THIS.
...
WHAT?
NO ONE ...

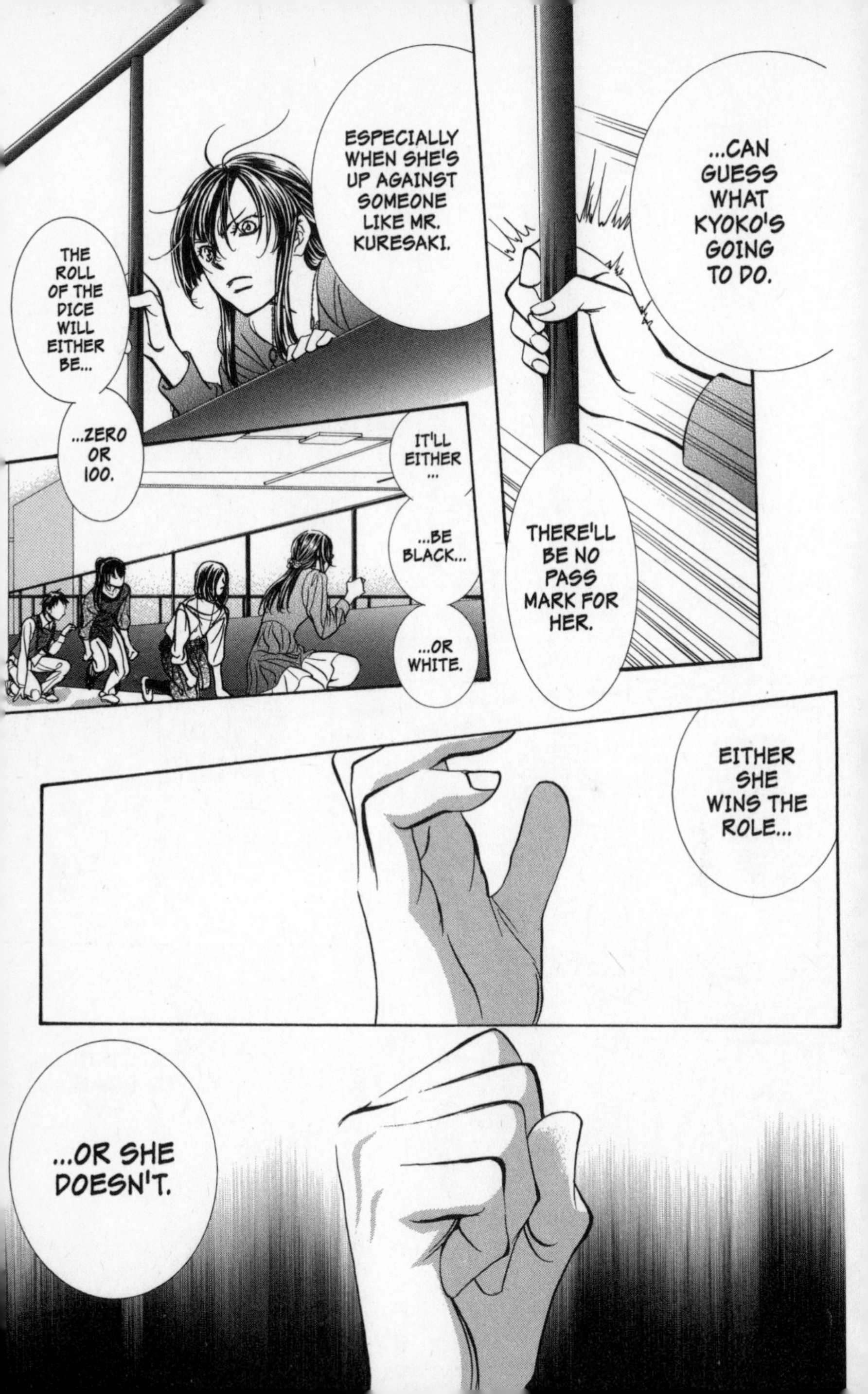
...CAN GUESS WHAT KYOKO'S GOING TO DO.
ESPECIALLY WHEN SHE'S UP AGAINST SOMEONE LIKE MR. KURESAKI.
THE ROLL OF THE DICE WILL EITHER BE...
...ZERO OR 100.
THERE'LL BE NO PASS MARK FOR HER.
IT'LL EITHER ...
...BE BLACK...
...OR WHITE.
EITHER SHE WINS THE ROLE...
...OR SHE DOESN'T.

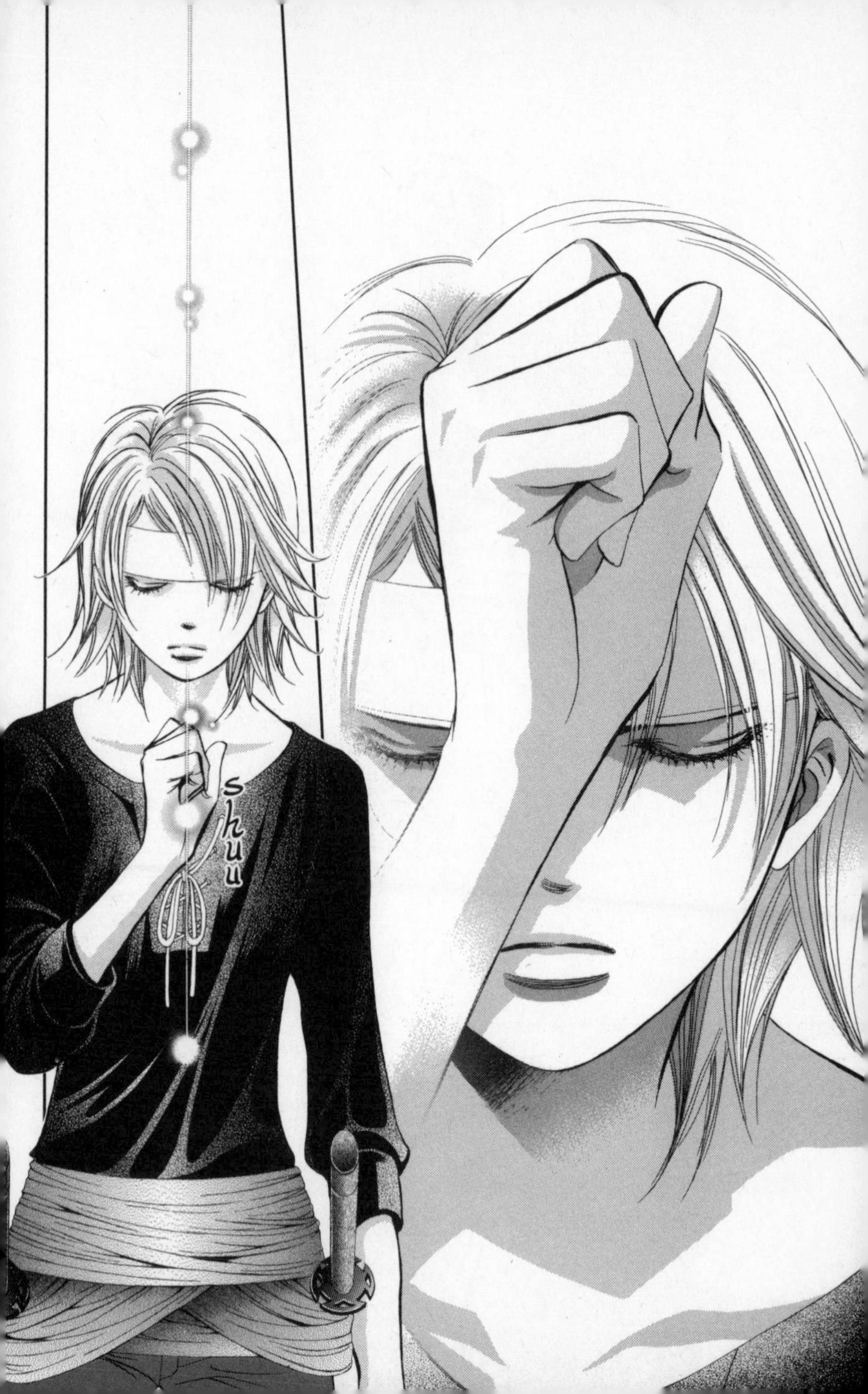
shuu

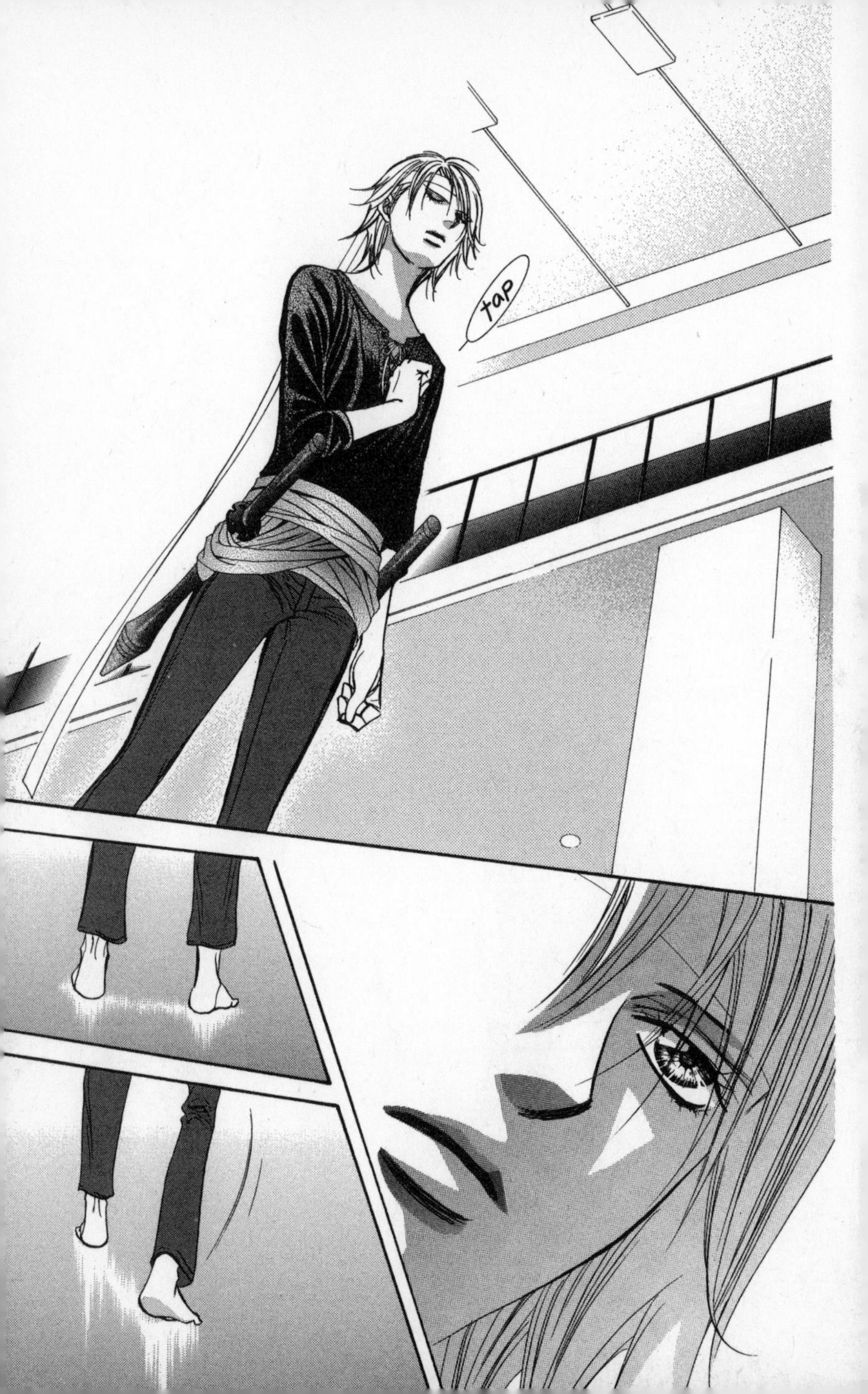
tap

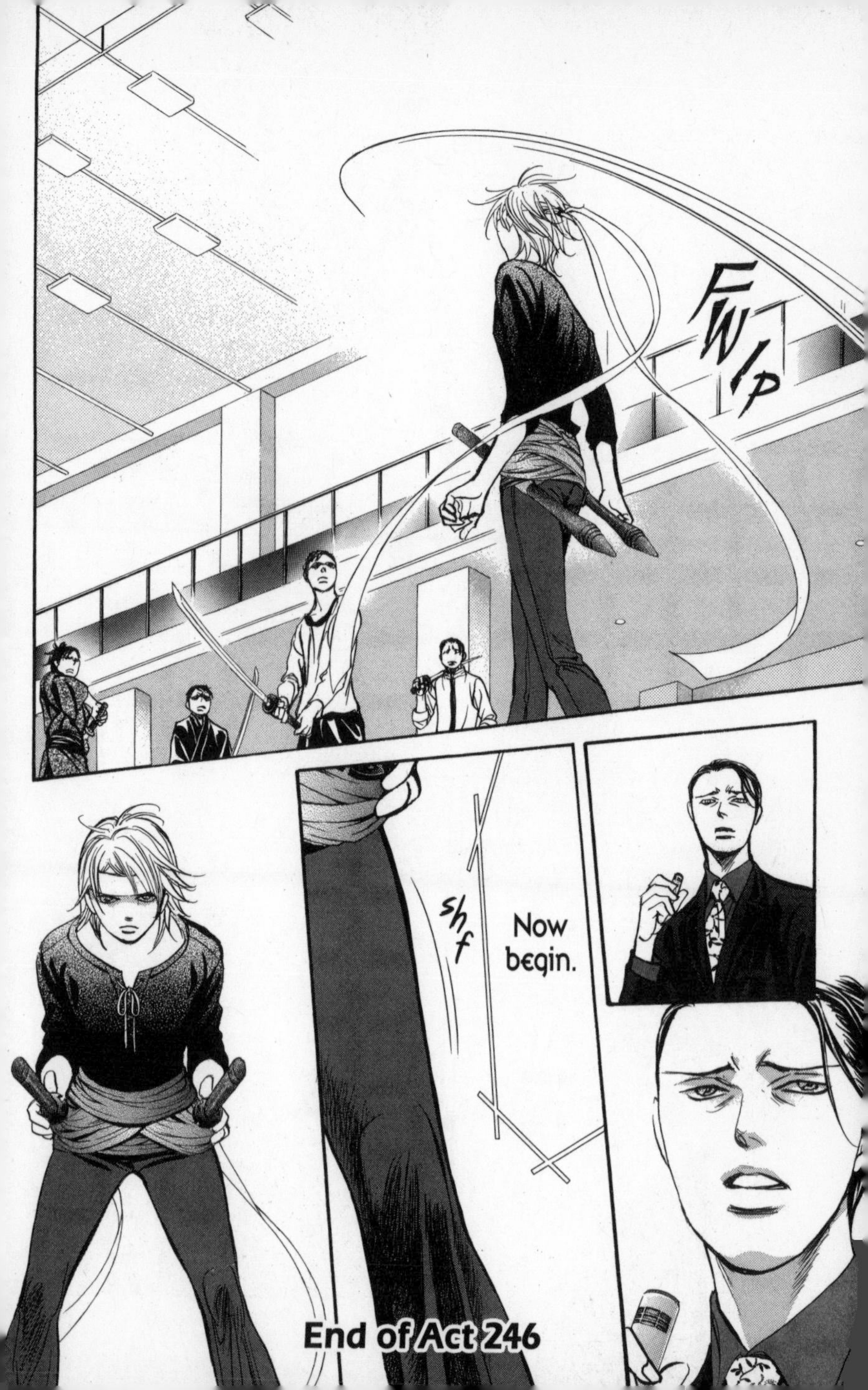
FWIP
Now begin.
shf
End of Act 246

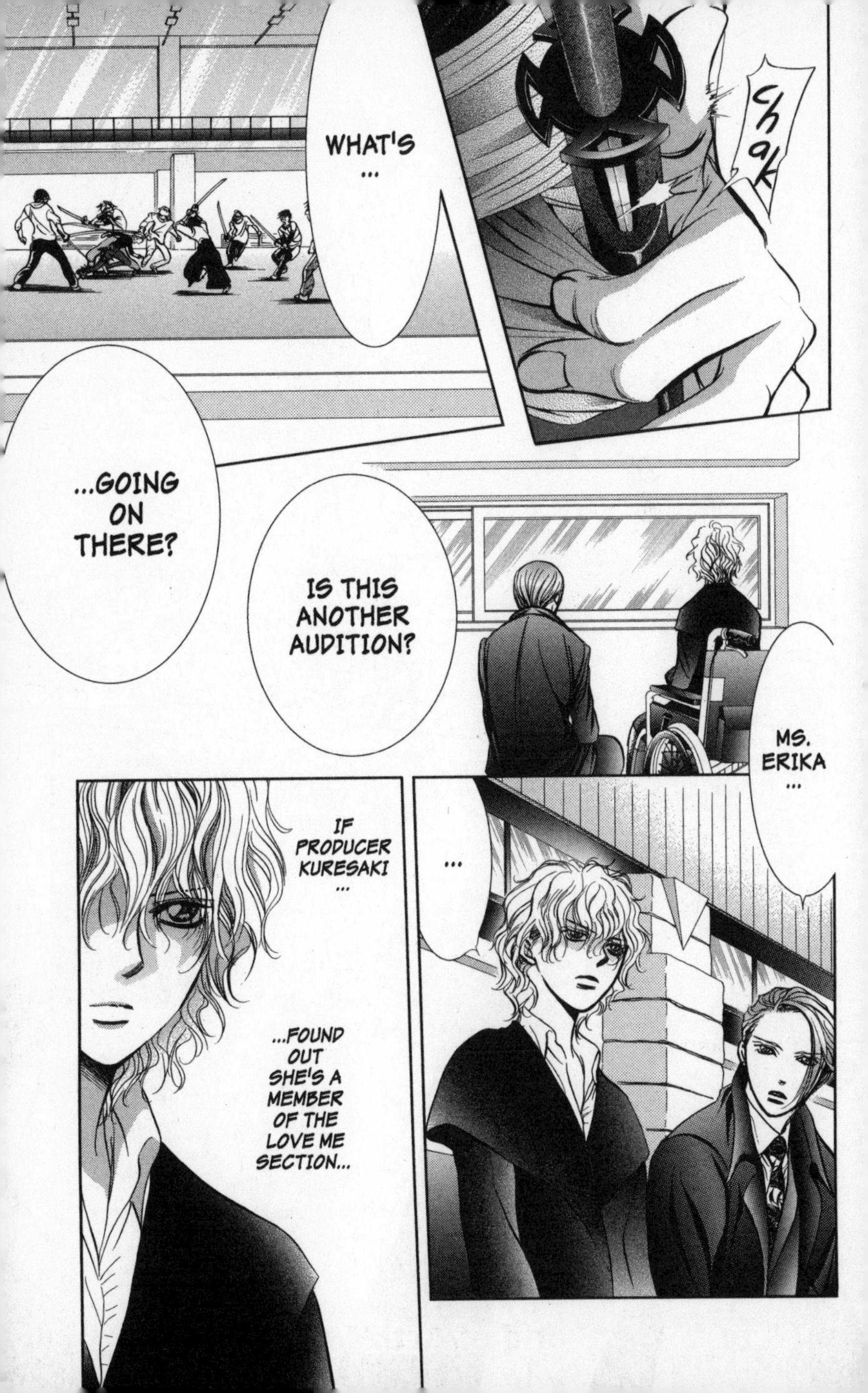
chak
WHAT'S ...
...GOING ON THERE?
IS THIS ANOTHER AUDITION?
MS. ERIKA ...
...
IF PRODUCER KURESAKI ...
...FOUND OUT SHE'S A MEMBER OF THE LOVE ME SECTION...

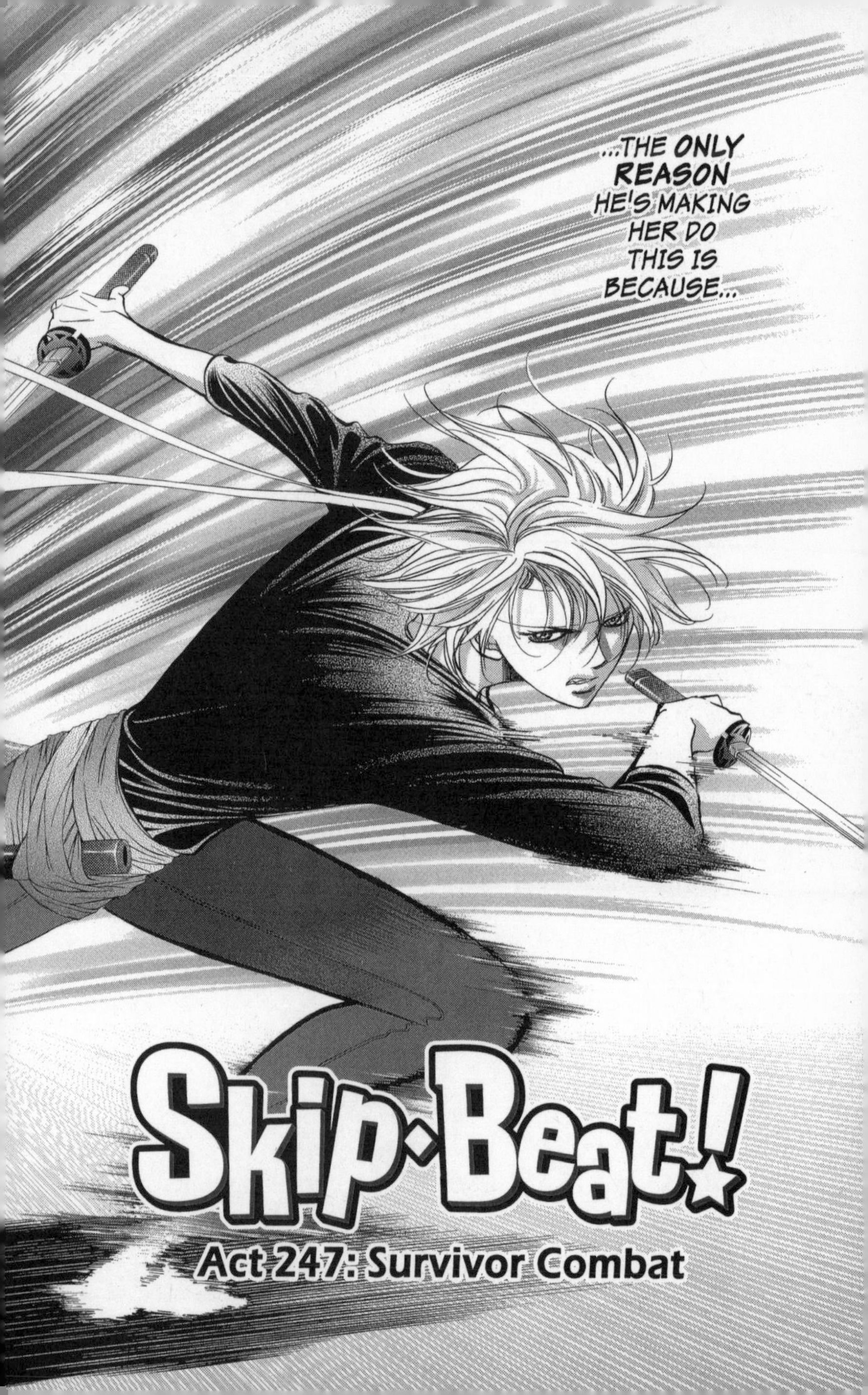
...THE ONLY REASON HE'S MAKING HER DO THIS IS BECAUSE...
Skip·Beat!
Act 247: Survivor Combat

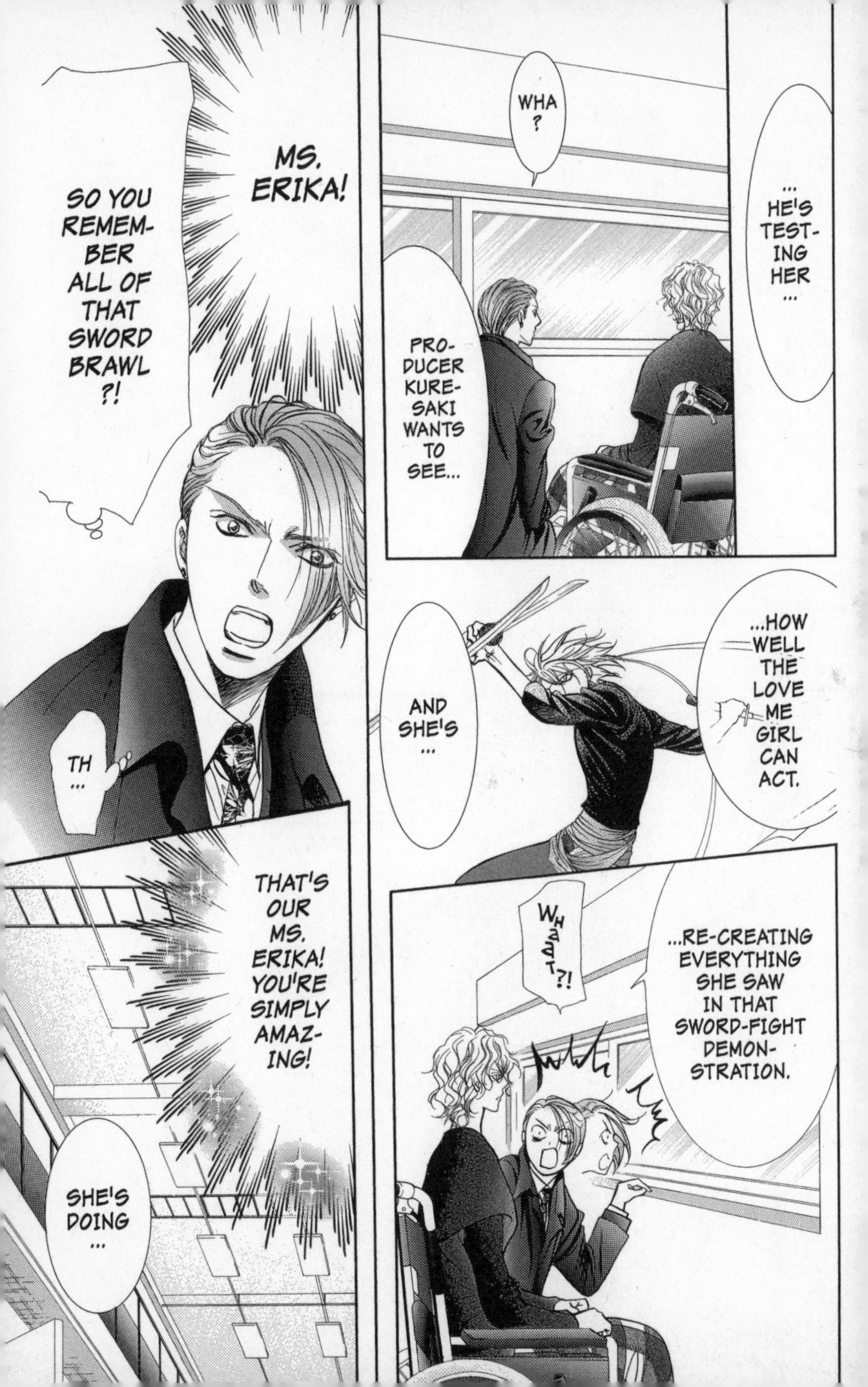
WHA?
...HE'S TESTING HER...
PRODUCER KURESAKI WANTS TO SEE...
...HOW WELL THE LOVE ME GIRL CAN ACT.
AND SHE'S...
...RE-CREATING EVERYTHING SHE SAW IN THAT SWORD-FIGHT DEMONSTRATION.
WHAAT?!
MS. ERIKA!
SO YOU REMEMBER ALL OF THAT SWORD BRAWL?!
TH...
THAT'S OUR MS. ERIKA! YOU'RE SIMPLY AMAZING!
SHE'S DOING...

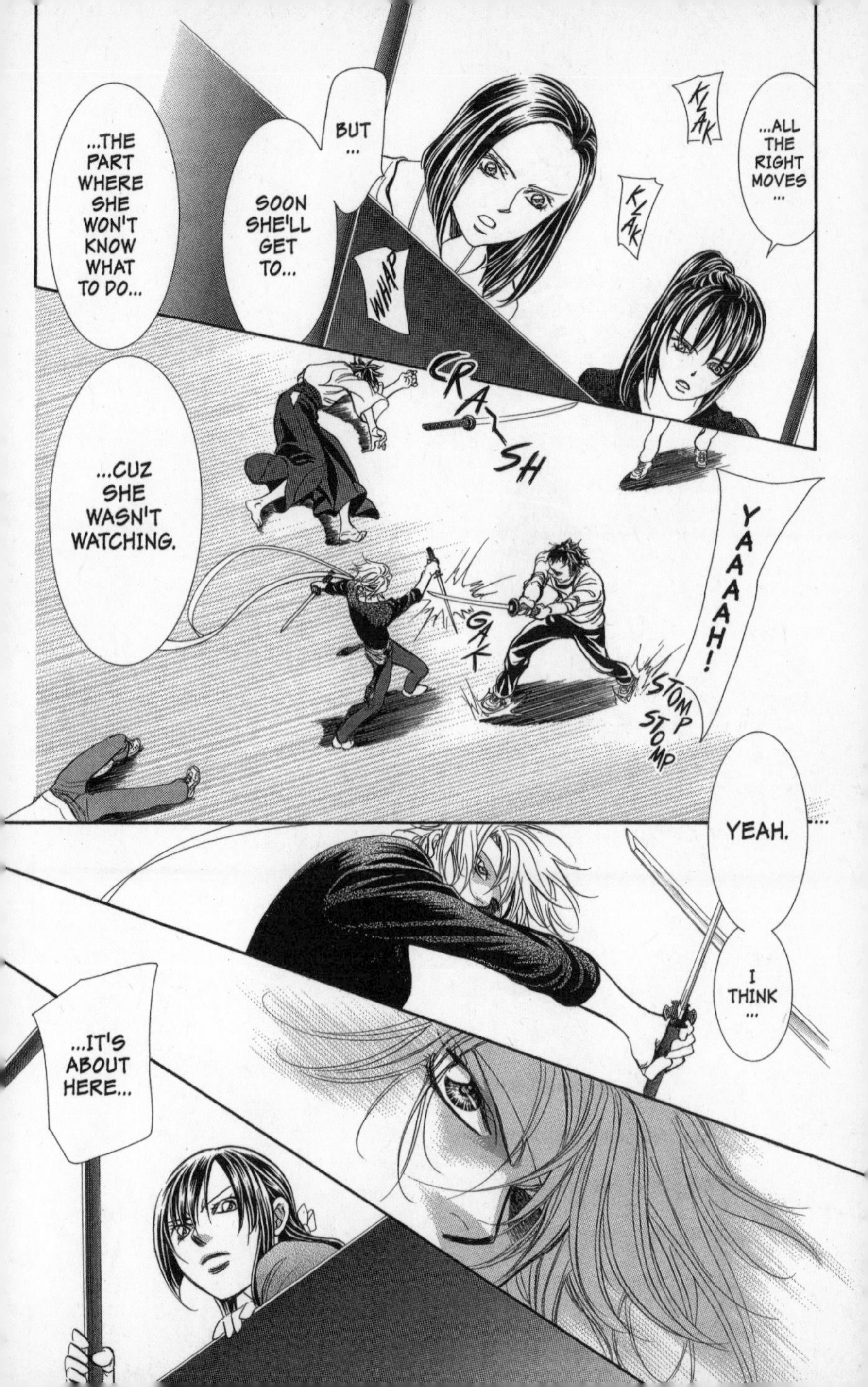

KLAK
...ALL THE RIGHT MOVES...
KLAK
BUT...
SOON SHE'LL GET TO...
WHAP
...THE PART WHERE SHE WON'T KNOW WHAT TO DO...
YAAAAAH!
STOMP STOMP
GAK
CRA-SH
...CUZ SHE WASN'T WATCHING.
YEAH.
I THINK...
...IT'S ABOUT HERE...

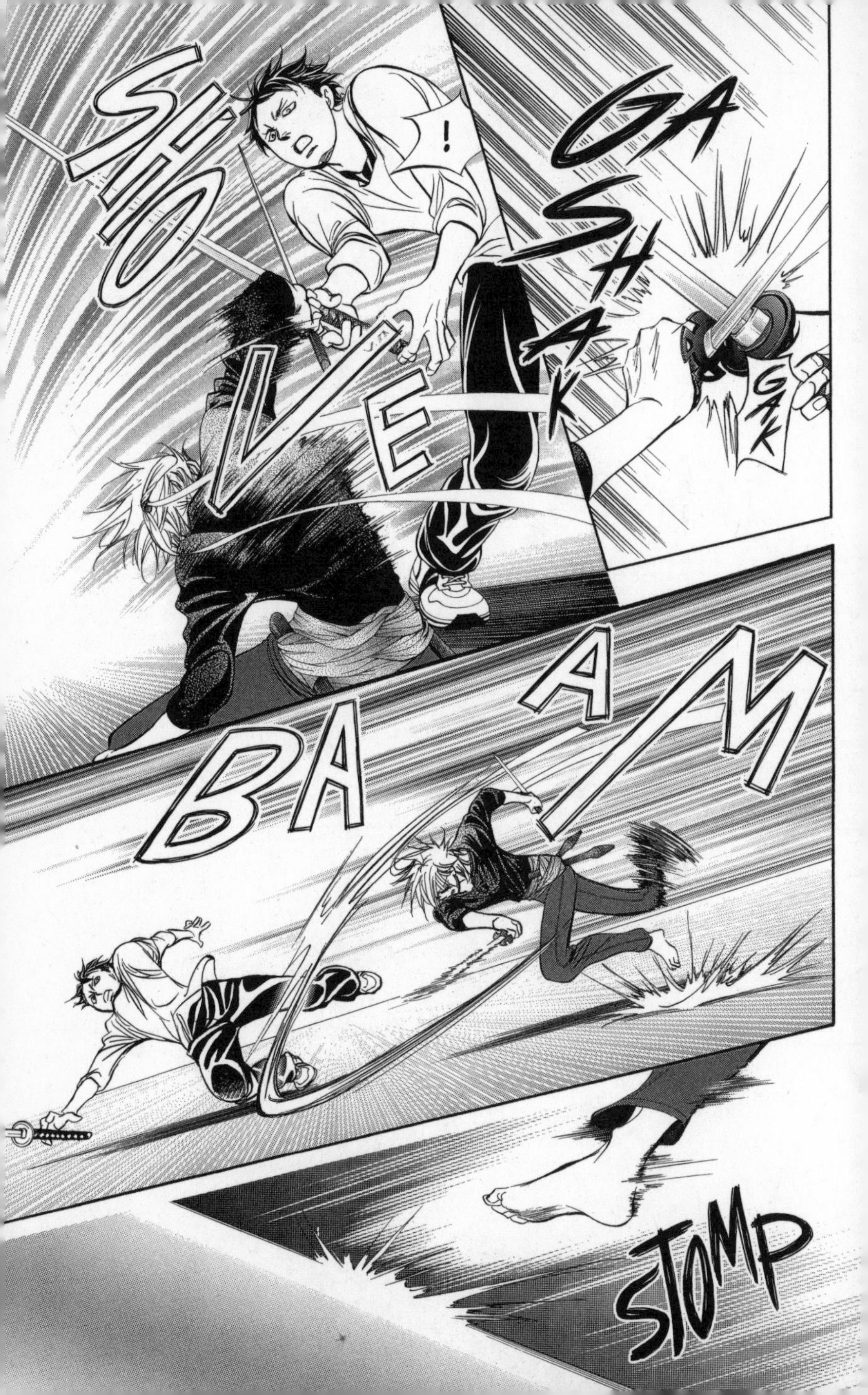
GASHAK
GAK
!
SHOVE
BAAM
STOMP

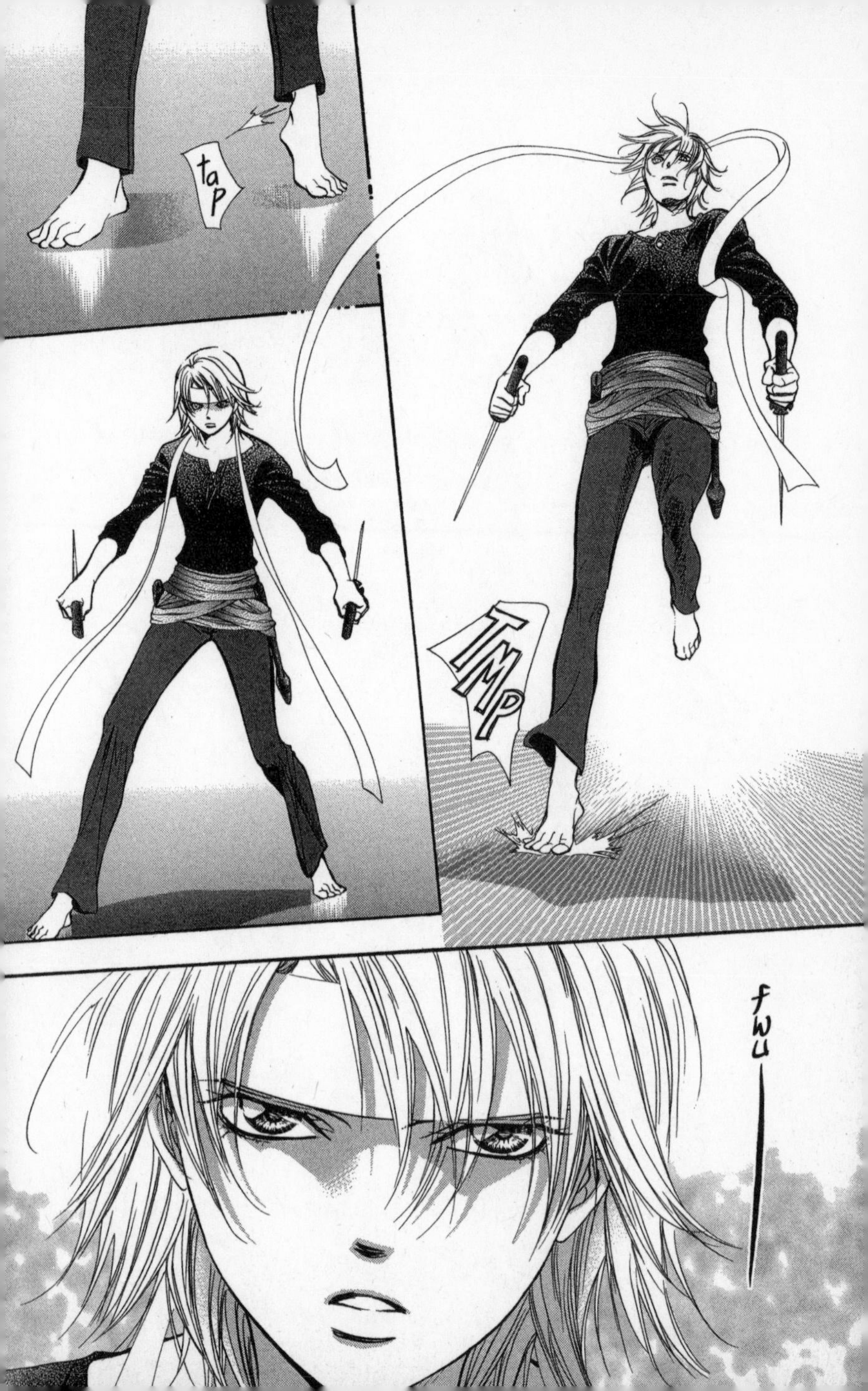
TMP
tap
fwu

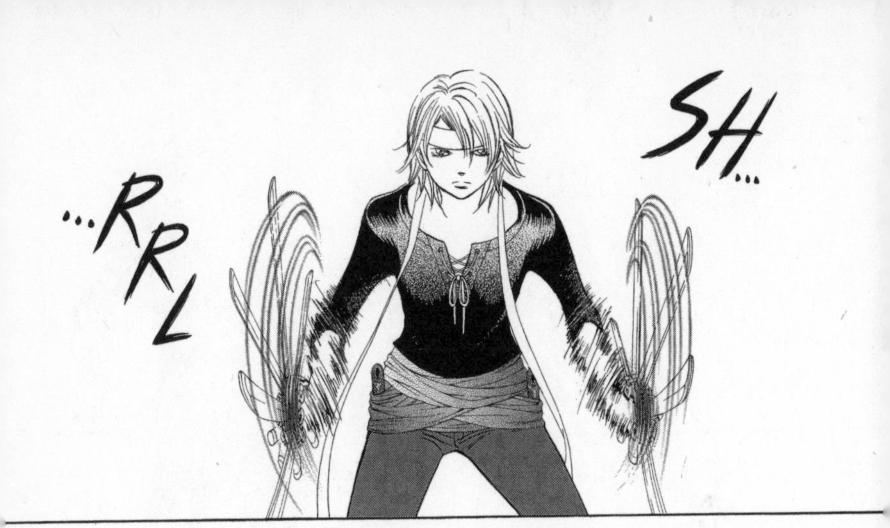
SH...
...RRL
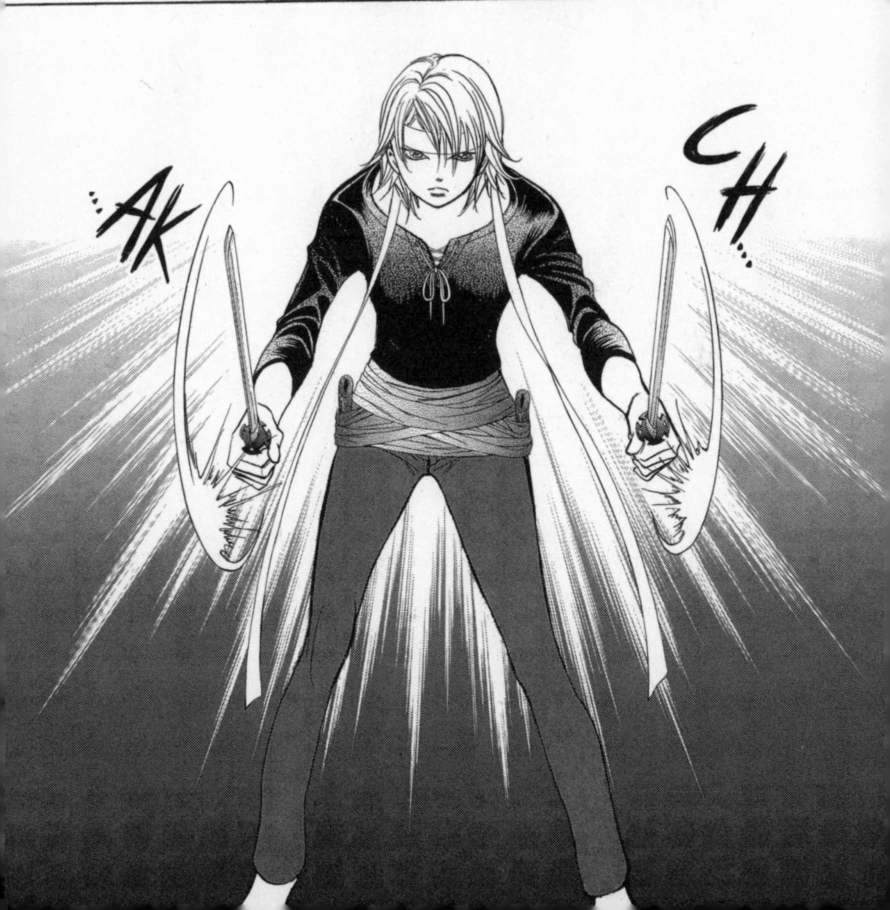
CH...
...AK

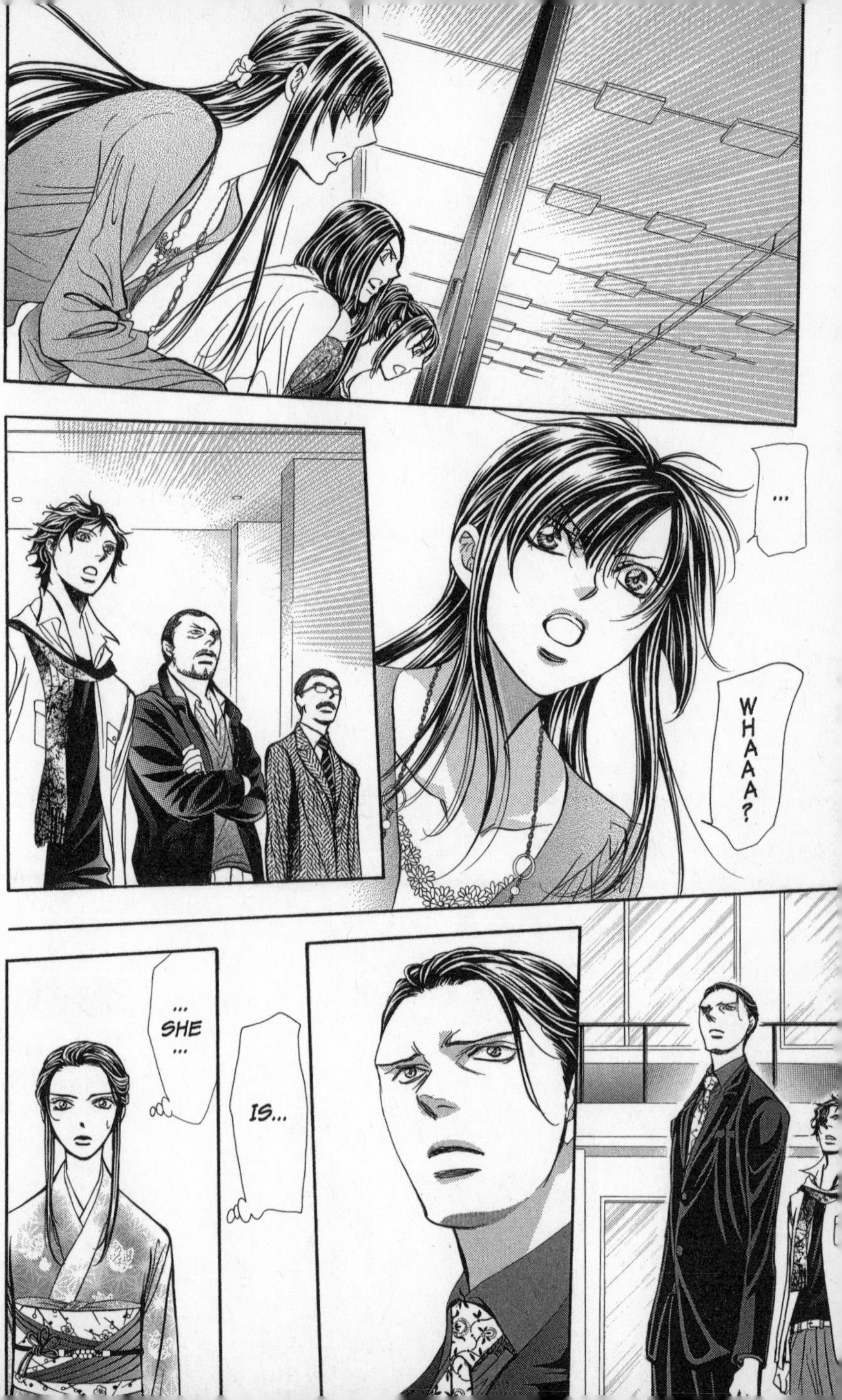
...
WHAAA?
... SHE ...
IS...

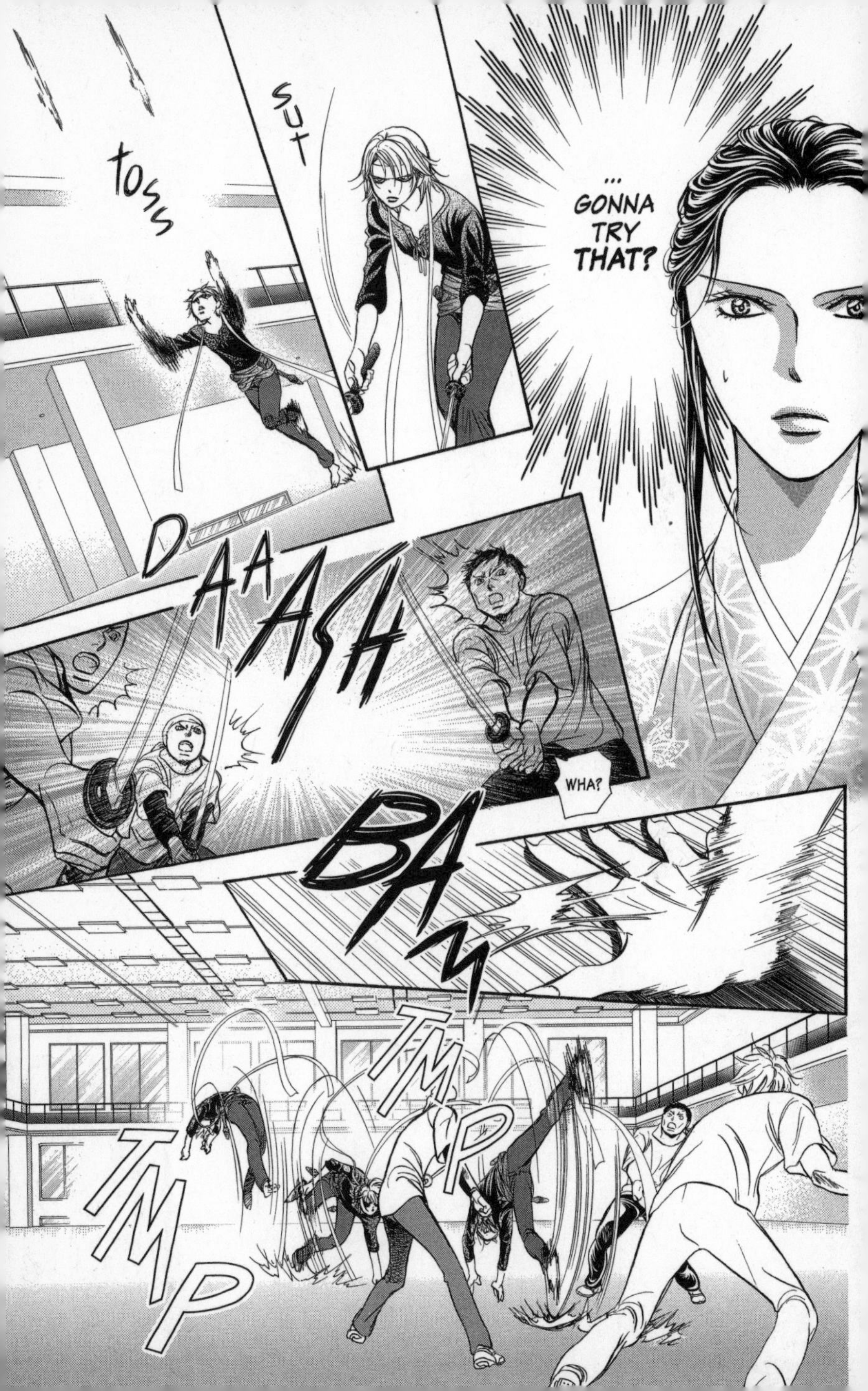
... GONNA TRY THAT?
SUT
TOSS
WHA?
DAAASH
BAM
TMP
TMP

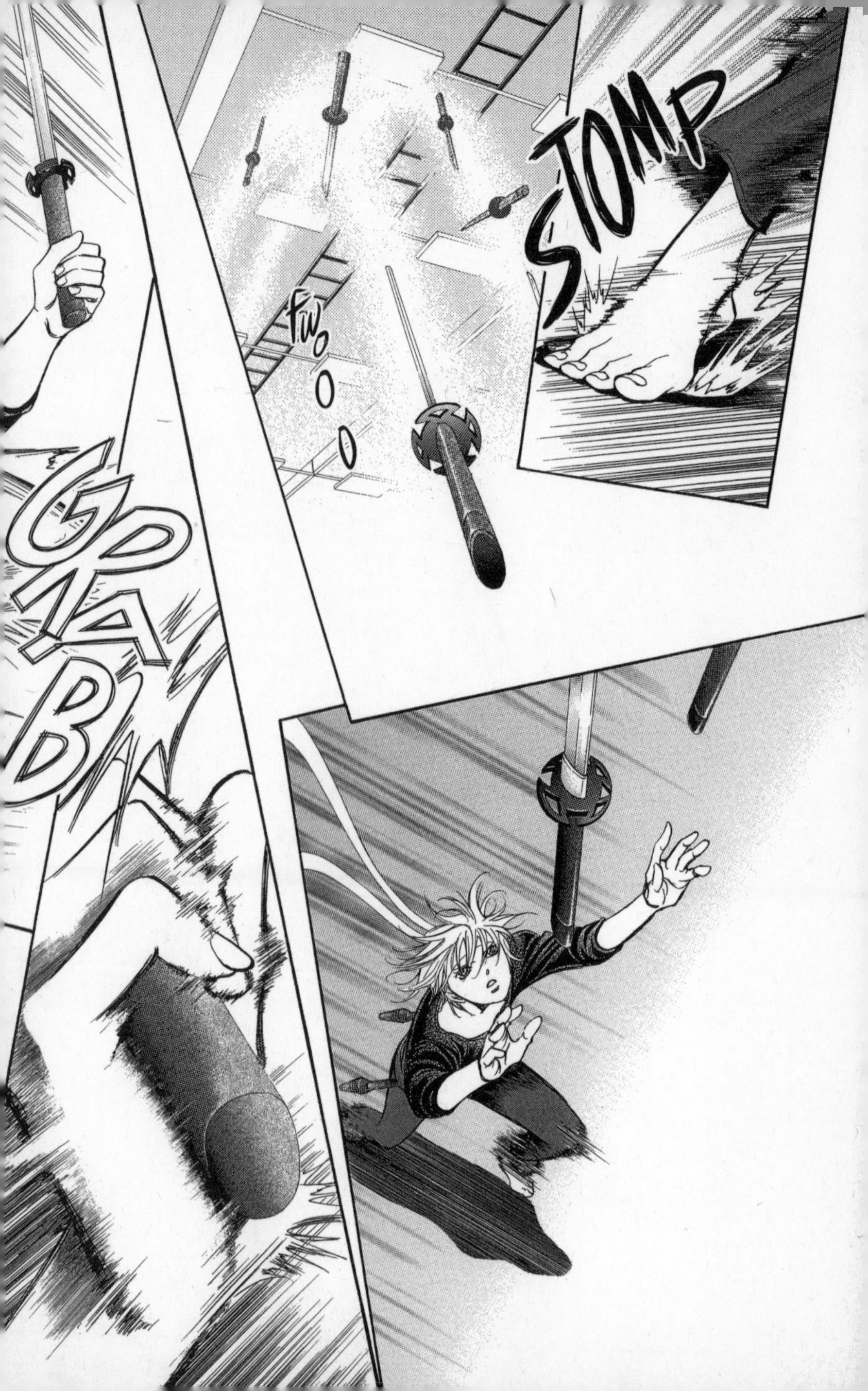
STOMP
FWOOO
GRAB

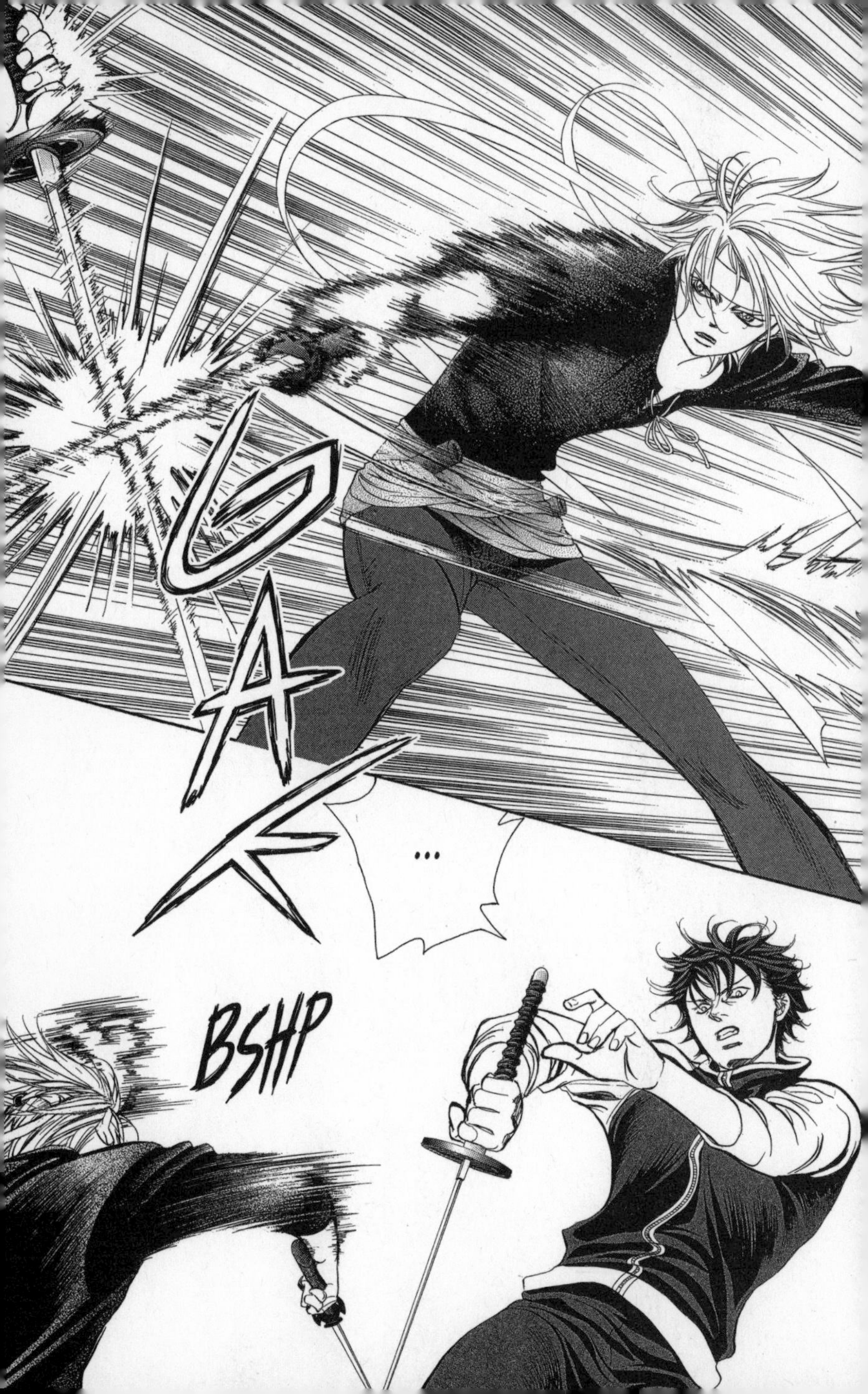
GAK
...
BSHP

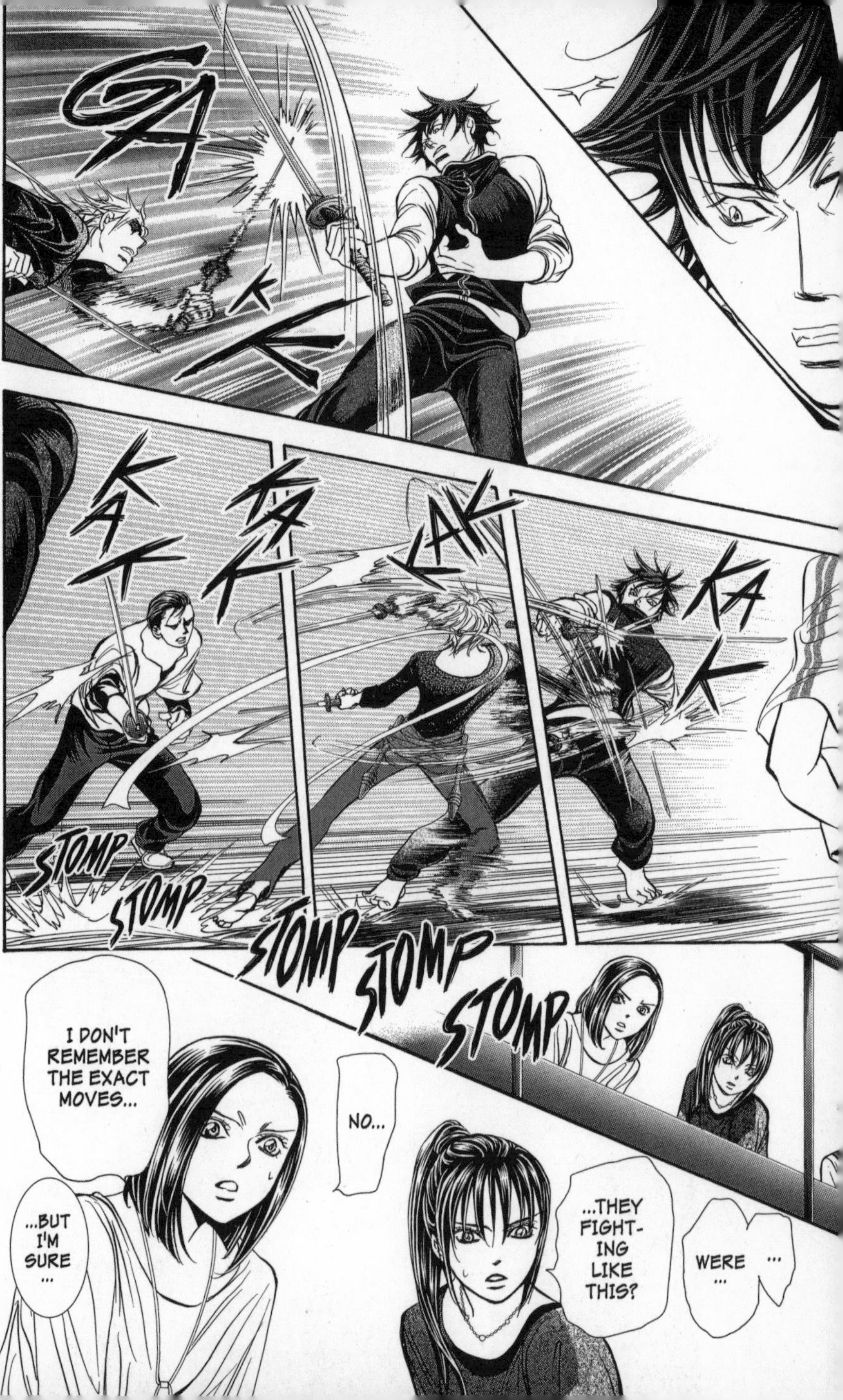
GAKK
KAKK
KAK
KAKK
KAKK
STOMP
STOMP
STOMP
STOMP
STOMP
WERE ... ...
...THEY FIGHTING LIKE THIS?
NO...
I DON'T REMEMBER THE EXACT MOVES...
...BUT I'M SURE ...

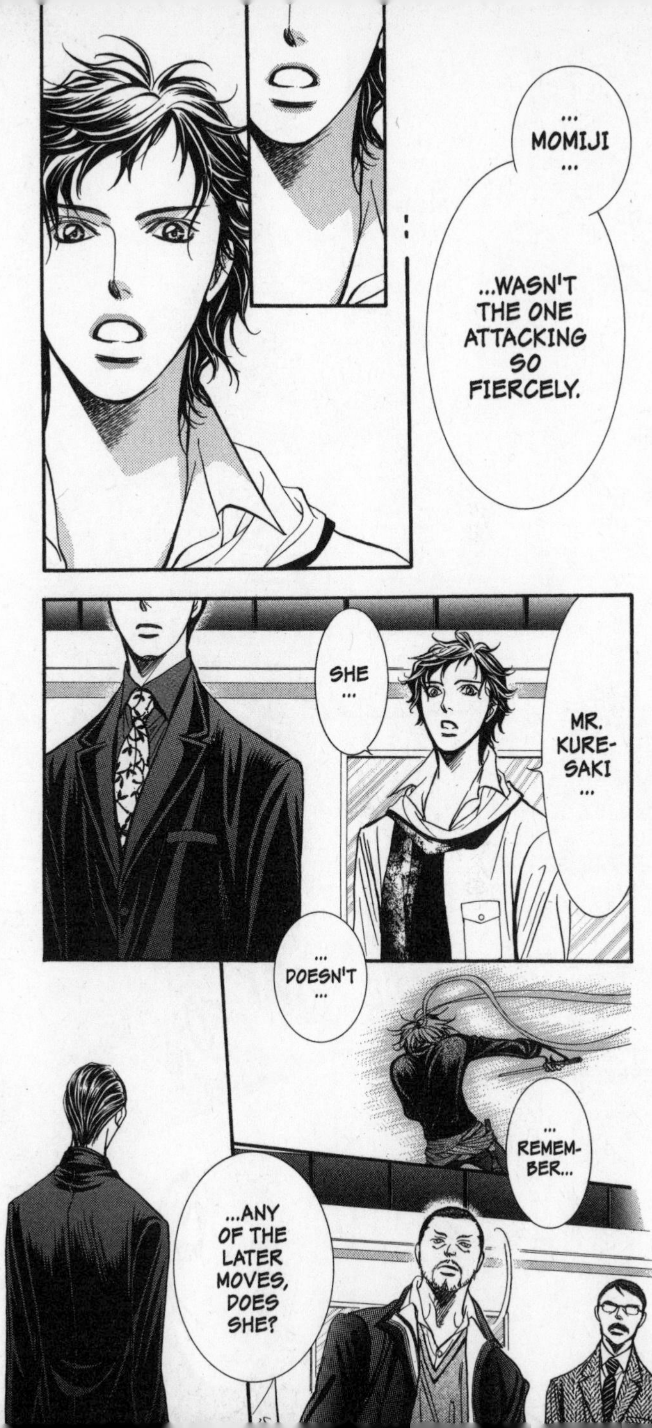

... MOMIJI ...
...WASN'T THE ONE ATTACKING SO FIERCELY.
MR. KURE-SAKI ...
SHE ...
... DOESN'T ...
... REMEM-BER...
...ANY OF THE LATER MOVES, DOES SHE?

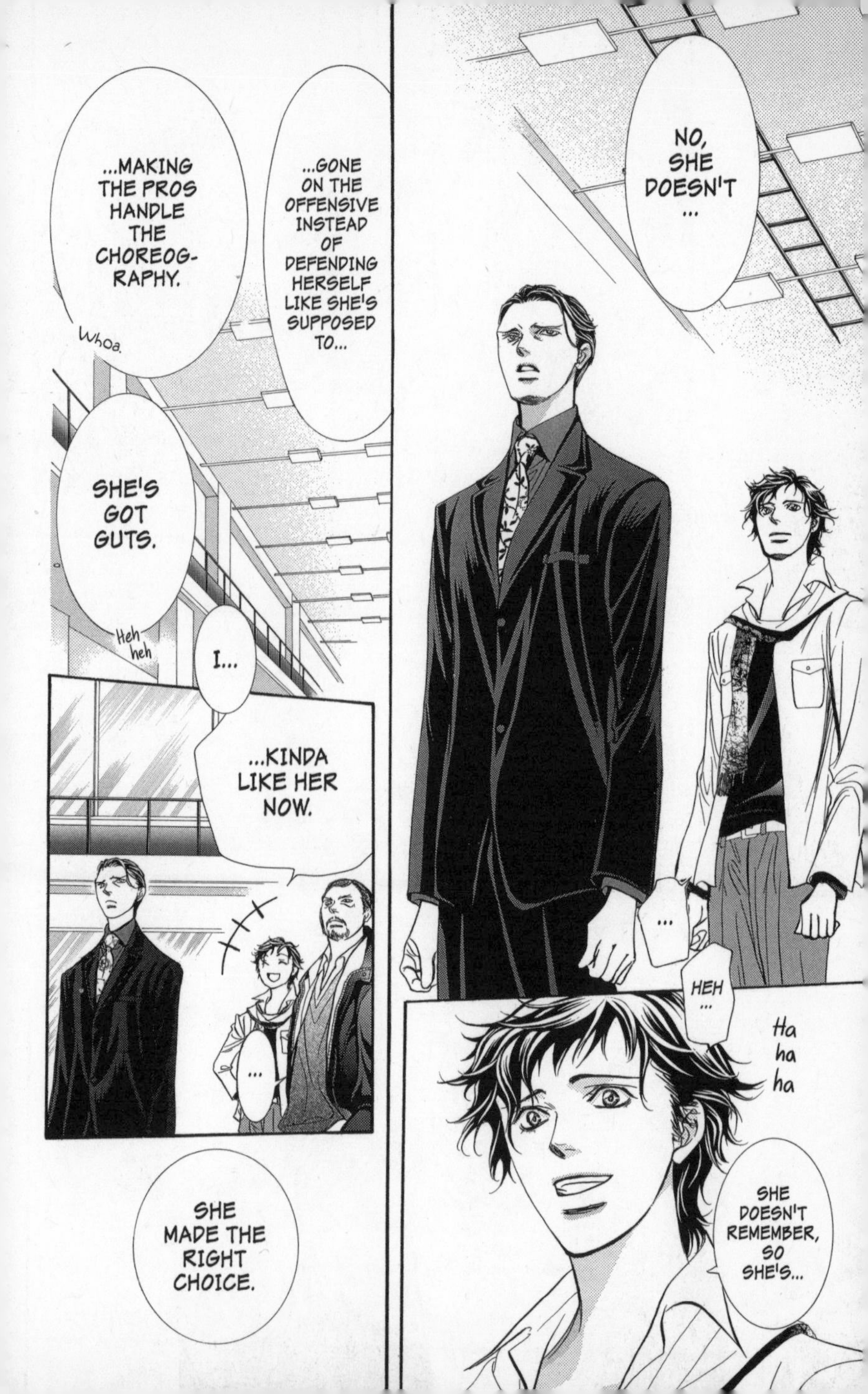
NO, SHE DOESN'T ...
...
HEH ...
Ha ha ha
SHE DOESN'T REMEMBER, SO SHE'S...
...GONE ON THE OFFENSIVE INSTEAD OF DEFENDING HERSELF LIKE SHE'S SUPPOSED TO...
...MAKING THE PROS HANDLE THE CHOREOG-RAPHY.
Whoa.
SHE'S GOT GUTS.
Heh heh
I...
...KINDA LIKE HER NOW.
...
SHE MADE THE RIGHT CHOICE.

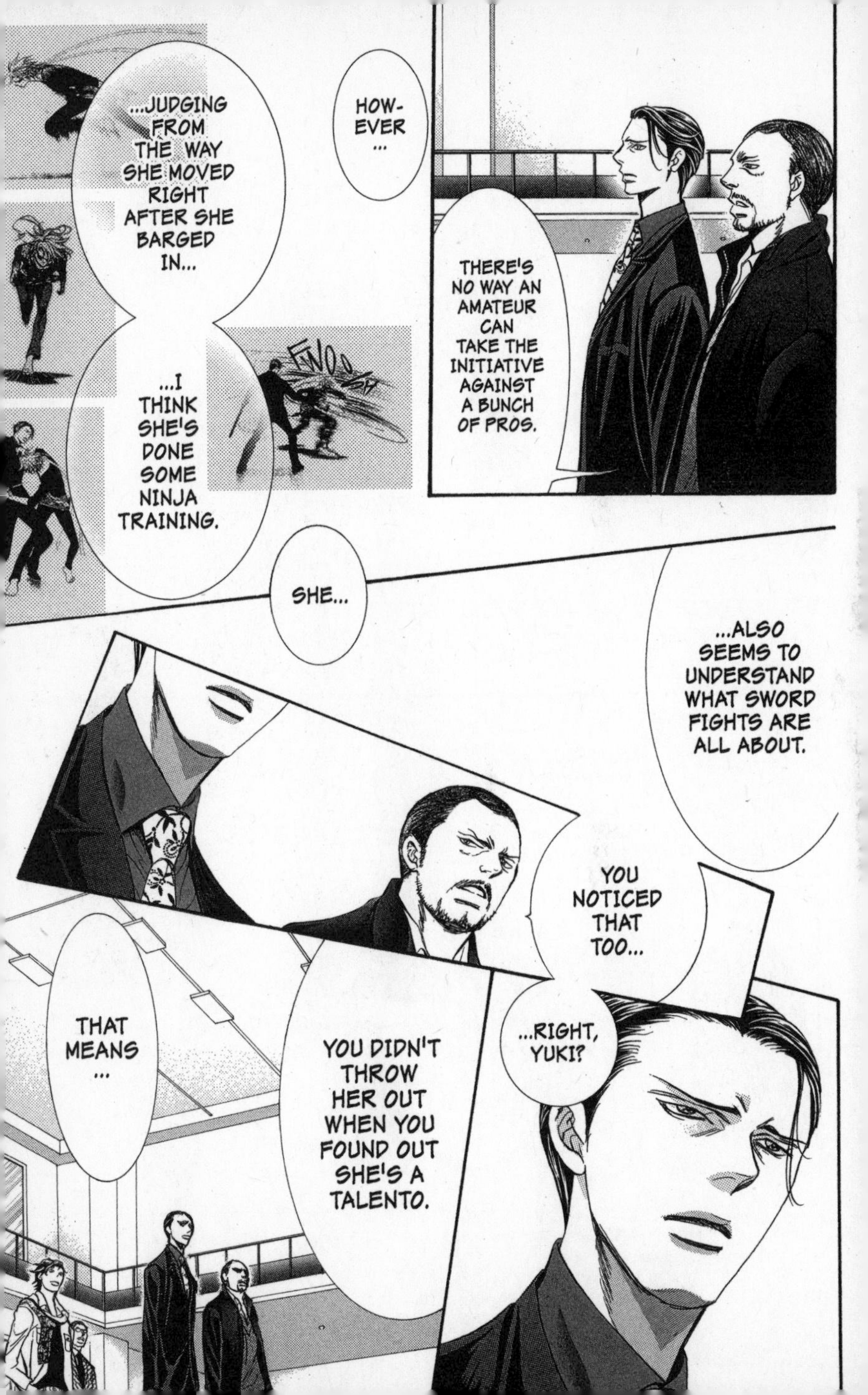
THERE'S NO WAY AN AMATEUR CAN TAKE THE INITIATIVE AGAINST A BUNCH OF PROS.
HOW-EVER...
...JUDGING FROM THE WAY SHE MOVED RIGHT AFTER SHE BARGED IN...
FWOOSH
...I THINK SHE'S DONE SOME NINJA TRAINING.
SHE...
...ALSO SEEMS TO UNDERSTAND WHAT SWORD FIGHTS ARE ALL ABOUT.
YOU NOTICED THAT TOO...
...RIGHT, YUKI?
THAT MEANS...
YOU DIDN'T THROW HER OUT WHEN YOU FOUND OUT SHE'S A TALENTO.

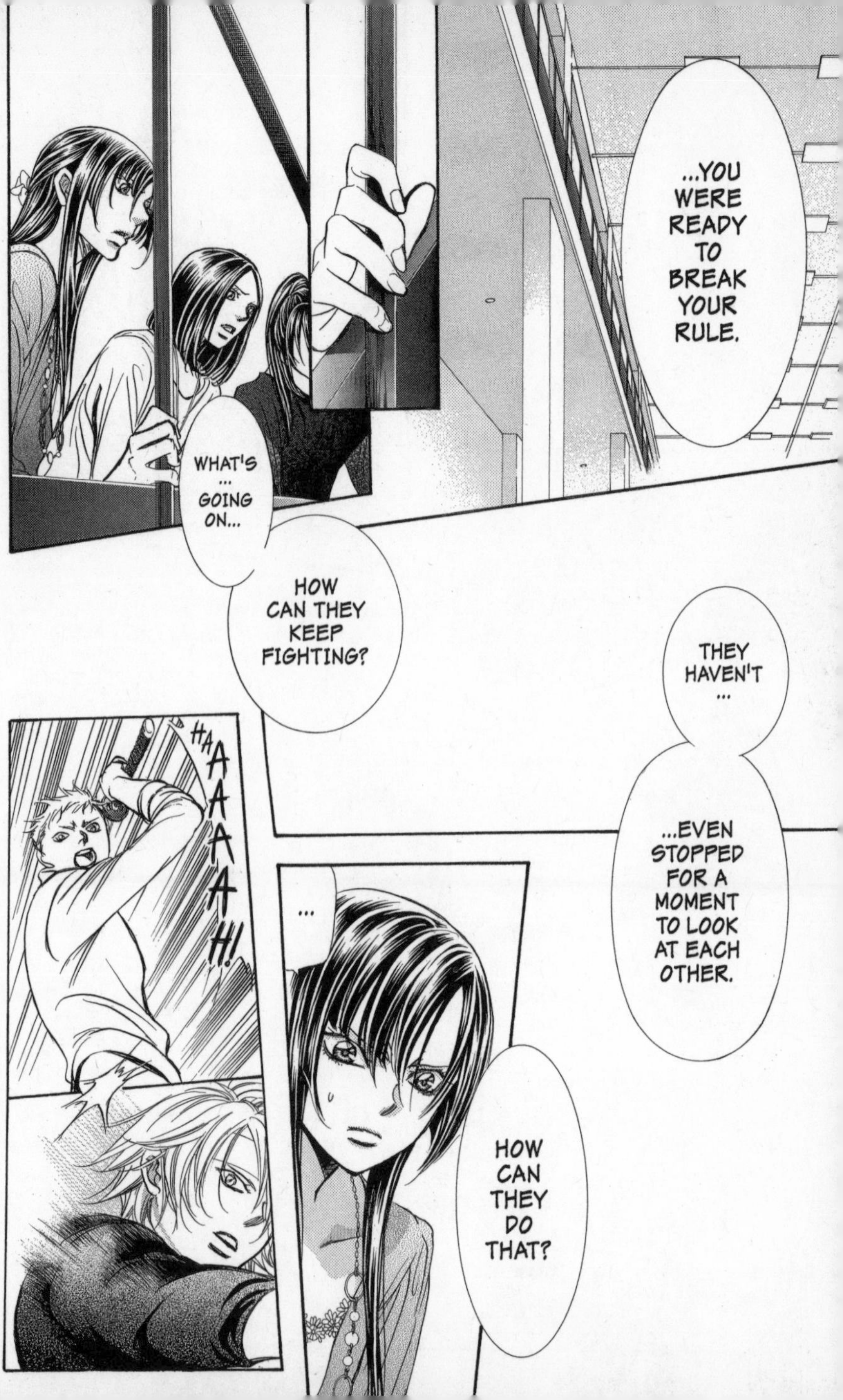
...YOU WERE READY TO BREAK YOUR RULE.
WHAT'S ... GOING ON...
HOW CAN THEY KEEP FIGHTING?
THEY HAVEN'T ...
...EVEN STOPPED FOR A MOMENT TO LOOK AT EACH OTHER.
...
HOW CAN THEY DO THAT?
HAAAAAAH!

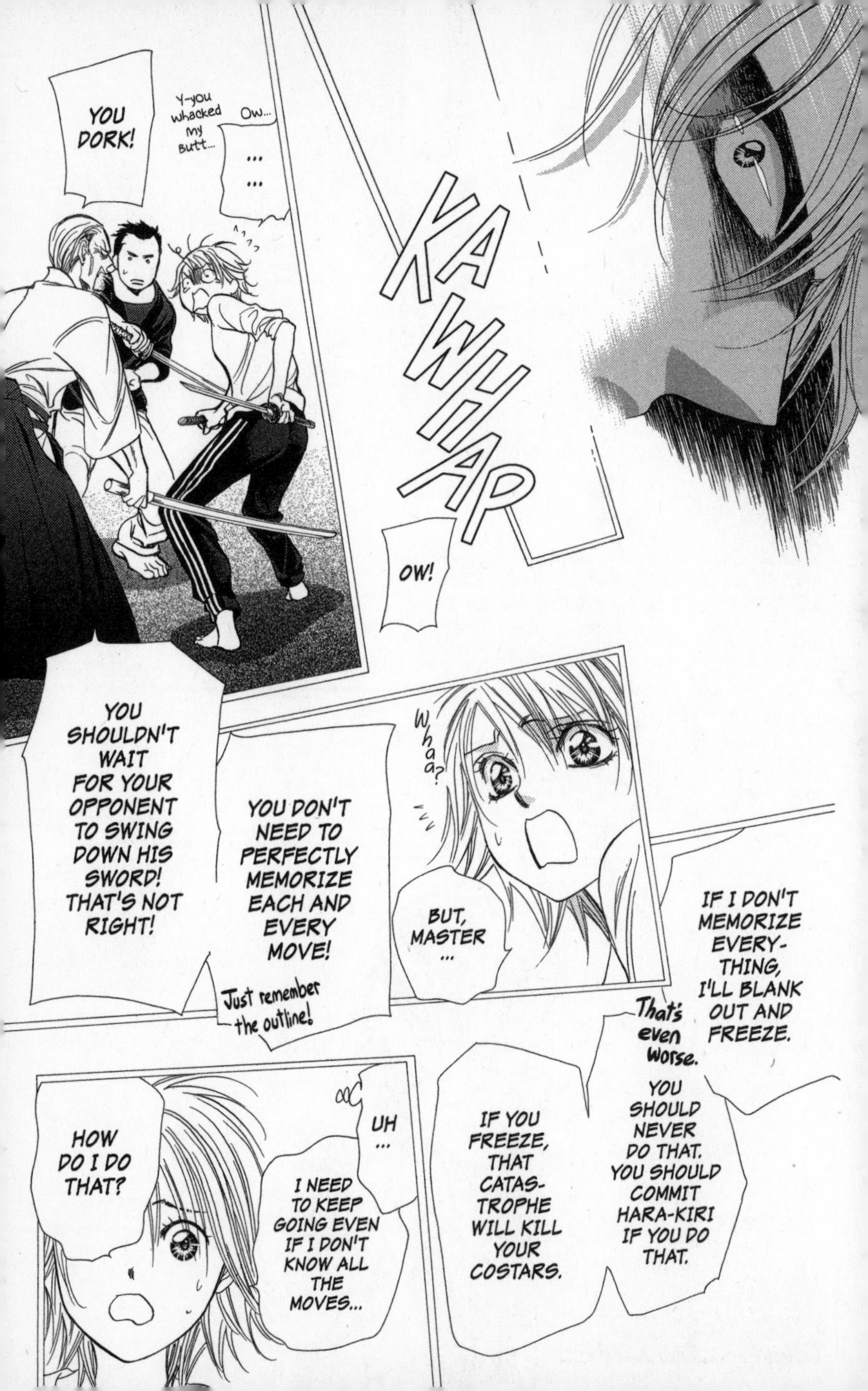
KA WHAP
OW!
YOU DORK!
Y-you whacked my butt...
Ow...
... ...
YOU SHOULDN'T WAIT FOR YOUR OPPONENT TO SWING DOWN HIS SWORD! THAT'S NOT RIGHT!
YOU DON'T NEED TO PERFECTLY MEMORIZE EACH AND EVERY MOVE!
Just remember the outline!
Whaa?
BUT, MASTER ...
IF I DON'T MEMORIZE EVERY-THING, I'LL BLANK OUT AND FREEZE.
That's even worse.
YOU SHOULD NEVER DO THAT. YOU SHOULD COMMIT HARA-KIRI IF YOU DO THAT.
IF YOU FREEZE, THAT CATAS-TROPHE WILL KILL YOUR COSTARS.
UH ...
I NEED TO KEEP GOING EVEN IF I DON'T KNOW ALL THE MOVES...
HOW DO I DO THAT?

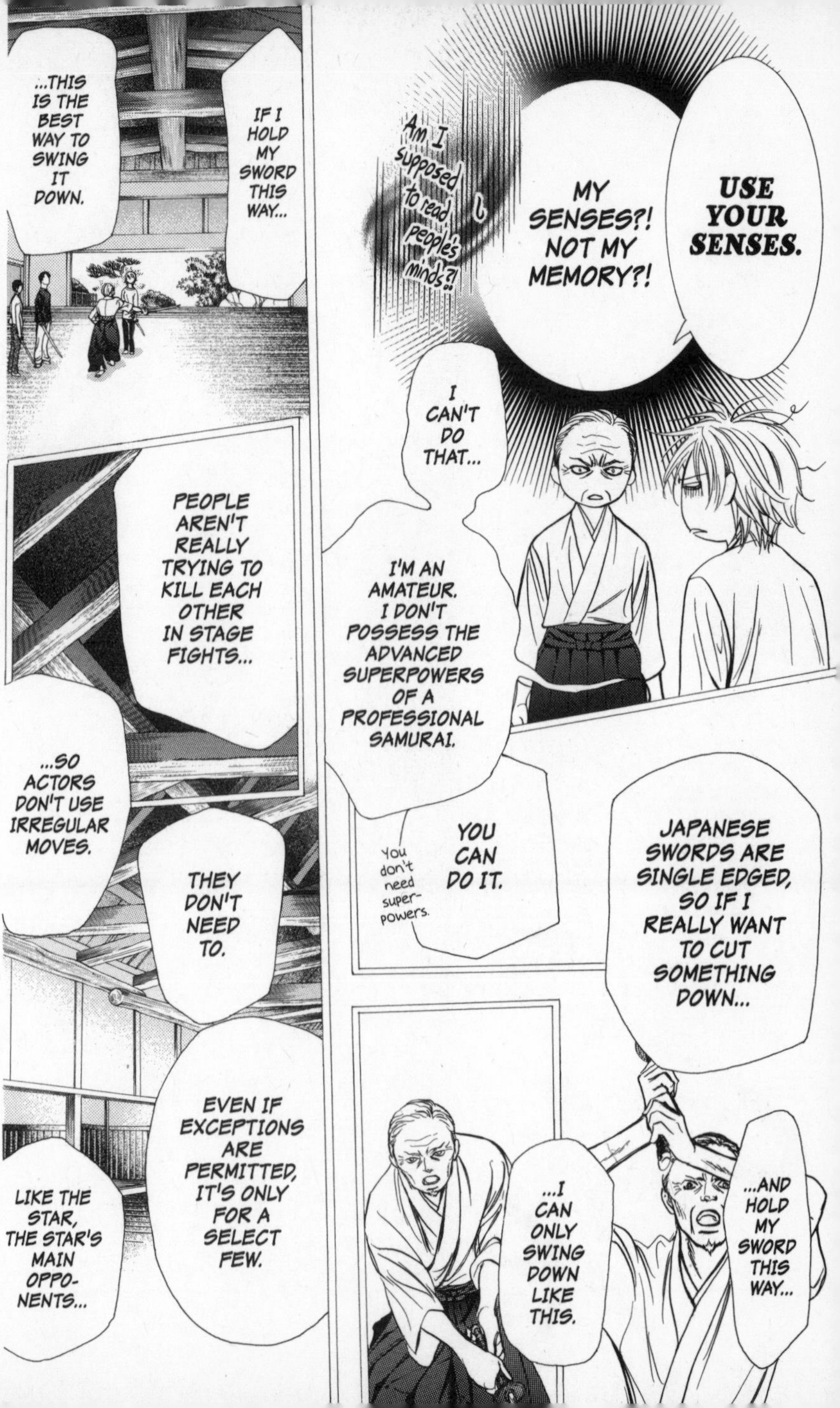
USE YOUR SENSES.
MY SENSES?! NOT MY MEMORY?!
Am I supposed to read people's minds?!
I CAN'T DO THAT...
I'M AN AMATEUR. I DON'T POSSESS THE ADVANCED SUPERPOWERS OF A PROFESSIONAL SAMURAI.
YOU CAN DO IT.
You don't need super-powers.
JAPANESE SWORDS ARE SINGLE EDGED, SO IF I REALLY WANT TO CUT SOMETHING DOWN...
...AND HOLD MY SWORD THIS WAY...
...I CAN ONLY SWING DOWN LIKE THIS.
IF I HOLD MY SWORD THIS WAY...
...THIS IS THE BEST WAY TO SWING IT DOWN.
PEOPLE AREN'T REALLY TRYING TO KILL EACH OTHER IN STAGE FIGHTS...
...SO ACTORS DON'T USE IRREGULAR MOVES.
THEY DON'T NEED TO.
EVEN IF EXCEPTIONS ARE PERMITTED, IT'S ONLY FOR A SELECT FEW.
LIKE THE STAR, THE STAR'S MAIN OPPO-NENTS...

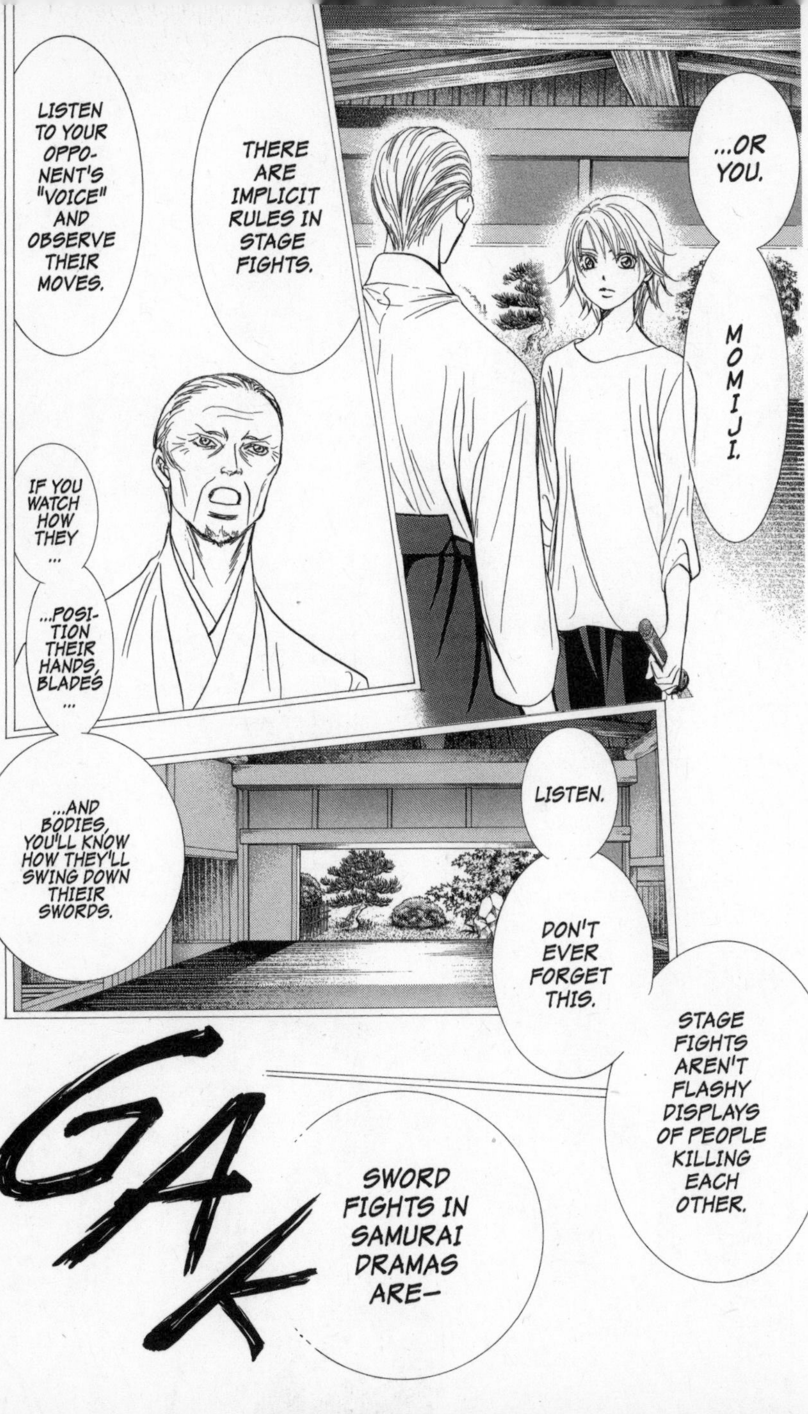
...OR YOU.
MOMIJI.
THERE ARE IMPLICIT RULES IN STAGE FIGHTS.
LISTEN TO YOUR OPPO-NENT'S "VOICE" AND OBSERVE THEIR MOVES.
IF YOU WATCH HOW THEY ...
...POSI-TION THEIR HANDS, BLADES ...
...AND BODIES, YOU'LL KNOW HOW THEY'LL SWING DOWN THIEIR SWORDS.
LISTEN.
DON'T EVER FORGET THIS.
STAGE FIGHTS AREN'T FLASHY DISPLAYS OF PEOPLE KILLING EACH OTHER.
SWORD FIGHTS IN SAMURAI DRAMAS ARE—
GAK

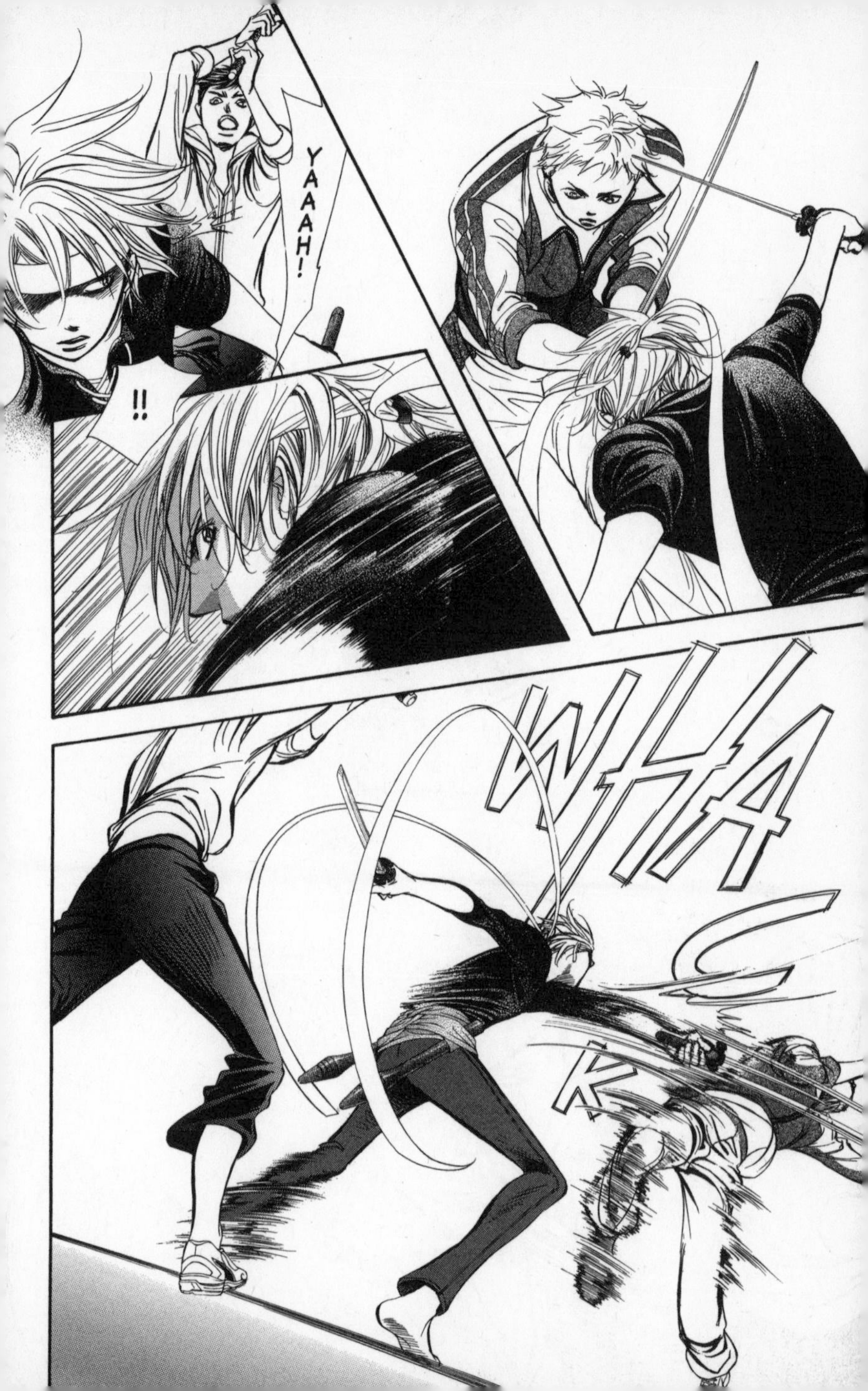
YAAAH!
!!
WHACK

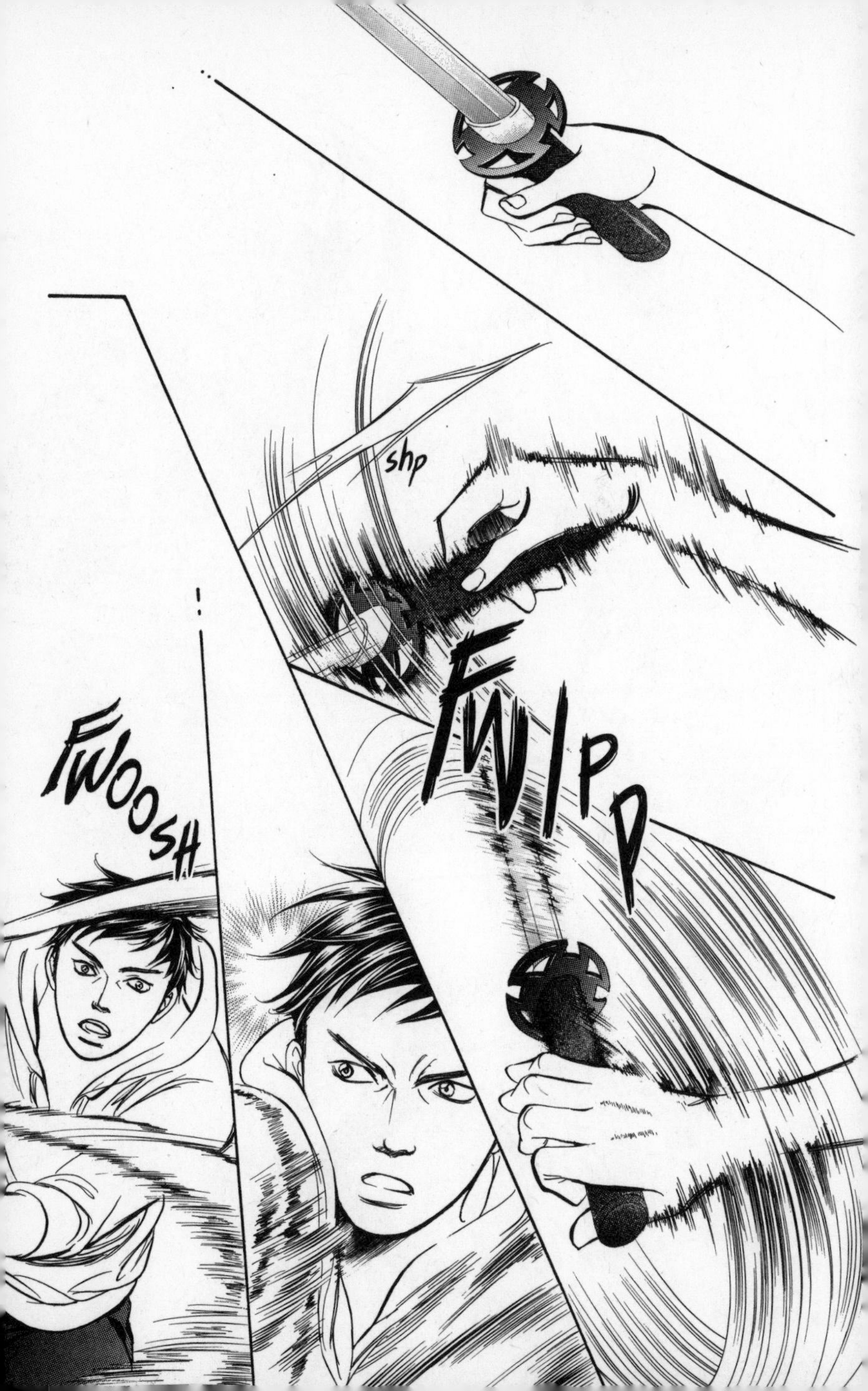
shp
FWIPP
FWOOSH

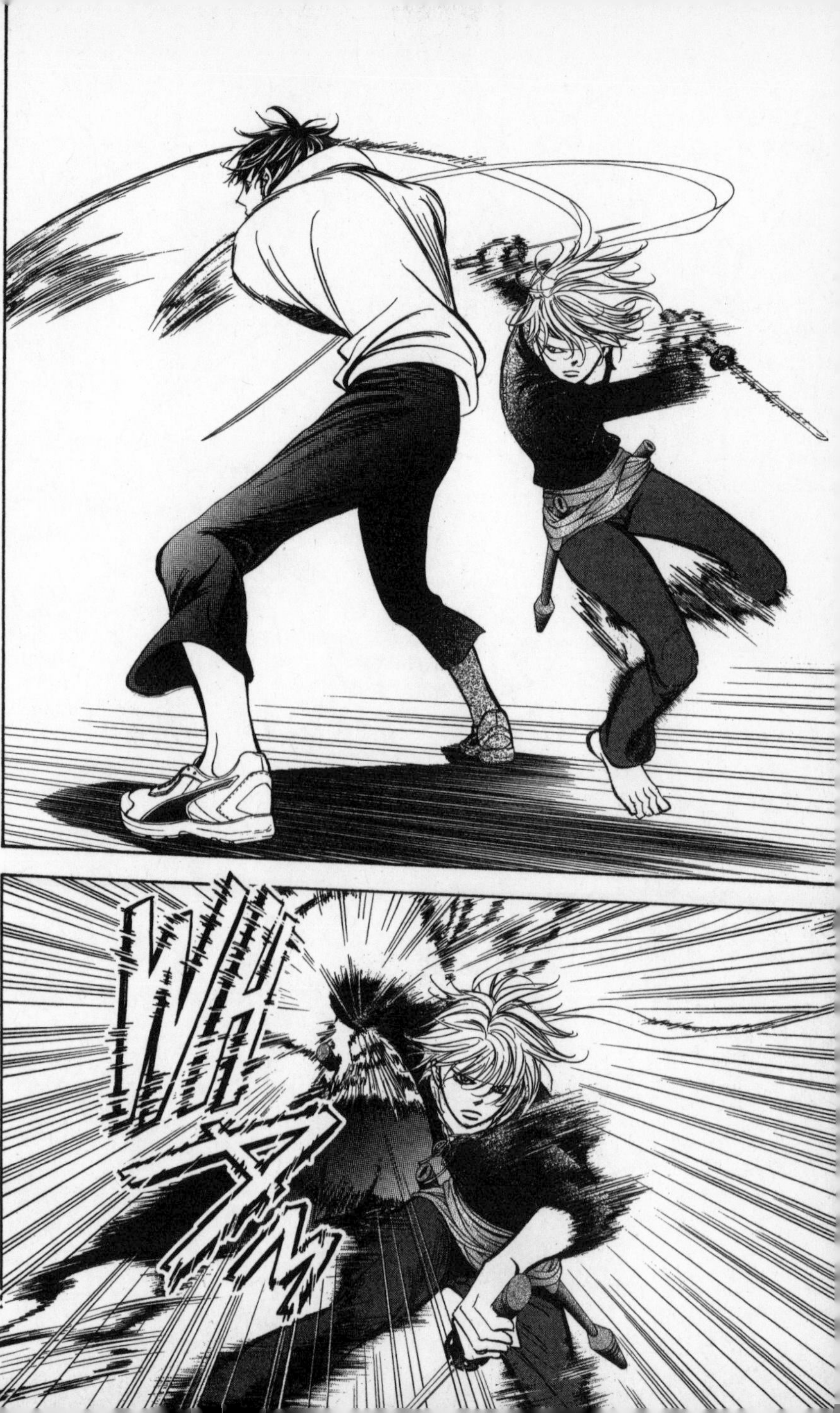
WHAM

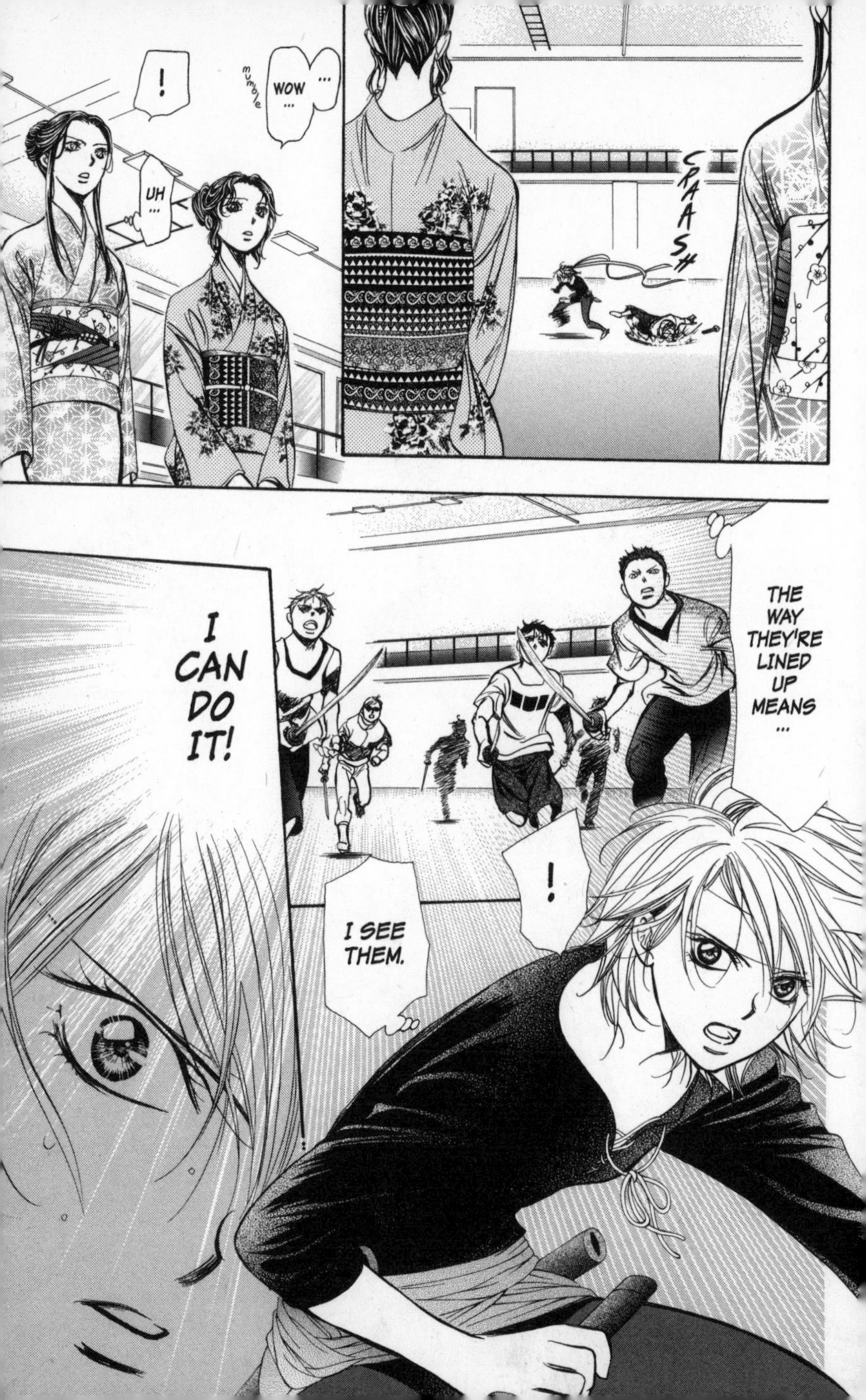
CRAASH
WOW ... ...
mumble
!
UH ...
THE WAY THEY'RE LINED UP MEANS ...
!
I SEE THEM.
I CAN DO IT!

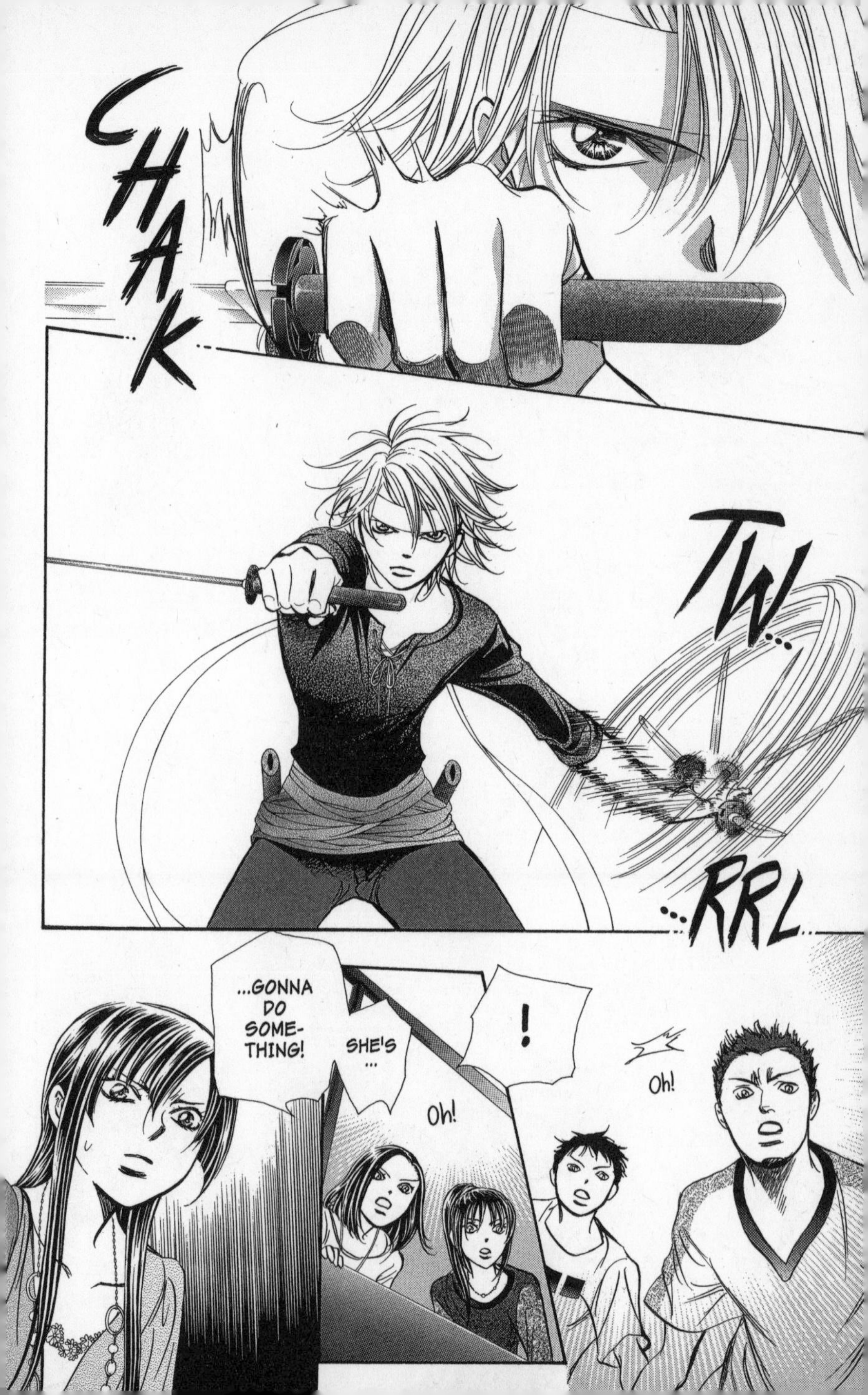
CHAK
TW...
...RRL
!
Oh!
Oh!
SHE'S ...
...GONNA DO SOME-THING!

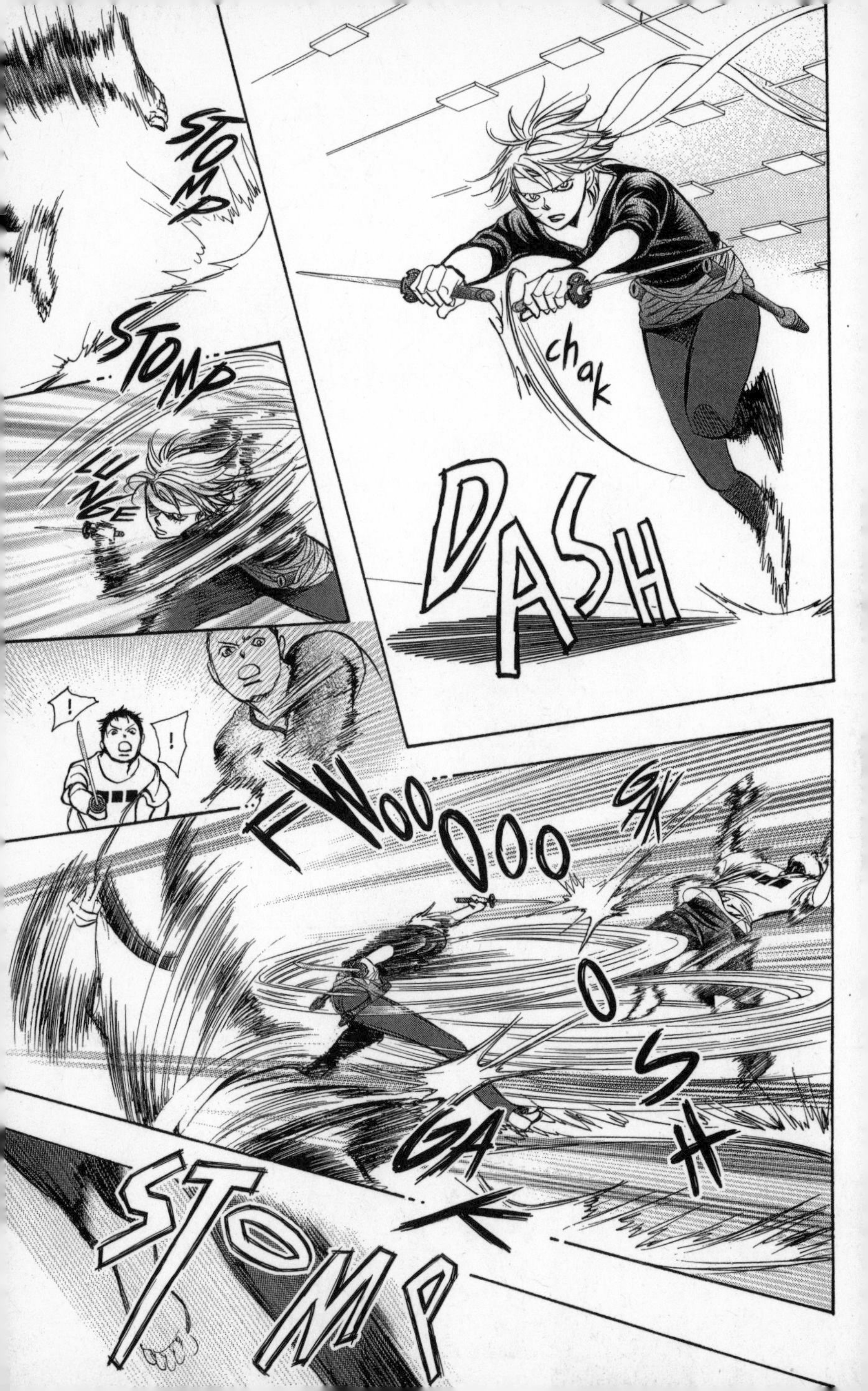
chak
DASH
STOMP
STOMP
LUNGE
!
!
GAK
FWOOOOOOOOSH
GAK
STOMP

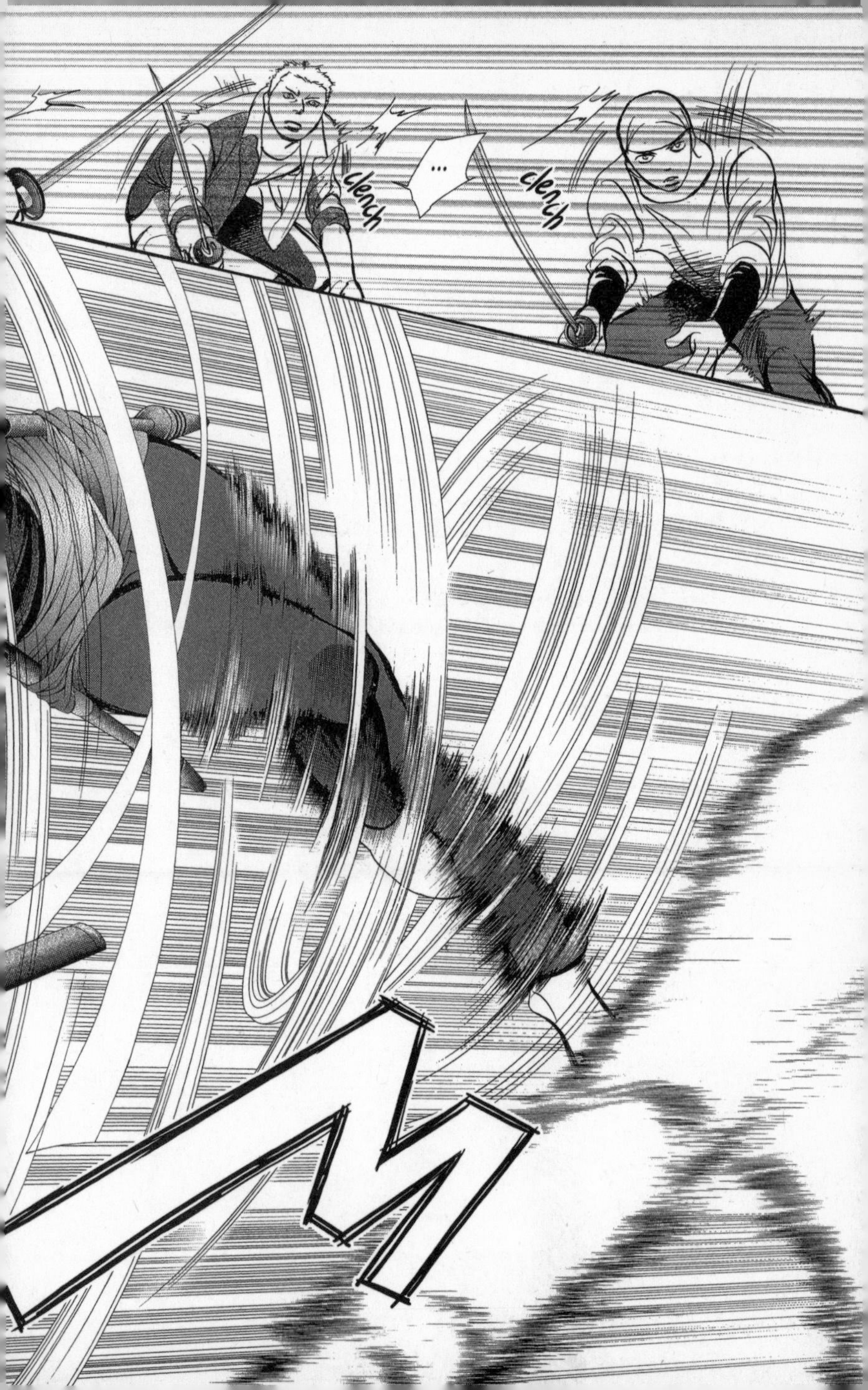
clench
...
clench

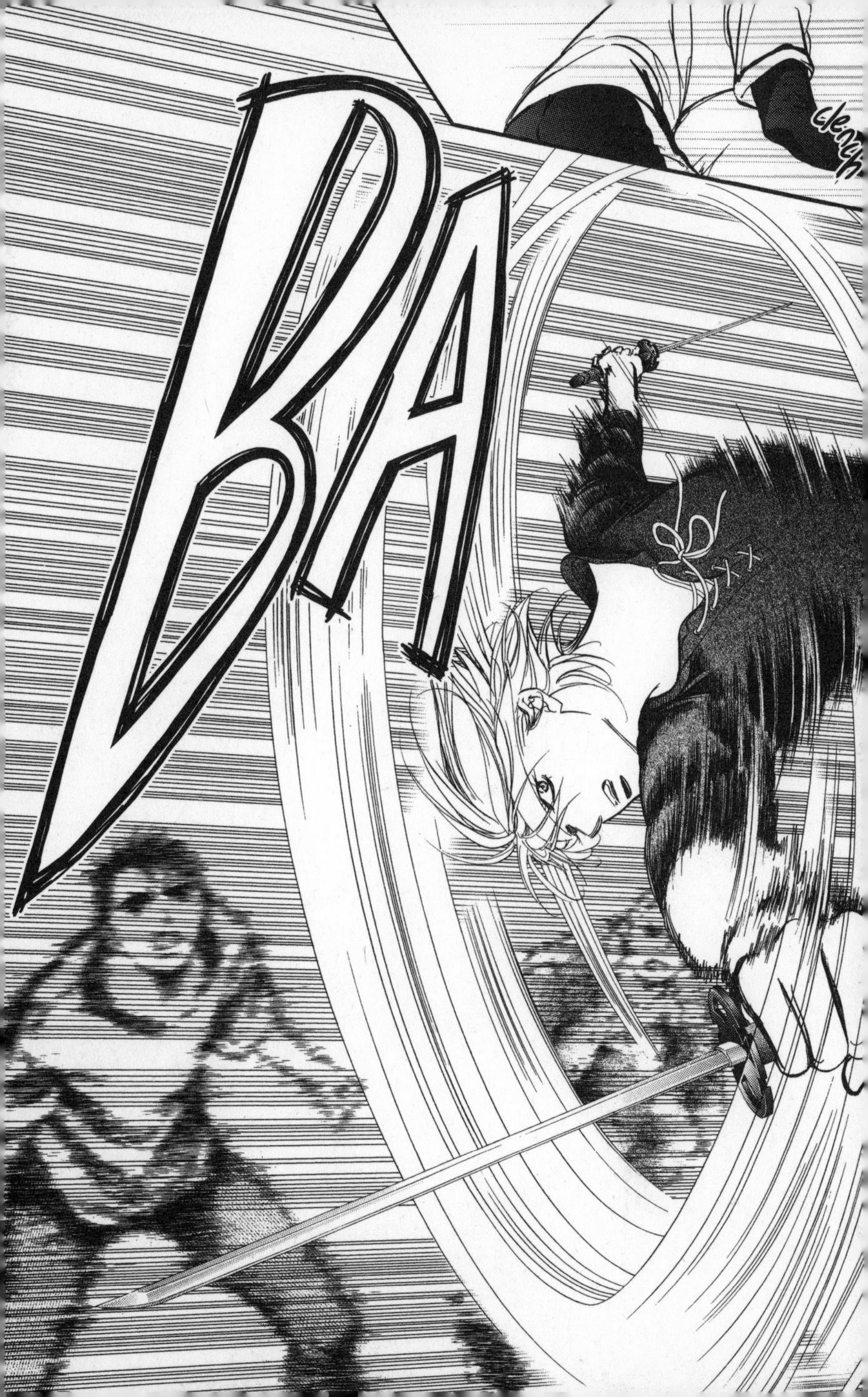
clench
BA

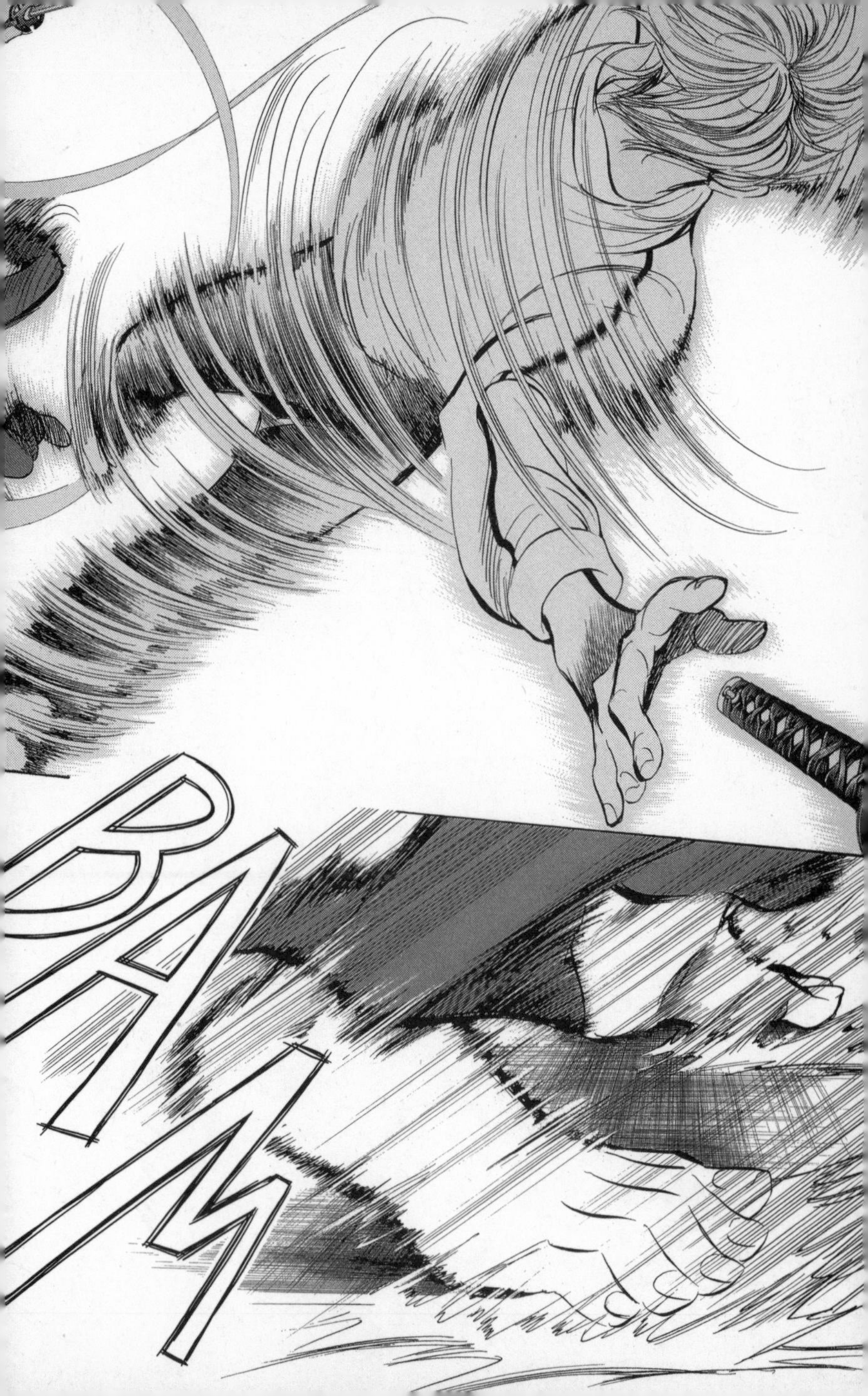
BAM

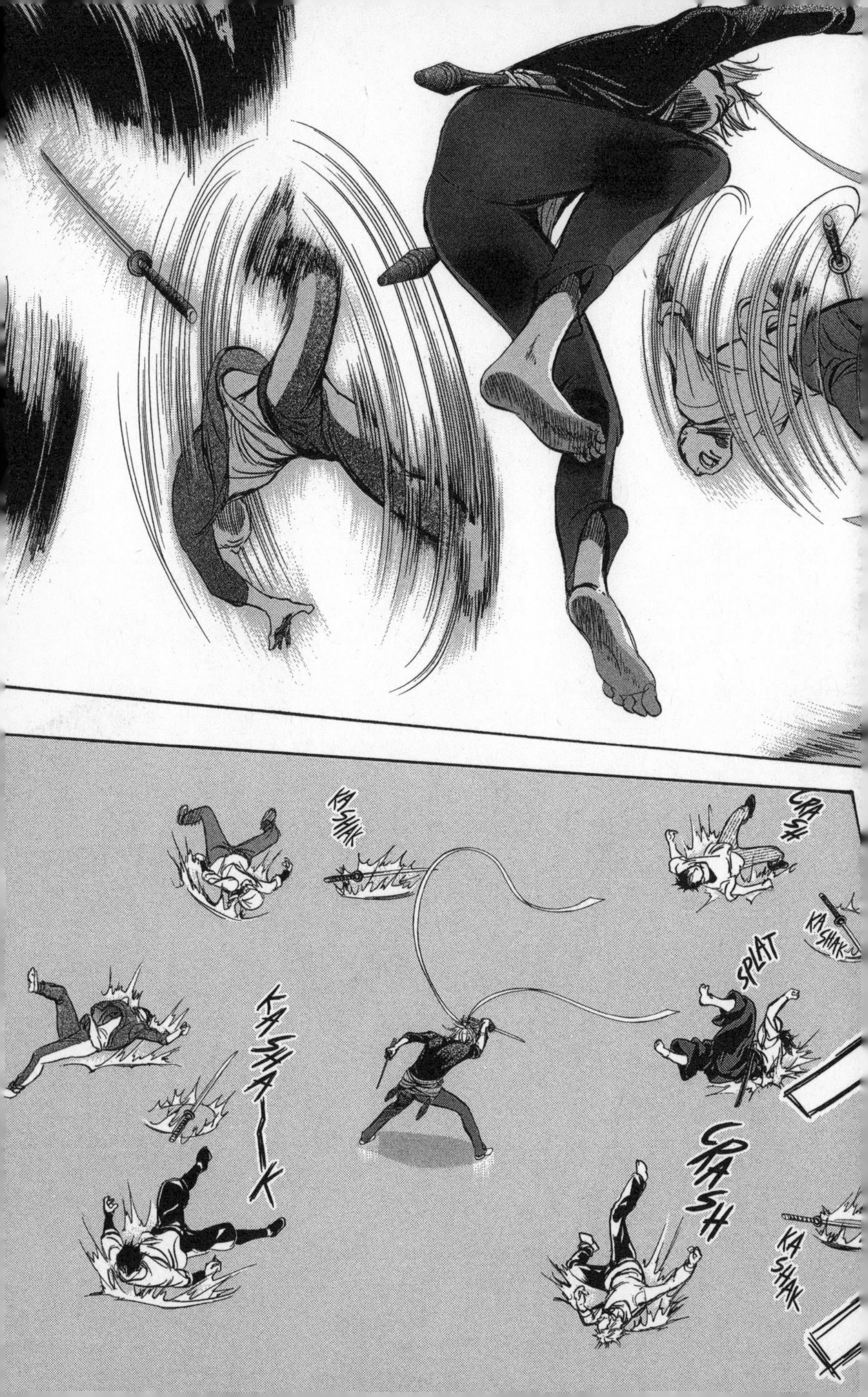
CRASH
KA SHAK
SPLAT
KA SHAK
CRASH
KA SHAK
KASHA—K

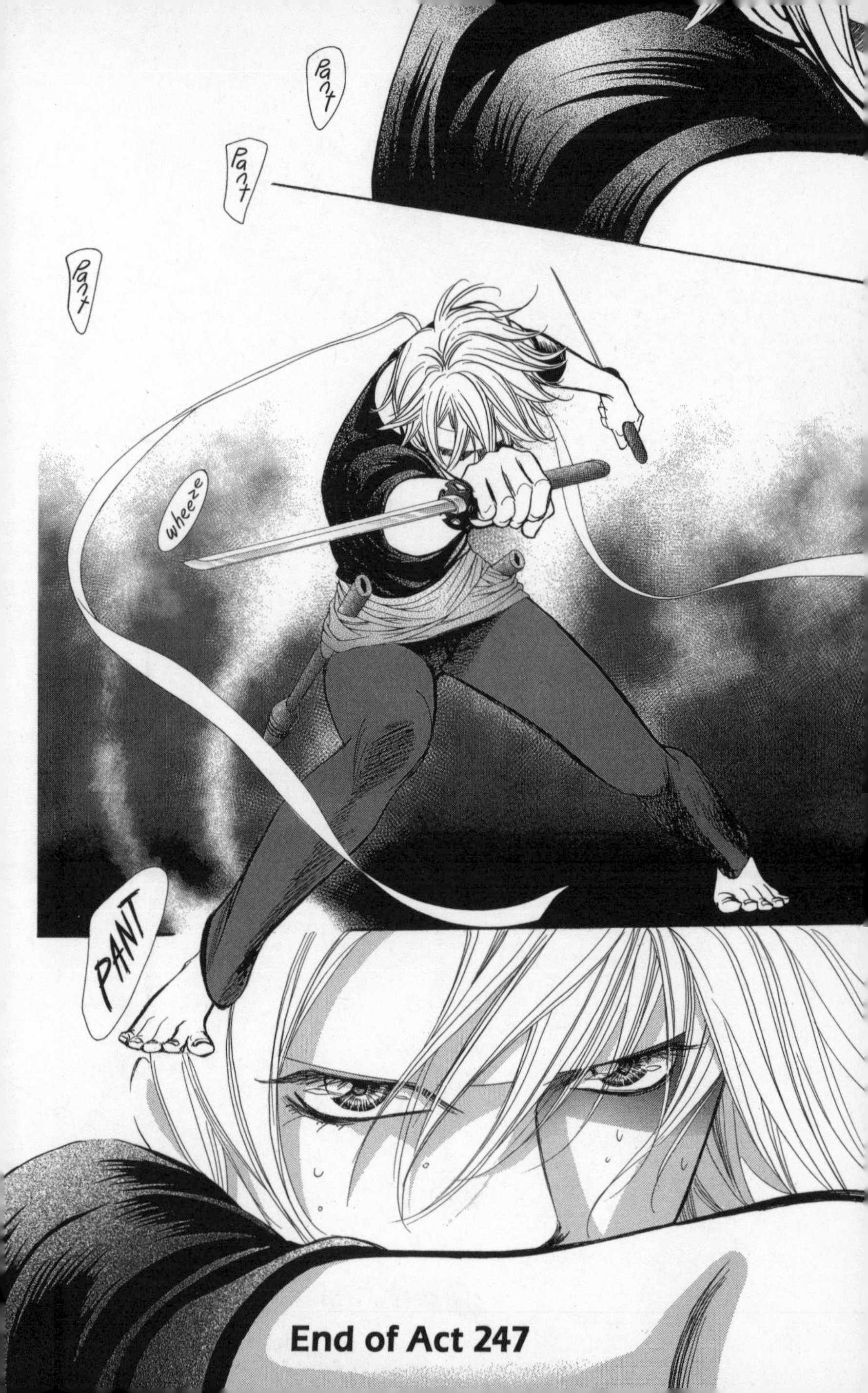
Pant
Pant
Pant
wheeze
PANT

End of Act 247

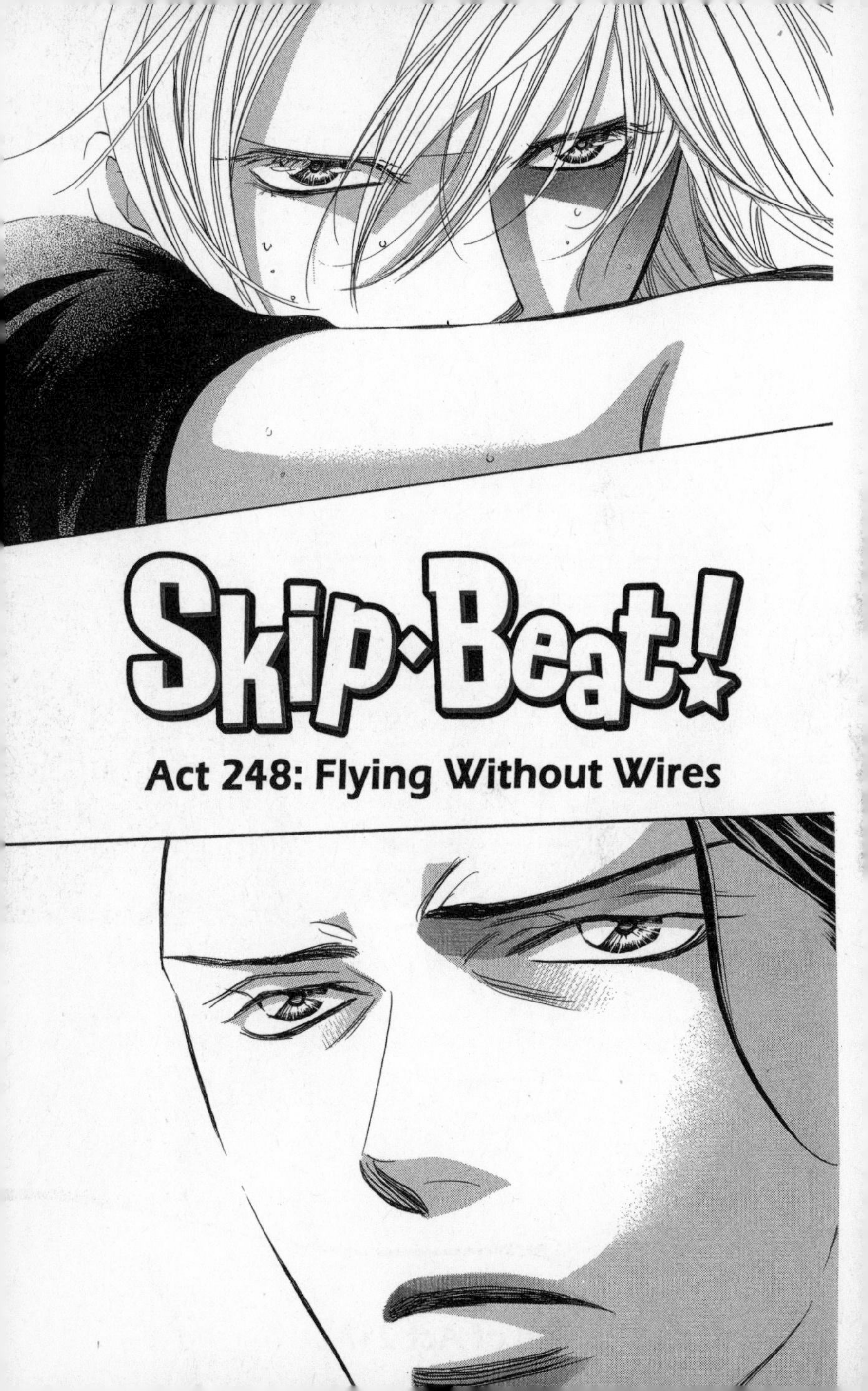
Skip·Beat!
Act 248: Flying Without Wires

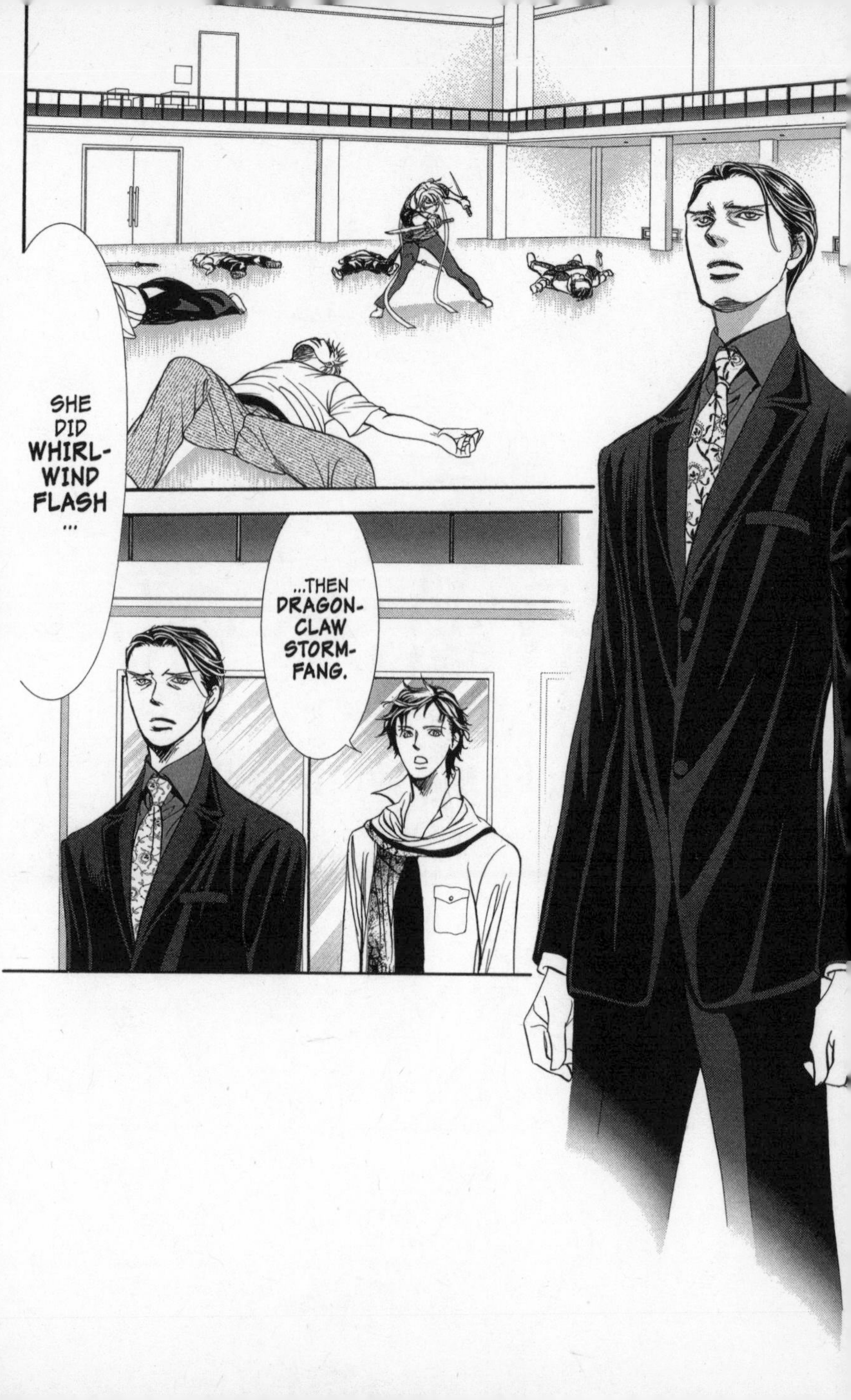
SHE DID WHIRLWIND FLASH...
...THEN DRAGON-CLAW STORM-FANG.

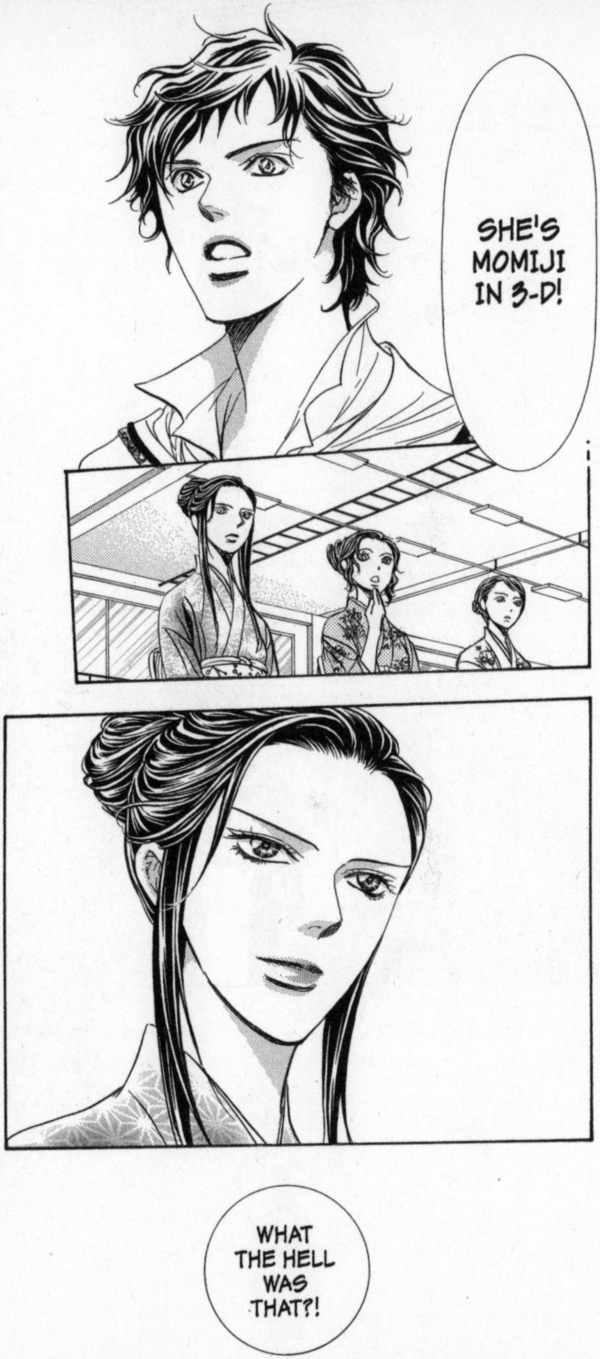
SHE'S MOMIJI IN 3-D!
WHAT THE HELL WAS THAT?!

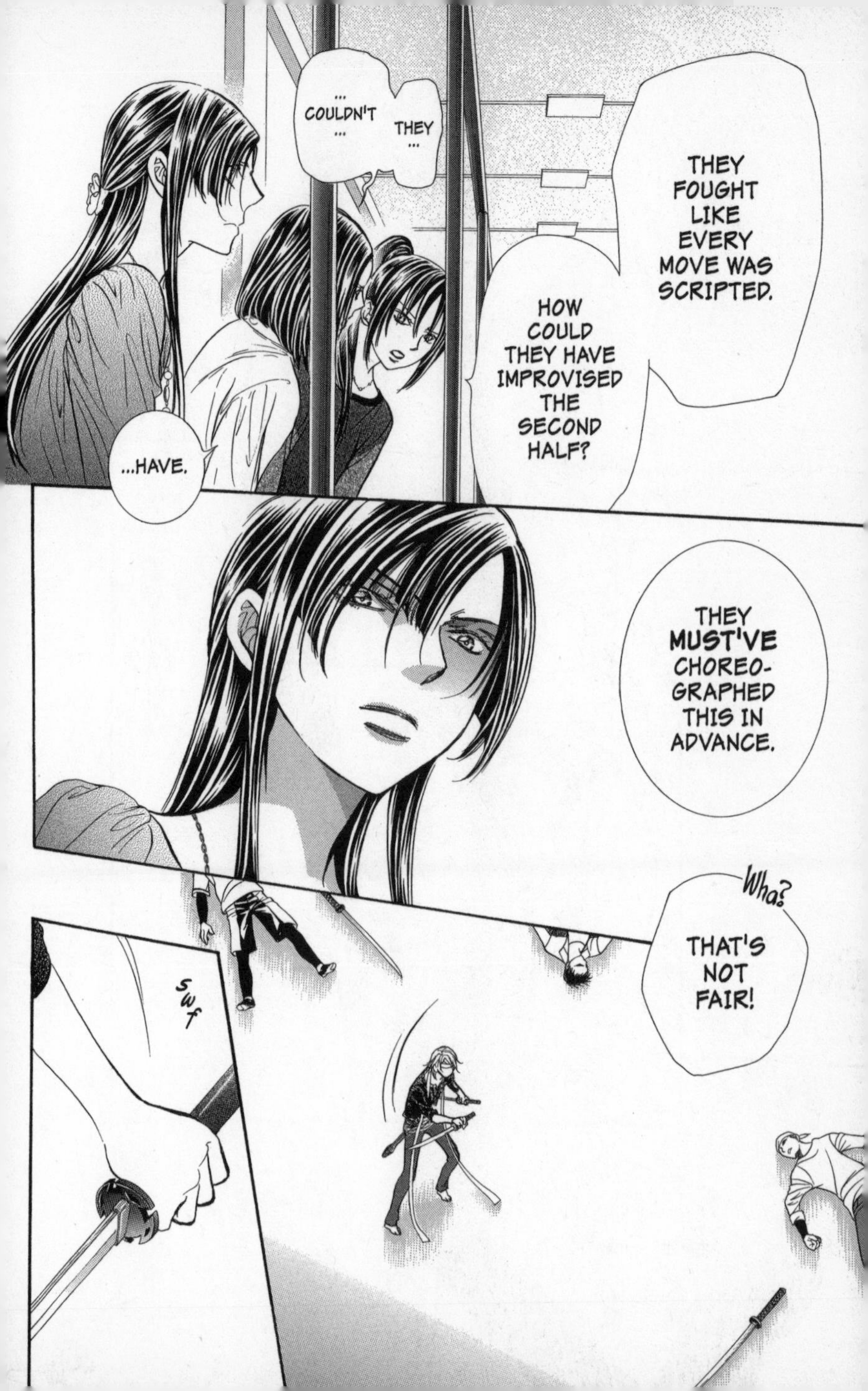
THEY FOUGHT LIKE EVERY MOVE WAS SCRIPTED.
HOW COULD THEY HAVE IMPROVISED THE SECOND HALF?
THEY ...
... COULDN'T ...
...HAVE.
THEY MUST'VE CHOREO-GRAPHED THIS IN ADVANCE.
Wha?
THAT'S NOT FAIR!
swf

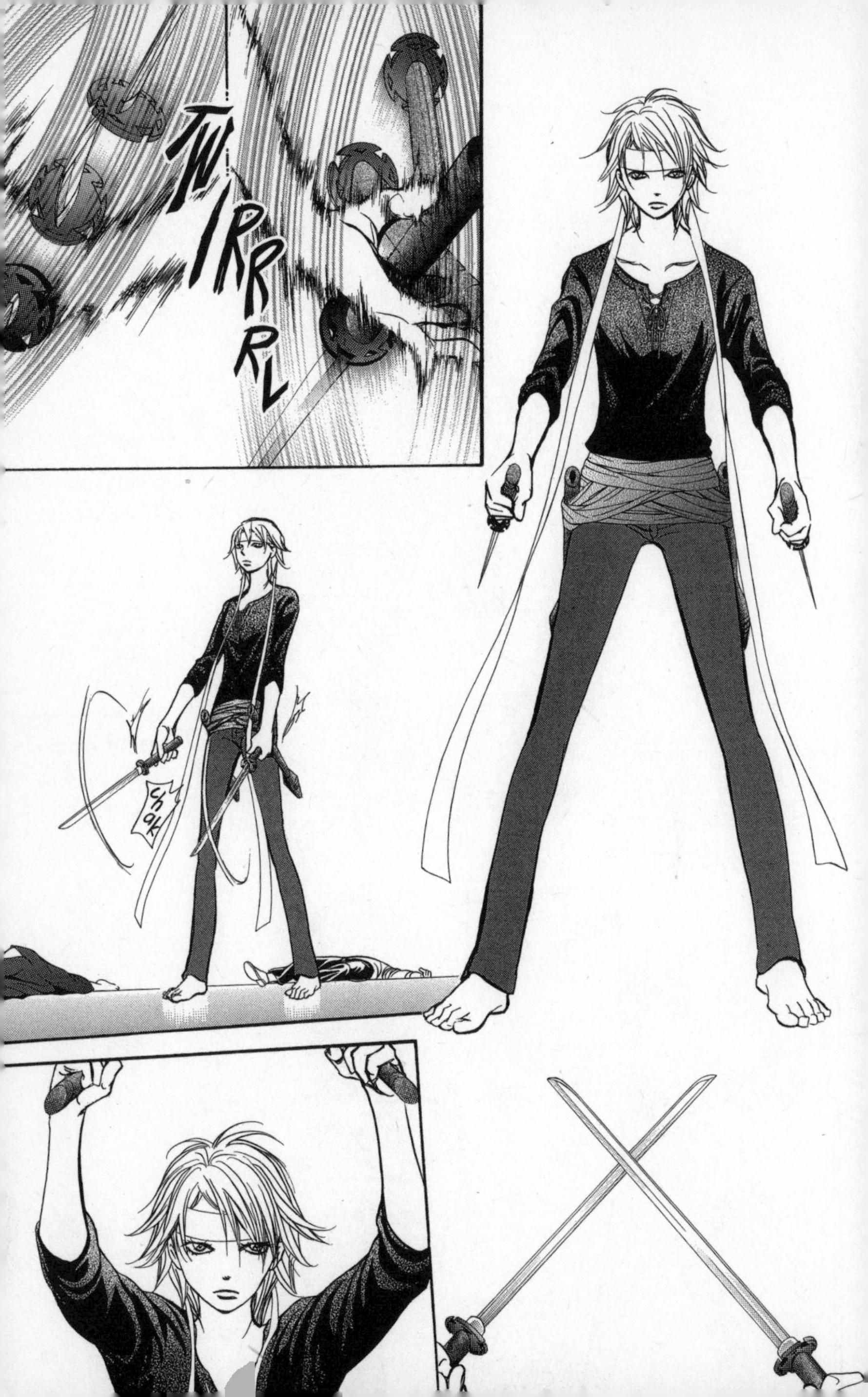
TWIRRRL
chak

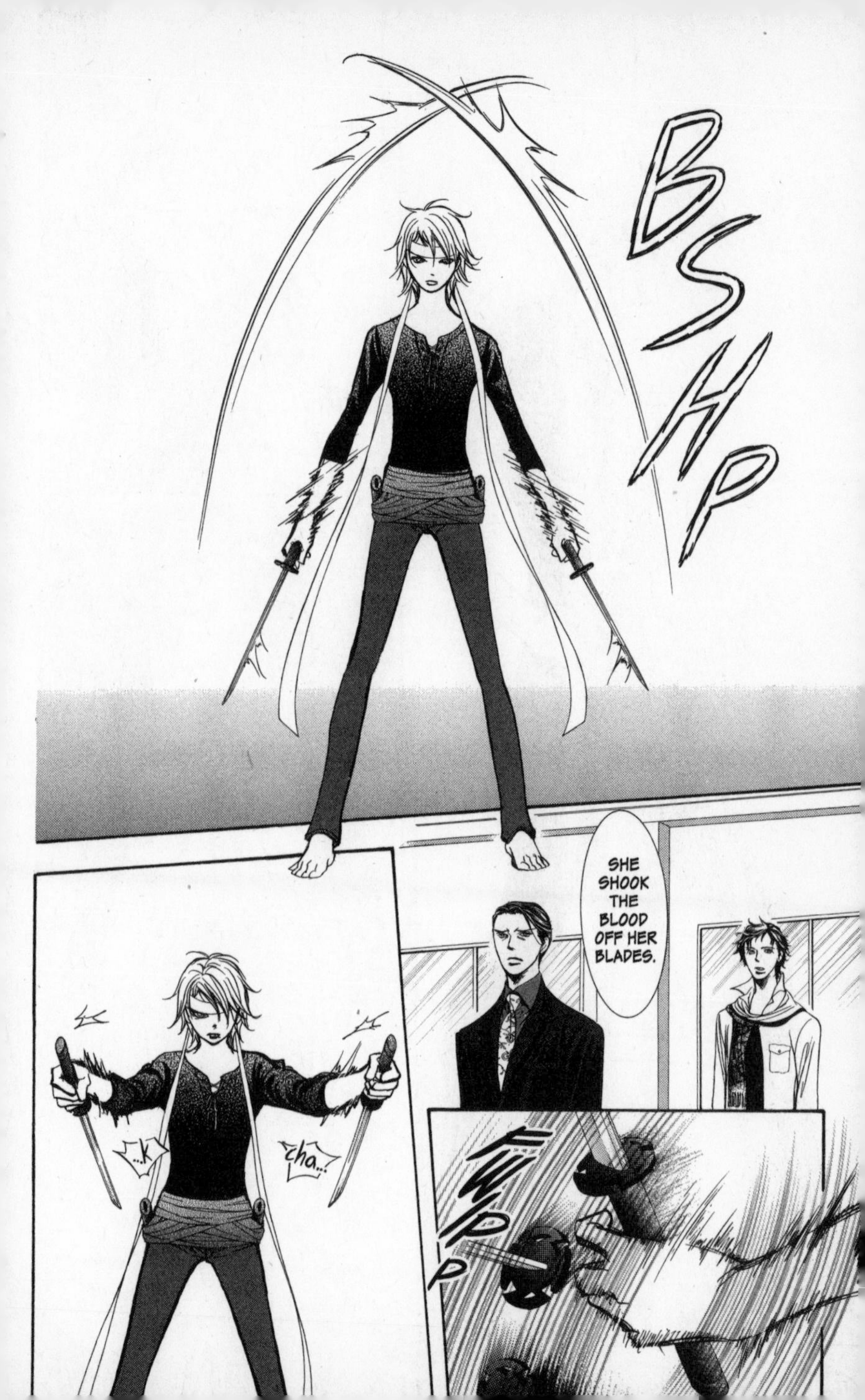
BSHP
SHE SHOOK THE BLOOD OFF HER BLADES.
FWIPP
...k
cha...

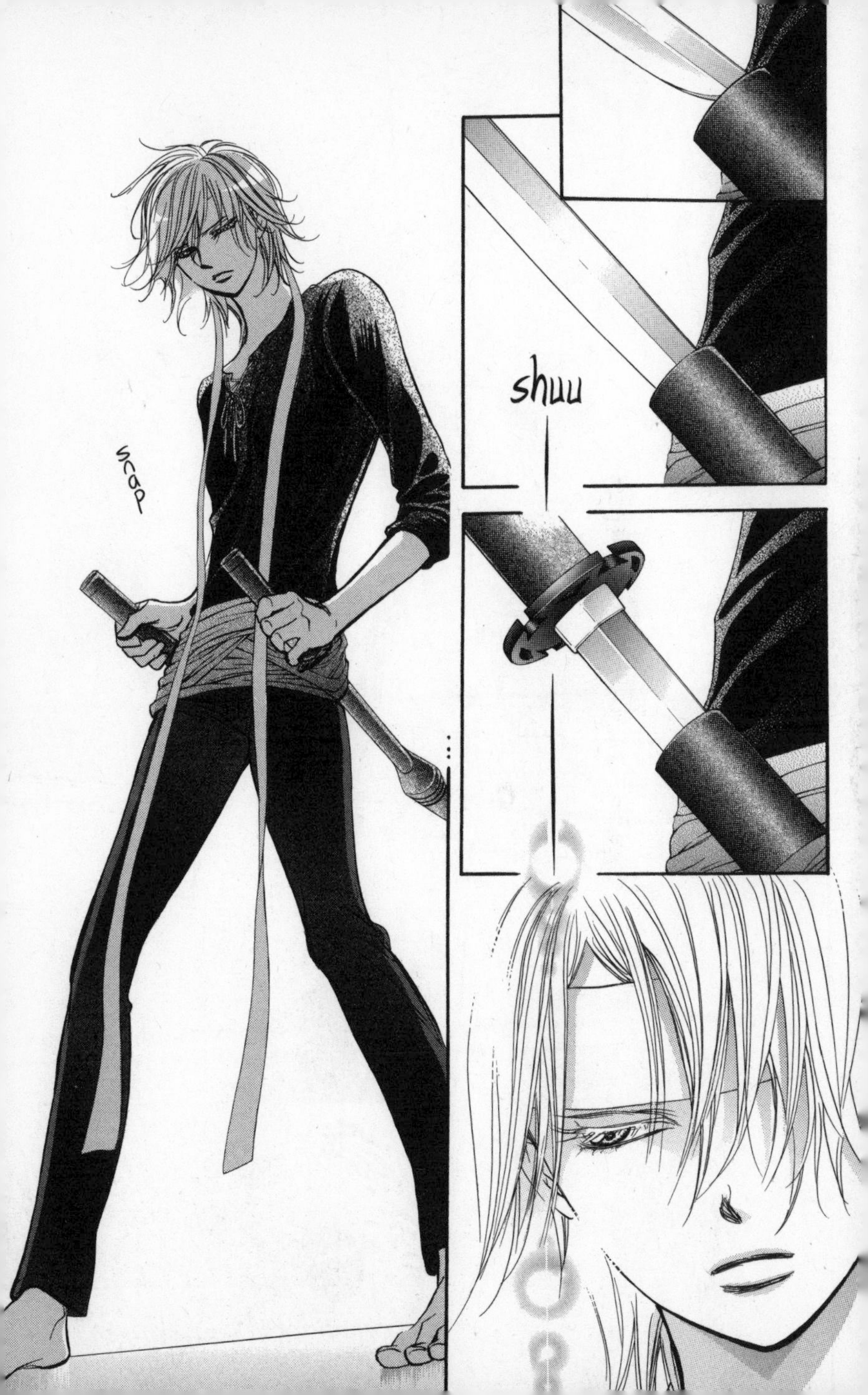
shuu
snap

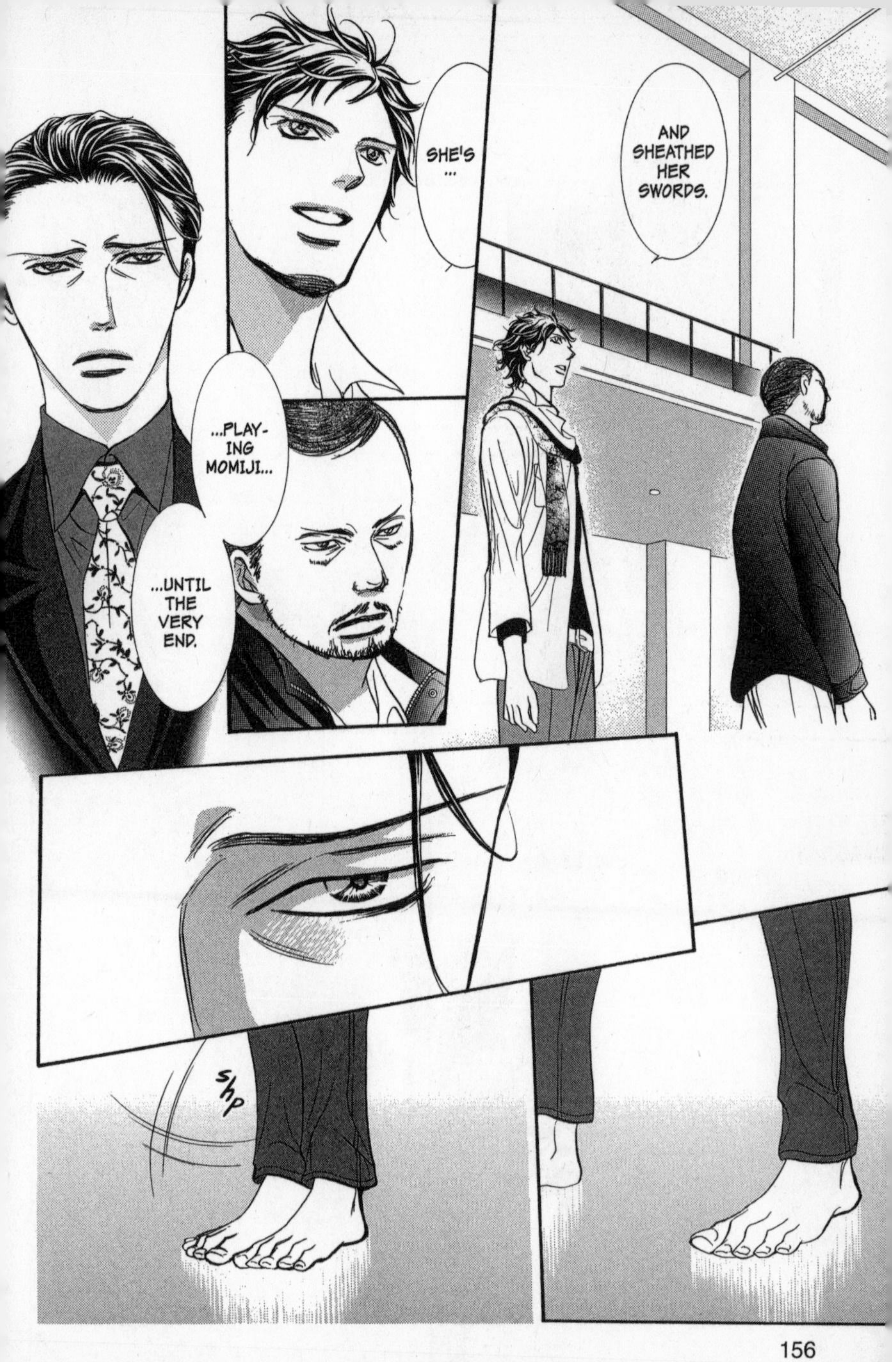
AND SHEATHED HER SWORDS.
SHE'S ...
...PLAYING MOMIJI...
...UNTIL THE VERY END.
shp

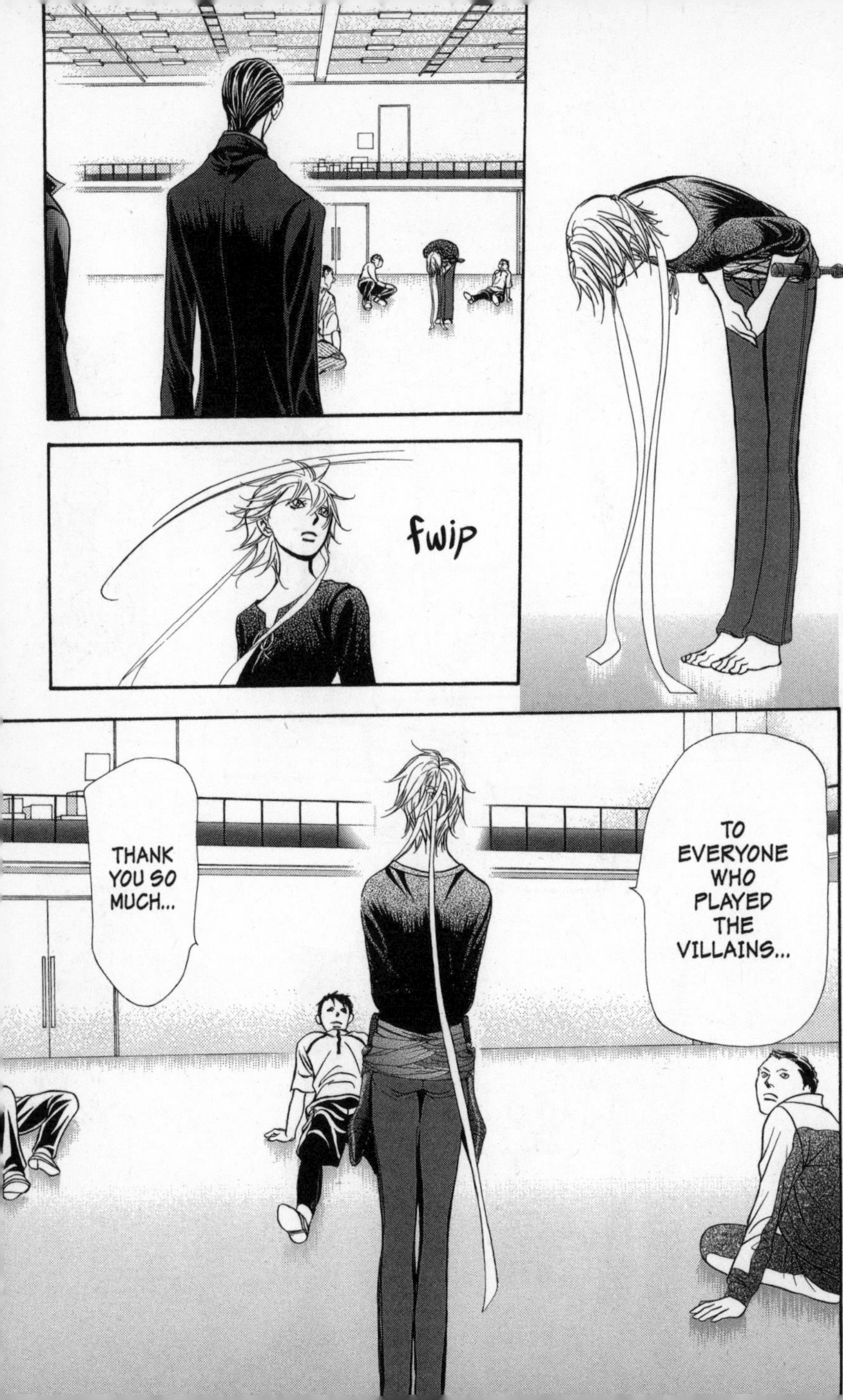
fwip
TO EVERYONE WHO PLAYED THE VILLAINS...
THANK YOU SO MUCH...

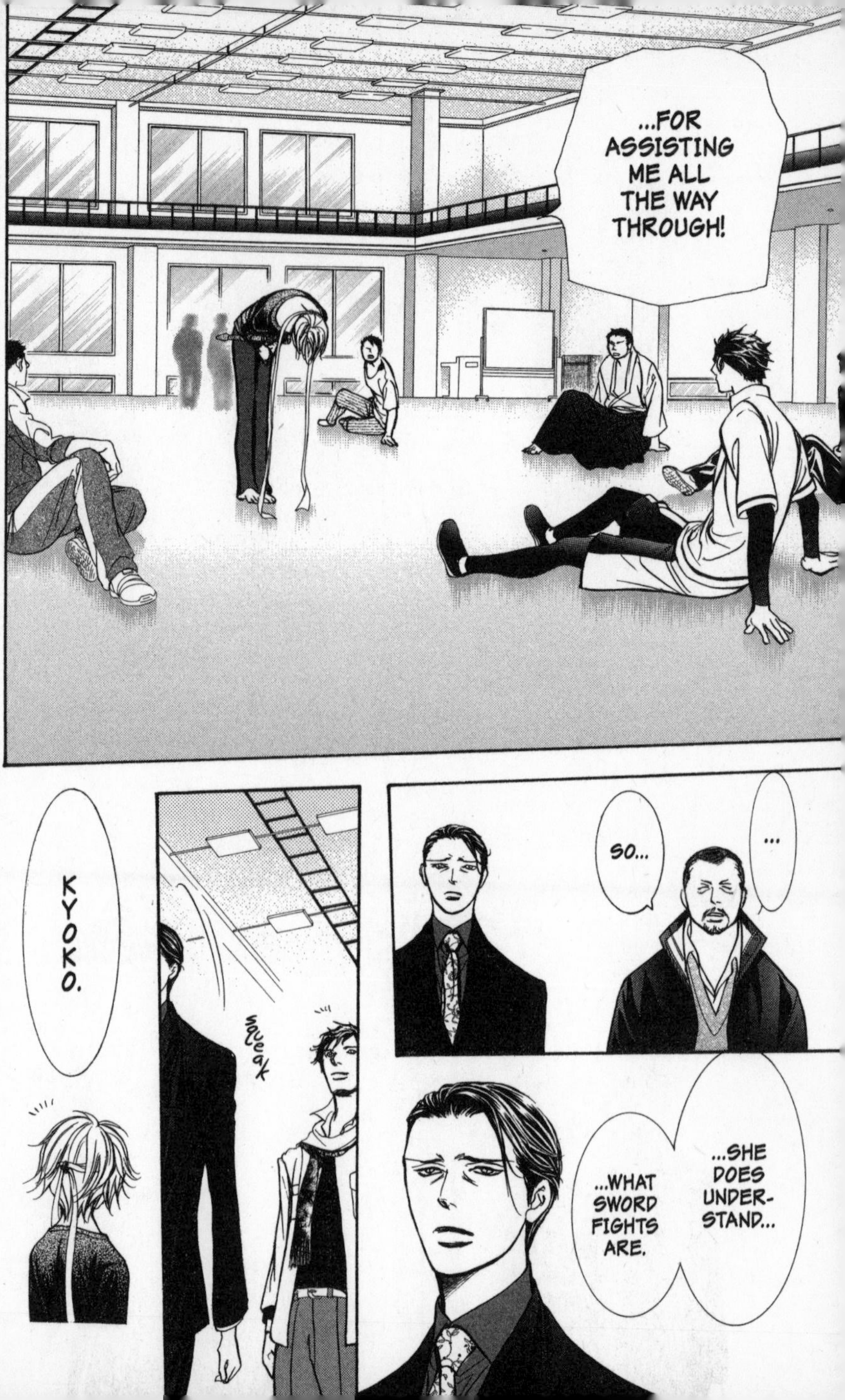
...FOR ASSISTING ME ALL THE WAY THROUGH!
...
SO...
...SHE DOES UNDER-STAND...
...WHAT SWORD FIGHTS ARE.
squeak
KYOKO.

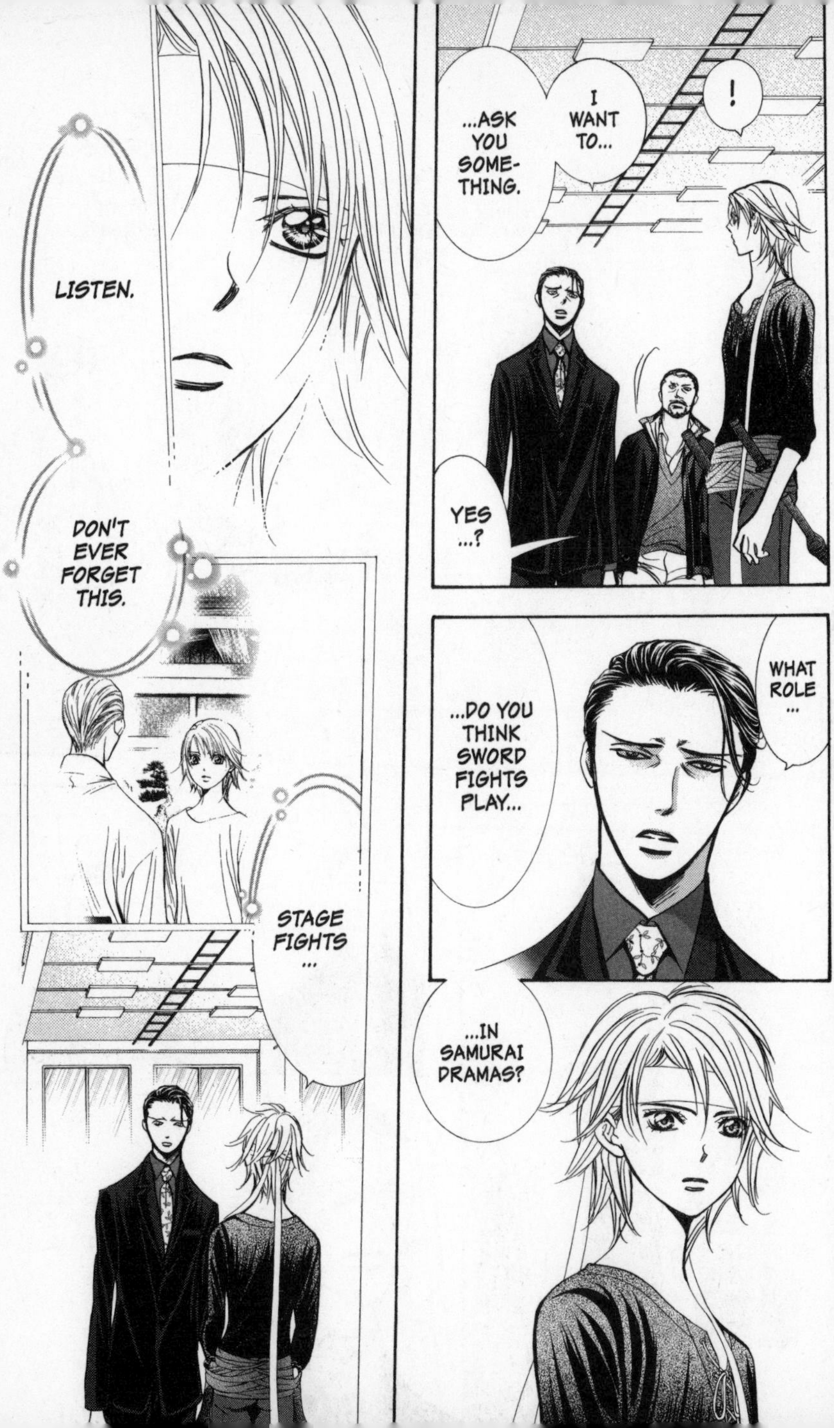
!
I WANT TO...
...ASK YOU SOMETHING.
YES ...?
WHAT ROLE ...
...DO YOU THINK SWORD FIGHTS PLAY...
...IN SAMURAI DRAMAS?
LISTEN.
DON'T EVER FORGET THIS.
STAGE FIGHTS ...

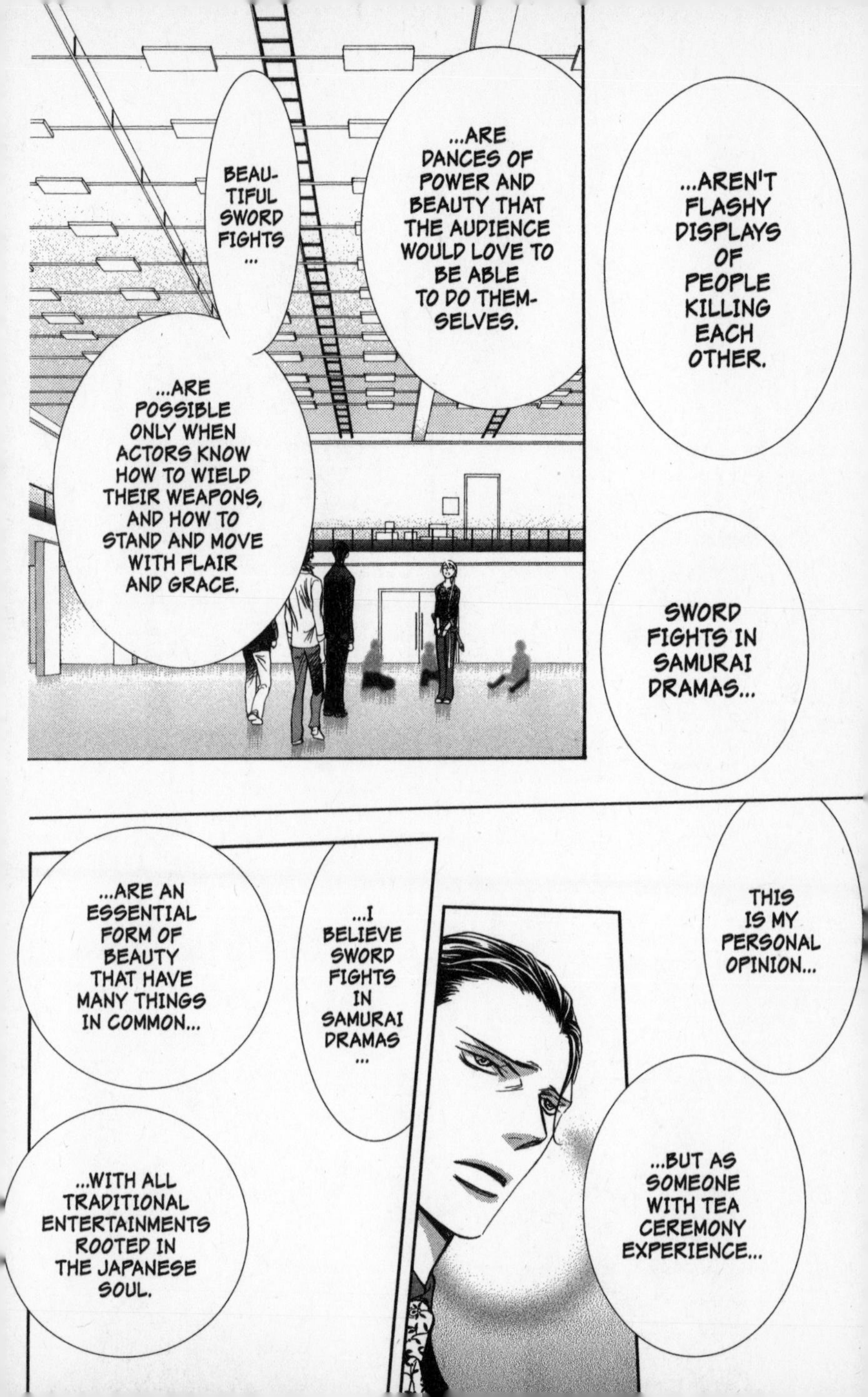
SWORD FIGHTS IN SAMURAI DRAMAS...
...AREN'T FLASHY DISPLAYS OF PEOPLE KILLING EACH OTHER.
...ARE DANCES OF POWER AND BEAUTY THAT THE AUDIENCE WOULD LOVE TO BE ABLE TO DO THEMSELVES.
BEAUTIFUL SWORD FIGHTS...
...ARE POSSIBLE ONLY WHEN ACTORS KNOW HOW TO WIELD THEIR WEAPONS, AND HOW TO STAND AND MOVE WITH FLAIR AND GRACE.
THIS IS MY PERSONAL OPINION...
...BUT AS SOMEONE WITH TEA CEREMONY EXPERIENCE...
...I BELIEVE SWORD FIGHTS IN SAMURAI DRAMAS...
...ARE AN ESSENTIAL FORM OF BEAUTY THAT HAVE MANY THINGS IN COMMON...
...WITH ALL TRADITIONAL ENTERTAINMENTS ROOTED IN THE JAPANESE SOUL.

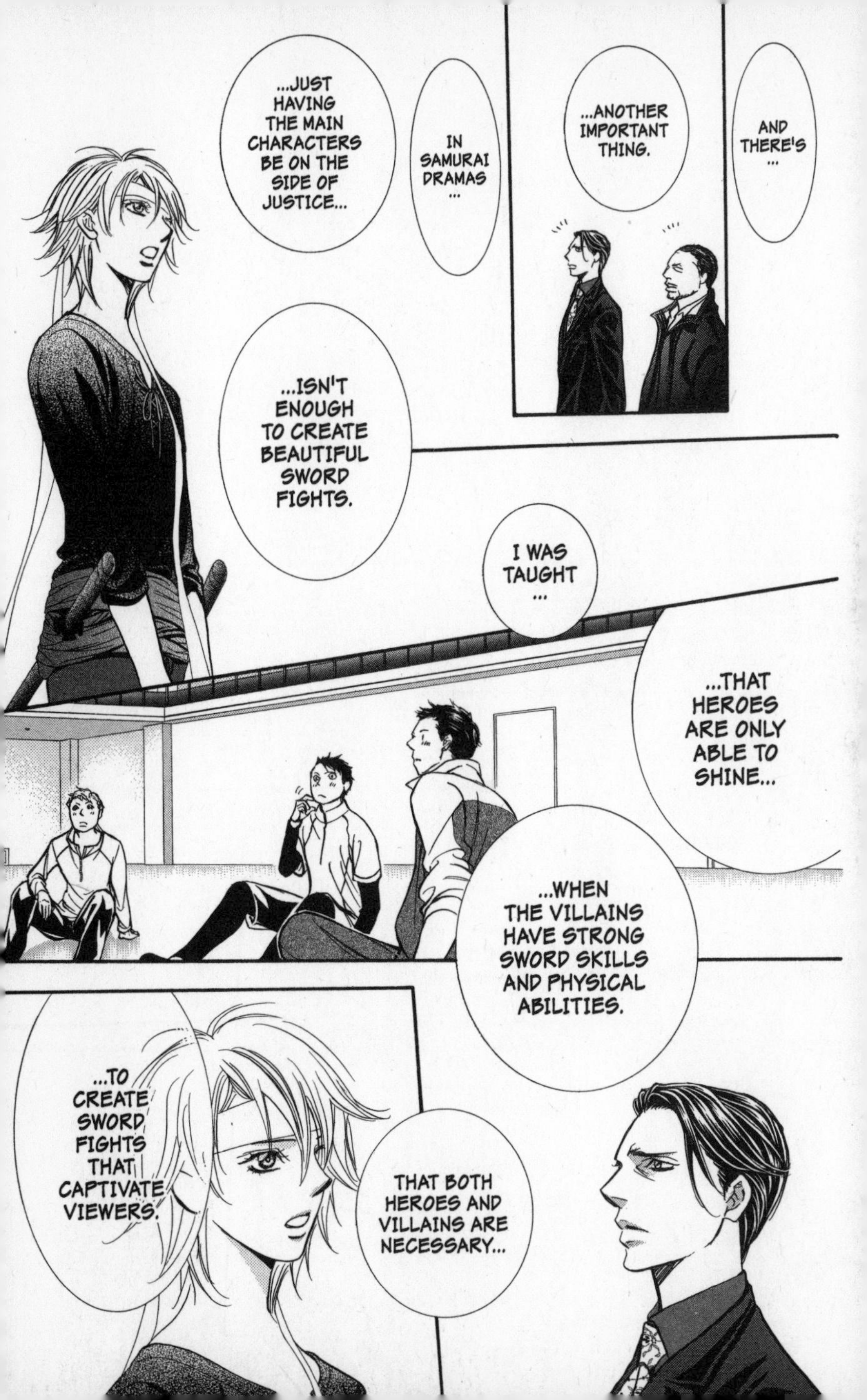
AND THERE'S ...
...ANOTHER IMPORTANT THING.
IN SAMURAI DRAMAS ...
...JUST HAVING THE MAIN CHARACTERS BE ON THE SIDE OF JUSTICE...
...ISN'T ENOUGH TO CREATE BEAUTIFUL SWORD FIGHTS.
I WAS TAUGHT ...
...THAT HEROES ARE ONLY ABLE TO SHINE...
...WHEN THE VILLAINS HAVE STRONG SWORD SKILLS AND PHYSICAL ABILITIES.
THAT BOTH HEROES AND VILLAINS ARE NECESSARY...
...TO CREATE SWORD FIGHTS THAT CAPTIVATE VIEWERS.

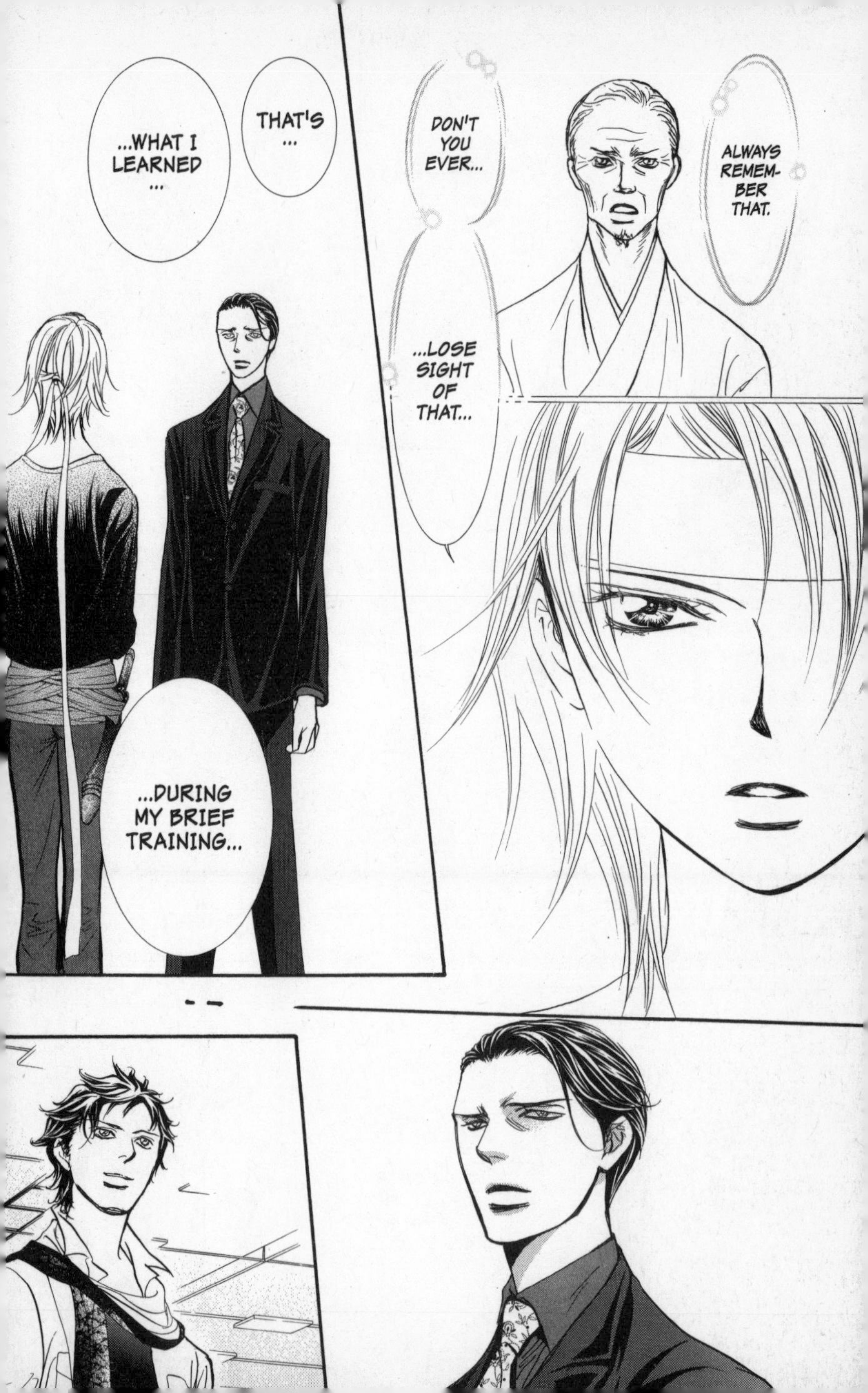
ALWAYS REMEMBER THAT.
DON'T YOU EVER...
...LOSE SIGHT OF THAT...
THAT'S ...
...WHAT I LEARNED ...
...DURING MY BRIEF TRAINING...

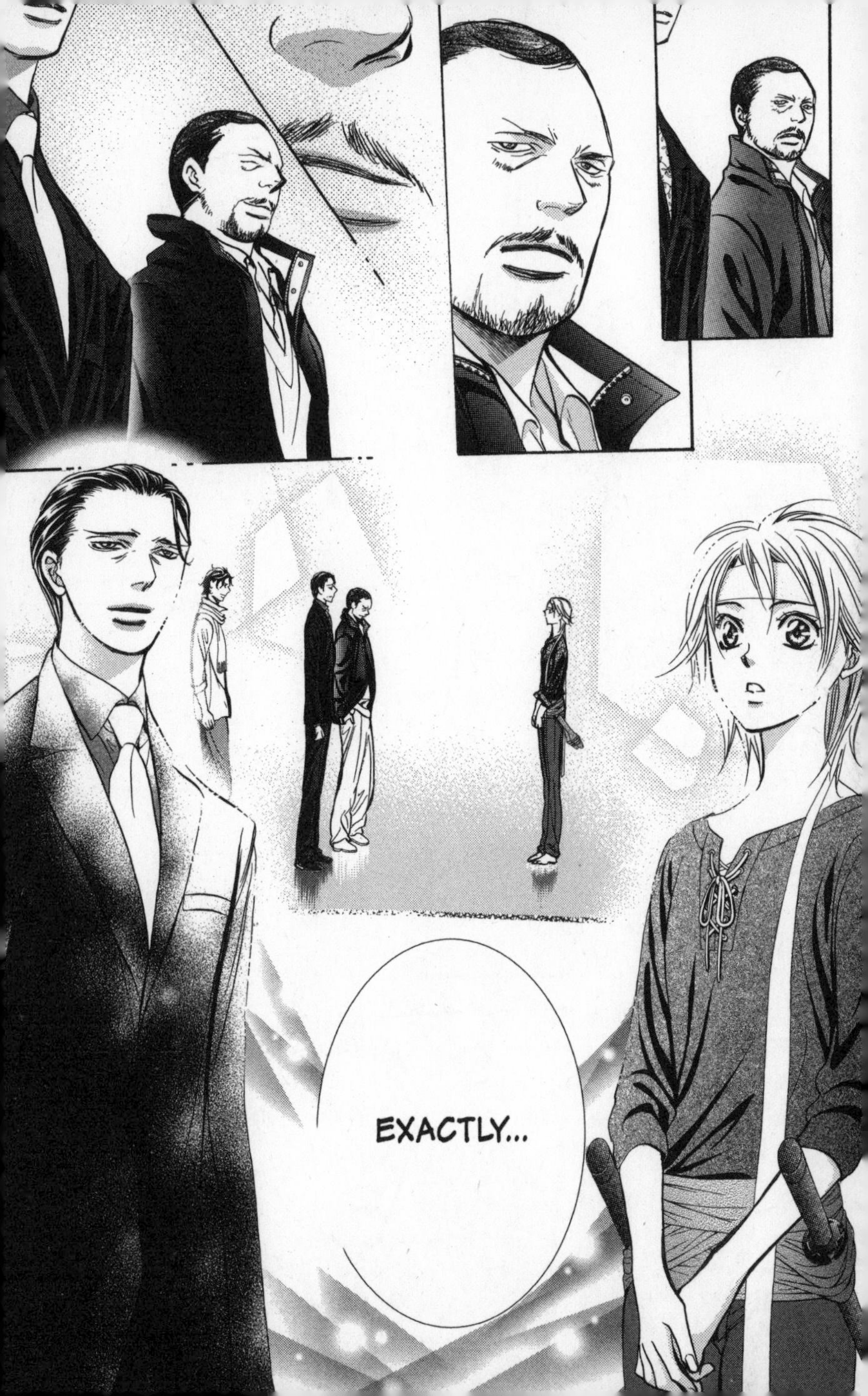
EXACTLY...

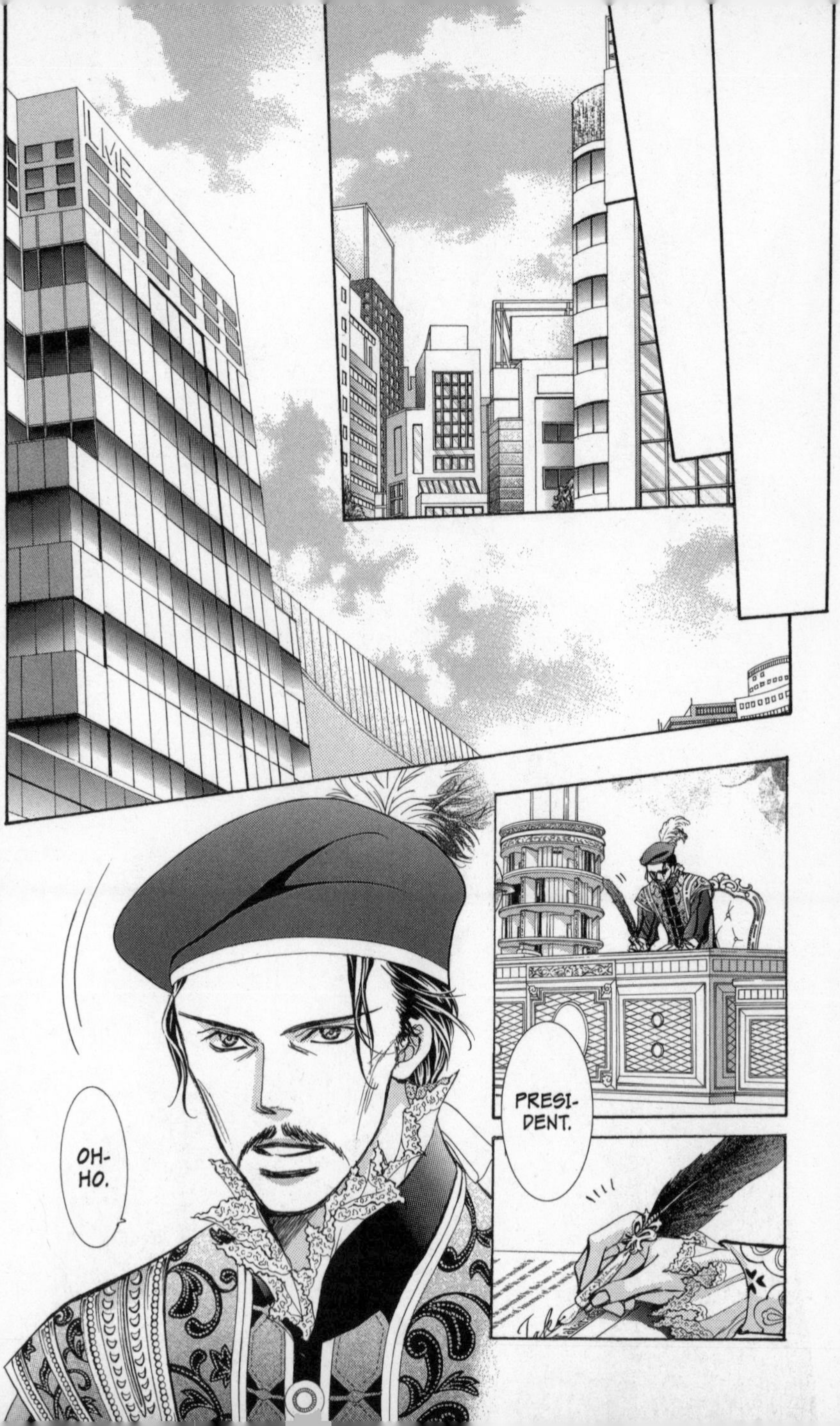
LME
PRESI-DENT.
OH-HO.

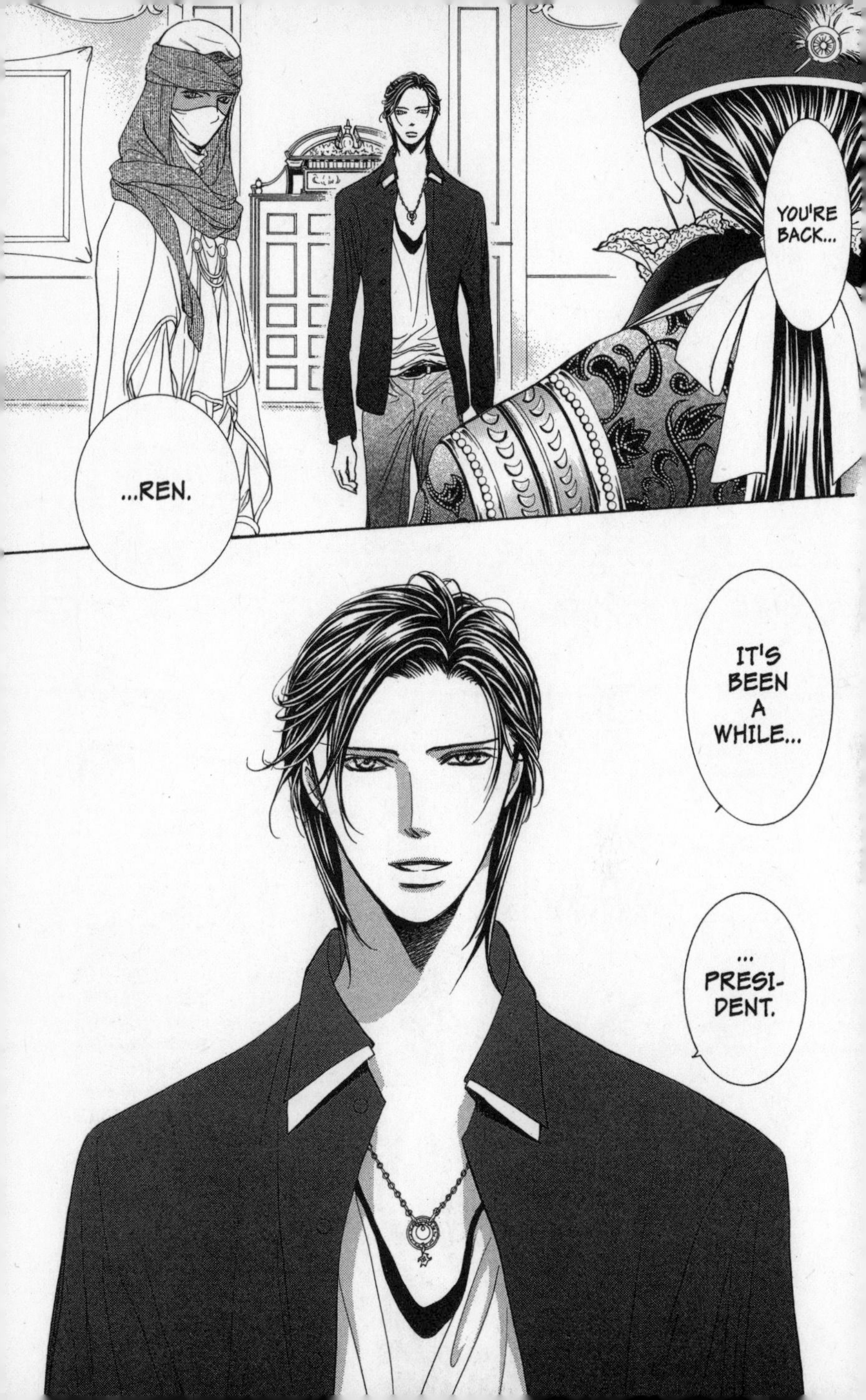
YOU'RE BACK...
...REN.
IT'S BEEN A WHILE...
...PRESIDENT.

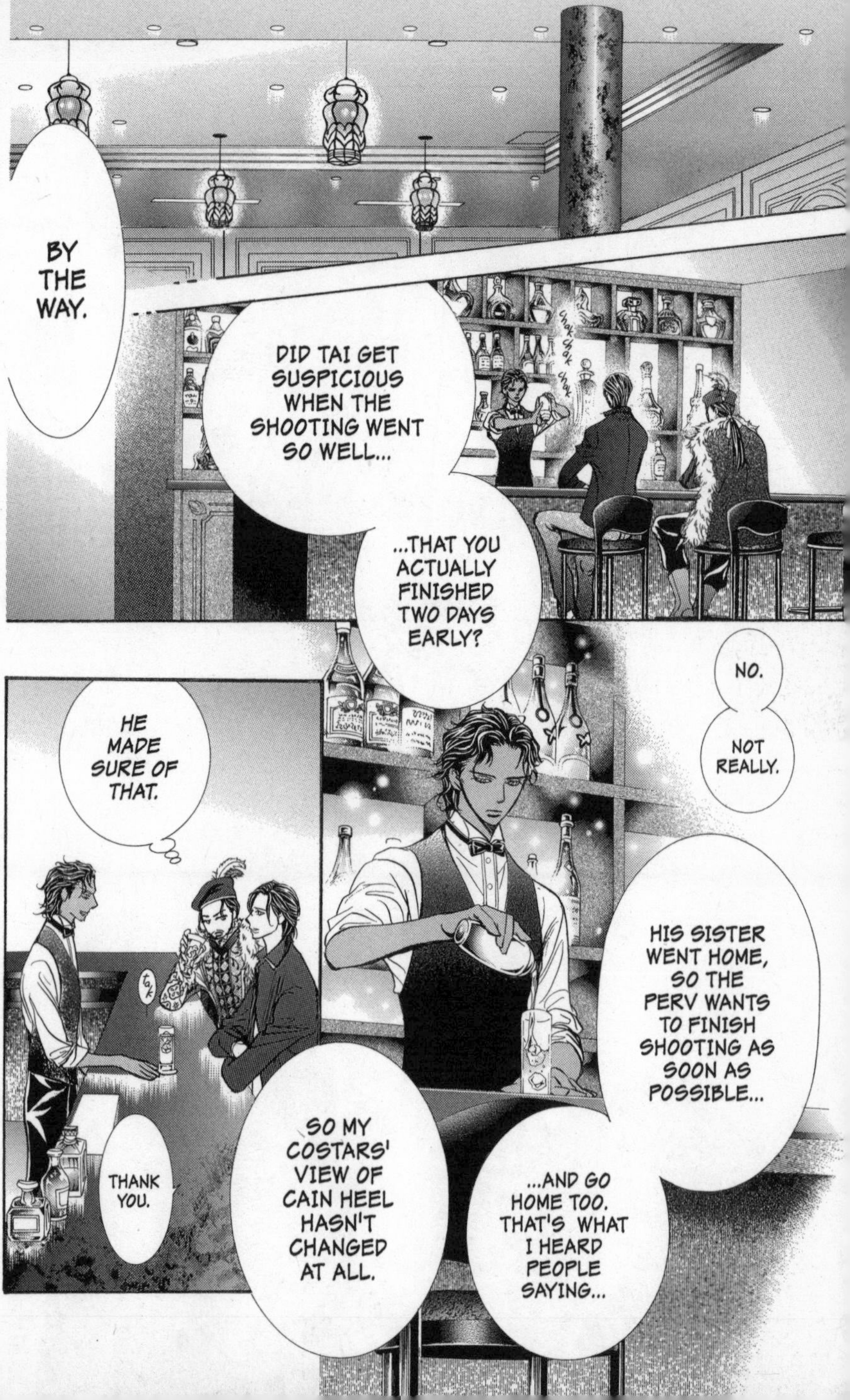
BY THE WAY.
DID TAI GET SUSPICIOUS WHEN THE SHOOTING WENT SO WELL...
shak shak shak
...THAT YOU ACTUALLY FINISHED TWO DAYS EARLY?
NO.
NOT REALLY.
HIS SISTER WENT HOME, SO THE PERV WANTS TO FINISH SHOOTING AS SOON AS POSSIBLE...
...AND GO HOME TOO. THAT'S WHAT I HEARD PEOPLE SAYING...
SO MY COSTARS' VIEW OF CAIN HEEL HASN'T CHANGED AT ALL.
HE MADE SURE OF THAT.
tak
THANK YOU.

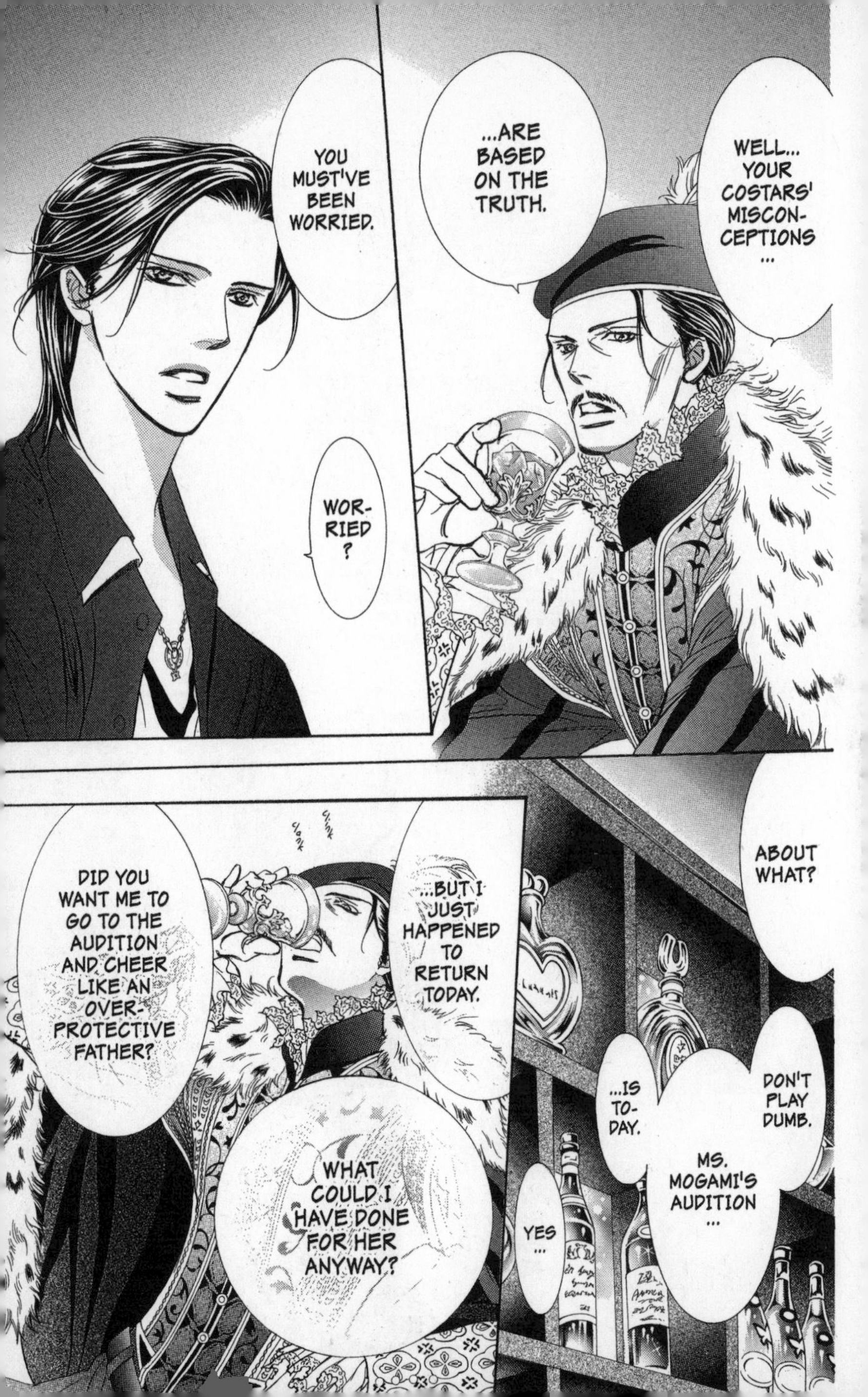
WELL... YOUR COSTARS' MISCONCEPTIONS ...
...ARE BASED ON THE TRUTH.
YOU MUST'VE BEEN WORRIED.
WORRIED?
ABOUT WHAT?
DON'T PLAY DUMB.
MS. MOGAMI'S AUDITION ...
...IS TODAY.
YES ...
...BUT I JUST HAPPENED TO RETURN TODAY.
clink
clank
DID YOU WANT ME TO GO TO THE AUDITION AND CHEER LIKE AN OVER-PROTECTIVE FATHER?
WHAT COULD I HAVE DONE FOR HER ANYWAY?

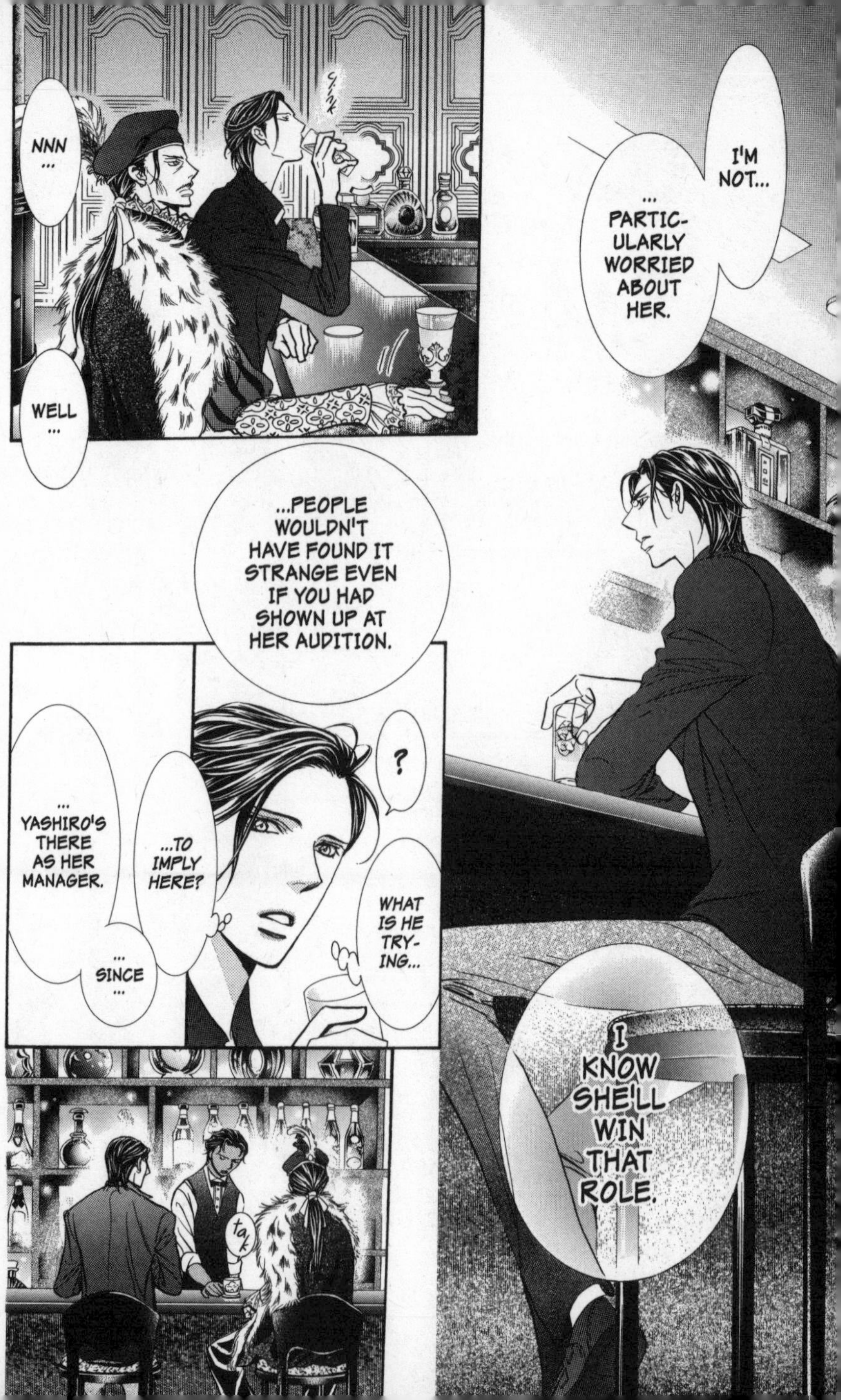
I'M NOT...
... PARTIC-ULARLY WORRIED ABOUT HER.
I KNOW SHE'LL WIN THAT ROLE.
NNN ...
WELL ...
...PEOPLE WOULDN'T HAVE FOUND IT STRANGE EVEN IF YOU HAD SHOWN UP AT HER AUDITION.
?
WHAT IS HE TRY-ING...
...TO IMPLY HERE?
... SINCE ...
... YASHIRO'S THERE AS HER MANAGER.
tak

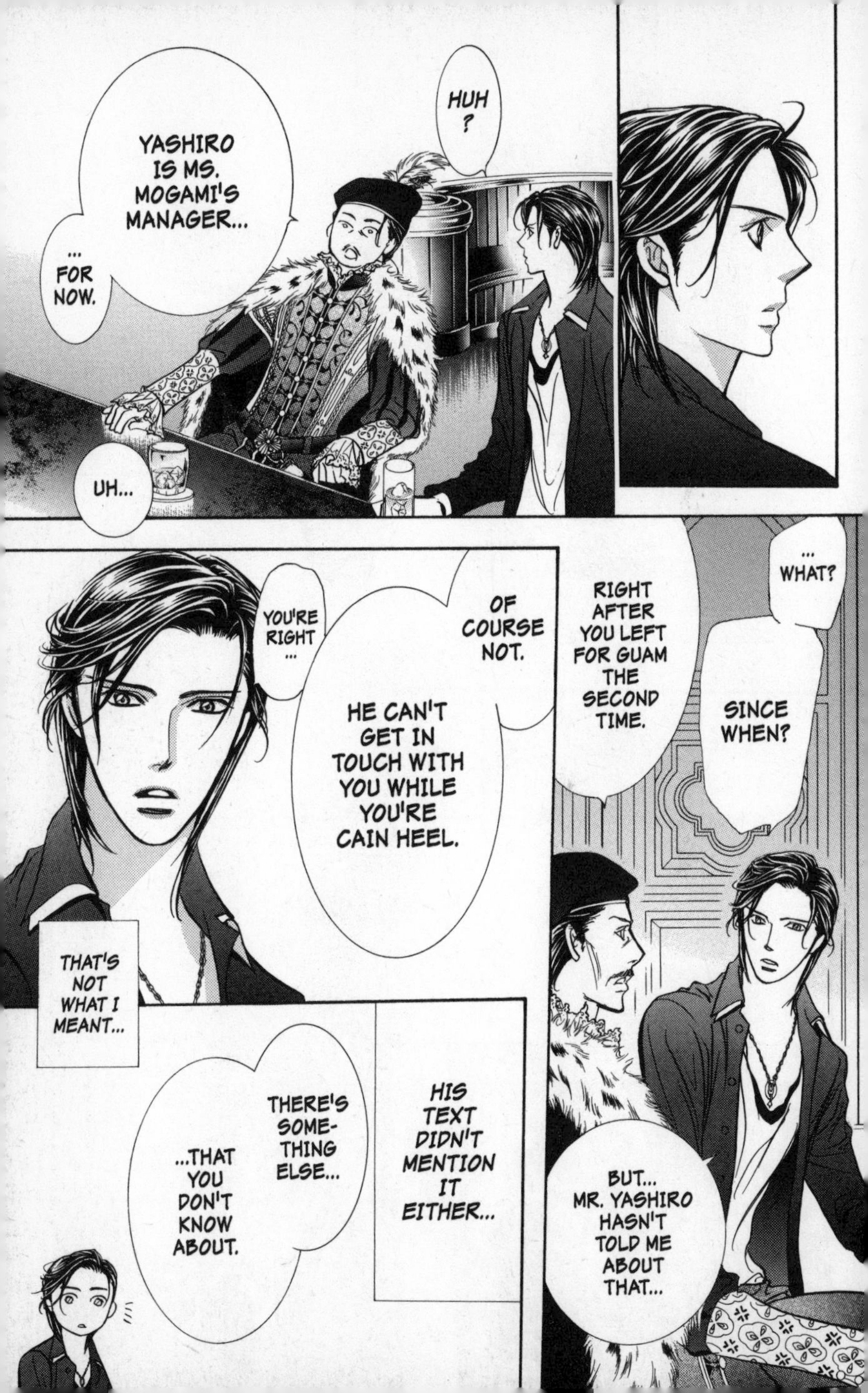
HUH ?
YASHIRO IS MS. MOGAMI'S MANAGER...
... FOR NOW.
UH...
... WHAT?
SINCE WHEN?
RIGHT AFTER YOU LEFT FOR GUAM THE SECOND TIME.
BUT... MR. YASHIRO HASN'T TOLD ME ABOUT THAT...
OF COURSE NOT.
HE CAN'T GET IN TOUCH WITH YOU WHILE YOU'RE CAIN HEEL.
YOU'RE RIGHT ...
THAT'S NOT WHAT I MEANT...
HIS TEXT DIDN'T MENTION IT EITHER...
THERE'S SOME-THING ELSE...
...THAT YOU DON'T KNOW ABOUT.

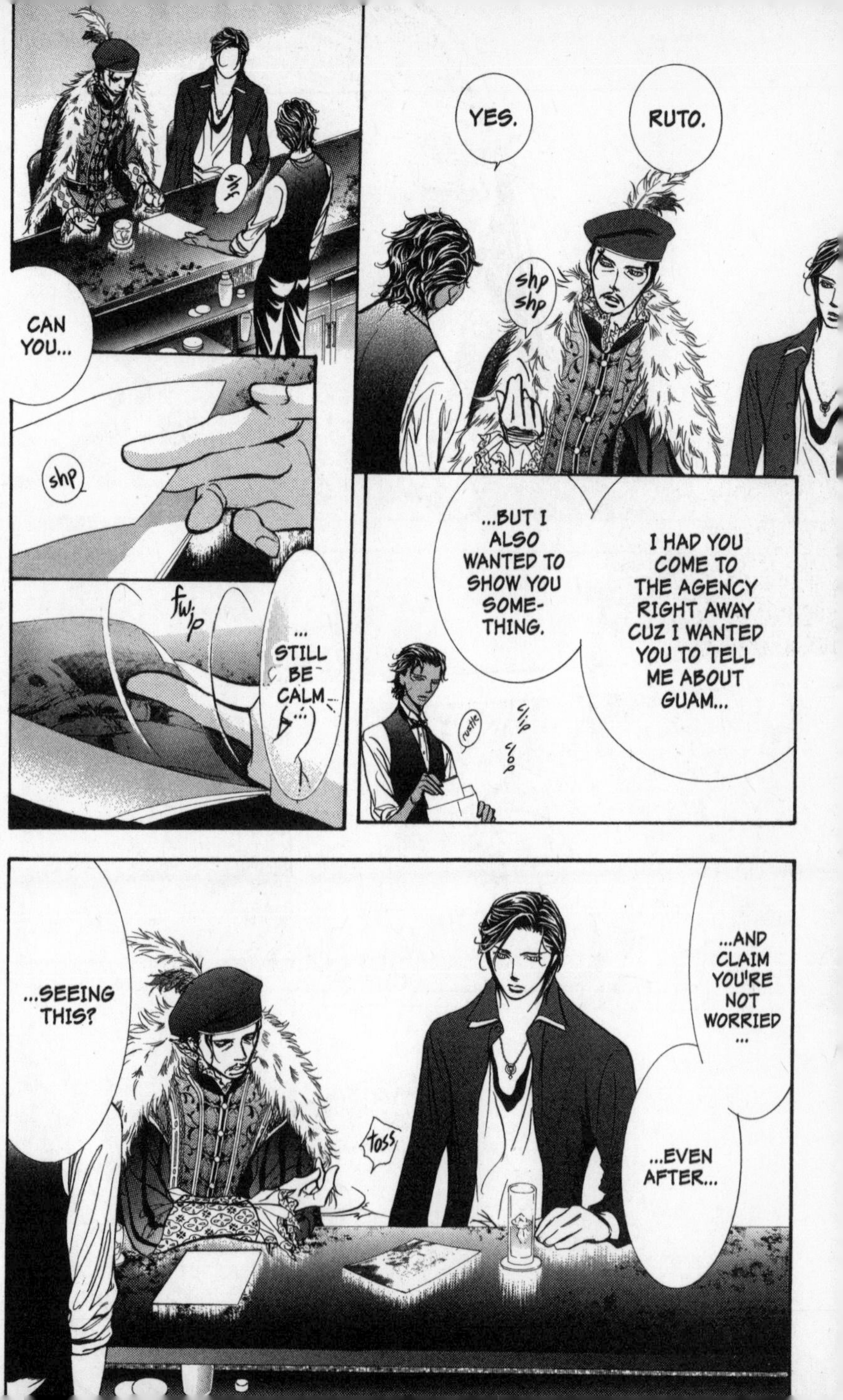
RUTO.
YES.
shp shp
I HAD YOU COME TO THE AGENCY RIGHT AWAY CUZ I WANTED YOU TO TELL ME ABOUT GUAM...
...BUT I ALSO WANTED TO SHOW YOU SOME-THING.
slip slop
rustle
shf
CAN YOU...
shp
...STILL BE CALM...
fwip
...AND CLAIM YOU'RE NOT WORRIED...
...EVEN AFTER...
toss
...SEEING THIS?

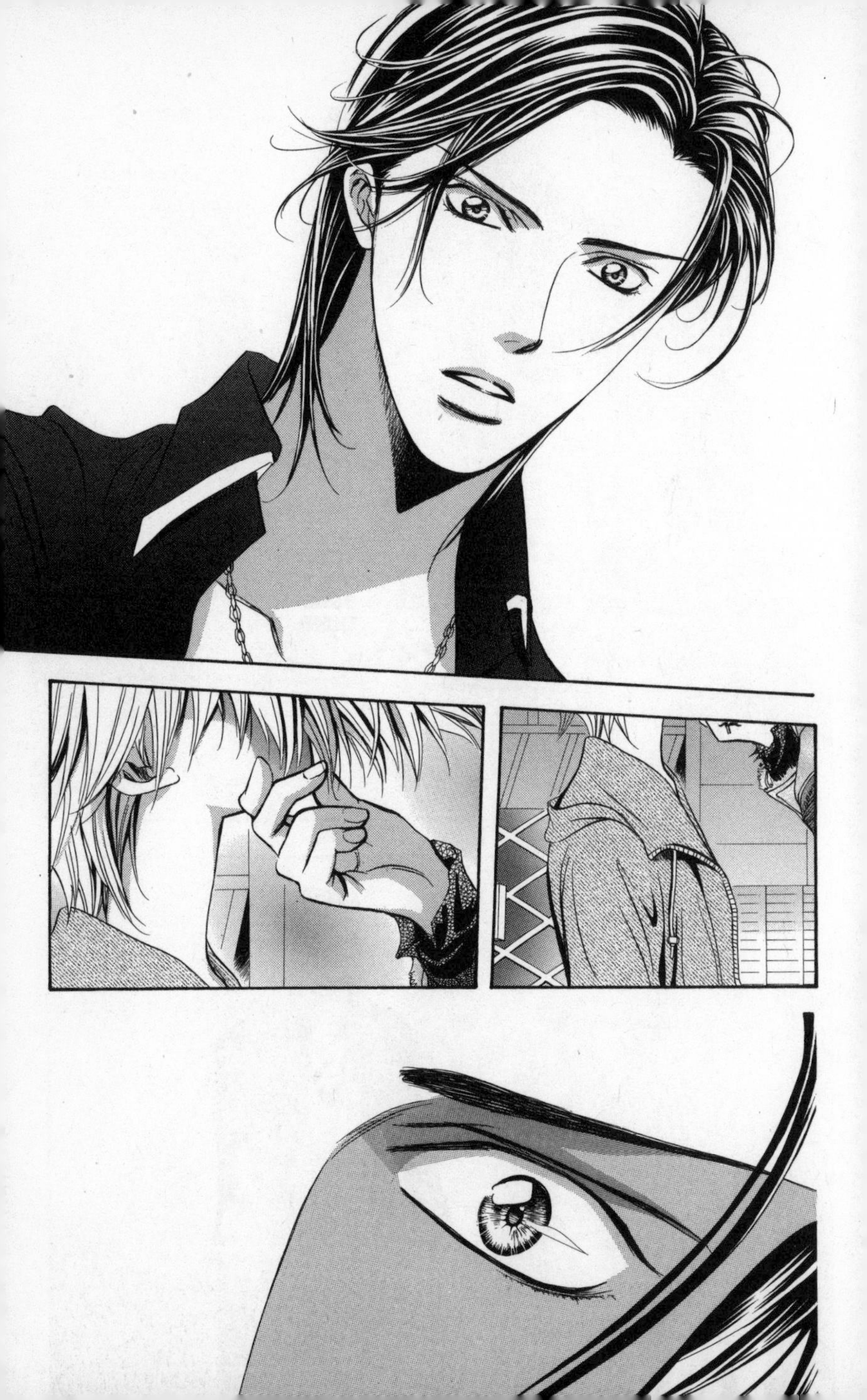

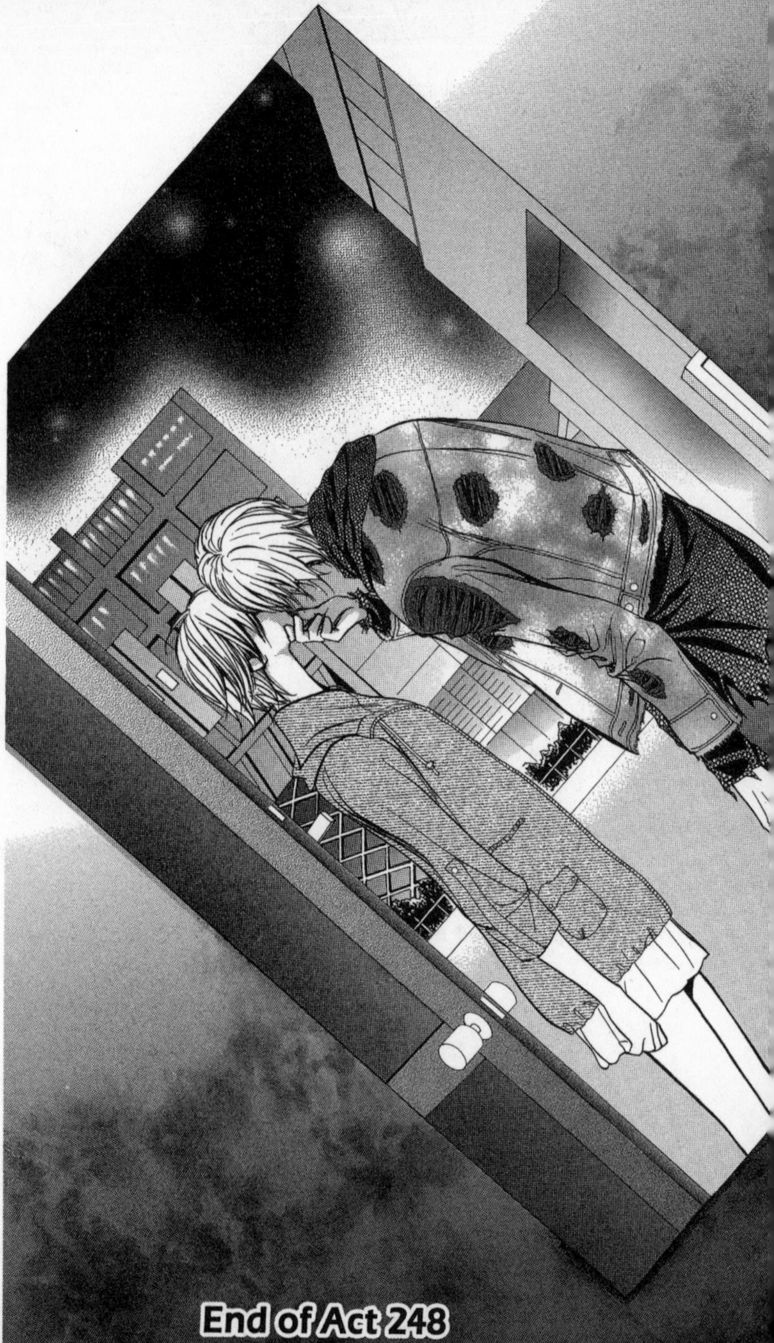

End of Act 248

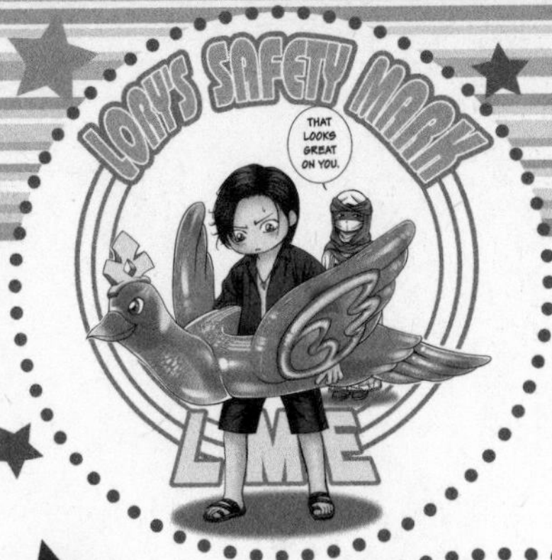
LORY'S SAFETY MARK
THAT LOOKS GREAT ON YOU.
LME

Yoshiki Nakamura is originally from Tokushima Prefecture. She started drawing manga in elementary school, which eventually led to her 1993 debut of *Yume de Au yori Suteki* (Better than Seeing in a Dream) in *Hana to Yume* magazine. Her other works include the basketball series *Saint Love*, *MVP wa Yuzurenai* (Can't Give Up MVP), *Blue Wars* and *Tokyo Crazy Paradise*, a series about a female bodyguard in 2020 Tokyo.

SKIP·BEAT!
Vol. 41
Shojo Beat Edition

STORY AND ART BY YOSHIKI NAKAMURA

English Translation & Adaptation/Tomo Kimura
Touch-up Art & Lettering/Sabrina Heep
Design/Veronica Casson
Editor/Pancha Diaz

Skip·Beat! by Yoshiki Nakamura © Yoshiki Nakamura 2017
All rights reserved. First published in Japan in 2017 by HAKUSENSHA, Inc., Tokyo.
English language translation rights arranged with HAKUSENSHA, Inc., Tokyo.

The stories, characters and incidents mentioned in this publication are entirely fictional.

Printed in the U.S.A.

Published by VIZ Media, LLC
P.O. Box 77010
San Francisco, CA 94107

10 9 8 7 6 5 4 3 2 1
First printing, September 2018

viz.com

shojobeat.com

IDOL *dreams*

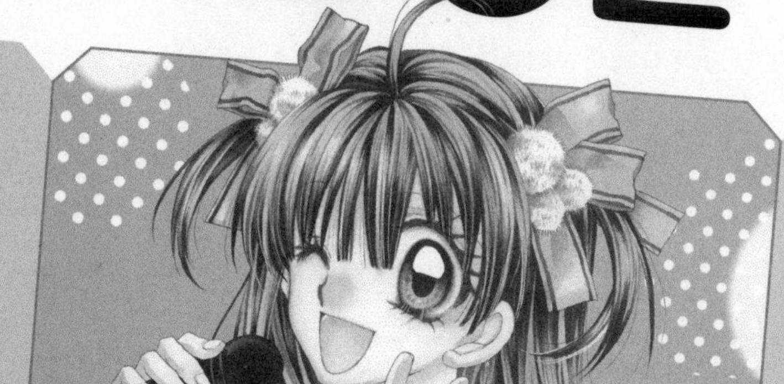
STORY & ART BY
ARINA TANEMURA

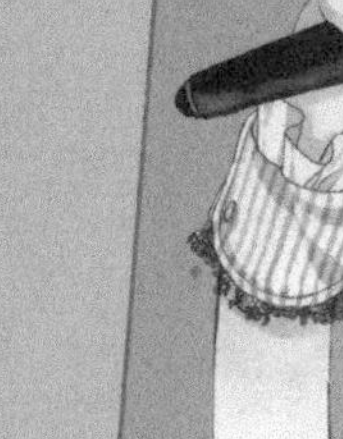
IDOL dreams
IDOL DREAMS
1
ARINA TANEMURA

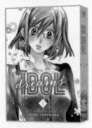

At age 31, office worker Chikage Deguchi feels she missed her chances at love and success. When word gets out that she's a virgin, Chikage is humiliated and wishes she could turn back time to when she was still young and popular. She takes an experimental drug that changes her appearance back to when she was 15. Now Chikage is determined to pursue everything she missed out on all those years ago—including becoming a star!

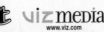

Shojo Beat VIZ MEDIA www.viz.com RATED T FOR TEEN ratings.viz.com

SURPRISE!

You may be reading the wrong way!

It's true: In keeping with the original Japanese comic format, this book reads from right to left—so action, sound effects, and word balloons are completely reversed. This preserves the orientation of the original artwork—plus, it's fun! Check out the diagram shown here to get the hang of things, and then turn to the other side of the book to get started!

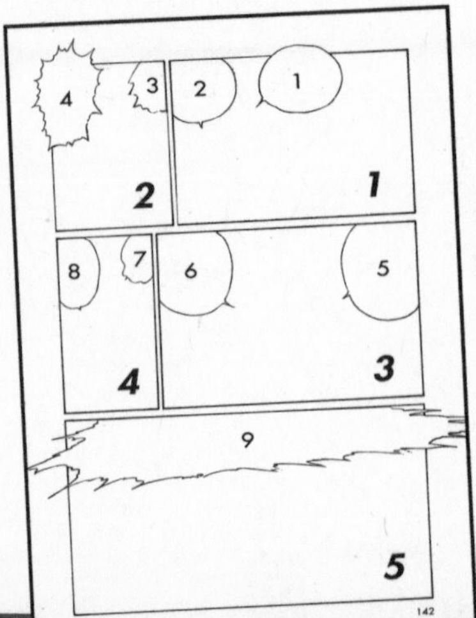
1
2
3
4
1
2
5
6
7
8
3
4
9
5
142

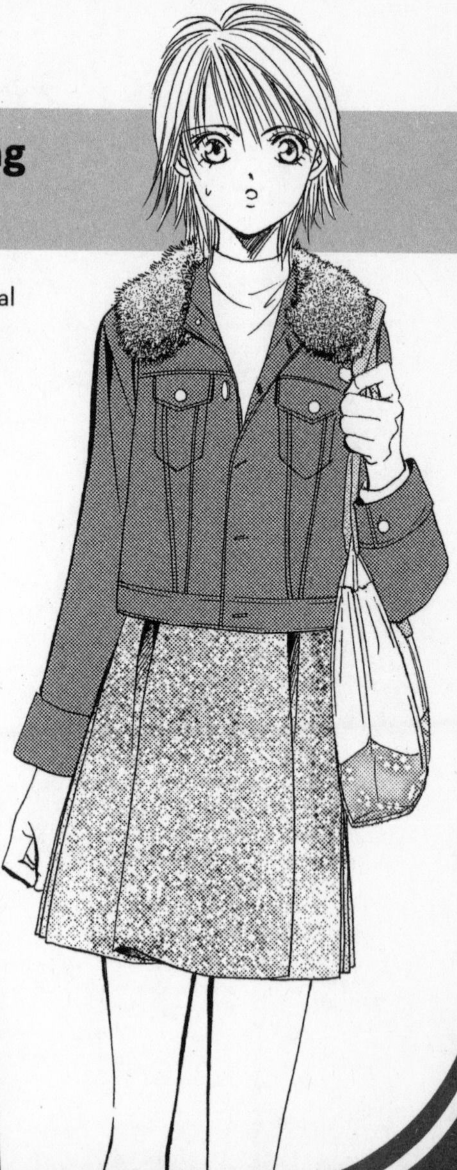